*See Journal 1, 1969 for amendments.

All communications with regard to the Society should be addressed to

THE HON. SECRETARY

English Place-Name Society
University College
Gower Street
London W.C.1

ENGLISH PLACE-NAME SOCIETY

GENERAL EDITOR
A. H. SMITH

ENGLISH PLACE-NAME ELEMENTS

PART II (JAFN–YTRI)

ENGLISH PLACE-NAME SOCIETY. VOLUME XXVI

ENGLISH PLACE-NAME ELEMENTS

BY

A. H. SMITH

PART II

THE ELEMENTS JAFN–YTRI

INDEX AND MAPS

CAMBRIDGE

AT THE UNIVERSITY PRESS

1956

PUBLISHED BY
THE SYNDICS OF THE CAMBRIDGE UNIVERSITY PRESS

London Office: Bentley House, N.W. 1
American Branch: New York

Agents for Canada, India, and Pakistan: Macmillan

Printed in Great Britain at the University Press, Cambridge
(Brooke Crutchley, University Printer)

CONTENTS

MAPS

(IN POCKET AT END)

The publication of these volumes on *English Place-Name Elements* has been most generously assisted by the Pilgrim Trust, and the researches involved in their preparation have been helped very materially by grants made to the Society by the British Academy and to the editor by the University of London.

J

jafn ON adj., 'even, level'. (*a*) Yanwath We (viðr). [~efen.]

jalda ON, 'a nag', found chiefly in poetry in the sense 'mare'. (*a*) *Yawdhole* Cu 407, *Yaldeflete, Yaldesik* YE. Cf. A. S. C. Ross, *Sagabook* xii, 5 ff.

jarl ON, 'a nobleman, an earl'. (*a*) *Gerlestre* YN (trēow), Yarlside La (sǽtr). [~eorl.]

Jewe, Jou ME, 'a Jew'. (*a*) Jewbury YE, Jubbergate Yk. Cf. Ekwall NoB xli, 174.

Jewerie ME, 'a place where Jews were segregated'. (*b*) The Jewry Ln, Jury Fm Sx.

jǫfurr ON, 'a wild boar'. (*a*) Gowerdale YN (dalr). [~eofor.]

justment, gistment ONFr, 'a piece of land of which the grazing is let'. (*b*) Justment D.

juxta Lat prep., 'near', often alternating with bi and ModE *near*, *next* (as in the spellings of Allerton Bywater YW, Thorpe By Water R, Thorpe next Norwich Nf). (*c*) Aston juxta Mondrum Ch, Norton juxta Twycross Lei, Norton juxta Kempsey Wo, etc.

K

kál ON, 'cole, cabbage', *v.* **cāl.**

kald ON adj., 'cold', *v.* **cald.**

kálfr ON, 'a calf', *v.* **calf.**

kambr ON, 'a comb, a crest', *v.* **camb.**

kapall ON, **capel** ME, 'a horse, a nag', introduced by Norwegian Vikings from Ireland (cf. OIr *capall* 'horse') and found chiefly in the NW (cf. Cu 465). (*a*) Capel Crag, Capplebeck Cu, Capplerigg We, The Crofts YE 65. [~Lat. *caballus.*]

karl ON, 'a freeman of the lower class', corresponding to OE **ceorl**, is well evidenced in p.ns. in Scandinavia, as in Swed *Karleby* (Hellquist, *Svenska Ortnamnen på -by* 76) which probably had much the same meaning as OE *ceorla-tūn* (*v.* **ceorl**) and the type *Akalby* (*á-karla-bý*, 'the river dwellers' **bý**', cf. Hellberg). The el. is apparently common in Danelaw p.ns., but not with distinctively Scandinavian els. It occurs chiefly in the numerous Carltons, ON *karla-tún*. In a good many instances this p.n., which is not found in Scandinavia, must be regarded as a Scand adaptation of the very common OE *ceorla-tūn*, for Charlton which is so common elsewhere is not usually found in that form in the Danelaw, and the ON word *karl* (except in the special compounds *butse-carl* and *hus-carl* 'servant') is not found in independent use in England before 1300. The p.n. may, of course, in a few instances be an Anglo-Scand equivalent of the Scand *Karleby*. The el. is sometimes difficult to distinguish from the ON pers.ns. *Karl*, *Karli* (Feilitzen 301–2), esp. in p.ns. like Carlsmoor YW. (*a*) Carleton Cu, La, Nf, YW, Carlton Bd, C, Du, L, La, Lei, Nb, Nt, Nth, Sf, Y (*freq*) (**tūn**), Carlbury Du (**burh**), Carlby L (**bý**), Carlecotes YW (**cot**).

karla-tún ON, *v.* **ceorl, karl, tūn.**

***kartr** ON, 'rough stony ground', surviving as Norw dial. *kart* 'rough rocky sterile ground'. (*a*) Cartmel La 195 (**melr**). [~**cert.**]

kaupa-land ON, 'purchased land', as opposed to *oðalsjorð* 'land that was acquired by customary law' (Lindkvist 145–6). (*b*) Copeland Cu 2, Du. [~**cēap**, ON *kaupa* 'to buy', **land.**]

kaup-maðr (**-manna** gen.pl.) ON, 'a merchant, a trader'. (*a*) Capernwray La (**vra**), Copmanthorpe YW (**þorp**), Coppingford Hu (**ford**), Cowmans Ess (**gehæg**). [~ON *kaupa* 'to buy', **cēap-mann.**]

kay OFr, **key** ME, 'a quay, a wharf'. (*a*) Key Street K, Wo, Quay Street Wt and other st.ns.; Kew Sr 58. (*b*) Newquay Co (nīwe), Torquay D (torr). [~cae.]

kelda ON, 'a spring, a marshy place', is common in the NCy and may in some cases be an ON adaptation of OE celde or possibly a replacement of wella; it is also common in ME f.ns. and minor names (e.g. YE 325, YN 328). (*a*) Keldholme YN (holmr), Kellet La, Kelleth We (hlið), Kelsick Cu (sīc). (*b*) Usually with significant words, as Akeld Nb (á), Calkeld La, Cawkeld YE, Cawkhill YW, Cold Keld YN (cald), Cop Keld YN (copp), Creskeld YW (cærse), Halligill, Hallikeld YN (hālig), Threlkeld Cu (þrǽll), Trinkeld La (pers.n.). [~celde.]

kerling ON, 'an old woman'. (*a*) Carling Gill Cu (gil), Carling Howe YN 151 (haugr).

kers ME, 'a fen', cf. Scots dial. *carse* 'fen, low wet land'. (*a*) Caistron Nb 37 (þyrne). [~kjarr.]

ketill ON, 'a kettle', which is difficult to distinguish from the common ON pers.n. *Ketill* as in Kettleby L, Lei, Kettlesing YW, Kettlethorpe YE, may replace OE cetel in (*a*) Kettleburgh Sf (berg), Kettlewell YW (wella).

kex ME, 'a dry hollow stalk, a large hollow-stemmed umbelliferous plant'; cf. dial. *kex* 'a teazel'. (*a*) Caygate L (gata), Kex Beck (R. Wharfe) YW (gil, bekkr), Kexwith YN (þveit). [~Swed *hundkäx*, cf. Ekwall, *Shakespeare's Vocabulary* 84.]

kicchen ME, 'a kitchen', *v.* cycene.

kide ME, 'a kid, a young goat'. (*a*) Kidsnape La (snap). [Possibly from ON *kið*.]

***kikall** ON adj., 'winding', as in Norw p.ns. like *Kikallvaagen* (NG xi, 88). (*a*) R. Keekle Cu 18 (also Corkickle Cu 482).

kil Corn, 'the back of the neck', probably also in a topographical sense 'a ridge'. (*a*) Colquite, Kilmenorth Co. [~cil, cūlo-.]

kíll ON, 'a narrow bay', probably also 'a narrow valley'; cf. Norw dial. *kill* 'a narrow triangular strip', Dan *kil* 'a narrow strip of land'. (*a*) Kildale YN 143 (dalr).

king ME, 'a king', *v.* cyning.

kirkja ON, 'a church', occurs in many p.ns. in the Danelaw, and in some of them when it is combined with OE els. as in Kirkham La, YE (hām), Kirkhaugh Nb (halh), Kirkstall YW (stall), Kirkstead L, Nf (stede), Kirton L, Nt, Sf (tūn), Peakirk Nth, Whitkirk YW, it has probably replaced OE cirice. But the form *kirk* was widespread as an appellative in ME and this is the immediate source in p.ns. of later origin like Kirklees YW and of *Kirk* as an affix. It was used of any religious building such as a monastery, as in Kirkham YE, Kirklees, Kirkstall YW, or a monastic cell, as in Skewkirk and Woodkirk YW, both cells of Nostell Priory. (*a*) Curthwaite Cu (þveit), Kirkdale La, YN (dalr), Kirkland Cu, La (land), the common st.n. Kirkgate (gata), the compound kirkju-bý. (*b*) As a final el. it is, like *cirice*, sometimes combined with (i) a significant word, as Bradkirk La (bred), Felkirk YW (fjǫl), Skewkirk YW (skógr), Woodkirk YW (wudu); (ii) a pers.n., as in Algarkirk L (said to have been founded by *Algar comes*, BCS 409), Ormskirk La; (iii) a saint's name, as in Bridekirk Cu (St Bride), Felixkirk YN (St Felix), Islekirk Cu (St Hilda), Peakirk Nth (St Pega), Oswaldkirk YN (St Oswald), Romaldkirk YN (St Romwald), and, with reversal of the els. in Cu, Kirkandrews (St Andrew), Kirkbrynnock (St Brynach), Kirksanton (St Sanctan). (*c*) As an affix *Kirk* prefixed to Deighton, Hammerton YW, Leavington YN.

kirkju-bý(r), 'a village with a church', as also in Scandinavian p.ns., is of frequent occurrence, and may sometimes have replaced an earlier OE *ciric-tūn*. (*b*) Kirby, Kirkby (*passim* in the Danelaw), in all about 40 examples, many of which are distinguished by affixes as in Monks Kirby Wa, Kirkby Overblow, Kirkby Wharfe YW, Kirkby Moorside YN, Kirkby Stephen We. [kirkja, -bý.]

kjarr ON, 'brushwood', ker ME, 'a bog, a marsh, esp. one overgrown with brushwood'; cf. Norw *kjerr*, *kjarr* 'wet ground, esp. where brushwood grows', Swed *kärr* 'fen, marsh', is very common in ME and later minor names and f.ns. in the Danelaw (e.g. Cu 481, Ess 583, Nt 286, Nth 265, YE 326, YN 328, etc.); it is frequent with OE and ME as well as ON els. (*b*) Mostly combined with (i) plant-names, as Ellerker YE (elri), Hezicar YW (hassuc), Humble Carr L (humli), Redcar YN (hrēod), Seavy Carr YE (sef); (ii) bird-names, etc., as Tranker Nt, Trencarr YN (trani); (iii) other words denoting location or shape, as Altcar La (R. Alt), Broadcarr Nf (brād), Cringle Carr YN (kringla), Dunscar La (dynge), Holme Carr Nt (holmr), Stone Carr YE (stān).

kjǫlr (kili dat.sg.) ON, 'a keel, a ridge (of hills)'. (*a*) Keelby L. (*b*) Keal L; Kelham Nt (dat.pl.); Withgill YW (víðir).

kjóss ON, 'a small creek, a valley, a recess' (cf. NGIndl 60 and ODan *kiūs recorded only in p.ns.). (*a*) Keasbeck YN, Kex Beck (R. Laver) YW (bekkr), Keasey YE (haugr), Keisley We (klif).

klakkr ON, 'a lump', probably also 'a hill', as in Swed *klack* 'hillock', Icel *klakkur* 'rock'. (*a*) Claughton Ch, La (tūn). (*c*) Cleckheaton YW.

kleggi ON, 'a haystack', probably also 'a hill'. (*a*) Cleggcliffe YW (klif). (*b*) Clegg La 56.

*kleif ON, 'a steep hill-side'. (*b*) Claife La 219. [~klif.]

klettr OWScand, 'a cliff, a rock', assimilated from earlier ON, ODan klint. (*a*) Cleatop YW (hop), Cleator Cu (erg).

* klif ON, 'a cliff, a steep hill', cannot be distinguished from OE clif, as in Rawcliffe YN 15 (originally rēad, clif). It may occur with other ON els. (*b*) Keisley We (kjóss), perhaps Rawcliffe La, Roecliffe YW (rauðr).

klint ODan, 'a rocky cliff' (cf. OSwed *klinter* 'hill'), used of 'a steep bank overlooking a river', and in dial. *clint* of 'a hard rock projecting on the side of a hill or a river-bank'. (*a*) *Clintway* C (weg). (*b*) Clint YW, Clints Nb, YN; Gaultney Nth (gǫltr), also in ME f.ns. (Wa 329, YE 326, YN 328). [~klettr.]

knabbe ME, 'a hill-top', occurs chiefly in late minor names. (*b*) *Cherche-knabbe* (now Castle Hill) Nth. [~ModE *knob*.]

* knapi ON, 'a youth, a servant'; ODan *knabe* denoted a nobleman of low rank, the equivalent of a dreng, as in Dan *Knovsnap* (DaSN Sj iii, 90). The el. may be found in some Danelaw p.ns., esp. those with habitative terminals, in contrast to OE cnafa, which had a menial significance; it may have affected both the form and meaning of *cnafa* in the Danelaw. It is difficult to distinguish from the ON pers.n. *Knapi*. (*a*) Knapthorpe Nt (þorp), Knaptoft Lei (topt).

knarre ME, 'a rugged rock', *v.* cnearr.

kné ON, 'knee', *v.* cnēo(w).

kniȝt ME, 'a knight', *v.* cniht.

knorre ME, 'a knot or excrescence on the side of a tree', perhaps used of 'a gnarled tree'; it is difficult to distinguish from the related cnearr. (*a*) Knar Lake C. (*b*) Knarr Fm C 281.

knǫttr ON, 'a ball', cnotta OE, 'a knot', knot ME, 'a hard mass of something' and so 'a hillock, a rocky hill, a cairn', found chiefly in both literary documents and p.ns. in the NW (cf. Ekwall, Scands-Celts 40). (*b*) Knott Cu, Knott End La; Blow Knott La, Dry Stone Knott Cu. [~knútr. The relation of OE *cnotta* and ON *knǫttr* is doubtful; in view of the distribution, the ON word is probably the immediate source, but it must be a late borrowing in English, as the back-mutated form *knott* (and not *knat*) is retained, as in **hǫfuð**, **hǫldr**.]

knútr ON, 'a knot, a rocky hill', probably used in much the same way as **knǫttr**. (*b*) Hard Knott Cu 343 (**harðr**).

kofri ON, 'a hood, a cap', used of 'a hill' and related to ON *kúfr* 'a rounded summit'. (*b*) Core La 143.

kokkr ON, 'a lump', used in some topographical sense or as a pers.n., is possible in (*a*) Caxton C (**tūn**). [~ **ceacce** or possibly **cocc**[1].]

kol ON adj. 'coal-black' (of streams); cf. NElv 30. (*a*) Cowldyke YN 58 (**dīc**, near *Colebecke* and R. Dove, *v.* **dubo-**). [~ **col**[1].]

kollr ON, 'a hill, a top, a summit'. (*b*) Cowlam YE 126 (dat.pl.), *Othecolle* ib. 326. An OE **coll* 'hill', connected with ME *collen* 'to poll' and related to *kollr* which also meant 'head, crown of the head', has been suggested; it might be found in OE *Colhill* BCS 361 and Cowling YW (**-ing**[2]).

kona (**kvenna** gen.pl.) ON, 'a woman'. (*a*) Whenby YN (**bý**). [~ **cwene**.]

konungr ON, 'a king', *v.* **kunung**.

koppari ON, 'a joiner, a turner'. (*a*) Coppergate Yk (**gata**).

kot ON, 'a hut', common in Icel p.ns., may be found in some Danelaw p.ns., but it cannot be distinguished from **cot**. It is used in La with the meaning 'sheep-cote', usually prefixed by a p.n. as Irelethcote, Waltoncote La. (*b*) Sculcoates, Southcoates YE (with ON pers.ns.). [It may be noted that this el. appears in the ODan compound *Kaldekot*, which seems, however, to have been introduced from the Danelaw, that is, from Engl *Caldcote* cf. **cald**, **cot**.]

krá ON, 'a nook, a corner of land'. (*a*) Crathorne YN 174 (**þorn**).

kráka ON, **crake** ME, 'a crow, a raven', enters into some p.ns., but an OE word **craca*, corresponding to *kráka* and G dial. *krake*, may also have existed, as the el. is found mostly with OE els. as in (*a*) Crackpot YN (**pott**), Cracoe YW (**hōh** or **haugr**), Crakehall, Crakehill YN (**halh**), Crakemarsh St (**mersc**), Crakethorn YN (**þorn**).

kriki ON, 'a nook, a bend', **crike** ME, 'a creek, an inlet', is found in minor names like *Sayercryk* YE, *Scaldecryke* L, and (with ME lengthening of *-i-* to *-ē-* in an open syllable) Creek C 254, Welton Creek YE. An OE word corresponding to this and to Du *krēke* 'creek, bay', may have existed in Creeksea Ess, but it would be difficult to distinguish from **crūc**[1].

kringla ON, 'a circle', used of 'the circular sweep of a river, a round hill, anything of circular shape'. Ekwall La 27 thinks there might have been an OE adj. *_cringol_ 'twisting' (which he connects with OE _cringan_ 'to die') in some p.ns. with OE els. (_a_) Crindledike, Cringledyke Cu (**dīc**), Cringleber (**beorg**), Cringlebrook (**brōc**) La, Cringle Carr YN (**kjarr**), Cringleford Nf (**ford**), Cringlethwaite Cu (**þveit**); also in ME f.ns. (Nt 286, YE 326).

kroked ME adj., 'crooked', _v._ **croked.**

krókr ON, 'a crook, a bend', usually denoting 'land in the bend of a river', but also in later f.ns. and minor names 'a nook, a secluded corner of land'; it is common in f.ns. (Du, Nb, etc., cf. also C 334 Nt 286, YN 328), and usually found as a simplex p.n. (_a_) Crook Dumble Nt, Croglin Cu, Crookhurst La. (_b_) Crook La, We, Crooks Nb, YW; Crookham Nb (dat.pl.); Coppy Crook (**copped**), Crawcrook Du (**crāwe**).

kross ON, 'a cross', _v._ **cros.**

kross-bý, krossa-bý ON, 'a farmstead or village with a cross or crosses'. The stone crosses sometimes remain, as at Little Crosby La where there are six. (_b_) Crosby Cu, La, We, YN, YW, Crosscanonby Cu. [**cros, bý.**]

kuml ON, 'a burial-mound, a cairn' (as in Scand p.ns. like Swed _Kumla_). (_a_) _Cumelkeldfot_ Cu 378.

kunung ODan, **konungr** ON, 'a king', is frequently found, but in some p.ns. with OE els. it may have replaced OE **cyning**, as it certainly has done in Coniscliffe Du (_Ciningesclif_ ASC 778 DE). The older OEScand form _kunung_ is very common in the early spellings of most p.ns., and the form _Coning-_ may also be for _kunung_ with the OFr, ME spelling _-o-_ for _-u-_. (_a_) with ON els., Coneythorpe YW (**þorp**), Coningsby, Conisby L (**bý**), Conjure Alders Nt (**vað**), Cunscough La (**skógr**); with OE els. (where it may have replaced _cyning_), Coney Street Yk (**strǣt**), Coney Weston Sf, Congerston Lei, Conington C, Hu, Coniston La, YE, YW (**tūn**), Conisbrough YW (**burh**), Conisford Nf (**ford**).

kvenna ON gen.pl., 'of women', _v._ **kona.**

kvern ON, 'a hand-mill, a mill, a mill-stone'. (_a_) Quarmby YW (**bý**). Quernhow YN (**haugr**). [~ **cweorn.**]

kví ON, 'a pen, a fold'. (_a_) Whaw YN (**hagi**), Wheyrigg Cu (**hryggr**).

kýr ON, 'a cow'. (_a_) Kitley Hill YN (**dalr**). [~ **cū.**]

L

lā[1] ODan, 'water along the sea-coast, a creek', has been suggested for Goxhill L, YE 66, Sixhill L, but there are topographical as well as philological objections to this; it is otherwise unknown in England.

la[2] OFr def.art. 'the', *v.* **le**.

lāc OE, 'play, sport', is possible in Lockinge Brk (**-ing**[2]); the usual OE word is **plega**. [~**leikr**.]

lache ME, 'a slow stream', *v.* **læcc**.

***lachet** ME, 'a small muddy hole, a bog'. (*b*) Latchet's Shaw Ess 135. [~**læcc**, **-et**.]

lacu OE, 'a stream, a water-course', surviving in that sense in dial. *lake* (NED s.v. *lake* sb. 3); Toller (BTSuppl) cites significant uses which show that this el. is not to be confused with ME *lake* 'lake, pool' (from Lat *lacus*). It is well evidenced in OE charters (Forsberg 4 ff) and in ME f.ns. (Bk 258, C 334, Ess 583, L, Mx 201, Nth 266, Sr 362, W 438, Wa 329, etc.). (*a*) Lackham W 103 (**hām**). (*b*) Lake W; Lacon Sa (dat.pl.); usually combined with significant words, as Charlock Nth (**cald**), Fishlake YW (**fisc**), Frostley L (**forsc**), Harlick Co (**horig**), Hartlake So (**heorot**), Kerslake Co (**cærse**), R. Medlock La (**mǣd**), Shiplake O (**scēap**), Standlake O (**stān**); occasionally with pers.ns., as Bablock Hythe O, Mortlake Sr. [~**lacuc**, **læcc**, **licc**, OE *leccan* 'to water, to irrigate'.]

***lacuc** OE, 'a small stream', is suggested (DEPN) for (*b*) Lacock W 102, Laycock YW, and a lost *Lakoc* in K, though there may be topographical difficulties with the Y place, which stands on a steep hill-side away from the stream. [~**lacu**, **-uc**.]

(ge)lād OE, 'a water-course, a passage over a river'.

(1) There is evidence for both *lād* and *gelād*, though the two were already coalescing in OE; only in a few cases where medial *-i-* in compounds reflects the old prefix *ge-* (as in Framilode Gl and occasional ME spellings of other p.ns.) has *gelād* survived.

(2) Ekwall (DEPN) thinks that the two forms also had distinctive meanings, *lād* 'a water-course' and *gelād* 'a passage over a river', but unfortunately the evidence is none too good; the situation of places called *gelād* on larger rivers like the Severn or the Thames makes Ekwall's suggestion for that word at least probable. In later

times, however, there is no distinction when *lād* and *gelād* fell together as ME *lode*. The meaning 'passage over a river, a ferry, a ford' for WCy dial. *lode* (EDD s.v.) is probably not that of a genuine local appellative, but merely a meaning established by p.n. usage, for many places on the Severn ferries happen to be found at places called 'lode', such as Framilode, Abloads Court, Wainlode, Lower Lode and Upper Lode Gl. On the evidence of a 1494 document about 'the fery otherwhyles called the loode of Apley with the were to the same fery or lode belongyng', Forsberg 22 would narrow the meaning to 'ferry', and calls attention to cognates like OE *lid* 'a ship', *lida* 'a sailor', *līðan* 'to travel (by sea or water)', which may well associate *gelād* with 'a passage across a river effected by boat'. This use is limited to England.

(3) Mod dial. *lode* (whether from *lād* or *gelād*) is otherwise used of 'a water-course, a channel, a fenland drainage channel'; this meaning is well attested in the fenland districts of the east, esp. in minor p.ns., such as *Oldelode*, *Waterlode* L, *Geynlode*, *Newlod* C 335, etc., and is also enjoyed by Continental parallels (Forsberg 20); in names of many places on small streams like the Evenlode, a meaning of this kind is obviously more likely than 'ferry'.

(4) There is some evidence for the meaning 'track' in OE poetry, as in *uncuþ gelad* in *Beowulf* 1410 and *Exodus* 313 (cf. also *Fates* 92, *Genesis* 1841); other contexts where this meaning might occur refer, however, to journeys over the water, as in *micel is lad ofer lagustream* 'great is the passage over the ocean' (*Andreas* 845), *ofer deop gelad* 'over the deep way' (that is, over the deep ocean, ib. 380).

(5) The modern form is *lode* in dial. and p.ns. like Clevelode, Evenlode Wo; *-lade* in Cricklade W or Lechlade Gl is irregular and probably arises from shortening of the vowel in the final el. at a very early period with subsequent lengthening in an open syllable or it is merely a traditional spelling and spelling pronunciation.

(6) (*b*) Load So, Lode C, Gl; Aquilate St (āc), Clevelode Wo (clif), Crollode Hu (crāwe), Evenlode Wo (pers.n.), Framilode Gl (a passage across R. Severn where it is joined by R. Frome), Lechlade Gl (a passage across R. Thames where it is joined by R. Leach), Linslade Bk (hlinc), Northload So, Portslade Sx (port 'harbour'), Shiplate So (scēap), Whaplode L (cwappe), Yanflet K (gegn, cf. also *Geynlode* C). (*c*) Curry Load So.

*ladda OE, 'a servant, a menial servant', later 'a youth, a young man', is not evidenced before the 14th century except in the late OE by-name of *Godric Ladda* (cf. Tengvik 256–7). (*a*) *Ladgate* (gata), Ladhill (dæl) YN. [Origin unknown, cf. NED s.v. *lad*; Tengvik connects it with OE *hlæd* 'load' as more befitting the older meaning 'servant', Whitehall with Goth *lauþs* from the root *leudh-* 'grow'.]

*læc(c), *læce *lec(c), *lece OE, lache, leche ME, 'a stream, a bog', surviving in NCy and NWMidl dial. *lache*, *letch* 'a stream flowing through boggy land, a muddy hole or ditch, a bog', occurs in OE only in charter material, and it is difficult to determine either its original form or its original meaning. OE spellings are *lec*, *lece*, *lecc*, *læcce*, and ME spellings chiefly *lache* or *lach*, occasionally *leche*; if anything, these point chiefly to an OE *læce*, *lece*, a fem. *i*-stem (cf. Forsberg 73). The word is certainly a derivative of lacu (either as an *i*-stem *læce* or a geminated *ja*-stem *læcc*), and the primary meaning might therefore be 'stream'; its use in dial. of 'a slow-moving stream' is topographically generally applicable when it is a final el.; in a few cases 'swampy boggy land' may be correct. The el. is commonest in NWMidl p.ns. It is sometimes difficult to distinguish from other els. such as lǣce, læcce, etc., esp. as a first el. in p.ns. like Latchmere Sr, Latchmoor, -more D, Ess, Ha, Sr, W *et freq*, Letchmoor Hrt (all from mere), where if it is *læcc* it would denote 'a swampy pool' (cf. G *lache* 'a pool, a puddle'). (*a*) Lashbrook O (brōc), Latchford Ch (ford), Latchley Co (lēah). (*b*) Lach(e) Ch, R. Leach Gl (hence Eastleach, Northleach, Lechlade Gl), *The Leche* Wo; Blacklache (blæc), Brindle Heath (brende) La, Cawledge Nb (pers.n.), Cranage Ch (crāwe), Fulledge La (fūl), Shocklach Ch (scucca); also in ME f.ns. (C 334, Ess 583).

*læcce (læccan gen.sg.) OE, 'a trap' or the like, has been suggested (DEPN) for (*a*) Latchingdon Ess (OE *Læce-*, *Læcendune*), but the OE spellings do not favour this; cf. *læcen. [~ OE *læccan* 'to catch'.]

lǣce[1] OE, 'a physician', perhaps used as a by-name, may be found occasionally as in (*a*) Lesbury Nb 134 (burh), Lexham Nf (hām).

lǣce[2], lyce OE, 'a leech, a blood-sucking worm', is possible as a first el. in some p.ns. like (*a*) Latchmere Sr, Latch Moor D, etc. (mere) and some others like Lashbrook O (brōc), but it is difficult to distinguish from læcc. *v.* Forsberg 33ff, Wt 284.

*læcen OE adj., 'abounding in water-channels' or 'having well-watered ground' (retaining something of the sense of OE *læccan* 'to irrigate'), has been suggested for (*a*) Latchingdon Ess 216 (dūn), though adjs. of this kind are not as a rule formed from topographical els. [~ lacu, læc(c), -en.]

***lǣd** OE, 'a drain, a water-course', not recorded in this sense before 1541 (NED s.v. *lead*), is difficult to distinguish from hlēda, but is possible in (*a*) *Ledhok* K 171, Leads House YE 43. [~ (ge)lād.]

lǣfer, lēfer OE, 'a rush, a reed, a yellow iris, levers', probably also used collectively (like hrēod) of 'a reed bed'; cf. *le leuer bedde* KCD 632 W and *Laurefen* Ess 579 (fenn). (*a*) Larden Sa (denu),Larford Wo (ford), Learmouth Nb (mūða), Leverton L (tūn). (*b*) Lever La 45; R. Dikler Gl (originally an old f.n. *Thickeleure* 'dense reed-bed', from þicce).

lǣge OE adj., 'fallow, unploughed, lying untilled', found in OE only in compounds such as *on þone lægæcer* BCS 964, *þam ealdan læg-hrycge* ib. 924, is in more general use in ME as *leye*, *laye* (cf. NED s.v. *lea* adj. and *lea-land*) and in such f.ns. as *Laiacre* Ess (cf. Forsberg 39) (*a*) Laylands YN, Lealands Ess, Leyland La 133 (land), Layriggs Cu (hrycg). [~ lágr, MHG *læge* 'low, flat, poor'.]

lǣl, lǣla OE, 'a twig, a switch', probably used of withies or the like. (*a*) Laleham Mx (hām), Lelley YE (lēah). (*b*) Lealholme YN 133 (dat.pl.).

læppa, lappa OE, 'a lap, the skirt of a garment', was also used in a topographical sense 'district' in the Laws (*v.* BT s.v.), and as an alternative to ende it glosses Lat. *ora* 'border, boundary, edge'; 'land at the end or edge of an estate or parish' or the like would seem to be implied. (*a*) Lapal Wo (hol), Lapland D (land), Lapley St (lēah), Laployd D (flōd), Lapscombe Sr 220 (cumb, on the edge of the parish), Lapworth Wa 288 (worð). (*b*) Cherry Lap Nth 159.

lǣs (lǣswe gen.,dat.sg.) OE, 'pasture, meadow-land', now dial. *lease* (from the nom.) and *leasowe* (from the obl. *lǣswe*), is found in ME and later f.ns. (Bd 295, Cu 482, L, Nt 286, *et passim*); in the pl. it is sometimes difficult to distinguish from lēah; it is not common in p.ns. (*a*) Leziate Nf (geat), Lissett YE (set). (*b*) Laisure Copse Sr, Leasowe Ch (dat.sg.); Cunlease So (cū), Eccles K (āc), Summerlease Co, Summer Lesure C (sumor), Whitrigglees Cu (p.n.).

(ge)lǣt, (ge)lǣte OE, 'a junction of roads', is in OE usually found in compounds like *oþ þæra stræta gelæto* BCS 945, *æt þære wege gelæton* ib. 801, *on weg gelætan* ib. 604, etc.; it glosses Lat *competum* (cf. þrop). Forsberg 43–4 shows that most examples can be identified with particular cross-roads. It is also probable that another meaning, that of dial. *leat* 'a conduit for water', is also old, as in OE *wæter-gelæt* glossing Lat *colimbus* and *concrematus* (WW 211.13) and OHG *wazzer-gilāz* 'conduit' and ME f.ns. in C 335. Both meanings are found in p.ns. (*a*) Ledburn Bk 81 (cross-roads, burna). (*b*) Leat D 172 (a mill-conduit), Longleat W (lang, a stream), Radlett Hrt (rād), Dunton Wayletts Ess 155 (a crossroads, weg).

* lǣte (lǣtan wk. obl.) OE adj., 'lonely, deserted', possibly with the meaning 'fallow, left alone', recorded only in OE *ǣ-lǣte* 'deserted, desolate'. (*a*) Netley Ha (OE *Lætanlia*, lēah).

lætt (latta gen.pl.) OE, latte, laþþe ME, 'a lath, a beam'. (*a*) Lathbury Bk 8 (burh).

lǣwerce OE, 'a lark', *v.* lāwerce.

* lāf OE, 'remains, what is left, a bequest', is also used in the compound *yð-lāf* of 'a shore, a beach' (that is 'what is left by the waves'). A similar sense is possible in (*b*) Marlow Bk 187 (mere, 'what is left by the draining of a mere'), but the meaning of *andlang lauen* BCS 1187 and *la Papelafe* O 146 is obscure.

lāferce OE, 'a lark, *v.* lāwerce.

*lagge OE, probably 'a marsh' or the like, recorded only in OE *in lacgeburnan* BCS 219 (*laggeburnan* KCD 1313), a Wo stream, is apparently the source of So, Sr dial. *lag* 'a narrow marshy meadow by a stream' and f.ns. such as *Lagge(s)* (Sr 369, W 260). (*a*) Lagham Sr 318 (hām). [~ME *bilagged, laggyd* 'made wet or muddy', cf. Forsberg 52.]

lágr ON adj., 'low'. (*a*) Laskill YN (skáli), Lodore Cu (duru). (*c*) StdE *low* frequent as an affix (often interchanging with *Nether*, *Inferior*) as in Low Buston Nb, Low Hutton YN, etc., and *lower* in Lower Slaughter, Lower Swell Gl, etc.

lagu (laga gen.,dat.sg., *læge dat.sg.) OE, 'sea, flood, water', is found only in OE poetic texts, esp. of 'the ocean', and in the p.n. Laver Ess (fær). This, and a by-form *lag(a)*, is found in *to þam ealdan lagan* BCS 705 W and *on secg lages strod* ib. 1282 Wo, but the precise meaning which should be something like 'stream' or 'pond' is difficult to determine. In ME the word is represented by *laȝe* (*lawes* pl.) 'lake, pool' and by a secondary form *ley*, *laie* which may be from an OE dat.sg. *læge* (cf. NED s.v. *lay* sb. 1) and this survives as dial. *lay* 'pool' and in Slapton Ley D 330 (a large lake).

laie ME, 'a pool', *v.* lagu.

lain ME, 'a layer of soil', *v.* leyne.

*laity Corn, 'a dairy-farm'. (*b*) Laity Co (*freq*).

lām OE, 'loam, clay', is often difficult to distinguish from lamb, esp. when followed by els. beginning with *b-* like brōc, burna, etc.; in OE charters *lām-pytt* 'clay pit' is common (Forsberg 57). (*a*) Lamarsh Ess, Lamas Nf (mersc), R. Lambourn Brk (burna), Lambrook So (brōc), Lamerton D 185 (burna), Lamphill Co (pyll), Lampitts Hrt 229, Loampit Sr (pytt), Lomer K (mere).

lamb (lambra, lamba gen.pl.) OE, 'a lamb', sometimes difficult to distinguish from lām. (*a*) Lambden K (denn), Lambeth Sr (hȳð), Lambley Nb, Nt (lēah), Lambrigg We (hryggr), Lambton Du (tūn), Lambwath YE (vað); the gen.pl. *lambra* is probable in Lamberhurst K (hyrst).

lan Corn, 'an enclosure, a sacred enclosure, a church', usually with saints' names. (*a*) Lamellan, Lamorran Co, Landkey D, Laneast, Launcells, Launceston, Lewannick Co. [~lann.]

land, lond OE, land ON, 'land'.

(1) This el. has in p.ns. a variety of meanings of which the principal ones are:

(i) 'a part of the earth's solid surface (as distinct from water), earth, soil, dry land', which may be the sense required when it is a first el. in p.ns. like Landbeach C (as distinct from Waterbeach), and as a final el. in some like Swarland Nb where the first el. is descriptive of the soil.

(ii) 'a tract of land of considerable extent', as in county names like Cumberland, Northumberland, Westmorland, and regional names like Cleveland YN or Holland L.

(iii) 'an estate or smaller tract of land', which is no doubt the common one in p.ns.; Rutland, for example, was originally a large single *soc* or estate.

(iv) 'a strip of arable land in a common-field', very common in ME and later f.ns. (Bd 295, Bk 258, C 335, Ess 584, L, Nt 286, W 439, YE 326, YN 328, *et passim*); these sometimes survive as p.ns., as Wrangling C.

(2) (*a*) As a first el. it is not common and its meaning difficult to determine, as in Lambrook So (brōc), Landwade C (gewæd); in Landbeach C, Langrick YE it probably denotes 'dry land, soil' or the like, and in Landmoth YN 'district' (gemōt); cf. land-gemære, land-riht, land-scearu.

(*b*) As a final el. it is combined with:

(i) Words describing the character of the soil, as Callowland Mx (calu), Dryland K (drȳge), Greetland YW (grēot), Soyland YW (sol), Stainland YW (stān), Swarland Nb (swǣr), as well as f.ns. like *Stonilond* (stānig) Bd, *Saltlond* L (salt), etc.

(ii) Words denoting shape, location or similar features, as Broadlands C *et freq*, Longlands Nt, Wt *et freq*, Shortlands C, Southlands Sr, Uplands K, Wrangling C (wrang); also in f.ns., such as *Longelonde*, *Wrongelond* Bd, *Woghelande* Bk (wōh), etc.

(iii) Words denoting a characteristic or nearby feature of the landscape, as Brooklands Sr (brōc), Cleveland YN (clif), Fenland C (fenn), Holland L (hōh), Litherland La (hlið); *v.* also ēa-land, ēg-land.

(iv) Words denoting the state of cultivation, as Laylands C *et freq* (lǣge), Newland(s) *passim* (nīwe, 'land newly brought into use'), Nomansland Mx *et freq* ('waste or deserted land'), Tyland K (tēah), Willand D (wilde), Woodlands Do *et freq* (wudu), Woolland Do (wynn).

(v) Words for crops and vegetation, as Balland C (bēan), Flaxland Sr (fleax), Lawkland YW (laukr), Oatland Sr (āte), Osierland K ('osier'), Ryeland(s) Nt, Wo *et freq* (rȳge), and esp. in f.ns. such as *Barlilond*, *Henepland* Bd, *Flexlond*, *Linlond*, *Rielond* Bk, *Beneland*, *Peseland* L, etc.

(vi) Words for animals, etc., as Darland K (dēor), Strickland We (stirc) Studland Do (stōd), Swilland Sf (swīn), Yaverland Wt (eofor).

(vii) Words denoting the kind of tenure or ownership, as Threapland Cu (þrēap), bōc-land, folc-land, kaupa-land.

(viii) The names of peoples and individuals, as Cumberland (Cumbre), Northumberland (Norðhymbre), Westmorland (west, mōr, -ingas); Priestland Sr (prēost); pers.ns. in Cooksland St, Gilsland Cu, Goathland YN, Marsland Co, Rutland.

(ix) The meaning 'strip of land' is implied in names like Acrelands, Twentylands Nt, and Headlands *passim* (*v.* hēafod).

land-gemǣre OE, 'a boundary'. (*a*) Ladywell Bd, Lamberhead La. (*b*) Landermere Ess, Laundimer Woods Nth. [land, (ge)mǣre.]

land-riht OE, 'land rights, the law of the land, rights connected with the ownership of an estate', possibly in allusion to a place where the law of a district was exercised or, as Ekwall suggests (DEPN), 'a property involving such rights'. (*b*) Rollright O 371 (pers.n.). [land, ~riht.]

land-scearu OE, 'a land-mark, a boundary, a share of land'. (*a*) Lancercombe (cumb), Landskerry (gehæg), Langsford (ford) D, Lanshare Lane W, Launcherley So (lēah); also in OE and ME f.ns. (D 690, W 440). [land, scearu.]

lane, lone, lanu OE, 'a lane, a narrow road', in both urban and rural usage, something less than a strǣt; it is common in minor st.ns. in towns and villages everywhere (cf. also C 337, Sr 363, Wa 330, etc.), but rare in p.ns. In York it usually replaces geil. (*b*) Laneham Nt (dat.pl.); Markland La, Redlane Do; in R. Asland La 126 (askr), it refers to 'the course of a stream in meadowland' (as in Scots dial. *lane*).

lanergh Corn, 'a glade' (as Welsh *llanerch* 'glade'). (*b*) Landrake, Larrick Co.

lang[1] (langan wk. obl.) OE adj., langr ON adj., 'long', in p.ns. usually means 'extending over a great distance', and in ford- and bridge-names it refers to the distance from bank to bank of the river (as distinct from brād); with tree-names it usually means 'tall, high' (as it does occasionally in OE and ME in relation to people); as an affix it generally alludes to the great length of a village main street. The OE and ON words cannot be distinguished but ON *langr* may be assumed with other ON els. The form *long-* is commonest in WMidl and in p.ns. of late origin which have StdE *long*; elsewhere *Lang-* and *Long-* both occur, except in NCy where *Lang-* is normal. There are occasional traces of WMidl over-rounding to *lung-* in the spellings of some p.ns.; Lumley YW has this form. (*a*) Ford-names, etc., as Langbridge Wt, Langford Bd, D, Ess, Nf, O, So, W *et freq*, Longford Db, Gl, He, Mx, W, Langwith Db, Nt, YE, Langworth L (vað); villages, farmsteads, etc., as Langham Do, Nf, R, Sf (hām), Langton Do, K, L, Lei, We, YN, Longton La, St (tūn); enclosures, clearings, woods, etc., as Langar Nt (gāra), Langtoft YE (topt), Longthwaite Cu (þveit), Longland(s) *freq* (land), Langley Bk, Brk, Db, Du *et passim*, Lumley YW (lēah), Llangrove He (grāf), Longwood *passim*; topographical features, as Langcliffe YW (clif), Langden YW, Longden, -don Sa, St, Wo (dūn), Langrigg Cu (hryggr), Longhoes K (hōh), Longney Gl (ēg); trees, as Langthorne YN (þorn), Langtree D, La, Longtree Gl (trēow), Longnor Sa, St (alor). (*c*) As an affix, *Long* prefixed to Ashton So,

Compton Wa, Ditton Sr, Marston Gl, Hrt, Stanton C, Sa, Stow(e) C, Hu; Longhope Gl.

lang[2] ME, 'a long strip of land', found in f.ns. such as *Le Langes, Southlong, Sourelonges* Nt 287 (cf. also C 337, Hrt 257, Nth 267, Sr 363, Wa 330, YE 326, etc.), and in **furlang**.

***langet** OE, 'a long strip of land', has been suggested for (*a*) Lansdown So (**dūn**), but there are phonological and other difficulties (cf. Forsberg 60); it does, however, occur as a f.n. *the Langet* He 111, and may be the source of dial. *langate* (cf. NED s.v. *languet*). [**lang, -et.**]

laning, loning ME, 'a lane, a right of way', surviving as NCy, Scots dial. *loaning*. (*a*) Loaningdale YE, Lonning Head Cu. (*b*) Haythwaite Lane Cu. [**lane, -ing**[1].]

lann OWelsh, 'an enclosure, a yard' and esp. 'a church' in p.ns., **llan** Welsh, 'a church', very common in Wales and fairly well-evidenced in Cu and the Welsh border counties, sometimes replacing **stōw**, with which it is equated; it is freq. with saints' names (as is Corn **lan**) or with other ecclesiastical words. It is ultimately from Brit **landā*. It mostly appears as *L(l)an-* in English p.ns. (cf. Jackson 511–3), but occasionally *land* occurs, as in OE *Landcawet* (Lancaut Gl). (*a*) Landican Ch, Landkey D, Llancillo, Llancloudy, Llanwarne He (Welsh *gwern* 'swamp'), Llanyblodwell, Llanymynech Sa (MWelsh *myneich* 'monks'). (*b*) Hentland He (Welsh *hen* 'old'). [~**lan, land, launde.**]

lappa OE, 'lap, edge', *v.* **læppa.**

látr ON, 'the lair of an animal', is probable in some p.ns., but may be difficult to distinguish in the NW from OIr *lettir* 'slope'; phonologically it is more likely even in Latrigg Cu 321. (*a*) Latterbarrow La 194, Latterhead Cu. (*b*) Hulleter La, *Swynlatermire* We, possibly Whinlatter Cu. [~Norw *lettre* 'a shelter for animals'.]

laðung OE, 'a calling together, a gathering of people', dial. *lathing*. (*a*) Laytham YE 239 (**holmr**). [~OE *laðian* 'to summon', **-ing**[1].]

lauf ON, 'a leaf, foliage'. (*a*) Loweswater Cu (**sǣ, wæter**), Lowick La (**vík**). [~**lēaf.**]

laukr ON, 'a leek, garlic'. (*a*) Lacra Cu (**vrá**), Lawkland YW (**land**), Loughrigg Cu, We (**hryggr**). [~**lēac.**]

laun ON, 'secrecy, concealment', with adj. function 'secret' in compounds like ON *laun-dyrr* 'secret door', ModE dial. *lown-hill* 'the lee-side of a hill' (though the latter may be from ON *logn* 'calm weather') (*a*) *Launland* La 253 (land), Longthwaite Cu 334 (þveit), *Lounlithgate* Yk (hlið[3]).

launde OFr, ME, 'an open space in woodland, a forest glade, woodland pasture', sometimes difficult to distinguish from land. (*b*) Laund Lei, YW; Blanchland Co, Nb, New and Old Laund La, Mill Lawn Co, Kingsland Wo; freq. with older p.ns. as Deanfield Lawn Nt, Corse Lawn Gl, Danby Lawns YN; it occurs in ME f.ns. (C 337, Hrt 257, Mx 201, Nt 287, W 440, Wa 330). [Ultimately a loan in Fr from OCelt **landā* and cognate with lann, land.]

lausa ON, 'a slope', difficult to keep apart from lauss. (*a*) Lowesby Lei (bý). (*b*) Possibly Backleys YN (bæc or bakki).

lauss ON suffix, '-less, without'. (*b*) *Footlessgale* Yk ('footless', that is 'a cripple', geil), R. Gaunless Du (ON *gagnlauss* 'useless', Watlass YN ('waterless', vatn). [~ lēas.]

laut ON, 'a small valley, a hollow' (NGIndl 64), also used in Swed p.ns. in some such sense as 'a small grass plot, pasture-land, a sheep enclosure' (Sahlgren, NoB vii, 102ff). (*a*) Loatland Nth 114 (lúndr).

lāwerce, lǣwerce, lāferce OE, 'a lark', usually reduced to *lark.* (*a*) Lar-, Larkborough W, Wo (beorg), Larkbeare D (bearu), Larkdale Nt (dæl), Larkfield K (feld), Larkhill C, Ess, W (hyll), Larkton Ch (tūn), Laverstock, -stoke Ha, W (stoc), *Lavertye* Sx (tēag), Lorden Wt (dūn). (*c*) Lark Stoke Gl.

laye ME, 'a pool', *v.* lagu.

le, la OFr def.art., 'the', is in English p.ns. usually a translation of the ME def. art. þe.

(1) In ME it is used in names, and esp. simplex names, where the els. still have an appellative function, as in Barns Nb (*le Bernes* 'the barns'), Biggin Bk 134 (ME *la Bygginge*), Hale K (*de la Hale*, *atte Hale*) or Roundhay YW (*le*, *la Rundeheie*); it survives occasionally as in Lamua Hundred Bk 51 (mūga), Delamere Ch (*foresta de la mere*), Delapre Nth (pre).

(2) It is much used also in affixes, where its use originates in the translation of ME prepositional phrases with the article and a common appellative; Spital le Street L was *Spitel oþþe strete*, *super stratam* and *on le Stret*, Thornton le Street YN was *in le Strete.* At a later date the preposition was lost, leaving the article as a kind of connective particle and used as such in Haughton le Skerne Du, St Mary le Bow Ln, but there is no evidence that it is connected in

any way with the OFr prep. *lès* 'near' found in Fr p.ns. like Plessis-lès-Tours. Many examples of *le* in affixes occur, as Bolton le Sands La, Burgh le Marsh L, Chapel en le Frith Db, Chester le Street Du, Hamble le Rice Ha, Hutton le Hole Y, Marham le Fen L. Cf. Zachrisson, IPN 95, Angl xxii, 308 ff.

lēac OE, 'a leek, garlic'. (*a*) Leckhampstead Bk, Brk (hām-stede), Leckhampton Gl (hām-tūn), Lickfold Sx (fald), Lickhill Wo (hyll); lēac-tūn. [~laukr.]

lēac-tūn OE, 'a leek enclosure', hence 'a herb garden' (glossing Lat *ortus olerum*, WW 270.8, 460.30); there is no evidence for the more general meaning 'kitchen garden, vegetable garden' until later in ME (cf. NED s.v. *leighton*), when it is also found in f.ns. (C 337, Ess 585, Hrt 257, Nt 287, Wa 330). (*b*) Lacton K, Latton Ess, Laughton L, Lei, Sx, Leighton Bd, Ch, Ha, K, Sa, So, Letton He, Sa; Wormleighton Wa. [lēac, tūn.]

lēaden OE adj., 'leaden', usually referring to lead roofing. (*a*) Leadenhall Ln (hall). (*c*) Leaden Roding Ess 493 (rendered Lat *plumbata*, also *Ledenechirche*). [OE *lēad* 'lead', -en.]

lēaf OE, 'a leaf, foliage'. (*b*) Redleaf K 92 (rēad). [~lauf.]

lēah (lēages, lēas gen.sg., lēage, lēa(e) dat.sg., lēagas, lēas nom.pl., lēagum, leaum dat.pl.) OE masc., lēah (lēage gen.sg.) OE fem., lǣh (Angl), 'a wood, a clearing in a wood', as long ago pointed out by Leo.

(1) Apart from OE charter p.n. material which is extensive (Mdf 86–8) OE *lēah* is infrequent in literary use, and the few examples that occur are not decisive as to meaning, apart from the gloss of *hriðra leah* as Lat *campus armentorum* 'field of oxen' (BCS 322). The sense 'meadow, open land, lea' given in BT and NED s.v. *lea* sb. 1 is really a very much later one found chiefly in poetic usage and in this usage there has been some confusion of meaning with lǣs 'meadow', which seems to have been regarded in later times as the plural of *lēah*. Apart from this there are certain indications that associate the term with 'woodland':

(i) The el. is extremely common, but it is esp. so in districts that were once heavily forested, such as Ha, Sr, Sx, Ch; in some counties such as C, Gl, etc. which had very varied types of landscape they are concentrated in particular areas which were once well wooded. On the other hand, *lēah* is nothing like so common in sparsely wooded regions like the mountains and moorlands of Y or the fenlands of L and EAngl.

(ii) In a great many p.ns. *lēah* is combined with tree-names, with words for 'pole, staff' and the like (probably in allusion to woods in which they were cut), and the names of wild creatures, etc. (cf. § 5 *infra*), all of which point to woodland rather than open country. It is also combined with words that denote burning (which suggests the clearing of woodland by this means) and with other words for cultivated crops and other vegetation, as well as the names of domestic animals, all of which indicate cleared land of some kind in various stages of exploitation either as pasture-land or as arable land.

(iii) As pointed out in EPN s.v., the Weald Forest K is in OE called both *Andredesweald* and *Andredesleage*, where *lēah* is clearly used in much the same way as wald 'forest', whilst BCS 669 records a grant *cum silva campisque ad eam jacentibus quae Earneleia dicitur*, which suggests that the *leah* of *Earneleia* was 'a wood with its adjacent open ground'. Similarly, Cheveley C 125 is called *villam silvosam* in 1022 and *silva* 'wood' from DB onwards, and *Waltonelega* La 14 is described as *nemus* 'grove'. This meaning of 'wood' is also evident in BCS 361, where the boundary of Salwarpe Wo goes *betwenan acwudu and wulle leah and swa æfre betwyx ðam twam wudan in Alrabroce*, 'between *ac-wudu* and *wulle-leah* and so continuing between the two woods to *Alrabroce*'.

(iv) The cognate words in other languages include ON ló 'a glade, a meadow', OHG *lōh* equated with Lat *lucus* 'a grove', MHG *lōh* 'low brushwood, a clearing overgrown with brushwood' and Lat *lucus* itself; Ekwall La 14 also notes that the meaning 'wood' was also current in the Netherlands (NGN i, 155).

(2) In most p.ns., therefore, the meanings most likely to occur are (*a*) 'a wood, woodland'; (*b*) 'a rough uncultivated natural open space in a wood, a glade'; (*c*) 'a rough clearing in a wood'; (*d*) 'a cultivated or developed glade or woodland clearing, esp. one used for pasture or arable'; and in later times (*e*) 'a piece of open land, a meadow'. Ekwall's suggestion that in a great many p.ns. *lēah* should be rendered 'woodland glade' rather than 'clearing' has much to commend it, in view of the evidence of the types of compounds, the OE usages and the cognates in other languages.

(3) The forms of *lēah*, which occur chiefly as a simplex p.n. or as a final el., as a rule present no difficulty. But in some NCy p.ns. such as Healaugh YW, Helmsley YN, Wensley YN, ME spellings

in *-lagh*, later *-laugh*, probably go back to an Angl *lǣh*, which was shortened to *-læh* in the unstressed position and so normally became ME *-lagh*; but it is not always easy to distinguish from ON lǫgr, as in Skirlaugh YE. Also in the NCy, a reduced dat.pl. form in ME *-lum*, later *-lam*, is fairly common, as in Acklam YE, YN, Cleatlam Du, Farlam Cu, Leam Nb, Streatlam Du. There is also some confusion through stress-shifting with hyll and -el in p.ns. like Okle He, etc. (cf. Smith, LMS i, 48–55).

(4) There is not much evidence to show how long the el. continued in living use. Some compounds with group-names in *-inga-* and a few with heathen associations (cf. § 5 (vii, xiii) *infra*) carry its use back to the early centuries of the English settlement, whilst a few compounds with ON and OFr pers.ns. (cf. § 5 (xiv) *infra*) bring its living use down to the period of the Norman Conquest; Brinsley Nt 117 may well be named from *Brun* who held the land there TRE. Many p.ns. like Leigh, Lee, etc. which in ME have forms like *la Legh*, etc., or Thurleigh Bd (from *atter Leghe*), where the use of the def. art. is thought to show that the final el. was still a significant word (*v.* atter, le), may indicate that it remained a p.n. appellative in ME, though, as pointed out (§ 1 *supra*), there is little enough literary evidence for this; but it occurs in a good many ME minor p.ns. (C 337, Ess 585, Hrt 257, Mx 201, Nt 287, *et freq*).

(5) (*a*) The el. is not used as a first el. with any certainty.

(*b*) As a simplex p.n., often apparently of post-Conquest origin, probably with the later meaning 'piece of open land, a meadow', in Lea L, Lee Bk, Ess, Ha, K, Sa (from dat.sg. *lēa*), Leigh Brk, Ch, D, Ess, Gl, Ha, K, So, Sr, W *et passim* (from nom.sg. *lēah* or dat.sg. *lēage*); Leece La, Leese Ch (nom.pl. *lēas*); Leam Du, Nb, Lyham Nb (dat.pl. *lēum*, *lēagum*).

In compounds, *lēah* is combined chiefly with the following categories of els.:

(i) Descriptive adjs. referring to location, shape, appearance, soil or other features, as Bradley *passim* (brād), Doiley Ha (diger), Fairlee Wt (fæger), Gringley Nt (grēne), Handley Do, Healaugh YN, YW, Healey YW *et freq*, Henley O *et freq* (hēah), Hardley Ha, Wt (heard), Langley *freq* (lang), Marley K (myrig), Olney Nth (ān), Rowley D, Du, St, YW (rūh), Shenley Bd, Bk (scēne), Shirley Wa *et freq* (scīr), Softley Du (sōfte), Sudeley Gl (sūð), Whitley *freq* (hwīt).

(ii) Tree-names, as Acklam YE, YN (dat.pl.), Acle Nf, Eagle L, Oakleigh K, Oakley Bd, Bk, Wo *et freq*, Ocle He (all with **āc**), Apley Nt, St, Appley Wt (**æppel**), Ashley Bk, C, Ch, D *et passim* (**æsc**), Apsley Bk, Aspley Bd, Nt, St (**æspe**), Berkeley Gl, Berkley So (**beorc**), Boxley K (**box**), Elmley Wo, Embley Nb (**elm**), Heasley Wt, Hesley Nt (**hæsel**), Lindley YW (**lind**), Parley Do (**peru**), Sawley YW (**salh**), Sapley Hu (**sæppe**), Thorley Hrt, Wt, Thornley Du (**þorn**), Uley Gl (**īw**), Weedley YE, Weethley Wa, Withiel So (**wīðig**), Willey Ch, He, Sa, Wa (**wilig**).

(iii) Words for other types of wild vegetation, as Bentley St, Wo, YW (**beonet**), Bromley K, Wo (**brōm**), Cleatlam Du (dat.pl., **clǣte**), Farleigh K, So, Farley St, Farnley YW (**fearn**), Gorsley Gl (**gorst**), Hadleigh Ess, Sx, Headley YW (**hǣð**), Himley St (**hymele**), Hoathly K (**hāð**), Mistley Ess (**mistel**), Notley Bk, Nutley Ess (**hnutu**), Riseley Bd, Brk, Risley Db, La (**hrīs**), Sloley Nf, Wa (**slāh**), Wyrley St (**wīr**).

(iv) Words for cultivated crops, as in Beanley Nb (**bēan**), Barlow Du (**bere**), Flaxley Gl, YW (**fleax**), Hailey Bk (**hēg**), Lindley YW, Linley Sa (**līn**), Oteley Sa (**āte**), Ryley La (**rȳge**), Whatley So, Wheatley Ess, La, Nt, YW (**hwǣte**).

(v) Words denoting 'stakes', etc., as Pilley YW (**pīl**), Staveley La, We, YW (**stæf**), Yardley Wo (**gerd**); cf. also Spoonlets K (**spōn**), Tiley Do (**tigel**).

(vi) Words implying 'clearing' (esp. one made by burning or cutting down trees), as in Brilley He (**bryne**), Brindley Ch, YN (**brende**), Ridley Ch, Nb (**rydde**), Stewkley Bk (**styfic**).

(vii) Words indicating use or religious or other association, as Bitterley Sa, Butterley He (**butere**), Edgeley Ch, Sa (**edisc**), Fawley He (**fealo**), Hawley K (**hālig**), Loosley Bk, Luzzley La (**hlōse**), Spetchley Wo (**spǣc**), Wensley Db (**Wōden**), Whistley Brk (**wisc**), Weeley Ess, Weoley Wo, Willey Sr (**wēoh**).

(viii) Words denoting the type of ground, as Horley Wt (**horu**), Loatleys YE (**lort**), Migley Du (**micge**), Scarle Nt (**scearn**), Slaley Nb (**slæf**) Stainley YW, Stanley Db, Du, Gl, St, W (**stān**).

(ix) Names of wild creatures, as Bagley Brk, Sr, So, YW (**bagga**), Bewley W (**bēaw**), Brockley So (**brocc**) Catley He (**catt**), Crawley Bd, Bk (**crāwe**), Corley Wa, Cornley Nt (**corn**), Durleigh So, Durley Ha (**dēor**), Foxley He (**fox**), Hartley Do, K, So (**heorot**), Marley YW (**mearð**), Pinsla Co (**pinca**), Rockley W (**hrōc**),

Shrigley Ch (scrīc), Ulley K (ūle), Woolley Brk, Hu, YW (wulf), Wormley L (wyrm), Yaxley Hu (gēac).

(x) Names of domestic animals, as Booley Sa, Bulley Gl (bula), Bulkeley Ch (bulloc), Calveley Ch, Calverley YW (calf), Cowley Gl, Kyloe Nb (cū), Gateley Nf (gāt), Horseley Db, Gl, Nb, Sr, St, YW (hors) Lambley Nt (lamb), Oxley St (oxa), Shepley YW, Shipley Db, Du, Sa, Sx, YW (scēap), Stirchley Sa (stirc), Warley, Worley Wo (weorf); cf. also Studley O, W, Wa, YW (stōd).

(xi) Topographical els., r.ns. and p.ns. and names of other local objects or features, indicating location, as Barley Wo, Burley He, YW *et freq* (burh), Cameley So (a r.n., Cam Brook), Coaley Gl (cofa), Horley Sr (the p.n., Horne Sr), Marcle He (mearc), Morley Db, Du, Nf, YW (mōr), Pauntley Gl (pant), Redmarley Wo (hrēod, mere), Semley W (R. Sem), Shelley Ess, St, YW (scelf), Streatlam Du (dat.pl., strǣt), Woodleigh D (wudu).

(xii) Words denoting ownership, etc., as Childerley C (cild), Frosterley Du (forester), Knitsley Du (cniht), Manley Ch (gemǣne), Swanley K (swān).

(xiii) Folk-names in *-inga-*, as Bardingley K, Finningley Nt, Hastingley K, Knottingley YW, Oddingley Wo.

(xiv) Pers.ns., which are fairly common, as in Asgardsley St, Alwoodley YW, Barclay K, Barnsley Do, Gl, Wt, Butleigh So, Cheveley Ch, Edgarley So, Goodmansleigh So, Gumley Lei, Offley Hrt, St, Otley Sf, YW, Poughley Brk, Wansley Nt, Wembley Mx; occasionally a woman's name, as in Alveley Sa, Bugley Do, an ON pers.n., as in Osmotherley YN, or an OFr pers.n. as in Mawdesley La.

*leaht OE, probably 'a channel', is possible in (*a*) Leckford Ha (ford). [~lacu; cf. Mansion s.v. *lecht*, Forsberg 68.]

leahtric OE, 'a lettuce'. (*a*) Laughterton L, Leighterton Gl (tūn).

lēap OE, 'a basket, esp. one for catching fish' (cf. cȳpe). (*a*) Lapford D (ford).

✱ lēas OE, -lēs ME, adj. suffix, '-less, without', as in Headless Cross Wo and in affixes such as Stratton Strawless Nf (strēaw), Westley Waterless C (wæter); *v.* also þēawleas. [~lauss.]

leax OE, 'a salmon'. (*a*) *Lexmere* YN (mere).

*lece OE, 'a brook', has been suggested for certain p.ns. (Ekwall, DEPN 278, Forsberg 34 ff); it is hard to differentiate from læcc in p.ns. like Latchford Ch and, with ON influence, from lœkr in p.ns. like Leake YN, Legbourne L, *Lekeley* Cu. [~ læcc, ON *leka* 'to drip, to leak'.]

lēfer OE, 'a rush', *v.* lǣfer.

leger OE, 'a burial place, a grave', in later times also 'lair', is possible in (*b*) Layer Ess 316, though this p.n. might be an old r.n. It is difficult to distinguish from leirr as in Layerthorpe YE 292.

leik ON, 'play, sport, a place where animals play'. (*b*) Cocklakes Cu 164, 466 (cocc), Ullock Cu 315, 367, Wooloaks Cu 204 (wulf). [~ lāc.]

leirr ON, 'mud, clay', leira ON, 'a clayey place'. (*a*) Lair Hill(s) L, YE (hyll), Larbrick La (brekka), Larpool YN (pǽla), Layerthorpe YE (þorp), Lear Ings YW (eng). (*b*) Lairs YE.

leið ON, 'a road, a track'. (*a*) Leagram La 142, Legram, *Laithgryme* YW (gríma[1]).

leme ME, 'an artificial water-course', first evidenced as *Leme* YW (from 1310) and surviving as dial. *leem* 'slime', *leam* 'an artificial river'. (*a*) Leam Bank L.

*lemo- Brit, 'an elm'; cf. RN 243–5 and on the forms *v.* Jackson 282, etc. (*b*) R. Leam Wa, Lem Brook Wo, Lymn L, Lympne K.

len, lin Corn, 'a pool, a lake'. (*a*) Lanyon. (*b*) Harlyn, Pellyn Co. [~ Welsh *llyn*, lindo-.]

lencten OE, 'Spring, Lent', as in OE *lencten-erðe* 'land ploughed in Spring' (WW 105.7). (*a*) Lentney So (gehæg).

lending ON, 'a landing place'. (*b*) Lendal Street, Marygate Landing Yk, *Cnarlending* (Selby) YW (ON *knǫrr* 'a warship'), all on R. Ouse Y. [~ land, -ing[1].]

lēode OE, 'folk, people'. (*a*) Leatherhead Sr (ride).

lēoht OE, lēht, līht (Angl), adj., 'light, bright, light-coloured', usually with tree- and wood-names. (*a*) Leagrave Bd (grāf), Leighton Nb (dūn), Light Birks Nb (birce), Lightcliffe (clif), Lighthazles (hæsel) YW, Lighthorne Wa (þyrne), Lightollers La (alor), Lightridge YW (hrycg), Lightshaw La (sceaga), Lightwood Wo (wudu).

les Corn, 'a residence', *v.* lisso-.

*lēto- Brit, llwyd Welsh adj., 'grey'. (*a*) Lichfield St, Lytchett Do (cēto-).

lettir OIr, leitir Gael, 'a hill, a slope', suggested for some Cu p.ns. such as (*b*) Whinlatter Cu 409 (hvin) (*v.* Latrigg Cu 321), but beside phonological difficulties it is difficult to distinguish from látr.

ley ME, 'a pool', *v.* **lagu.**

leyne, lain ME, 'a layer, a tract of arable land', is freq. in later f.ns. and is evidenced from the 13th century (Cu 482, W 439, Wo 391). The precise meaning is not known. (*b*) *Monklanes* Gl, Rolvenden Layne K 354, Tenant Lain Sx 310. [*v.* NED s.v. *lain*(*e*).]

leysingi ON, 'a freedman', used also as a pers.n. (Feilitzen 319). (*a*) Lazenby YN, Lazonby Cu (**bý**), Lazencroft YW (**croft**), *Laysingthorpe* L (**þorp**). [~**lauss**, ON *leysa* 'to loosen, to free', **-ing**[1].]

līc OE, 'a body, a corpse', mostly in allusion to places where a corpse has been found or possibly sometimes where skeletal remains in old burial places have been unearthed. (*a*) Leech Lake So (**lacu**), Lickpit Ha (**pytt**), Litchborough Nth (**beorg**), Litchardon D (**dūn**), Lychpole Sx (**pōl**).

-lic, -loc OE noun suffix of unknown origin, used to form the plant-names **bærlic, cerlic, hymlic** (ME *hemeluc*); it may be the common suffix **-uc** added to themes already ending in **-(e)l.**

***lic(c)** OE, 'a stream', is possible in (*b*) Beverley YE 192 (**beofer**). [~**lacu, læcc**, cf. Forsberg 102.]

* **līc-tūn** OE, 'a burial ground'. (*b*) Litchaton D. [**lic, tūn.**]

lida OE, 'a sailor', possibly also as a pers.n. (*a*) Lydney Gl (**ēg**). [~**(ge)lād.**]

lieu OFr, 'a place', usually with **bel.** (*b*) Beadlow Bd, Beaulieu Co, Ha, Bewley K, Nb (**bel**[2]), Rewley O (AN *real* 'royal').

lifer OE, 'liver', probably used in the sense 'thick, clotted water' (cf. OE *lifrig*, ME *livered* 'clotted, coagulated'), possibly sometimes as a stream-name. (*a*) Livermere Sf (**mere**), Liverpool La (**pōl**, etc.), Liversedge YW (**secg**).

līm OE, 'lime'. (*a*) Limehouse Mx (**āst**), Limekiln Nt, Sx, YW (**cyln**).

līn OE, **lín** ON, 'flax', sometimes difficult to distinguish from **lind**, esp. in Linton C, He, YE, and **hlynn.** (*a*) Linacre(s) C, La, Nb, Lenacre K (**æcer**), Linley Sa (**lēah**), Linthwaite YW (**þveit**), Linton Db (**tūn**), Lyford Brk (**ford**), Lylands YW (**land**), Lyncombe So (**cumb**), Lyneham O, W (**hām**).

lind OE, ON, 'a lime-tree'. (*a*) Limber L (**beorg**), Linby Nt (**bý**), Lind-, Lyndhurst Ha, K, Nt (**hyrst**), Lindley YW (**lēah**), Lindrick Nt, YW (**ric**), Lindridge K, Wo (**hrycg**), Lindsell Ess (**gesell**), Linwood Ha, L (**wudu**). (*b*) Lyne Sr, Lynn St; *Lindon* Wo (dat.pl.).

linden OE adj., 'growing with lime-trees'. (*a*) Lindfield Sx (feld). [lind, -en.]

*lindo- Brit, *linn PrWelsh, llynn Welsh, 'a pool, water'. On the forms, *v.* Jackson 512–13, 543, etc. This el. would be difficult to distinguish from hlynn (some of the examples cited s.v. hlynn might well belong here). (*a*) Lincoln (*Lindon* Ptolemy, *Lindum colonia* RavGeog, *colonia* 'colony'), Lindsey (*Lindis-*, ēg) L, Lindisfarne Nb ('the Lindsey (way)farers'). (*b*) King's Lynn Nf.

-ling OE diminutive suffix, *v.* -ing[1, 2].

*lisc OE, 'reeds, reedy marsh' or the like, cognate with OHG *lisca*, Du *lisch* 'reeds', and found in OE *Liscbroc* KCD 730 Do (Ekwall, Studies[1] 109, Forsberg 141). (*a*) Lyscombe Do (cumb). (*b*) Redlynch So (hrēod).

*lisso- Brit, llys Welsh, 'a hall', lis, les Corn, 'a court, a residence, the chief house in a district'. (*a*) Liscard Ch, Liskeard, Lesnewth Co. (*b*) Helston Co, Liss Ha.

lītel OE adj., 'little', *v.* lȳtel.

litestere, listere ME, 'a dyer' (Fransson 105). (*a*) Listelow Wa (lēah).

lítill ON adj., 'little', *v.* lȳtel.

ljóss ON adj., 'light, bright, bare'. (*a*) Leashore (haugr), R. Liza (á), Lyzzick (eik) Cu. [~lēoht.]

llan Welsh, 'a church', *v.* lann.

llanerch Welsh, 'a glade'. (*a*) Lanercost Cu 71.

llwyd Welsh adj., 'grey', *v.* lēto-.

llynn Welsh, 'a pool', *v.* lindo-.

llys Welsh, 'a hall', *v.* lisso-.

ló ON, 'a glade, a meadow'. (*b*) Belleau L (pers.n.). [~lēah.]

*lobb OE, 'something heavy or clumsy', used in p.ns. in a topographical sense not determined. The el. is found chiefly in D where most places are on or near steep slopes. (*a*) Labdon (tūn), Labworth Ess (wereð), Lobhill, Lopwell D (wella). (*b*) Lobb D 33, O 129.

loc OE, 'a lock, a bolt, a fold', loca OE, 'an enclosure', are difficult to keep apart in p.ns., though *loca* is better attested; since it would usually be reduced to *loc* as the first el. of a compound, it is uncertain whether *on lochylle* is from *loc* or *loca*. In some p.ns. where *loc* appears to be combined with a word for 'an enclosure', it may have the primary meaning of 'lock, bolt' (that is 'an enclosure that can be locked'). As a final el., it clearly denotes 'a fold' or 'an enclosure'; and in Ess minor names it is used of 'a lock, a river-barrier' (Ess 585). (*a*) Laughton L (tūn), Locka La, Locko Db, Lockwell Nt (haga), Lockham YE (holmr), Lockwood YN (viðr), YW (wudu). (*b*) Challock K (cealf), Harlock Ess (horu), Parlick La (pirige), Porlock So (port). [~lycca.]

***lōcere** OE, **lōkere** ME, 'a keeper, a shepherd', used also as a by-name (Fransson 146), as in OE *loceresweg* BCS 866, *Lokeresleag* KCD 687. (*a*) Lockerley Ha (lēah). [~OE *lōcian* 'to look', -ere.]

loddere OE, 'a beggar', in p.ns. usually referring to places like roads, fords, bridges, etc. frequented by beggars, as in OE *to loddera stræt* BCS 895, *Lodreswei* KCD 1367, *Loderesbrugg* C; cf. Bd 55 s.n. Beggary. (*a*) Lattiford So (ford), Leatherlake Sr (lacu), Lothersdale YW (denu), Lotherton Bridge D (tūn).

lǿkr, lǽkr ON, 'a brook, a rivulet', much used instead of bekkr in Iceland, but not very common in Norway (NGIndl 67), is difficult to distinguish from lece. (*b*) Leake L, Nt, YN, Leck La, Leek St, Wa.

loge OFr, **log(g)e** ME, 'a hut, a small house', later 'a house in a forest for temporary use, a house at the entrance to a park', common in late minor names. (*b*) Lodge Fm Mx, Sr *et freq*, Lodge Copse Nth, etc.

lǫgr ON, 'a law, a district administered under one law'. (*a*) Laffog La 109 (āc). (*b*) Possibly Skirlaugh YE (scīr 'shire'); *v.* býjar-lǫgr.

lollarde ME, 'a mumbler', in later ME 'a heretic', in p.ns. possibly used as a by-name. (*a*) Loosedon D 373 (dūn, from DB). [~MDu *lollaerd* 'a mumbler, a member of a religious fraternity'.]

lond OE, 'land', *v.* land.

lone OE, 'a lane', *v.* lane.

loning ME, 'a lane', *v.* laning.

loppe OE, 'a spider', difficult to distinguish from ON *hloppa* (Swed *loppa*), ModE dial. *lop* 'a flea'. (*a*) Lop Lane Yk 293.

lopped ME adj., 'lopped, having the branches cut off', with tree-names; it is first found in p.ns. in the 13th century. (*a*) Lapthorne D, Lopthorne Co, D (þorn). [~ModE *lop* 'a small branch, a twig' (cf. NED s.v. *lop* sb. 3), -ed.]

lopt ON, 'a loft, an upper chamber', is used with this meaning in p.ns. denoting buildings, esp. in lopt-hús. In Norw p.ns. it is also used of 'something elevated, esp. a hill' (NGIndl 66), and this sense may occasionally but not certainly occur in English p.ns. (*a*) Loftmarishes YN (merisc), Loscoe Db, YW, Loskay YN (skógr), Lothwaite (þveit), Low Scales (skáli) Cu. [~ON *loft*, OE *lyft* 'the air, the sky'.]

lopt-hús ON, 'a house with a loft or upper chamber' (the lower part being used as a stable or barn), usually found in the pl. (*b*) Lofthouse YW, Loftus YN, YW, Loftsome YE (all dat.pl. originally). [lopt, hús.]

***lort(e)** OE, 'dirt, mud, a muddy place, a swamp', has been suggested for certain OE charter p.ns. such as *to lortan hlæwe* BCS 705, *to lortenwille* b. 923, etc. (cf. Forsberg 158ff, RN 259ff, Zachrisson, SNPh v, 50), and it corresponds to OSwed *lorter*, Dan, Norw *lort* 'dirt'. (*a*) Lark Lane Nth, Lurk Lane YE (lane), Larport He (port) Lertwell Brk, *Lortewell* Nth (wella), Loatleys YE (lēah), *Lortemere* (mere), Lortepole (pōl) Sx, Lothburgh C 45, *Lurtebourne* Sx 4 (burna).

lost Corn, 'a tail'. (*a*) Lostwithiel, Lestow Co.

lufu OE, **love** ME, 'love', probably in allusion to places, esp. secluded lanes, considered suitable for love-making. (*a*) Luccombe Wt (cumb), Lusted Sr 337 (stede), and the common Love Lane *passim*; cf. also mægden.

luh OE, 'a lough, a lake, a pool', a loanword from Brit (cf. Welsh *llwch* and *v.* Förster KW 130), chiefly in the NCy. (*a*) Lutton L (tūn). (*b*) *The Loughe*, Lough Cu 160, Lowes Forest Nb 137.

lúka (lúkar nom.pl.) ON, 'the hollow of the hand', used topographically of 'a hollow' as in Norw p.ns. (NG iii, 195). (*b*) Lucker Nb 137 (nom.pl.).

***lum(m)** OE, 'a pool'; ModE dial. *lum* 'a deep pool in the bed of a river' is not recorded before the 18th century, except in p.ns., which carry it back to OE. (*a*) Lomax La 62 (halh), Lumford Db (ford), Lumley Du (OE *Lummalea*). (*b*) Lumb La 62, YW. [Origin unknown.]

lumber ME, 'lumber, odds and ends', first recorded in 1552 (NED) (*a*) Lumbercote YE 45 (cot, from 1150).

lundi ON, 'a puffin'. (*a*) Lundy Island D (ey).

lúndr (lúndar gen.sg.) ON, 'a small wood, a grove', also 'a sacred grove, one offering sanctuary'; in Scandinavia it is sometimes combined with the name of a heathen god as in Swed *Närlunda*

(*Nerthus*), Dan *Tislund* (~Tīw), *Torslunde* (*Þórr*), and a religious association is found in Plumbland Cu 309 in which, according to Reginald of Durham, *lund* was *nemus paci donatum* 'a grove given to peace'; there is historical evidence for a similar use in Sweden on a rune-stone at Eklunda near Lundby which was a grove where the outlaw Gunner settled (cf. Smith, LSE i, 72–5). The el. is combined with OE as well as ON els.; it is already recorded in OE in p.ns. and is found in ME minor names (C 338, Nt 287, Nth 267, YE 327, YN 329). Normally the modern form is *-land* finally. (*a*) Londonthorpe L (gen.sg., þorp), Lumby YW (bý). (*b*) Lound L, Nt, Sf, Lund La, YE, YN, YW, Lunt La. In compounds it is usually found with (i) tree-names, as Alderlands L (alor), Birklands Nt (birki), Ellerlands YN (elri), Plumbland Cu (plūme), Shrubland Sf (scrybb); Timberland L (timber); (ii) other significant words, as Holland Hu 220 (hagi), Kirkland La (kirkja), Morland We (mōr), Owlands YN (úlfr), Rockland Nf (hrōc), Rowlands Db (rá); (iii) pers.ns. frequently, both OE and ON, as Boyland Nf, Cowsland Nt, Natland We, Osland Nt, Snelland L, Sutherland YN, Swanland YE, Toseland Hu. (*c*) Upsland YN 221 (olim *Upsale*).

lūs OE, lús ON, 'a louse', may be found in some p.ns. where it denotes a place infested with lice, or is used as a pers.n. But, as Forsberg 182ff points out, it is found with words denoting 'barrow, hill', as in OE *on lusa beorg* BCS 699, *on lusebeorg* ib. 748, *to lusdune* ib. 1023, as well as in Continental p.ns., where 'louse-infested' may not be altogether appropriate; it has therefore been suggested that *lūs* was used to describe something small and insignificant. (*a*) Loosebarrow Do (beorg), Loose Howe YN (haugr), Lousehill So (hyll), Luscott D (cot), Luston He (tūn).

lūs-þorn OE, 'a spindle-tree', recorded as OE *on lusthorn* BCS 1215 *of lusðorne* ib. 1282, and ME *Lusethorne* YN, etc.; cf. also ME *Lousithorn*(*e*) Bk, O and *v.* Forsberg 188–9. It is possible in (*a*) Lostiford Sr 255, Lus Hill W. [lūs, þorn.]

*lūtegār OE, 'a trapping spear, a spear set as a trap for impaling wild animals', a compound word connected with OE *lūtian* 'to hide, skulk', *lytig* 'crafty', MHG *lūze* 'fishing net', etc., and OE gār 'spear'. Tengstrand 222ff, suggests this el. (and notes several Swed words for trapping devices of this kind) to explain the difficult series of p.ns., Ludgershall Bk, W, Luggershall Gl,

Lurgashall Sx, *Lotegoreshale* Ess (which all contain the final el. halh).

Of the various suggestions made for these names, two others may be noted:

(1) Ekwall (DEPN s.n.) proposes a combination of lȳt 'little' with a compound word gærs-halh; but, though some ME spellings of these p.ns. might fit this etymology, the genuine and contemporary OE spelling, *æt Lutegaresheale* 1015 ASWills, cannot possibly accord with this; ME spellings with *Lot-* (which occur in these p.ns.) are very unlikely developments of *lȳt*; it seems curious that *-gærs-halh* should almost always be *-gares-* in the spellings, and it would be remarkable that the doubtfully evidenced gærs-halh should always be found in combination with lȳt or lȳtel 'little'. Similar phonological difficulties arise with a suggestion of Mawer's (*Problems of Place-Name Study* 87) that the names may contain OE *hlyte* 'lot' and mean 'grassland on a healh allotted by lot'; Wallenberg (KPN 333–4) notes these difficulties and gets round them by other proposals such as OE **hlut* (a by-form of hlot 'lot, share') or an old stream-name related to holt 'wood'.

(2) The second major proposal (by Mawer) is that this series of names consists of a pers.n. *Lutegar* and halh (Bk 104–6, Sx 111, W 367–8). This does of course explain certain formal difficulties, but it makes others. Although the pers.n. *Lutegar* may be found as the first el. of ME *Lutgaresberi*, the old name of Montacute So, and as the surname of Thomas *Lotegar* (Tengstrand 224), it is unlikely to be of English origin, for *Lut(e)-* is certainly not an OE pers.n. theme, and if, as is likely enough, it is of Continental Germanic origin its appearance in a p.n. recorded in Old English and its repetition in others over such a wide area would be improbable. There is also some difficulty in the coincidence of so rare a pers.n. and one so doubtfully evidenced (even Thomas *Lotegar's* surname may originate in a local place-name) being so often combined with halh.

(3) It would therefore seem that Tengstrand's proposal of a word *lūte-gār* 'trapping spear' combined with halh is the best solution of all the orthographic and composition difficulties, and its regular occurrence with halh is not here problematic, for 'a nook of land' is precisely the place where such a trap would be set. The persistent genitive *lutegares-* in the p.ns. offers no

serious problem of composition. The element may also enter into *Lutgaresberi* (with beorg, burh, or even burg 'burrow') and also be the source of Thomas *Lotegar's* surname.

*lycce OE, 'an enclosure', possibly evidenced in OE in *on lychagan* KCD 1309 (cf. Forsberg 192–4), corresponding to ON *lykkja*, Swed *lycka* 'enclosure', OHG *luccha* 'a gap', is suggested by Ekwall, Studies[2] 182ff, for several p.ns., but it is hard to keep apart from līc. (*a*) Lessland Wt 154 (land), Letchworth Hrt (worð), Liscombe Bk (cumb). [~loc, OE *lūcan* 'to lock'.]

lyng ON, 'ling, heather'. (*a*) Line Croft Nt (croft), Ling Hill YN (haugr). (*b*) Ling L, Nf, Lingwood Nt.

lȳt OE adj., 'little'. (*a*) Litchurch Db (cirice). [~lȳtel.]

lȳtel, lytel, lītel (lytlan wk. obl.) OE adj., lítill ON adj., 'little, small', are generally indistinguishable from each other in the Danelaw. (*a*) Littleborough La, Nt, Littlebury Ess (burh), Littlecote Brk, W (cot), Little Dale Cu (dæl), Littleham D (hām), Littleton Do, Gl, Ha, Mx *et freq*, Litlington Sx (tūn), Littleworth Bk (worð). (*c*) As an affix *Little* (often rendered by Lat *parva*) prefixed to Aston St, Bampton Cu, Carlton L, Compton Wa, Dean Gl, Mayne Do; Littlehampton Sx. [OE *lȳtel*, *lytel* and OE *lītel*, ON *lítill* are radically different forms, *v.* NED s.v. *little*.]

lȳðre OE adj., 'bad, wretched, worthless'. (*a*) Leatherfield Hrt (feld).

M

mǣd (**mǣdwe** obl.sg., **mǣdwa** nom.pl., **mǣdwum** dat.pl.) OE (WSax), **mēd** (Angl, Kt), 'a meadow', originally 'a piece of meadowland kept for mowing', is very common in OE, ME and later f.ns. (cf. Mdf 91, Bd 295, Bk 259, Cu 484, Nt 287, etc.). The common later form is *meadow* from the OE obl. cases, *mead* from the OE nom.sg. being now mostly poetic and dialectal. (*a*) Madehurst Sx, Medhurst K (**hyrst**), Meadle Bk (**hyll**), Meads Sx (**efes**), Medbourne Lei, W (**burna**), R. Medlock La (**lacu**), Metfeld Sf (**feld**). (*b*) In compounds, it is found with (i) descriptive adjs., as Breightmet La (**beorht**), Hormead Hrt (**horu**); (ii) appellatives, etc., as Dolemeads So (**dāl**), Foulmead K (**fugol**), Runnymede Sr (**rūn**, **ēg**), Shipmeadow Sf (**scēap**); (iii) words denoting people, as Bushmead Bd (**bisceop**), Presteign He (**prēost**); (iv) pers.ns., as Hardmead Bk, White Ox Mead So. [~**mǣð**, OE *māwan* 'to mow'.]

mæddre, **mædere** OE, 'madder' or some similar plant. (*a*) Maddacombe (**cumb**), Maddacleare (**clif**) D, Mayfield St (**feld**). [~**maðra**.]

mægden (**mægdena** gen.pl.) OE, 'a maiden'.

(1) This el. generally denotes 'a maiden, a young unmarried woman', in p.ns. usually in allusion to places owned by them, to places thought suitable for their use, or to places which they habitually frequented (as in lanes or at bridges, fords and the like), as in p.ns. incorporating words for 'youth', like **cild**, **cniht**, sometimes to places owned by houses of religious females.

(2) The use of the word with **burh** and **castel** is fairly widespread (cf. Cu 255, R. E. M. Wheeler, *Maiden Castle, Dorset*, Oxford 1943, 6–14). In a few instances like Medbury Bd 71, where there is no evidence of earthwork or old fortification, it may simply denote 'a manor held by maidens', but usually such places are the sites of ancient earthworks. In many of them the suggestion that they signify 'a fortification so strong that it could be defended by girls' or 'one that has never been taken' would no doubt be possible; but this kind of description would hardly be applicable to some of the earthworks which must have long passed into disuse when these names were created. The sense may well be that implied in other names like the common Love Lane (cf. *Maiden Lane oth. Lovers Lane* in Penrith Cu 231 and **lufu**), namely, 'a place frequented by

maidens, a secluded place where maidens could indulge their fancies unobserved'. This kind of meaning is also likely in other p.ns. formed with topographical els. like cumb, dūn, etc.

(3) The el. usually remains as *maiden*, but a shortened form *maid* (which is not to be derived from mægð[1] 'maiden') also occurs, as in Maidenhead Brk (olim *Mayden-*, *Mayde-*), Maidforth Nth; this loss of *-en* would be paralleled by byden.

(4) (*a*) Madley Wo (lēah), Maidencombe D (cumb), Maidencourt Brk (cot), Maiden Down D (dūn), Maidenford D, Maidford Nth (ford), Maidenhatch (hæc), Maidenhead (hȳð) Brk, Maidenwell Co, L, Maidwell Nf (wella, perhaps in allusion to 'fertility' springs); Maidens Bridge Mx, Maybridge Wo (brycg, cf. also *mægidna brycg* BCS 428); Maiden Castle Cu, Do, Castle Hill (Saxton) YW (olim *Maidanecastell*), also Maiden Castle, Edinburgh (olim *Castrum Puellarum*, cf. NED s.v. *maiden* 5) (from castel); Maidenburgh Ess 371, Medbury Bd 71, *Maidebury* C 314 (burh), cf. also mǣge.

(*b*) Rigmaiden We (hryggr, an inversion-compound).

(*c*) As an affix *Maiden* prefixed to Bradley W (from the nuns of Amesbury), Morton Bk 45 (from two maiden ladies who built the church), Newton Do, Winterbourne W.

mǣge OE, 'a kinswoman, a maiden', used in much the same way as mægden. (*a*) Mawbray Cu 296 (a Roman fort), Mayburgh We (burh).

mægen OE, 'might, power', used as a prefix in compound words in the sense 'mighty, huge', as in OE *mægen-stān*, 'a huge stone, a monolith', in *Boethius Metr.* 5.16 (where the prose has *micel stan*) and *to mægenstanes dene* BCS 727, might be confused with Welsh maen 'stone' in some p.ns., esp. in the WCy. (*a*) Mainbow D (boga), Mainstone D, Db, He, Sa, Sr (stān).

mægð[1] OE, 'a maiden', occurs in a few OE p.ns. like *Magþeford* BCS 672 Gl, *Mægþeford* ib. 906 Brk, and was used in much the same way as mægden, by which it would generally be replaced later. It may be found in (*a*) Maidstone K 140 (stān), but it cannot be distinguished from mægð[2].

mægð[2] OE, 'folk, people', is possible in (*a*) Maidstone K 140 (stān), which would be equivalent in meaning to Folkestone K from folc, but *v.* mægð[1]. Cf. *Meanware mægð* (OEBede) for the Meon district Ha.

mægðe OE, 'may-weed', difficult to distinguish from mægð. (*a*) Maidford W (ford), Mayfield Sx (feld), Maytham K (hamm).

mǣl[1] OE (WSax), mēl (Angl, Kt), 'a sign, a cross', had a variety of meanings, the chief of which in p.ns. is probably 'cross, crucifix', as also in cristel-mǣl, but it would be difficult to keep apart from mǣl[2] and mǣle. (*a*) Malden Sr, Maldon Ess, Mauldon Bd, Meldon Nb (dūn); Trimdon Du (þrēo, dūn).

mǣl[2] OE, 'speech', a shortened form of mæðel, may be found in some p.ns. but it cannot be separated from mǣl[1].

mǣle, (ge)mǣl (mǣlan wk. obl.) OE adj., 'dyed, stained, multi-coloured' (cf. OE *unmǣle* 'unspotted, immaculate'), is difficult to distinguish from mǣl (and perhaps also from OE *mǣle*, 'bowl, bucket', used in some topographical sense); it may occur where ME spellings are *Mele-* rather than *Mel-*. (*a*) Melbury D, Do (*freq*) (burh), Meldon D 203 (dūn), Melhuish D (hīwisc), Mellersh's Fm Sr (ersc), Milbury D, Millbarrow Ha (OE *mælanbeorh*, beorh).

maen Welsh, mên Corn, 'a stone, a rock', from Brit **mag(e)no-* 'a stone, a rock', may be difficult to distinguish from mægen in compounds with 'stone'. (*a*) Manuels Co. (*b*) Mayne, Broadmayne Do, Penmayne, Tremayne Co.

(ge)mǣne (mānan, mǣnan wk. obl.) OE adj., 'common', in p.ns. denoting property or land owned or held communally, was occasionally used as a noun 'common land'. Many places with names containing this el. are to be found on the outskirts of parishes. It is common in ME f.ns. (C 338, Ess 585, Hrt 260, Mx 202, W 441). (*a*) Manaton D, Manton Nt, R, W (tūn), Manadon D (dūn), Mangreen Nf (grēne), Manley Ch (lēah), Man-, Menwood W, Manhood Sx, Meanwood YW, Monwood Wa (wudu), *Meaning Way* O (weg), Meneatt, Menith Wo (geat), Menmarsh O (mersc), Menwith YW (viðr). (*b*) The Mean K, *West Mean* Wt. [~mann.]

(ge)mǣnnes OE, 'community', used of 'common land, a common holding'. (*v.* Mawer, Problems 57); cf. also its use in ME f.ns. in Sx 560 (s.v. *menesse*). (*b*) The Minnis K, Minnis Rock Sx 536, 560, Rhodes Minnis K. [(ge)mǣne, -nes.]

(ge)mǣnscipe OE 'a community, a communal possession'. (*a*) Mansditch D 130 (dīc), Manships Shaw Sr 292 (sceaga). (*b*) Minskip YW (with ON *-sk-*); cf. also *Manship* W 441. [(ge)mǣne, -scipe.]

mǣre OE adj., 'famous'. (*a*) Merstow Wo (stōw).

(ge)mǣre OE, 'a boundary, a border', and in f.ns. 'the balk of a ploughland', surviving as dial. *meare* 'a strip of grassland forming a boundary, a boundary road', is of very common occurrence in

OE charters as an el. prefixed to the names of objects (like āc, brōc, dīc, pōl, pytt, stān, þorn, weg, etc.) which marked the boundaries of estates; it is also common in ME f.ns. in many counties. It survives mostly in p.ns. which can for the most part be identified with boundaries; thus, Maesbrook, Maesbury and *Merset* Sa are all near Offa's Dyke, Didmerton and Tormarton Gl are on the Gl-W county boundary, and Meersbrook YW forms part of the boundary of Y and Db. The el. is sometimes difficult to keep apart from mere, unless the topography is decisive for one or the other. (*a*) Marbrook, Mere Brook W, Marlbrook Sa (brōc), Marden K (denn), Sx (dūn), Mareway C (weg), Marley D, Mearley La (lēah), Martin Nt (on the county boundary) and perhaps Marton in some cases (tūn), Merbach He (bece), Mereburn Nb (burna), Merridge So (hrycg). (*b*) Udimore Sx, land-gemǣre.

maes Welsh, 'a plain, a field'. (*a*) Maisemore Gl (mawr).

mǣte (mǣtan wk. obl.) OE adj., 'mean, poor, bad', is possible in (*a*) Metham YE 254 (hām).

mǣð OE, 'mowing, the cutting of grass or corn', as in ModE *aftermath*, hence 'mowing grass, crop', ME f.ns. (C 338). (*b*) Meeth(e) D, Wheatmath Field C. [~OE *māwan* 'to mow', -ð(e), mǣd.]

mæðel OE, 'speech, assembly, council', also perhaps in a short form mǣl[2], is used in p.ns. that denote the meeting place of an assembly or council. (*a*) Malton YN (tūn), Matlask Nf (æsc, askr), Matlock Db (āc).

mǣðere OE, 'a mower'. (*a*) Madresfield Wo (feld). [~mǣð, -ere.]

mǣw OE, 'a sea-gull'. (*a*) Measham Co, Mew Stone D.

*mǣwe OE, 'a meadow', *v.* māwe.

magna Lat. adj., 'great', often used, esp. in medieval documents, for *Great*, *Much*, etc. in affixes, as (*c*) Ashby Magna Lei.

main, mesne, ME, 'demesne land, home farm' (often in pl.). (*b*) *Maynes* Cu 166, 484, Mainsbank Nb, Mesne Close Nt 288. [OFr *demeine*; *mesne* is an AFr law spelling.]

māl[1] late OE, 'a law-suit, bargaining', also 'tax, rent', thought to be a loan from ON *mál*, cognate with mǣl[2], may in view of its provenance be simply a variant of the latter, contracted from *maðel* as distinct from mæðel, and so perhaps have in p.ns. also the sense 'speech, council'. (*a*) Molash K (æsc), Mole Drove L (drāf), Molland K, Mollands Ess (land, cf. ModE *molland* 'land held by payment of rent instead of service').

mal[2] OFr adj., 'bad'. (*a*) Malpas Ch (OFr *pas* 'passage'), Malzeard YW (assart).

*malgr ON, 'a gravelly or stony place', related to malu, melr, mǫl 'gravelly soil', Swed *mal* 'stones' and the Swed lake-name *Maljen* (olim *Malghe*); cf. Ekwall, DEPN 297. (*a*) Malham Moor (olim *Malghemore*), Malham Tarn (*Malgewater*) and (*b*) Malham YW (dat.pl.). The exact meaning is not known, and it is difficult to decide which aspect of the remarkable scenery at Malham it describes. The allusion might be to loose boulders or the like.

malm OE (Angl), mealm (Kt, WSax), 'sand, sandy or chalky soil, soft stone', málmr (málmar gen.sg.) ON, 'sand, sandy field'. OE *malm* is found only in the derivatives *mealmeht* 'sandy', *mealmstān* 'sandstone' (*a*) Manton L (tūn), possibly Melmerby YN 219 (with ON gen.sg., bý). [~Goth *malma* 'sand'.]

*malu (*malwe dat.sg.), *mealu OE, 'a gravel ridge', as in ME f.ns. such as *Malwe* Wa, *le longemalewe* Nth, *Gretmale* C 338. (*a*) Mawsley (lēah), (*b*) Wythemail Nth 129. [~malgr.]

man-drēam OE, 'revelry, festivity', probably used of a place where festivities were held. (*b*) Mondrum Ch.

mangere OE, 'a trader, a merchant'. (*a*) Mangersford D (ford), Mangerton Do (tūn), and in st.ns. such as *Haymongergate* (hēg), *Ketmongergate* (ON *kjǫt* 'flesh') Yk, etc. [~OE *mangian* 'to trade' (from Lat *mango* 'trader'), -ere.]

manig, monig OE adj., 'many'. (*a*) R. Manifold St (OE *manig-fald* 'with many folds'), Manningtree Ess (trēow), Moneyhull Wa (hyll), Monyash Db (æsc).

mann, monn OE, maðr (mans gen.sg., manna gen.pl.) ON, 'a man', is found in some p.ns. denoting in the pl. (i) 'community', as in almenn and p.ns. like Monmore St (mere), Montford Sa (ford), when it is sometimes difficult to distinguish from (ge)mǣne and the OE pers.n. *Manna*, or (ii) 'dwellers, inhabitants', as in Brockmanton He ('tūn of the brook-dwellers'), Eastmanstreet W ('eastern dwellers', strǣt), Westmancote Wo, Westmanton D ('western dwellers', cot, tūn), possibly Woodmancote Gl (cot, 'dwellers in the wood', but *v.* wudu-mann). It is found in the sg. in Noman's Land Sx, Wo ('no man's land', that is, 'deserted land') and in many compounds such as man-drēam, æcer-mann, æsc-mann, bed-mann, gafol-mann, hunda-maðr, sacu-mann, scīr-mann, sōc-mann, sulh-mann, wæðe-mann, wudu-mann.

***mapel, *mapul** OE, 'a maple-tree', found only in OE in the compound *mæpel-trēow* (recorded only in charter material, as in *ðæt ruge mapeltreow, ðonne mapultre* KCD iii, 379, 381). The usual OE word is mapuldor. (*a*) Maplebeck Nt (bekkr), Mappleton Db, YE (tūn).

mapuldor OE, 'a maple-tree'. (*a*) Maperton So, Mapperton Do (tūn), Mapledurham Ha, O (hām), Mapledurwell Ha (wella), Maplehurst K (hyrst), Maplescombe K (camp), Maplestead Ess (stede), Mapperley Db (lēah), Mappleborough Wa (beorg). (*b*) Mappowder Do. [~mapel, -dor.]

māra OE adj., 'greater, bigger', is rare. (*a*) Marwood Du (wudu).

mare Lat, 'the sea' (cf. LatAdd 338). (*c*) Bradwell juxta Mare Ess, Weston super Mare So.

mareis OFr, ME, 'a marsh'. (*a*) Morris Fen C. (*c*) Stow Maries Ess 229 (from a surname). [~mersc.]

market ONFr, late OE, merket ME, 'a market', esp. in st.ns. (*a*) Market Place, Market Street *passim*, *Marketshire* Yk (scīr), Martholme La (holmr). (*b*) Newmarket Sf, Saturday Market YE, Thursday Market Yk. (*c*) Stowmarket Sf, S. Cave YE (olim *Marched Caue*), Thorpe Market Nf, Market Bosworth, Market Harborough Lei; cf. forum.

marle OFr, ME, 'marl'. (*a*) Marl Pit K (pytt). (*b*) Blanch YE (olim *Blanchmarle*).

marlede ME adj., 'marled, fertilized with marl'. (*a*) Marland Bridge Sx (land).

marling ME, 'a marl pit' or 'a marled place'. (*b*) Marling Place, Marling Shaw, Marlpit Shaw Sx (cf. Sx 386, 560, Hrt 258). [marle, -ing[1].]

marr[1] ON, 'a fen, a marsh' (recorded in the sense 'the sea' but only rarely), survives as Swed dial., Dan *mar* 'bog, fen'; it is common in f.ns. in YE 327, YN 329. It interchanges with the cognate OE mere, as in Eelmere, Fimber, Redmere YE, Whitwood Mere YW. (*a*) Marfleet YE (flēot), Marton YN (*freq*) (tūn). (*b*) The Marrs YE, Kelmer YN (kelda).

márr[2] ON, 'a horse' (only in poetry), is possible in (*a*) Marrick YN 294 (hryggr).

māse OE, 'a titmouse', is possible in (*a*) Macefen Ch (fenn).

māððum, māðm OE, 'treasure, a gift', perhaps used in the same way as gifu, gift. (*b*) Mathon Wo 65. [~Goth *máiþms* 'gift'.]

maðra ON, 'madder'. (*a*) Matterdale Cu (dalr). [~mæddre.]

maurr ON, 'an ant'. (*a*) Moor Isles La 82 (hygel).

*māwe, *mǣwe OE, 'a meadow'. (*b*) Dunmow Ess 475 (dūn). [~OE *māwan* 'to mow', -e.]

mawr Welsh adj., 'big, great' (from PrWelsh **mōr*). (*a*) Morchard D (cēto-), Mordiford He (ty), Morfe St (tref). (*b*) Maisemore Gl (maes).

mearc OE, 'a march, a boundary' and as a final el. 'a boundary mark'; forms with *mark* are regular, *mearc* being a fem. *ō*-stem. Ekwall (DEPN 299) explains the palatal *ch* in March C as due to the name being an old locative in *-i* (**marki*). It is sometimes difficult to separate this el. from Merce (which is a derivative). (*a*) Marcle He (lēah), Marden W (denu), Mark So (ærn), Markham Nt (hām), Marksbury So (burh, probably in reference to the Wansdyke), Markwich Sr (wīc), Marraton Co (dūn), Marsden Gl, YW (denu). (*b*) Mirk Bk 243, Chilmark Wt (cegel), Shiremark Sr, Sx (scīr 'shire'), The West March Cu; it is also found in ME minor names (C 339, Mx 202, etc.). [~mǫrk.]

meargealla, mergelle OE, 'gentian' (cf. Ekwall, Studies[2] 110). (*a*) Marldon D (dūn), possibly Malborough D, Marlborough W (beorg), Marwell D (wella).

mearð OE, 'a marten, a weasel', as in OE *mearðeshrycg* BCS 455. (*a*) Marefield Lei (feld), Mardleybury Hrt, Marley YW, Martley Sf, Wo (lēah).

mēd OE (Angl, Kt), 'a meadow', *v.* mǣd.

medume, meodume OE adj., 'middle, of medium size'. (*a*) Meadfield Sr (feld), Medmenham Bk (hām), Medmerry Fm Sx, Modney Nf (ēg). (*b*) R. Meden Nt 6 (the middle one of three rivers).

mēl[1] OE (Angl, Kt), 'a cross', *v.* mǣl[1].

*mēl[2] PrWelsh, moel Welsh, *moil, *muil PrCorn, adj., 'bald' (from Brit **mailo-*, later **mēlo-*, cf. Jackson 328). The sense in p.ns. may be compared with that of calu. (*a*) Mallerstang We, Malvern Wo, Melchet Ha, Mellor Db, La, Plenmellor Nb, Watermillock Cu. (*b*) Fontmell Do (funta).

*melce OE (Angl), milce (WSax), mi(e)lch ME adj., 'milch, yielding milk'; in OE it occurs only in *þri-milce* 'May' (the month when cows can be milked thrice a day); in p.ns. it is probably used in the same way as meoluc. (*a*) Melchbourne (burna), *Melcheheg* Bd 16 (gehæg), *Melcheburnfeld* Mx (burna). [~meoluc, -e.]

melde OE, 'orach', is suggested by Ekwall (DEPN) for (*a*) Melbourn C (burna); in C 58 it is noted that orach would not be found in the locality; although on formal grounds both Melbourn and Meldreth C 60 are from *melde*, the word may denote some other plant than orach, to which it is first recorded as applying *c.* 1450 (NED s.v. *milds*).

*melin Corn, 'a mill' (cf. Welsh *melin*). (*a*) Mellingey, Millendreath. (*b*) Tremellan Co. [Lat *molina*, myln.]

melr ON, 'a sand-bank, a sand-hill'. (*a*) Meaux YE 43 (sǽr). (*b*) Meols Ch; Cartmel La (kartr), North Meols La (norð), Rathmell YW (rauðr); with pers.ns., as Argarmeles La, Ingoldmells L, Ravensmeols La. [~malgr.]

*menehi Corn, 'sanctuary'. (*b*) Manhay, Tremenhee Co. [Lat *monachia*, Bret *menechi* 'sanctuary'.]

meneth Corn, 'a hill'. (*b*) Menna, Penmenna Co. [~minid.]

meoluc, meolc, milc OE, 'milk', probably used of rich pastures and the like yielding good milk; in stream-names it may denote a turbid nature or milky colour or streams which run through rich pastures. (*a*) Melcombe Do (cumb, cf. *meoluccumb* BCS 620 Ha), Melkridge Nb (hrycg). Milkhurst Sx (hyrst), Milkwell Du (wella), Mulbarton Nf (bere-tūn). [~melce.]

mēos OE, 'a moss, a marsh, a bog'. (*a*) Meesden Hrt (dūn), Moseley Bk, Mosley Nt (lēah), Muswell Bk (wella). (*b*) R. Mease Lei (with Measham), Meece St. [~mýrr, OHG *mios*, and mos by ablaut.]

meox OE, 'dung', *v.* mix.

Merce (Mercna gen.pl.) OE (Angl), Mierce (WSax), 'the Mercians' (cf. Ekwall, NoB xli, 141), the English tribe settled in the West Midlands, difficult to keep apart from mearc, but possible (with -*k*- from gen.pl. *mercna* or due to ON influence) in (*a*) Markenfield YW (near Markington, *v.* ingas), Markfield Lei (feld). [~mearc.]

mercels OE (Angl), miercels (WSax), 'a mark', probably 'a boundary mark, a boundary'. (*a*) Marsden La 86 (denu). [~mearc, -els.]

mere[1] OE, mær(e) (ONb), 'a pool', occasionally 'a sea pool', and in Margate K, Mersea Ess (*igland...ute on þære sæ* ASC) 'the sea, the ocean'. The secondary ONb form *mær*, ME *mar*, limited in p.ns. to Y, L, Nt, cannot be distinguished from marr[1], which may have replaced *mere* in these Danelaw counties. It is also difficult to separate from (ge)mǣre, except when the topography specifically indicates one word or the other. It is common in ME minor names (C 339, Ess 586, Mx 202, Nt 287, *et passim*).

(*a*) Marbury Ch (burh), Mardale We (dæl), Marlow Bk (lāf), Marten W, Martin Ha, K, L, Wo *et freq*, Marton Ch, La, L, Wa, Y *et freq*, Merton D, Nf, O (tūn).

(*b*) Maer Co, St, Meare So, Mere Ch, L. In compounds, it is combined with (i) descriptive words, as Fennymere Sa (fennig), Lomer K (lām), Ringmer Sx (hring), Seamer YN, Semer Nf, Sf, Semerwater YN (sǣ), Stanmer Sx, Stanmore Mx (stān), Thirlmere Cu (þyrel); (ii) vegetation names, as Grasmere We (gærs), Redmarley Wo, Redmire YN (hrēod), Rushmere Sf (risc), Widmere Bk (wīðig); (iii) the names of living creatures, as Almer Do (ǣl), Buckmere K (bucca), Cranmore So (cran), Cromer Nf (crāwe), Eldmire YN (elfitu), Enmore Do (ened), Fowlmere C, Fulmer Bk (fugol), Keymer Sx (cū), Pickmere Ch (pīc), Tadmarton O (tāde); (iv) words denoting people, as Fishmere L (fiscere), Walmer K (Walh); (v) pers.ns. occasionally, as Dedmar K, Offmoor Wo, Peasemore Brk, Tusmore O, Windermere La.

mere[2] OE (Angl, Kt), miere (WSax), 'a mare', difficult to distinguish from mere[1], is possible in some p.ns. such as (*a*) Marden K, but no certainty is possible.

merece OE, 'wild celery, smallage', has been proposed for (*a*) Marcham Brk (hām), Marchington St (hǣma-tūn), Marchwood Ha (wudu).

merket ME, 'a market', *v.* market.

mersc, merisc OE, 'watery land, a marsh', is common in most parts, except that in some areas of the Danelaw such as Nt (as contrasted with L or YE) ON kjarr is more frequently used. The older form *merisc* is found in some p.ns. such as Marishes YN; in the Danelaw ME *mersk* (as in Marske YN) has ON *-sk*, and numerous spellings like *Mars-*, *Mers-* are AN. It is common as *mershe*, *mersk* in ME f.ns. (*passim*).

(*a*) Marshfield Gl (feld), Marshwood Do (wudu), Marston Bd, Bk, Ch, Gl, He, L, Lei, Nth, O, So, YW *et passim*, Merston K, Sx, Wt (tūn).

(*b*) Marsh Sa, Sx, Marsh Gibbon Bk, Marske YN (2). In compounds, it is usually found with (i) a descriptive word, as Lamarsh Ess, Lamas Nf (lām), Michelmarsh Ha (micel), *Owstmarsk* YE (austr), Rawmarsh YW (rauðr), Saltmarsh Gl, He, Sx, YE (salt), Widemarsh He (wīd); (ii) older p.ns., as Denge Marsh, Romney

Marsh K; (iii) bird-names, etc., as Crakemarsh St (craca), *Henmarsh* (now Moreton in Marsh) Gl (henn), Owmers Nb (ūle); (iv) pers.ns., as Gunneymarsh YE, Titchmarsh Nth.

(*c*) Burgh le Marsh L, Marsh Baldon O.

[~mere, -isc, from WGerm **marisk-*, which was borrowed as Lat *mariscus*, whence mareis.]

mesne AFr, 'demesne land', *v.* main.

meðal ON adv., 'among, between', in p.ns. with adj. function 'middle', mostly found replacing OE middel as in the spellings of Middleton YW (OE *middel-*, *meðeltun*, ME *Mid*(*d*)*el-*, *Mitheltun*). (*a*) Medlar La (erg), Melbourne YE (burna), Melton L, Lei, Nf, YE (tūn), Melwood L (wudu), Methwold Nf (wald).

micel, mycel (miclan wk. obl.), OE adj., 'big, great', usually remains *Mickle-* in p.ns., but occasional spellings like ME *Muchele-* and *Much-* (with ME loss of *-el*) come from the OE variant *mycel.* Spellings with medial *-k-* are NCy or NMidl in origin or are due to the influence of ON mikill. (*a*) Michel Grove Sx (grāfa), Michelmarsh Ha (mersc), Mickfield Sf, Micklefield YW (feld), Micklebring YW (brink), Mickleton Gl, YN, Muggleton Wt (tūn), Mickley Nb (lēah), Muchelney So (ēg), Muckleford Do (ford), Mucklow Wo (hlāw). (*c*) Mitcheldean Gl, Much Dewchurch He, and sometimes in the older spellings of p.ns. which now have *Great*, as Great Bourton O (olim *Muchele-*). [~mikill.]

* micge OE, 'liquid drainings from manure', as in OE *micghæma gemæra* KCD 636, now NCy dial. *migg*. (*a*) Migley Du 142 (lēah).

mid OE prep., adv., 'among, amidst', probably used also in an elliptical fashion, as of the land between two ridges or valleys (as in Midridge So). It is sometimes influenced by ON miðr. (*a*) Mid(d)ridge Du, So (hrycg), Middop, Midhope YW (hop), Midhurst Sx (hyrst), Midsyke YN (sīc).

middel (midlan wk. obl.) OE adj., 'middle', midlest OE adj. sup., 'middlemost'. The el. is often replaced by ON meðal in the Danelaw. (*a*) Middleham Du, YN (hām), Middleney So (ēg), Middlesex (Seaxe), Middleton Db, Du, Ess *et passim*, Milton Bd, Bk, Brk, C *et freq* (tūn); the sup. *midlest* is found in Milston W 369 and some forms of Middlewich Ch. (*c*) Middle Aston, Middle Barton O, etc.

midding ME, 'a midden, a dung-heap' (cf. NED s.v. *midden*). (*b*) Blackmiddingmoor Nb, *Burdatt Midding* YE.

mid-sumor, -er OE, ME, 'Midsummer'. (*c*) Midsomer Norton So (in allusion to the festival of St John, the patron saint of the parish church).

Mierce OE (WSax), 'the Mercians', *v.* Merce.

miere OE (WSax), 'a mare', *v.* mere^{2}.

mikill ON adj., 'big, great', difficult to distinguish in the NCy and NMidl from micel. (*a*) Mickleby YN (bý), Micklethwaite Cu, YW (þveit).

milce OE (WSax) adj., 'milch', *v.* melce.

mīl-gemearc OE, 'a mile-mark' (recorded in *Beowulf* 1362 only, meaning 'measurement in miles'), no doubt with the sense 'mile-stone' or the like in (*b*) *Milemerke* YN 331.

mīl-gemet OE, 'a mile distance', possibly 'a mile-stone', found in OE in *to mil gemete* BCS 955, *on ðæt milgemæt* KCD 673. (*b*) Milemead D 219 (1 mile from Tavistock).

*mīl-stān OE, 'a mile-stone'. (*b*) Milestone Wood Sx.

minid OWelsh, mynydd Welsh, 'a mountain', usually becoming *myned* in OE. (*a*) Mendip Hills So, Mindrum Nb, Minehead So, Mindton, Minton Sa. (*b*) Meend Gl, He, Sa, Minn Ch, The Mynde He; Longmynd Sa, Pen Cross D. [Brit **monijo-*, ~ meneth Lat *mons* 'mountain'.]

minte OE, 'mint'. (*a*) Minety W (ēg), Minstead Ha, Sx (stede), Minterne Do (ærn). [~ Lat *mentha*.]

*mispeler OE, 'a medlar-tree'. (*a*) Misperton YN 75 (tūn). [~ OHG *mespila*, ME *mespile(r)*.]

mist OE, 'mist'. (*a*) Misdon (dūn), Mis Tor (torr) D 150, 195.

mistel OE, 'mistletoe', is possible in (*a*) Mistley Ess (lēah), *Mystelfelde*, *Mystlehawe* Sr (feld, haga).

miðr ON adj., 'middle', sometimes replaced mid. (*a*) Meathop We, Mythop La (hop).

mix, meox OE, 'dung, filth'. (*a*) Maxted K (stede), Mixehill Bd 163 (weg). (*b*) Misk Nt 119. [~ mixen.]

mixen OE, 'a dung-hill'. (*a*) Mixbury O 230 (burh), Mixenden YW (denu). (*b*) Mixon St, Oldmixton So. [mix, -en.]

mjór ON adj., 'thin, narrow, small'. (*a*) Measand We (sand), Muker YN (akr).

moel Welsh adj., 'bald', *v.* mēl^{2}.

~~*moil PrCorn adj., 'bald', *v.* mēl^{2}.~~

*moke ME, 'a stump, a log', cf. ModE dial. *mock* 'stump'. (*a*) Mock Bridge Sx 217. [Origin unknown.]

mǫl (malar gen.sg.) ON, 'gravel, gravelly soil'. (*a*) Mawthorpe L (þorp). [~malgr.]

molda OE, *moldi ON, 'the crown of the head', used as a hill-name in Norw p.ns. (*a*) Mockerkin Cu 410 (pers.n.), possibly Mouldsworth Ch (worð).

molde OE, 'earth, soil', in f.ns., such as *Swartemolde* YN 329. (*a*) Moulderidge Db (ric). [~mylde.]

molle ME, 'a mole' (recorded from 1398, NED), is possible in (*a*) Molecombe Sx 78 (cumb, from 1278).

mōna OE, 'the moon', in some undetermined application. (*a*) Moonhill Sx 264 (hyll).

monachus Lat, 'a monk' (cf. munuc). (*c*) Buckland Monachorum D.

mōnandæg OE, 'Monday', perhaps sometimes difficult to separate from the surname *Mund*(*a*)*y*, which appears in Mundie's Fm Sr 280. (*a*) Monday Dean Bk. Cf. Sr 410–11.

monig OE adj., 'many', *v.* manig.

monn OE, 'a man' *v.* mann.

mons (montem acc.sg.) 'a hill' (cf. LatAdd 339), sometimes replacing hyll as an affix in early spellings. (*c*) Thorpe sub Montem YW.

mont OFr, ME, munt(e) ME, 'a mount, a hill', in p.ns. mostly of Fr origin, some being transferred from France, as Kirmond L (Fr (*Chèvremont*), Richmond YN (Fr *Richemont*); OE munt 'hill' is hardly likely to enter into these p.ns. (*a*) Mount Ferrant YE, Mount Grace YN. (*b*) Beamond Bk, Beaumont Cu, Ess, Nb (bel), *Eglemont* Bd (egle), Grosmont YN (gros), Ridgmont Bd, YE, Rougemont YW (rouge), St Michael's Mount Co. (*c*) Mount Bures, Theydon Mount Ess. [~Lat *mons*, *montem*.]

montaigne OFr, monteyne, muntayne ME, 'a mountain, a lofty hill'. (*b*) Mountain Fm, Wood D, Sr. [~mont.]

mōr[1] OE, mór ON, 'a moor', originally 'barren waste-land', which in the SCy and Midl and the fenlands of the east came to mean 'marshland' and in the NCy (esp. along the Pennines) 'a high tract of barren uncultivated ground'; the meaning 'marshland' was, however, also current in low-lying parts of NCy. There is no distinction in p.ns. between the OE and ON words. It is a common el. in ME f.ns. (*passim*).

(*a*) Moorby L, Moreby YE (bý), Morborne Hu (burna), Moredon W, Morden C, Do, Sr, Mordon Du (dūn), Moreton Bk, Brk *et freq*, Morton Db, Du, L *et passim*, Murton Du, Nb, We, YN (tūn), Morland We (lúndr), Morley Db, Du, Nf, YW (lēah), Morthen YW (þing), Morwick Nb (wīc), Mosbrough Db (burh), Murcot(t) O, W (cot).

(*b*) Moor(e) Ch, Ess, Wo *et freq*, More Sa. In compounds, it is found with (i) significant words, usually descriptive, as Blackmoor La (blæc), Quernmore La (cweorn), Rodmore Nth (hrēod), Sidemoor Wo (sīd), Swarthmoor La (sweart), Tranmoor YW (trani), Wedmore So (wǣðe), Wildmore L (wilde); (ii) older p.ns. and r.ns., as Dartmoor, Exmoor D, Fordham Moor C, Ilkley Moor YW, Shore Moor La; (iii) pers.ns., as Dunsmore Wa, Easemore Wo, Portsmoor Ess; (iv) folk-names, as Spaldingmoor YE (Spaldas, -ingas).

(*c*) Moor Allerton, Moor Monkton YW, Appleton le Moor YN, Bolton le Moors, Clayton le Moors La, Buckland in the Moor D, Norton in the Moors St.

*mōr[2] PrWelsh adj., 'great', *v.* mawr.

*morgen-gifu OE, 'a morning gift', that is, 'a piece of land or the like given by a man to his bride on the morning after their marriage' according to OE custom (cf. ASWills xiii, xv). The compound is freq. in Sx and Ess and is recorded in other counties such as K, L, Nth, Sr, W, Wa, and esp. in ME f.ns. (cf. C 339, Ess 276, Nth 274, Sx 519). (*a*) Marraway Wa, Moor Fm Ess 276. (*b*) Mooray W 186, Morgay Sx, Morghew, Murrein Wood K, *Morngifts* L, Morrif Wa 354. [OE *morgen* 'morning', *gifu* 'gift', gipt.]

mōrig OE adj., 'swampy, marshy'. (*a*) Moordale YN (deill), Morralee Nb (lēah). [mōr, -ig.]

mǫrk ON, 'a border, a boundary'. (*a*) *Danmark* L (Danir). [~mearc.]

*mort ME, 'a young salmon', recorded from the 16th century (NED s.v.) may be found in (*a*) Mortlocks Ess 513, Mortlake Sr 26 and a lost *Mortelake* Hrt (all with lacu), but the origin of these and other p.ns. in *Mort*, such as Morcombelake Do, Mortham YN, Morte Point, Morthoe, Murtwell D, is obscure; in some a pers.n. *Morta* is possible, or some word connected with dial. *murt* 'a stumpy person', MHG *murz* 'a stump'.

morð OE, 'murder', as in OE *morþhlau* BCS 1234. (*a*) Morpeth Nb (pæð). Mortgrove Hrt (grāf).

mos OE, mosi ON, 'moss, lichen', also 'a bog, a swamp', found chiefly in the NCy and NWMidl. (*a*) Mosedale Cu (dæl), Moseley YW (lēah, near Moss), Moss Beck YN (bekkr), Mosser Cu,

Mozergh We (erg), Mosswood Du (ford), Moston Ch, La, Sa (tūn). (*b*) Moss YW, Moze Ess, Chat Moss, Rathmoss La. [~mēos by ablaut.]

mōt, gemōt OE, **mót** ON, 'a meeting, an encounter', are used in p.ns. with two distinct meanings:

(i) 'an assembly of people, esp. one concerned with judicial matters', found frequently in combination with words for 'hill' (hlāw, beorg) and other places where such assemblies could conveniently meet. (*a*) Mettle Hill C, Moat Low Db, Mutlow C, Ch, *Motelowe* Nth 142, the meeting-place of Wymersley Hundred, *Motlowe*, that of Thriplow Hundred C 82 (hlāw), Mobberley Ch, Modbury D (burh), Modbury Hundred Do (beorg, cf. OE *gemotbeorh* BCS 392 Wt), Motcombe Do (cumb), Mutford Hundred Sf (ford), Mutley D (lēah, cf. OE *in gemotleage* BCS 476); *v.* also mōt-stōw. (*b*) Landmoth YN (land), Portsmouth Wo 217 (port, the part of Pershore belonging to Westminster Abbey); *v.* also halimote, scīr-gemōt.

(ii) 'a river-confluence', a sense not recorded in OE and therefore no doubt an ON borrowing; it occurs only in the NCy. (*b*) Ameshaugh Cu, *Aymot* YN (á), Beckermonds YW (bekkr), *v.* also ēa-mōt.

[~OE *mētan* 'to meet'.]

mote OFr, 'an embankment', **mote** ME, 'a moat, a protective ditch filled with water around a building'. (*b*) Moat Court, Fm, Hall, etc. Ess, Sx, Wo, etc.

mōtere OE, 'a speaker at an assembly'. (*a*) Mottistone Wt 164 (stān), possibly Moulter Hill Nt 153. [mōt, -ere.]

mōt-stōw OE, 'a meeting-place, a place where a judicial assembly met'. (*b*) Motstow Wa, Moustows Sx, Munster Mx, *Mustouwe* Ess 314. [mōt, stōw.]

mudde ME, 'mud', not evidenced before the 13th century (NED s.v.), but cf. muddig. (*a*) Muddipit D (pytt), Mudwall Ess (wall).

***muddig** OE adj., 'muddy'. (*a*) Mudford So (ford, from 1086 DB). [~mudde, -ig.]

mūga OE, 'a stack, a heap', recorded with the meaning 'a heap of earth, a mound' from the 15th century (NED s.v. *mow*). (*b*) Mow Cop Ch (a hill on a boundary, perhaps referring to a boundary cairn), Lamua Hundred Bk 51 (le) (probably 'a mound where the hundred met').

muk ME, 'dung, muck, dirt'. (*a*) Mucklands Nth (lúndr). [~mykr, mix.]

mūl OE, **múll** ON, 'a mule', is possible in some p.ns. but it is difficult to separate from the OE, ON pers.ns. *Mūl*(*a*), *Múli*, as in (*a*) Moulsecoombe Sx (cumb), Moulsford Brk (ford), Moulsham Ess (hām), Moulton Ch, L, Nf (tūn), Mowthorpe YN (þorp), Mulwith YW (vað). The pers.n. seems more likely. [Lat *mulus*.]

múli ON, 'a snout', also 'a headland, a jutting crag', is possible in (*a*) Mulgrave YN (gryfja), but cannot easily be distinguished from mūl or the pers.ns., *Mūla*, *Múli*.

mund OE, 'security, protection', appears to be found in some p.ns., and a connexion between this word, probably used in a concrete sense as in OE *mund-beorg* (*Psalms* 124.2), and ModE *mound* 'hedge, fence, tumulus' has been suggested (cf. Ess 220); it might well be related to OE *mand* 'a basket' and denote some kind of a woven palisade. (*a*) Munden Hrt (denu), Mundon Ess (dūn), Munstead Sr 199 (stede).

munnr ON, 'the mouth of a river, etc.', occurs in minor p.ns. as (*b*) *Dalemun*, *Depedalemun* YE 327 (dalr). [~mynni.]

munt OE, 'a mount, a hill', would be difficult to distinguish from OFr mont. (*b*) The Mount K. [Lat *mons*, *montem*.]

munuc OE, **monke** ME, 'a monk', in p.ns. usually with reference to monastic institutions which can mostly be identified; many of these p.ns. are of post-Conquest origin. In SCy p.ns. a new ME wk. pl. *munken*(*e*) often replaces the more regular *monkes*. (*a*) Monkgarth Pool Cu (garðr, a fishery owned by Calder Abbey), Monkroyd La (rod, belonging to Pontefract Priory), Monkton D, Do, Du, K, So, YW (tūn), Monkwith YE (wīc). (*c*) As an affix (often rendered by Lat *monachorum*, OFr *moines*) in Monkland He, Monkleigh D, Monksilver So, *Monk* prefixed to Bretton, Fryston YW, Hesleden Du, *Monks* to Eleigh Sf, Kirby Wa, Risborough Bk. [~Lat *monachus*.]

mūs OE, **mús** ON, 'a mouse, a field-mouse', used of places infested with mice, sometimes difficult to distinguish from the OE, ON pers.ns. *Mūs*(*a*), *Músi*, and from must. (*a*) Moseley Wo, Mowsley Lei (lēah), Mouseberry D, Musbury D, La (burh), Mousehole D (hol), Mowshurst K (hyrst), Muscoates, -cott YN, Nth (cot), Musden La (denu), Muston Lei, YE (tūn).

must OE, 'must, new wine', could no doubt be used of 'a muddy stream', as in *Must* BCS 1280, and is possible in that sense in some p.ns., though it would be sometimes difficult to keep apart from mūs, in p.ns. like Musden La, Muston Lei, YE.

mūða OE, 'the mouth of a large river, an estuary'. (*b*) In compounds it occurs with (i) significant words, as Learmouth Nb (**lǣfer**), Portsmouth Ha (**port**), Widemouth Co (**wīd**), Yarmouth Wt (**ēaren**), but mostly with (ii) r.ns., as Alnmouth Nb (R. Alne), Cockermouth Cu (R. Cocker), Jesmond Nb (a r.n. *Yese*, now Ouseburn), Stourmouth K (R. Stour), Tynemouth Nb (R. Tyne), Wearmouth Du (R. Wear), Weymouth Do (R. Wey), Yarmouth Nf (R. Yare). [~**munnr, mynni, (ge)mȳðe**.]

mycg OE, 'a midge, a gnat', in allusion to place infested by such insects. (*a*) Midge Hall La (**halh**), Midgell So (**hyll**), Midgeham Brk (**hām**), Midgley YW (**lēah**).

mykr (**mykjar** gen.sg.), **myki** ON, 'dung, muck'. (*a*) Mickering La (gen.sg., **eng**). [~**muk**.]

***mylde** OE (Angl, WSax), ***melde** (Kt), 'soil, earth', usually combined with colour-words, esp. in ME f.ns. such as *Blakemildes* YE 327, *Blak*(*e*)-*mild*(*e*), etc. Nt 288, Nth 268, Sx, Wa 331 (**blæc**), *Red-mylde* Nth (**rēad**). (*b*) Redmile Lei, Rodmell Sx 325 (**rēad**). [~**molde, -e**, cf. Swed *mylla* 'loose earth'.]

myln, mylen OE (Angl, WSax), **meln** (Kt), 'a mill', usually reduced to *mill* in ME. It is frequent with words for 'stream' and the like, and is common in ME minor names (*passim*). (*a*) Melcombe So (**cumb**), Melplash Do (**plæsc**), Milbourn(e), -burn Do, Nb, So, W, We *et freq* (**burna**), Milford Db, Ha, W, YW (**ford**), Millbrook Bd, Ha (**brōc**), Millington Ch, YE, Milton Db, Kt, Nb, Nt, Nth, St (**tūn**), Millthorpe L, Miln(e)thorpe Nt, We, YW (**þorp**). (*b*) Mells Sf, So, Melles Sf; Millom Cu (dat.pl.); Chilmill (**cild**), Cuddymill (**cutted**) K, Cutmill Wo (**cut**), Drockmill Sx (**þroc**), Shottermill Sr, Windmill Hill, etc. *passim*. [~Lat *molina*.]

myncen (**myncena** gen.pl.) OE, 'a nun'. (*a*) Minchen Down D (**dūn**), Minchington Do (**tūn**). (*c*) Minchin Buckland (also called Buckland Sororum) So, Minchinhampton Gl, Barrow Minchin So. [~**munuc, -en**.]

mynni ON, 'the mouth of a river where it joins another or runs into a lake or the sea'. (*b*) Airmyn (R. Aire), *Niddermyn* (R. Nidd) YW, Stalmine La (**stell**). [~**munnr**.]

mynster OE, 'a monastery, the church of a monastery or other religious body, a church served by secular clergy'; these are the usual meanings in p.ns. In ME the word came to denote 'a church of considerable size, a cathedral church', as in Beverley Minster YE 195 (hence Minster Moorgate, Minster Yard), York Minster (hence Minster Yard YE 294). (*a*) Minsterley Sa (**lēah**), Minsterworth Gl (**worð**, belonging to St Peter's, Gloucester), Misterton Nt 36 (**tūn**). (*b*) Minster K, Minster Lovell O (both monastic foundations). In compounds, it is combined with either (i) words denoting location, esp. r.ns., as Axminster D (R. Axe), Charminster Do (R. Carne), Emstrey Sa (**ēg**), Exminster D (R. Exe), Leominster He (*Leon*, a district name), Southminster Ess (**sūð**), Sturminster Do (R. Stour), Westminster Mx (**west**), or (ii) pers.ns., as Beaminster Do, Bedminster So, Buckminster Lei, Kidderminster Wo, Lyminster Sx, Yetminster Do, probably all named after their founders or owners; saints' names do not occur. [Lat *monasterium*.]

mynydd Welsh, 'a mountain', *v.* **minid**.

myrig (**myrgan** wk. obl.) OE (Angl, WSax), **merig** (Kt), adj., 'pleasant, sweet, agreeable'. (*a*) Marley K (**lēah**), Marvell Wt, Merrifield Co (**feld**), Merevale Wa, Merryvale He (**val**), Meriden Wa, Merridale St (**denu**), Merriall Nt (**helde**), Merrington Sa (**dūn**), Moorlinch So (**hlinc**).

myrkr ON adj., 'dark, muddy'. (*a*) Mirk Booths (**búð**), Mirkholme (**holmr**) Cu, Mirk Fell (**fjall**), Murk Head (**hēafod**) YN.

mýrr ON, 'a mire, a bog, swampy ground', common in ME f.ns. (as YN 329) and becoming ME *mire*, which is the immediate source of Yendamore D 100. (*b*) It is usually found with (i) a descriptive word, as Gormire (**gor**), Rudmoor (**rotinn**) YN; (ii) a plant-name, as Dockmire YW (**docce**), Goldmire La (**golde**), Redmires Du (**hrēod**), Starnmire (**stǫrr**), Thackmire (**þak**) Cu; (iii) some other significant word, as Walmer La (**wald**), Wragmire Cu (**vargr**).

***mysni** ON, a water-plant (cf. Swed *missne* 'water lily'), is possible in (*b*) Misson Nt 87. [~**mysse**.]

***mysse** OE, a water-plant (cf. Dan *mysse* 'water lily' and **mysni**), is suggested (DEPN) for (*a*) R. Misbourne Bk (**burna**, hence Missenden), Miswell Hrt (**wella**). [~**mos**.]

(ge)mȳðe OE, 'the mouth of a river where it runs into another, a confluence of rivers'. (*a*) Midford So, Mitford Nb (**ford**), Mitton La, Wo, YE, YW, Myton YE, YN, Mytton Sa (**tūn**). (*b*) Meeth(e) D, The Mythe Gl; Mytham Db, La, Mytholmroyd YW (dat.pl.). [~**mūða**, **-e**, **-mynni**.]

N

ná- ON adv. prefix, 'near', is possible in (*a*) Naburn YE (**burna**), *Nathwait* Cu (**þveit**), but it is difficult to distinguish from other els. [~OE *nēah* 'near'.]

nabbi, nabbr ON, 'a projecting peak, a knoll, a hill', occurs chiefly in minor names as *Nab* (cf. Cu 486, Nt 288, YE 327); its ME form may have occasionally been influenced by OE *nebb* 'beak'. (*b*) Nabbs Nt, Fordham YE 131 (olim *-nab*), Gascow Nab La, Killing Nab Scar YN, Nab Lane Nth.

nacod OE adj., 'naked, bare'. (*a*) *Nakedale* Nb (**ēle**).

nǣddre OE, 'an adder'. (*a*) Netherfield Sx (**feld**).

nǣp OE (WSax), 'a turnip', *v.* **nēp**.

næss OE (Angl, WSax), **ness** (Kt, Merc), 'a promontory, a headland, a cape', also 'a projecting piece of high land, a piece of land round which a river flows to form a headland', is difficult to keep apart from ON **nes**, which has probably influenced its form in Danelaw p.ns. (*a*) Nassington Nth (**-ing²**, **tūn**), Neston Ch (**tūn**), Nazeing Ess (**-ingas**), Neswick YE (**wīc**). (*b*) Nass Gl, The Naze Ess, Ness Ch, Sa, YN. In compounds it is found with (i) significant words and p.ns., as Bowness Cu (**boga**), Claines Wo (**clæg**), Lessness K (**lǣs**), Outerness Hu (**ūterra**), Reedness YW (**hrēod**), Sharpness Gl, K (**scearp**), Sheerness K (**scīr**), Tockwith Ness YW (p.n.), Widnes La (**wīd**), and (ii) occasionally pers.ns., as Totnes D, The Naze Ess (OE *Eadwulfesnæss*). [~OE *nasu* 'nose', **nōs**, **nes**.]

næt** (natan** wk. obl.) OE adj., 'wet, moist', cognate with OHG *naz* 'wet', recorded in OE only in *Nataleahes æsc* BCS 299; in ME it might be confused with **nēat**. (*a*) Nateley Ha (**lēah**), Natton Gl (**tūn**), Notgrove Gl (**grāfa**).

nām OE, 'the taking (of land)'. (*b*) Binhamy Co; cf. **af-nám**, **in-nām**.

nant, nans Corn, **nant** Welsh, 'a valley, a brook'. (*b*) Pennance, Trenance Co.

nár ON, 'a corpse' (used in the same way as **līc**), is possible in (*a*) Naburn YE (**burna**), but is difficult to distinguish from **ná-**.

nattok ME, of unknown origin and meaning, but possibly a plant-name or the like in view of its formation with **-uc**; it is freq. in ME and later f.ns. (cf. Ess 586, Hrt 258, Nth lii, 277, Sr xlv, 364, W 442, in which counties it is so far evidenced). [Possibly related to næt 'wet', -uc; denoting some marsh plant.]

naut ON, 'cattle'. (*a*) Neat Marsh, *Noutdritlane* YE, Noutgate Yk, *Noutwath* Cu 241. [~nēat.]

nearu (nearwan wk. obl.) OE adj., 'narrow', possibly in (*a*) Narford Nf (ford).

nēat OE, 'cattle'. (*a*) Nafford Wo, Neatham Ha (hām), Netton D, W (tūn); the gen.sg. *nēates* is possible in Nesfield YW (feld, but cf. nezti). [~naut.]

nēd OE (Angl, Kt), nīed (WSax), 'distress, need, poverty', probably used in much the same way as hungor. (*a*) Needham C, Db, Nf, Sf (hām), Needwood St (wudu); also in the compound *nēd-ærn* 'a privy' or more generally 'a poor house', as in Netherne Sr. Cf. Löfvenberg 139.

neoðera, niðera OE adj., 'lower'. (*a*) Netherbury Do (burh), Nethercot(e) Nth, O (cot), Netherhampton W (hām-tūn), Netherton Nb, Wo (tūn). (*c*) *Nether* prefixed to Broughton Lei, Cerne Do, Langwith Nt, etc.

nēp OE (Angl, Kt), nǣp (WSax), 'a turnip', difficult to keep apart from hnæpp. (*a*) *Napsted* Ess (stede), Neopardy D (worðig), Nepicar K (æcer). [~Lat *nāpus*.]

*nēs[1] OE, nese ME, 'the nose', hence 'a headland, a promontory, a projecting piece of land formed in the bend of a river', cognate with MLG *nese*. (*a*) Neasden Mx (dūn), Neasham Du (hām), Nesbit(t) Nb (byht). [~nōs(e).]

nes[2] ON, 'a headland, a promontory', used in the same way as OE næss, which it may sometimes have influenced or replaced, as in Ness YN, etc. It is also used of extensive tracts of land in district names. (*b*) Amounderness Hundred (pers.n.), Crossens (cros), Furness, a district La 200, Ashness Cu (eski), Gunness, Skegness L (pers.ns.), Holderness Wapentake YE (hǫldr). [~næss.]

-nes, -nis OE noun suffix, used to form abstract nouns from adjectives (PrGerm *-inassu-*, *-nissi-*, Kluge §§ 138–9), as in (ge)hernes, (ge)mǣnnes.

ness OE (Merc, Kt), 'a headland', *v.* næss.

nest OE, 'a nest', sometimes used, esp. in *crow's nest* to denote the highest point in a district; it is often combined with bird-names. (*a*) *Arnesnest* YE (earn), Crowneast Wo 91, Crownest YW, Crowsnest D, Crow's Nest Hill Hu (crāwe), Culverness Wo (culfre),

Kite's Nest Sx (cȳta), Pinners Green Ess (pīe), Ramsnest (hræfen), Rooks Nest (hrōc), Storksnest (storc) Sr, Swan's Nest D (swan); cf. also Nth 268, W 442, Wa 331.

netel(e) OE, 'a nettle'. (*a*) Nettlebed O (bedd), Nettlecombe Do, So, Wt (cumb), *Nettleford* So (ford, now Nettlebridge), Nettleham L (hām), Nettlestead K, Sf (stede), Nettleton L (tūn), W (-ing[2], tūn), Nettleworth Nt (worð).

neðri ON comp.adj., 'lower'. (*a*) Netherby YW (bý). [~neoðera.]

nezti ON superl. adj., 'lowest', possibly replacing OE *niðemest* 'lowest', may be found in (*a*) Nesfield YW (feld), but *v.* nēat. [~neðri.]

nicor OE, 'a water-sprite', is found in f.ns. such as *Nikeresaker* C (æcer), *Nikersmadwe* Ess 598 (mǣd), *Nikerpoll* Sx 562, *Nycharpool* L, *Nykerpole* W 444 (pōl), *Nikirwells* L (wella). Cf. Dickins 159.

nīed OE (WSax), 'distress', *v.* nēd.

nīge (*nīgan wk. obl.) OE (Kt) adj., 'new', is a secondary form of nīwe, found in p.ns. in K, west Sx, Sr, Ha and Wt. It is independently evidenced in OE only in compounds *nig-slycod* 'glossy', *nige-cyrred* 'newly converted', *nifara* 'newcomer', etc. The replacement of *-w-* by *-g-*, which is paralleled by *hīgan* for hīwan, īg for īw, *Tīg* for Tīw, tige beside tiwe (cf. Luick § 243, Brunner § 234 n. 3 and esp. I. Dahl, *Substantival Inflexion in Early Old English* (Lund 1938) 95–105), occurs also in OSax *nigi* (beside *niwi*) and OFris *ny*, *ni* (cf. Mawer, Problems 16ff). It may well be a feature of the language of the Jutish settlers in K, Ha and Wt. It is sometimes replaced by the more common *nīwe*. (*a*) Newdigate Sr (wudu, geat), Newtimber Sx, Nyetimber Sx 95 (getimbre), Ninham Wt (hām), Niton Wt, Nyton Sx (tūn), Nizell's Heath K (gesell), Nyewoods Sx (wudu).

nigon OE num., 'nine'. (*a*) Highley Hill (hlāw), Nine Acre Wood (æcer) Hrt, Ninebanks Nb (benc), Noonstones Cu (stān), Nynehead So (hīd). (*c*) Stow Nine Churches Nth 30.

nimet OWelsh, nyfed Welsh, 'a shrine, a holy place', used sometimes in r.ns. (*a*) Nympton D (3) (from an old r.n., tūn), Nympsfield Gl (feld). (*b*) Nymet D (an old r.n.).

*niming OE, 'land taken into cultivation'. (*b*) Nimmings Wo 280. [~OE *niman* 'to take' (~nām), -ing[1].]

niðera OE adj., 'lower', *v.* neoðera.

nīwe (nīwan wk. obl.), nēowe OE adj., 'new', used in many p.ns. of buildings in the sense 'newly built', sometimes of plots of land in the sense 'newly acquired', 'newly cultivated' and chiefly 'newly reclaimed from waste'. The usual later forms are *New-* and *Newn-* (from the wk. obl. *nīwan*); the occasional *Naun-* is from the OE (Anglian) weak form *nēowan*; in ME this latter form became WMidl *nōwen*, from which *Naun-* is regularly derived; *v.* also **nīge**. (*a*) Naunton Gl, Wo, Neanton Sa, Newington Gl, K, Mx, O, Sr, Newton *passim*, Nowton Sf (**tūn**), Newark Nt, Nth, Sr (**weorc**), Newbald YE, Newbold Ch, Db, La *et freq*, Newbottle Du, Nth, Nobottle Nth (**bōðl**), Newball L (**bøle**), Newbiggin Cu, Du, Nb, We, YN (**bigging**), Newb(o)rough Nb, St, Newburgh La, YN, Newbury Brk (**burh**), Newby Cu, We, YN, YW (**bý**), Newcastle Nb, St (**castel**), Newerne Gl (**ærn**), Newhall Ch, Db (**hall**), Newham Nb, Newholme YN, Newnham Bd, C, Gl, Ha *et freq*, Nuneham O (**hām**), Newland(s) (often Lat *nova terra*) Cu, Gl, L, La, YW *et freq* (**land**), Newport Bk, D, Ess, Sa, Wt (**port**), Newsham, Newsholme Du, L, La, Nb, Y (*freq*) (**hūs**, dat.pl.), Newstead L, Nt, YN (**stede**). It is mostly used therefore with words for buildings. [~**nīge**, **nýr**.]

nōk ME, 'a nook', a nook of land, a triangular plot of ground' (cf. NED s.v. *nook*), is frequent in late f.ns. (Cu 486, Nt 288). It is also the first el. of the Shakespearean *nook-shotten* (cf. TLS 25 July 1935), which occurs as a f.n. in Wa 365 describing a field which has many angles and corners.

norð OE, ON adj., adv., 'northern, north', is very common, but it is not always possible to separate the adj. and adv. uses.

(1) The adj. is probable in the names of many places which lie to the north of an older place or face the north, as in (*a*) Norbiton Sr (**beretūn**), Norbury Ch, Db, Sa (**burh**), Norfolk (**folc**), Norham Nb (**hām**), Norland YW (**land**), Northolt Mx (**halh**), North Riding Y (**þriðungr**), Norton *passim* (**tūn**), Norwich Nf (**wīc**). (*c*) As an affix in Northampton Nth, Northleach Gl and *North* prefixed to many p.ns. like Ashley Ha, Aston O, Cave YE, Deighton YW, etc.

(2) The adv. use is probably best represented by **norðan**, but an elliptical use of **norð** '(land lying) to the north' of some feature is sometimes possible, as in Norrington W, Norton Wo 82 (OE *norð-in-tūne* 'north in the village', cf. **in**).

norðan OE adv., 'north, (lying) north of', used in p.ns. esp. of '(a place lying) north of some other place', sometimes with the prep. bī. (*a*) Narraway D 433 (weg), Norney Sr 199 (ēg), Nornay Nt (ēa), Northwood K (OE *bi northan uude* BCS 846, wudu). [~ norð.]

Norðhymbre OE, 'the Northumbrians, the English dwelling north of the R. Humber' in the OE period, the district being called *Norðhymbraland*. By the time of the Conquest Yorkshire had become a separate county and after the creation of the County Palatine of Durham at the end of the 11th century, this district name became restricted to the present county of Northumberland. [~ norð, R. Humber YE.]

Norðman (-manna gen.pl.) late OE (from ON Norð-maðr), 'a Northman, a Norwegian', seems to have been used in OE specifically of Norwegian Vikings, as evident from the distinction made in ASC 924A, *Ealle ða ðe on Norþhymbrum bugeaþ, ægþer ge Englisce ge Denisce ge Norþmen* 'all who dwell in Northumbria either English or Danish or Northmen', and it is used of the inhabitants of Norway in Ælfred's *Orosius* (cf. BT s.v.). A few p.ns. may contain the pers.n. *Norðman* (Feilitzen 331–2). (*a*) Normanby L (4), YN (3) (bý), Normancross Hu (cros), Normansburgh Nf (berg), Normanton Db (3), Lei (2), L, Nt (4), R, YW (tūn), Ormathwaite Cu (þveit). [norð, mann.]

norðmest OE adj., 'northernmost'. (*a*) Northmostown D (tūn).

* **nōs(e)** OE, 'a headland, a promontory', used in this sense in *Beowulf* 1892, 2083. (*b*) Dunnose Wt (dūn), Hackness YN 112 (OE *Hacanos*, haca). [~ nēse.]

nunne (nunnan gen.sg., nunnena gen.pl.) OE, 'a nun', in p.ns. generally in allusion to the possessions of post-Conquest nunneries. Some p.ns. may, however, be from the OE pers.n. *Nunna*. (*a*) Nunley Wa (lēah), Nunney So (ēg), Nunriding Nb (rydding), Nunton Nth (tūn), Nunwick Nb, YW (wīc). (*c*) *Nun* prefixed to Appleton YW, -burnholme YE, -eaton Wa, Monkton YW, -stainton Du.

nýr ON adj., 'new', is usually replaced by OE nīwe, as in Newball L, Newby Cu, etc., but traces of it may be found occasionally in ME spellings like DB *Nie-* in Newsham YN 45.

O

-oc OE noun suffix, *v.* **-uc.**

ōd ME, 'an ash heap', *v.* **ād.**

-od OE noun suffix, forming concrete nouns (from PrGerm *-uð-*, Kluge § 99), as in **falod, hēafod, weorod**; cf. **-ed.**

oddi ON, 'a point or tongue of land'. (*b*) Greenodd La (**grēne**), *Ravenser Odd* YE 16 (now Spurn Point). [~ **ord**, ON *oddi* 'the point of a weapon'.]

ofan OE adv., 'over', *v.* **ufan.**

ofen OE, 'an oven, a furnace'. (*b*) Noven Sx 342, King's Oven D (olim *furnum regis*).

ōfer[1] OE, 'a bank, a river-bank, the sea-shore'.

(1) This el. occurs in OE and ME literary contexts with only these meanings (cf. NED s.v. *over* sb. 1), the basic meaning appearing to be 'border, rim, edge', which is repeated in WGerm cognates OFris *ōvere*, MLG *ōver*, MHG *uover* (cf. Mdf 98–9). In OE it glosses Lat *margo* 'margin' and OE **ōra** 'shore', and it is an alternative to **brerd** as a gloss to Lat *crepido* 'rim' (WW 31.29, 461.26, 178.3). The meaning 'river-bank, seashore' is clear in *Maldon* 28, where the Viking messenger stood *on stæðe* 'on the shore' and delivered his threats to the earl *þær he on ofre stod* 'where he stood on the bank', and it is implied in phrases like *on ðære ea ofre* 'on the river bank', *on ofre ðæs foresprecenan streames* 'on the bank of the aforesaid stream', *of sæs ofre* 'from the sea's edge' (BT and Suppl, OEBede ii, 3, iv, 13, etc.), and in ME *þe sæ oure* (Laȝamon), *þe seis oure* (*Havelok*) which the contexts show to mean 'the sea-shore' (NED s.v.).

(2) Ekwall (DEPN 332) suggests that there might have been an extension of meaning from 'border, margin' to 'the edge of a hill', and even to 'hill, ridge', as there are many p.ns. which are ostensibly derived from *ōfer* but which do not topographically fit in with the established meanings of that word of 'river-bank, sea-shore'. But Ekwall's alternative suggestion that there was another OE **ofer**[2] meaning 'hill, slope' is preferable to explain such p.ns.

(3) Both **ōfer**[1] and **ofer**[2] are difficult to distinguish from each other and from other els. such as **ōra, ofer**[3], **ufer, uferra**; such p.ns. as Orton Lei, Nth, Wa, We, Overton Ch, Db, Lei, R, Sa, etc., are

ambiguous. The vowel of *ōfer* is usually assumed to be long, presumably from the many examples in OE documents where it is accented as *ófer* and from MHG *uover*; this should, of course, have become ModE *oover* [u:və], but such a form is not attested and presumably was influenced or replaced at an early period by *ofer*, esp. in compounds and final unstressed positions.

(4) Examples of *ōfer* where the meaning 'shore, river-bank' is confirmed by topography include: (*a*) Orton Hu, Water Orton Wa, Overton La, YN (tūn), Overstrand Nf (strand); (*b*) The Nower K, Over C; Bicknor Gl, He, Elmore Gl, Hedsor Bk, Northover So, Southover Sx, Spernal Wa, Westover Wt.

*ofer[2], ufer OE, 'a slope, a hill, a ridge', is difficult to distinguish from ōfer[1] and other els., but there are many p.ns. where the topography favours a meaning 'slope, hill' rather than 'river-bank' or the like, which is established for ōfer[1]. A good many early spellings like *Ufre*, *Uvre*, etc. point to the existence of a secondary form *ufer*, also related to yfer. Local topography points to the meaning 'slope, hill, ridge' in (*a*) Overton Ch, Lei (tūn). (*b*) Over Ch, Db; North-, Southowram YW (dat.pl.), all with occasional spellings *Ufre*, *Ufrun*; Ashover Db (æsc), Eastnor He (ēastan), Eastover So (ēast), Haselor Wa (hæsel), Heanor Db, Hennor He (hēah), Little-, Mickleover Db (olim *Ufre*), Okeover St (āc), Thorner YW (þorn), Wentnor Sa (pers.n.). [~ofer[3], uferra, yfer.]

ofer[3] OE prep., 'over, above, across', is infrequent and difficult to distinguish from ōfer[1] and ofer[2]; it is used in elliptical formations, '(land) over or across something'. (*a*) Overy O (ēa, '(land) across the river'). (*c*) Burnham Overy Nf (ēa), Burton Overy Lei (from a surname *Overy*, ēa).

* *ofes OE, 'an edge, a border', an unmutated form of efes, with which it interchanges in p.ns.; it probably meant 'the edge (of a wood)'. OE *be þære alra ofesce* BCS 462 (Wo 391) is no doubt an early example; it survives as So dial. *ovvis* 'edge'. (*b*) Ovis D, Treovis Co (tre), Woodovis D 220, Woodsaws Co (wudu). [~ōfer, -es.]

of-nam ME, 'a detached piece of land', *v.* af-nám.

ǫkull ON, 'ankle', used in Norw p.ns. in the sense 'slope', has been suggested for (*b*) Acklam YE 147, YN 162 (dat.pl.), but, as Ekwall points out, it would be unusual for the OWScand assimilation of *nk* to *k*, *kk* to be found in DB spellings (as these p.ns. are); *v.* āc, lēah.

-ol, -ul OE suffix, is used to form (i) concrete nouns such as fugol, gafol, hugol, scearpol, stapol, staðol, sticol, wapol (from PrGerm *-ula-*, Kluge § 89), and (ii) adjectives such as hamol, sticol, wacol (from PrGerm *-ula-*, Kluge §§ 191–3).

ǫmstr ON, 'a heap (of dung, corn, etc.)'. (*a*) Anserdale YN (deill).

on OE prep., 'on', esp. in affixes which refer to rivers, hills and the like; it sometimes replaces and is replaced by Lat super and ModE *upon*, as in official forms like Kingston upon Hull YE, Preston upon Stour Gl, etc. (*c*) Burton on Trent St, Newton on the Moor Nb, Newton on Ouse YN, Stanton on the Wolds Nt, Stockton on the Forest YN, Walton on Thames Sr.

ǫngul ON, 'a bend', *v.* angel.

open OE adj., 'open, unenclosed', is rare. (*a*) Openshaw La (sceaga).

ór ON adv., prep., 'away from, out of', probably meaning 'remote' (cf. ūt). (*a*) *Orwithfleet* YE 22.

-or OE noun suffix, forming concrete nouns (PrGerm *-ra-*, Kluge § 92), as cilfor, fōdor, foðor.

ōra[1] OE, 'a border, a margin, a bank, an edge'.

(1) This el. is rare in literary sources (cf. BT s.v.), but it is common in p.ns., which show that its topographical meanings were (i) 'river bank, shore, foreshore', as in Orford Sf, Oare K, Pershore Wo, Rowner Ha, and (ii) 'the brink or edge of a hill, a slope', as in OE *on hliþes oran* 'on the edge of a slope' (*Boethius* 21), Orcop He, Oare Brk, W, Boxford Brk. It has much the same meanings as ōfer[1] and ofer[2], with which it interchanges often in ME spellings; Batsford Gl, which is OE *æt Bæccesore*, has *-oure* and *-ofere* in ME. This el. is most common in southern counties and it does not appear to be found in the NMidl and NCy.

(2) (*a*) Orcop He (copp), Orford Sf (ford).

(*b*) Oare K, Brk, W, Ore Sx, Ower Do. In compounds it is found with (i) plant- and tree-names, as Ashover K (æsc), Boxford Brk (box), Elmsworth Wt (elm), Goldor O (golde), Pershore Wo (persc), Vexour K (feax); (ii) other significant words, as Bagnor Brk (bagga), Lynsore K (hlinc), Rowner Ha (rūh), Stonar K, Stonor O (stān), Upnor K (uppan), Wardour W (weard), Windsor Brk, Do (windels); (iii) pers.ns., as Bicknor K, Copnor Ha, Itchenor Sx, Lewknor O. [~ Lat *ōra* 'rim, bank, shore'.]

ōra[2] OE, 'ore', usually in allusion to places where bog-ore was got or to iron-workings. (*a*) Orgill Cu (gil), Orgrave La, Orgreave YW (græf), Orrell La (hyll), Orsett Ess (sēað).

* ***ōra-blāwere** OE, 'an ore-blower, a smelter'. (*c*) Kirkby Overblow YW.

orceard, ort-geard OE, 'a garden', later in OE 'an orchard'. (*a*) Orcheton D (**tūn**), Orchardleigh So (**lēah**). (*b*) Norchard Wo (**atten**), Orchard Co, D, So. [~Lat (*h*)*ortus* 'a garden', **geard.**]

ord OE, 'a point, a corner or spit of land, a projecting ridge of land'. (*a*) Orgreave St (**grāf**). (*b*) Ord Nb, Shamblers Wt, *Sword Point* Hu. [~**oddi.**]

orne OEScand, 'a boar'. (*a*) Ornthwaite YW (**þveit**).

orri ON, 'a black-cock', possibly used as a by-name. (*a*) Orby L (**bý**), Orton Cu (**tūn**).

***or-spring** OE, 'a spring', has been suggested for (*b*) Ospringe K, Oxspring YW, but the difficulty remains that ME spellings have *Ospring* and not *Orspring*. (OE *or-* pref. 'from', etc., often intensitive, **spring.**]

ort-geard OE, 'a garden, an orchard', *v.* **orceard.**

ōs OE, 'a god', *v.* **ēs.**

ōsle OE, 'an ouzel, a blackbird'. (*a*) Owzlebury Ha (**burh**), Ozleworth Gl (**worð**).

***ōster** OE, 'a hillock', a derivative of OE *ōst* 'a knot, a lump, protuberance', *ōstig* 'rough, knotty', may occur in some p.ns. such as (*a*) Osterland (**land**), Westenhanger (olim *Ostringe*) K (**hangra**), but it is difficult without OE spellings to distinguish it from later forms of **eowestre**, as in Osterley Mx, etc. The OE *Ostercumb* of BCS 622 cited as evidence for *ōster*, is later *Ostra-*, *Eustrecumbe* (13th), now Eastercombe Ha.

oter, otor OE, 'an otter'. (*a*) R. Otter So, Otter D (**ēa**), (hence Otterford So, Otterton D), Atterburne Wo, Otterbourne, -burn Ha, Nb, YW (**burna**), Otterham Co (**hamm**), *Otterpley* K (**plega**), Ottershaw Sr (**sceaga**), Otter's Pool La (**pōl**).

-oð, -að, -uð OE noun suffix (from PrGerm *-oþu-*, Kluge §135), used to form abstract nouns from Class II weak verbs, as in OE *fugeloð*, *huntoð*, *langoð*, and often extended to *-noð* with *-n-* from verbal forms as in **hlēonoð**; cf. **ēgeð.** The vowel variations in OE are merely scribal, as might be expected in an unstressed syllable.

ōðer OE adj., 'other, second'. (*a*) Otherton St (*alia villa* DB), Wo (**tūn**), Othery So (**ēg**).

Óðinn ON, the name of the principal god of heathen Scandinavia, corresponding to **Wōden.** (*a*) Roseberry Topping YN 164 (**under, berg**).

ovenam ME, 'a detached piece of land', *v.* **af-nám**.

oxa (**oxan** gen.sg., **œxen, exen** nom.pl., **oxna** gen.pl.) OE, 'an ox'. The usual gen.pl. *oxna* is freq. in p.ns. as *Oxen-*, but Ekwall (DEPN s.n.) suggests that Exfold Sx, Exton R may be from a secondary form **exna* which has been influenced by the nom.pl. *exen*. (*a*) Oxborough Nf (**burh**), Oxcombe L (**cumb**), Oxenbald Sa (**bōðl**), Oxendon Nth, Oxenton Gl (**dūn**), Oxenhall Du, Gl (**halh**), Oxen Hoath K (**hāð**), Oxenhope YW, Oxnop YN (**hop**), Oxford O (**ford**), Oxley St (**lēah**), Oxton Ch, Nt, YW (**tūn**), Oxwick Nf (**wīc**).

***ox-gang** OE, 'a measure of land' of 10–30 acres' extent, an eighth of a plough-land (*v.* **plōg-land**), occurs frequently in ME f.ns. (Nt 288, YN 329). [**oxa, gang**.]

P

***padde** OE, **padda** ON, 'a toad', first evidenced in ASC 1154, and in p.ns. from DB. (*a*) Padbrook K (**brōc**), Paddle Nth (**wella**).

paddock ModE, 'an enclosure', *v.* **pearroc.**

***padduc** OE, **paddok** ME, 'a frog'. (*a*) Padbrook D (**brōc**), Paddock Hill YE (**deill**). [~**padde, -uc.**]

***pǽla** ON, 'a dug-up place' (surviving as Icel *pæla*, Cleasby-Vigf s.v.), a derivative of ON *páll* 'a spade for peat or earth' (~**pāl**), and perhaps denoting a place where peats were dug or the like; it offers a better explanation than Norw *pøyla* 'pool' for the ME spellings *-pel* of Larpool YN 122 (**leirr**).

pæð OE (Angl, WSax), **peð** (Kt, Merc), 'a path, a track', glosses *dene*, *uallis* (*Rushw.Gosp.*, Luke iii. 5), which suggests that it denoted 'a path between banks', as in NCy dial. *peth* 'a hollow or deep cutting in a road'; usually, however, it glosses Lat *semita* 'footpath' and *callis* 'a cattle track' (as in WW 146.35–6). The NCy *peth* is a later dialectal form. (*b*) Peth Cu. It is combined with (i) descriptive adjs., as Roppa YN (**rauðr**), Sticklepath D (**sticol**); (ii) animal names, as Bagpath Gl (**bagga**), Doepath Nb (**dā**), Horsepath O (**hors**), Urpeth Du (**ūr**); (iii) words denoting special associations as Dupath Co (**þēof**), Morpeth Nb (**morð**), Soppit Nb (**soc**), Tolpits Hrt (**toln**); (iv) pers.ns., as Alspath Wa, Brancepeth Du, Hudspeth Nb. It is fairly common in similar combinations in ME minor names (C 340, Mx 202, Nth 268, W 442).

***pagol** OE, 'a stake', cognate with LG *pegel* 'a stake, esp. one to denote a high water mark'; cf. K, Sx dial. *paul* 'a measure of land' (perhaps from the idea of one marked out with stakes); in the sense 'small peg' as in MDu *pegel*, it may be the source of ModE *pawl*. (*b*) Paull YE 36.

pāl OE, 'a stake, a pole'. (*a*) Paulshot Sr (**scēat**). (*b*) Pole Elm Wo. [~Lat *pālus* 'a stake'.]

palant OE, 'a palace', later 'a district with palatine rights'. (*b*) The Pallant Sx 13 (a peculiar of the Archbishop of Canterbury). [LLat *palantia* 'palatinate'.]

paleis OFr, ME, 'a palace', usually only in modern names of important official royal or episcopal residences such as Fulham Palace,

Whitehall Palace, the Palace of Westminster Mx, Lambeth Palace Sr, Blenheim Palace O. [~Lat *palātium.*]

palis, paleis OFr, ME, 'a palisade'. (*a*) Palis Hall Nt. [~Lat *pālus* 'a stake', pāl.]

*pall OE (Angl), *peall (Kt, WSax), 'a ledge', cognate with ON *pallr* 'a step, a raised floor', Swed *pall* 'a footstool, a ledge' (cf. Ekwall, Studies[2] 145) and used of a hill with steep sides. (*a*) Paulton So (tūn). (*b*) Paul Wood So.

palster, palstr OE, 'a spike, a point', probably also 'a staff', cf. *palster* ME 'a pilgrim's staff'. (*a*) Palstre Court K (ēg). [pāl, -estre.]

*pamp OE, probably used of a hill, probably related to the ON by-name *Pampi*, Swed *pamp* used of thickset people, *pampen* 'swollen' (Ekwall, DEPN); perhaps also used as a by-name in Pampisford C 111. (*a*) Pamphill Do (hyll), Ponton L (tūn).

*pande ME, 'a pond', *v.* ponde.

panne OE, 'a pan', used topographically of something thought to resemble a pan in shape, as of a stone or a rounded valley. (*a*) Pannal YW (halh), Panston D (stān). (*b*) Mapstone, Mis Tor Pan D 480, 196.

pant Welsh, 'a valley'. (*a*) Pauntley Gl (lēah). (*b*) R. Pant Ess.

papi ON, 'a hermit'. (*a*) Papcastle Cu (ceaster). [~Lat *pāpa* 'pope, priest'.]

papol OE, 'a pebble', as in OE *papolstān* recorded only in Ælfric's *Homilies* i, 64. (*a*) Papplewick Nt 130 (wīc). [~popel, *v.* NED s.v. *pebble, pebblestone.* The relationship of *papol, popel,* ME *pibbil,* etc., is obscure; *pibbil* is probably from an OE **pyp(p)el,* an *i*-mutated variant of *popel,* which may lie behind OE *oð pippel riðiges, to pippel bricge* (v.l. *pyppel-*) BCS 906; *popel* itself may well be connected with ME *pople* 'to roll about, to flow in a tumbling manner, as water flowing over a pebbly surface' (cf. NED s.v. *popple* vb.); the relation of *papol* to these is obscure, but if the words are originally onomatopoeic, the variation would not be difficult.]

parc Corn, Welsh, 'a park, an enclosure'. (*a*) Parkangear, Parknowith Co. [A loan from OE pearroc.]

park OFr, ME, 'an enclosed tract of land for beasts of the chase', is common in that sense in minor names; it is also recorded in more recent times with the meaning of the related pearroc as 'an enclosed plot of ground, a paddock, a field' (*v.* NED s.v. *park*). It is probably the main source of *park* in p.ns. and in ME and later f.ns. (as

W 442, YE 327, etc.). (*a*) Parkfield C, Wa, Park Leys Nt. (*b*) Park Fm, etc. *passim*, Hill Park La, Hyde Park Mx, King's Park Wo, Old Park Hrt, Mx, Roydon Park Ess, Stot Park La, Westpark K, Wimpole Park C. [A Fr loan from WGerm **parruk-*, pearroc.]

paroche OFr, ME, par(i)she ME, 'a parish'. (*b*) Whiteparish W 387 (where it replaces *church*).

parva Lat adj., 'small'. (*c*) As an affix, often replacing litel, as in Ashby Parva, Thorpe Parva Lei.

pas OFr, 'a passage'. (*b*) Malpas Ch (mal).

pasture OFr, ME, 'a pasture, a piece of pasture-land', is fairly common in ME f.ns. (C 340, L, Nt 288, YE 327, etc.) from the 14th century and later. (*b*) North Pasture YW.

*pat(t)e OE, 'mud, marsh', related to OSwed *pata* 'low lying grass-land by water', etc. (cf. Löfvenberg 148). (*a*) *Patbroc* Nth 66, *Pattelake* Wo. (*b*) *la Patte* So, etc.

pavement OFr, ME, 'a pavement, a paved way'. (*b*) The Pavement Yk. (*c*) All Hallows on the Pavement Ln.

pāwa, pēa OE, 'a pea-fowl'. (*a*) Peamore D 496 (mere).

*pēac OE, 'a knoll, a hill, a peak', cognate with Norw *pauk* 'a stick', Swed dial. *pjuk* 'a point, a hillock', Du *pōk* 'a dagger', all suggesting 'something pointed'; it is established by several p.ns. besides The Peak Db (OE *Peaclond*, *Pecsæton*, etc.) and *Peak*, a common local name in St 114; *v.* Mawer, Problems 72. (*a*) Peak Db (land, etc.), Peckforton Ch (ford, tūn), Pegsdon Bd 176 (denu, dūn). (*b*) Peek D 285, Peke's House Sx, Ganton Peak YE 119.

*peall OE (Kt, WSax), 'a ledge', *v.* pall.

*pearr(e) OE, 'an enclosure', cognate with OHG *pharra* 'district, parish', related to ME *parren* 'to enclose, to fold (animals)', and surviving as dial. *parr* 'an enclosure for animals'. (*a*) Parham Sf (hām). (*b*) Parr La 109. [~pearroc.]

pearroc OE, 'a fence enclosing a piece of ground', glossing Lat *clatrum* (WW 140.8, etc.); this sense is the original one (cf. NED s.v. *parrock*), but later in OE it came to mean 'the ground enclosed with a fence, a small enclosure, a paddock'; it was also used of 'a fishing enclosure' in *la Parrok* in the Colne estuary Ess. The WGerm word was borrowed in OFr (*v.* park) and the OE word in Corn and Welsh (*v.* parc). Although it remained in use of 'a small enclosure' as *parrock* and the late variant *paddock*, it was never so widely current as the related OFr *park*. An *i*-mutated form **perric* is thought to lie behind Perching Sx 285 (-ingas). (*a*) Parkham D (hamm), Parkhall Hu 223 (halh, 'a fishing enclosure'). (*b*) Paddock Wood, Parrock Fm K, Parrox La. [~pearr, -uc.]

pece OFr, ME, 'a piece, a piece or plot of land', is freq. in later f.ns. such as *Flexpece* (fleax), *Geldenepece* (gylden), *Gorepece* (gāra), etc. (C 340, Nt 288, W 442, Wa 331).

peddere ME, 'a pedlar'. (*a*) Pether Hill YW (hyll).

pēl AN, ME, 'a stake, a palisade, an enclosure formed by a palisade', in minor names (Cu 486). (*b*) Peel Wood YN. [~Lat *pālus*, pāl.]

*penarth Corn, 'a headland, a promontory'. (*b*) Penare Co (*freq*). [~Welsh *penarth* 'headland'.]

pend OE (Kt), 'an enclosure', *v.* pynd.

pening, pending OE, peni, paneȝ ME, 'a penny', is used in p.ns. of 'something paying a penny rent'; it is sometimes difficult to distinguish from a pers.n., as in Penistone, *Penisale* YW, Pensthorpe YE. (*a*) Pennaton D, Pennington Ha, La, Penton Ha (tūn), Pennytoft L (topt), Pynamead D 378 (mǣd).

penn[1] OWelsh 'a height, a hill', *v.* penno-.

penn[2] OE, 'a small enclosure, a fold', later 'an enclosure for animals', is very difficult to distinguish from penno- and some doubtful examples mentioned there (§ 1) may well contain penn[2]. Forms with *pan* are from OE *pænn*, an older or alternative form of *penn*. (*a*) Pamber Ha (beorg), Penhurst Sx (hyrst). (*b*) Pann Wt, Penn Bk 229; Black Pan Wt (blæc), Hackpen D, W (haca), Kilpin YE (celf), Walpen Wt (wall); with pers.ns., Hampen Gl, Ipplepen D, Owlpen Gl. [Origin obscure, but possibly related by ablaut to OE *pinn* 'a pin, a peg', since the related ME *pennen* 'to pen, to fold' also meant 'to fasten (as with a bolt)'; the original meaning of *penn* therefore may have been a place which could be fastened up (cf. haca).]

*penno- Brit, penn OWelsh, pen Corn, Welsh, 'top, height, a hill', also an adj., 'chief'.

(1) This el. is very difficult to distinguish from penn[2], but it occurs in many p.ns. which have other Brit. els. and where the topography is appropriate, esp. in those where an OE el. such as hyll has been subsequently added, as in Pen Hill So (OE *of þam penne* BCS 1009). With other els. a measure of uncertainty remains as in Pemberton La (bere-tūn), Penwortham La (worð, hām), Pembridge He (brycg), Pencombe He (cumb), Pensby Ch (bý),

Pensnett St (snǣd), Pinhoe D (hōh), where the first el. could be either *penno-* or penn[2].

(2) The usual OE forms of this el. are *pen(n)*, *pænn*, *peon*. If any conclusion can be drawn from its use in the dat.pl. *æt Peonnum* for Penselwood So and its possible survival in Cu and Gl dial. *pen* 'a hill' (though these dial. uses may be revivals based on local place-names and have no continuous history from OE), the word may have been borrowed in OE as an appellative. For the most part, however, the Brit hill-names themselves were taken over by the English and other els. added according to the usual OE custom, for the many tautological examples with **hyll** suggest that the real meaning of *penno-* was then unknown. Such names were borrowed or created at different periods, those found in K, Sr, Sx, etc., being from Brit *penno-*, since some like Panshill Bk, Penge Sr, are combined with very early forms of **cēto-**; others like Pencoyd He (with later Welsh *coed* for *cēto-*) are clearly late borrowings or creations.

(3) (*a*) It is combined with other Brit els., probably sometimes with the meaning 'high, chief', as in Panshill Bk, Penge Sr, Penketh La, Penkhill St, Pencoyd He (**cēto-**, **coed**), Pencraig He (**creic**), Pen Cross D (**minid**), Penrith Cu (**rhyd**), Pensax Wo (**Saxones** 'the Saxons'); also Pennant, Penhale, Penheale Co.

(*b*) Original OE simplex p.ns. include Penn Hill So (2), Pendomer So, Penn St; Penselwood So (dat.pl.); combined with **hyll** in Pen Hall Wo, Penhill YN, Pendle Hill La (also Pendleton), Pendlebury La (all probably old simplex hill-names).

***pennuc** OE, **penok**, **pinnok** ME, 'a small pen', is found chiefly in W f.ns. from the 13th century. (*b*) Pinnocks W 443 [**penn**[2], **-uc**.]

***pentir** Corn, 'a headland'. (*b*) Pentire Co (*freq*). [~Welsh *pentir*.]

pēo, pīe (**pēona** gen.pl.) OE, an insect, a parasite of some kind, possibly used as a pers.n. sometimes. (*a*) Pymore Do (**mōr**), Pyon He (**ēg**), Pyworthy D (**worðig**).

***peren** OE adj., 'growing with pears'. (*a*) Parndon Ess (**dūn**), Parnham Do (**hām**), Prinstead Sx (**stede**). [**peru**, **-en**.]

permain OFr, ME, 'a pear' (cf. LöfvenbergME 68, from 1273). (*a*) Parmentley Nb 155 (**lēah**). [~Lat *Parmanus* adj. 'of Parma'.]

***perric** OE, 'an enclosure', *v*. **pearroc**.

***persc** OE, **persche** ME, 'a twig, an osier', surviving as Gl dial. *persh* (Ritter 133). (*a*) Pershore Wo 217 (**ōra**, OE *Perscoran* BCS

1282). (*b*) Persh Fm Gl. [Possibly from pearr, -isc, in allusion to hurdles or the like made from twigs or osiers.]

persone OFr, ME, 'a parson, a beneficed cleric', freq. in minor p.ns. (*a*) Parsonage Fields Ess, Parsons Green Mx.

*pertā Brit, perth Welsh, 'a wood, a bush, a brake'. (*a*) Pertwood W 176. (*b*) Peart So; Solpert Cu.

peru, pere, OE, 'a pear, the fruit of the pear-tree'; it is not used of 'the pear-tree' before 1400 (NED s.v.). (*a*) Parbold La (bōðl), Parham Gl, Sf (hām), Parley Do, Ha (lēah), Parton, Perton St (tūn), Pastead K, Prested Ess (stede), Spurshot Ha (scēat). [WGerm **pera-* from Lat *pirum.*]

pete ME, 'peat'. (*a*) Peatmoor (mōr), *Petegroves* Cu (gróf), Pedams Oak Du (mos, āc). (*b*) Peet Tie Hall Ess. [Origin unknown.]

pett OE (Kt), 'a pit', *v.* pytt.

pīc[1] OE, 'a point, a pointed tool', sometimes difficult to distinguish from the OE pers.n. *Pica*, as as in Pickhill YN, Pickworth R, Picton Ch, YN. It is recorded only in sense 'point' in OE, but later on it developed more specialized meanings which appear in p.ns., as (i) 'a prickle, a thorn', as in Pickthorn Sa (þorn); (ii) a fish 'the pike', as in Pickburn YW (burna), Pickmere Ch (mere); (iii) 'a pointed hill, a conical hill, a hill', extremely common in the NCy, where this particular meaning is thought to have been ensured by the influence of a cognate ON word which survives as Norw dial. *pik* used of conical or pointed mountains; but this meaning was probably also English, as examples of its use as a hill-name are found outside the Danelaw. In cases where it is followed by 'hill', the meaning 'point' would suffice (cf. pīced); (*a*) Pickhill Ess, Pick Hill K (hyll), Pickhurst K (hyrst), Pickup La (copp), Pickwick W (wīc), Pigdon Nb (dūn). (*b*) Red Pike, Stone Pike Cu, Rivington Pike La.

pic[2] OE, 'pitch, resin, mineral pitch'. (*a*) Picktree Du (trēow), Pitchcott Bk (cot), Pitchford Sa (ford, where there was a bituminous well). [~ Lat *pix, picem.*]

*pīced OE, piked ME, adj., 'having a point or pike, pointed', also in many f.ns. 'having sharp corners' (Mx 263, Nt 288, W 443). (*a*) Peaks Wood W, Picthall La, Picket How Cu, Pike Law La. [pīc[1], -ed.]

picen OE adj., 'pitchy, pertaining to pitch'. (*a*) Pitchcombe Gl (cumb). [pic[2], -en.]

*pide, *pidu OE, 'a marsh, a fen', recorded only in OE *Pidewællan* BCS 537; it is the source of pidele (cf. RN 324–6, where Du and LG parallels are adduced). (*a*) Pidsea YE 55 (sǣ).

*pidele OE, 'a fen, marshland' or the like, as in MDu *pedel* 'low-lying land, fenland' (cf. RN 324–6). In p.ns. it is recorded in OE spellings. From motives of delicacy the el. is sometimes replaced by puddel. (*b*) Piddle Brook, Ho, etc. D, Wo 14, R. Piddle D, Puddle Ho Nth, Puddle Do; Affpuddle, Tolpuddle Do (pers.ns.). [pide, -el.]

pīe[1] OE, an insect, *v.* pēo.

pīe[2] OFr, ME, 'a magpie'. (*a*) Pienest, Pinners Green Ess (nest) [Lat *pīca.*]

*pigga OE, pigge ME, 'a young pig', first evidenced independently in the 13th century; as a nickname and in p.ns. it is first known in 1086 DB (Tengvik 364); the general sense 'pig' is late. (*a*) Pickeridge (rið), Pickford (ford), Sx 272, 453, Pigsdown Co (dūn). [Origin unknown.]

pightel, pighel, pichel ME, 'a small enclosure, a croft', surviving as dial. *pightle*, is of obscure origin, and its original form is not easy to determine; *pightel* appears to be the earlier and commoner type. It is used mostly in f.ns. (Bd 295, C 340, Du, Nth 268, Sr 364, Sx 561, W 443, Wa 331, YE 327, YW, etc.); in some parts (Nt 288, Wa 331, etc.), the nasalized pingel is more frequent. (*b*) Pea Hill YE, Colepike Du.

piked ME adj., 'pointed', *v.* pīced.

pīl (pīla gen.pl.) OE, 'a spike, an arrow, a shaft, a pile', is fairly frequent in p.ns., but it cannot easily be distinguished from pill and an OE pers.n. **Pil*(*a*), nor can its various meanings be easily isolated in p.ns. In p.ns. like Pyle Bridge D it may refer to the piles on which a bridge was erected and with wood-names to places where shafts or stakes could be obtained; some may denote enclosures made with stakes, whilst in others such as those for 'marsh' or as a simplex p.n., it may simply denote a stake or a pile used as a landmark. (*a*) Pileholt K (holt), Pile Hill Sr, Pilemoor D (mōr), Pilham L (hām), Pillaton Co (tūn), Pilley YW (lēah), Pillwoods YE (ford). (*b*) As an original simplex p.n., Pilehays, Piley, Pilton, Pyle Bridge D, Pyle Wt.

*pil-āte, -ǣte (pil-ātan nom.pl.) OE, 'pill-oats' (*v.* Ekwall, Studies[2] 105); cf. ME *pilcorn* (LöfvenbergME 13–14). (*a*) *Pilatecroft* YW, Pillaton Hall St (halh).

pill ON, 'a willow' (cf. Swed *pil*), may be found in some Danelaw p.ns. but it cannot be distinguished from pīl.

*pinc OE, 'a minnow', surviving as *penk*, later *pink* (NED s.v. *pink* sb. 2), is probably identical with G dial. *pink*(*e*) 'minnow'; it may occur in some stream- and pool-names, but there are phonetic difficulties. (*a*) Pinchbeck L (bece), Pinchpools Ess 552 (pōl).

**pinca OE, 'a finch, a chaffinch', a variant of finca, which replaces it in Finchale Du (cf. Förster, Angl lxii, 662), is recorded in OE only in p.ns. such as *pincanhamm* BCS 665. (*a*) Pinkhurst Sr, Sx (hyrst), Pink Lane Ess, W (land), Pinkworthy D (worðig), Pinsla Co (lēah).

pingel ME, 'a small enclosure', a nasalized variant of pightel, occurs in ME f.ns. and frequently in later f.ns. in some areas (C 340, Cu 487, L, Nt 288, W 443, Wa xxi, 331). (*b*) Pickle Bank Cu, The Pingle Wa, Pingley Dyke Nt.

pinn (pinna gen.pl.) OE, 'a pin, a peg', probably enters into some p.ns. The original and the oldest recorded OE meaning is 'a wooden peg or pin, usually one holding a structure together', and no doubt this sense occurs in some p.ns. such as Pennicott, Uppincott D, Pincote C 66 (cot), which would denote 'a wooden cottage whose frame was held by pegs' or 'a shed where such pegs were made', whilst Pinn Wood D, might denote 'a wood where suitable wood for pegs could be obtained'. In other p.ns. like Pinn D, Pin Green Hrt, Pinham Sx, Pinley Wa, Pinton Wo, the meaning is obscure; an OE pers.n. *Pinna* would account for some, but some reference to a particular type of fence is possible. [~penn[2].]

pinnok ME, 'a small pen', *v.* pennuc.

pīn-trēow OE, 'a pine-tree'. (*a*) Pantry Bridge W.

pīot ME, 'a magpie', usually in NCy f.ns. (Cu 487). (*a*) Pye Close Du, Pyetmore Cu. [~pīe.]

pīpe OE, 'a pipe, a conduit', evidenced in ME minor names (C 340). (*a*) Pipewell Nth (wella). (*b*) Pipe He (near a stream Pipe Brook), St (a water conduit). [Lat *pīpa*.]

pīpere OE, 'a piper'. (*a*) Peppercombe Ha (cumb), Pepper Ness K (næss). [pīpe, -ere.]

pirige, pirge, pyrige OE, 'a pear-tree'. (*a*) Perreton Wt, Perton St, Pirton Hrt, Wo, Purton Gl, St, W, Pyrton O (tūn, possibly an OE *pirig-tūn* 'a pear orchard', cf. æppel-tūn), Pierce Hey YW (gehæg), Pirbright Sr (fyrhð), *Pirifield* K (feld), Pirehill St (hyll), Pyrford Sr (ford). (*b*) Perry Hu, K, St, Paulers-, Potterspury Nth, Water-, Woodperry O; Hartpury Gl (heard). [~peru, -e.]

*pirigen OE adj., 'growing with pear-trees'. (*a*) Parndon Ess (dūn), Parnholt Ha (holt), Purnish Sr 123 (ersc). [pirige, -en.]

pise (pisan), pisu, peosu OE, 'pease'. Most modern forms are from *pise* with ME lengthening of *i* to *ē* in the open syllable. (*a*) Peaseholmes La (holmr), Peasemore Brk (mere), Peasfurlang La (furlang), Peas Hill Nt, Pishill O (hyll), Peasmarsh Sx (mersc), Pusey Brk (ēg). [~Lat *pisum*.]

*pisen, *peosen OE adj., 'growing with pease'. (*a*) Peasenhall Sf, Posenhall Sa (halh). [pise, -en.]

place OFr, place, plas ME, 'an open space in a town, an area surrounded by buildings'; it is also frequent in later minor names in the senses 'a plot of ground, a residence', as Crakeplace Hall Cu, Knight's Place K, York Place Mx; cf. also C 340, W 443, YE 327. [Lat *platea* 'open space'.]

*plæsc OE, 'a pool', recorded only in OE charter names, as *plæsc*, *plesc* BCS 1119 Sa; it survives in ME f.ns. (Bk 259, C 341, Ess 587, Hrt 258, W 443, Wa 331) and as dial. *plash* 'a marshy pool' (cf. Ekwall, Studies[2] 117). (*a*) Plashford Co (ford). (*b*) Plaish Sa, Plash So, Splash Bridge Wo; Melplash Do (myln). [~plysc, plaschiet.]

plain OFr, ME, 'a great open tract', also 'a piece of flat meadowland', found occasionally in f.ns. (as Mx 203). (*b*) The Plains C, Salisbury Plain W. [~Lat *plānum*.]

plaisseis OFr, 'an enclosure made with fencing', *v.* plessis.

plaissiet OFr, 'an enclosure, a park', *v.* plessis.

planke ONFr, ME, 'a plank, a plank bridge'. (*a*) Plonk Barn Sx, Plonk's Hill Sr.

plas ME, 'an open place', *v.* place.

plaschiet, *plascquet OFr, 'a marshy pool', may occur in ME and later f.ns. as *Plashet* (W 443) and *Plasket* (Cu 487), but it is difficult to distinguish from plaissiet. (*b*) Plasket Plantation, Plasketlands Cu. [OFr *plaschiet* is a dim. of OFr *plascq* 'damp meadow', which is a loan from MLG *plas*, ~plæsc.]

plat[1] OFr, ME, 'something flat, a footbridge, a place, a spot'; it may be confused with plat[2]. (*b*) Platt, Platt Bridge La 31, 102.

plat[2] ME, 'a plot, a small piece of ground', is a secondary form of plot due to the influence of plat[1]; *plat* is not evidenced before 1511 except in p.ns. and f.ns. which carry it back to the 13th century (as in *Adamesplat* La 31 n., *Scortplat* Nt 288, etc.); it is fairly common in f.ns. (Nt, etc.). (*b*) Platt Wo 311.

plega OE, plæga, plaga (Angl), 'play, sport', used in p.ns. of 'a place for games or where animals played'. The later variants *Play-* and *Plaw-* are from *plega* and *plaga* respectively. (*a*) Playden Sx, Plowden Sa (denu), Playford Sf, Plyford D (ford), Playton Co (tūn), Plealey Sa, Pleyley Wo (lēah); *v.* also pleg-stede, pleg-stōw, etc. (*b*) Plawhatch Sx; in compounds usually with animal-names, as *Cockplaie* Cu 101 (cocc), Deerplay La, Deer Play YW, Durpley D (dēor), Hemplow Nth (hind), *Otterpley* K (oter).

*pleget OE, 'a place for games', is probable in (*a*) Plaitford Ha, W 383 (ford). [plega, -et.]

*pleg-stall OE, 'a play place', probably meaning much the same as pleg-stōw, is found only in f.ns. in Ess 587. [plega, stall.]

pleg-stede OE, 'play place', found in OE as *plægstede* KCD vi, 244 and in later f.ns. (W 444). (*a*) Chapel Plaster W 83.

pleg-stōw OE, 'a sport place, a place where people gathered for play', glossing Lat *amphitheatrum*, *palaestra* and *gymnasium*, is also found in f.ns. (C 341, Ess 587, Mx 203, W 443). (*b*) Plaistow D, Db, Ess, Plaistows Hrt, Plaxtol L, Playstow K, Plestowes Wa, Pleystowe Sr. [plega, stōw.]

plek ME, 'a small plot of ground', chiefly in f.ns. (Nt 289, Nth 268, W 444, Wa 331, etc.). (*b*) The Pleck He, Meadow Place Db (mǣd). [~ Du *plek*, MLG *plecke*.]

plessis ONFr, plaisseis OFr, 'an enclosure made with interlaced fencing', and a derivative plaissiet OFr, 'an enclosure, one made with wattles, a park'. (*b*) Plashes Hrt, Plashet(t) Ess, Sr 280, Sx 356, Plassett Nf, Platch He, Pleshey Ess 488, Plessey Nb 158. [Lat *pless-*, *plassetum* 'a small wood, a park'.]

*plisc OE, 'a pool', *v.* plysc.

*plōc OE, 'a log, a club', surviving as ME (Scots) *ployk* 'a club' and dial. *plock* 'a log, a block of wood'. (*a*) Plockwoods YN (wudu).

plodde ME, 'a pool, a puddle', *v.* pludde.

plógr ON, plōg, plōh late OE, 'a plough', eventually ousted the usual OE word sulh. (*a*) Ploughfield He (feld).

plógs-land ON, plōg(a)-land late OE, ME, 'a ploughland', was a measure of land, in ON an acre; in the Danelaw it was about 120 acres and was the equivalent of the carucate of DB or what a team of oxen could plough in the year. (*b*) Ploughland YE. [plógr, land.]

plot late OE, ME, 'a small piece of ground', found in f.ns. (as Bd 295, C 341, Ess 587, Hrt 258, Mx 203, Sr 364, Sx 561, W 444, etc.); cf. **plat**[2]. (*b*) Plot(s) Fm Nt.

pludde, plodde ME, 'a pool, a puddle', surviving as dial. *plud* 'the swampy surface of a wet ploughed field' (So), 'temporary pools of water' (Sa), found chiefly in the WCy in f.ns. (as W 444). (*b*) Pludd, Pludda D. [Origin unknown, unless it is a metathesized form of **puddel**.]

plūme OE, 'a plum, a plum-tree'. (*a*) Plompton YW, Plumpton Cu, K, La, Nth, Sx (**tūn**, perhaps an OE *plūm-tūn* 'a plum orchard', cf. **æppel-tūn**), Plumber Do (**bearu**), Plumford K (**ford**), Plumbland Cu (**lúndr**), Plumley Ch (**lēah**), Plumstead K, Nf (**stede**), Plungar Lei (**gāra**). [~ Lat *prunum*, **plȳme**.]

plūm-trēow OE, 'a plum-tree'. (*a*) Plumtree Nt (2). [**plūme, trēow**.]

plȳme OE, 'a plum, a plum-tree'. (*a*) Plympton (**tūn**), Plymstock (**stocc**), Plymtree (**trēow**) D. [~ **plūme, -e**.]

***plysc, *plisc** OE, 'a pool', surviving as dial. *plish* (EDD). (*a*) Plusha Bridge Co (**brycg**). (*b*) Plush Do. [~ **plæsc**; the exact relationship is obscure as both *plæsc* and *plysc* are probably onomatopoeic in origin; cf. Fris *plas(se)*, *plis* 'a pool'.]

pode ME, 'a toad'. (*a*) Podder Nt (**gehæg**), Poddimore So, Podmore St (**mōr**). [~ **padde**; **pode** is found from c. 1250 and is probably formed from *padde* on the analogy of ME *tode* (OE *tāde*) by the side of OE *tadde*; cf. **tādige**.]

***pofel** OE, meaning and origin unknown; in Scotland *poffle* is used of 'a small parcel of land' (NED). (*a*) Pollington YW (*Pouelingtun* DB, ME). (*b*) Pool YW (OE *on pofle*), *Prestpofle* (1391 a st.n. in Hexham Nb), Maxpoffle Scotl (*Maxpoffil* 1317).

pohha, pocca OE, 'a pouch, a bag', used in some undetermined sense in p.ns., possibly as a by-name. (*a*) Polebrook Nth (**brōc**), Poughill Co, D (**hyll**), Poughley Brk (**lēah**).

***pokere** ME, 'a hobgoblin', said to be from ON (cf. NED), or 'one who has to do with a poke' (cf. **beggere**). (*a*) Pokerly, -ley Nb, Sx (**lēah**).

pōl[1], **pull** OE, 'a pool, a pond, a pool in a river', possibly also 'a creek'; p.ns. also suggest that it might also have meant 'stream, rivulet'. Normally OE *pōl* and *pull* remain distinct, but in some p.ns. like Liverpool La and when used as a first el. there has been some interchange of the two forms. The relationship of *pōl* and

LG *pōl* to *pull* and other variants like pyll, ON *pollr*, Welsh *pwll*, etc. is obscure. (*a*) Polsloe D (slōh), Polstead Sf (stede), Poolhampton Ha (hǣma-tūn), Poulton Ch, Gl, K, La (*freq*) (tūn), Pulford Ch (ford), Pulham Do (hām). (*b*) Pool D, Poole Ch, Do, Gl, YW; Poolham L (dat.pl.); Bathpool Co (bæð), Blackpool La (blæc), Bradpole Do (brād), Drypool YE (drȳge), Hampole YW (hana), Harpole K (horu), Otterpool K (oter), Walpole Nf (walh), Yarpole He (gear); it is common in ME minor names (*passim*).

~~pol[2] Corn, 'a pool, a hollow, a pit'. (*b*) Penpoll, Trempoll Co. [poll, pwll.]~~

poll PrWelsh, Ir, Gael, 'a hole, a pit, a pond', a by-form of pwll Welsh 'a pool, a pond, a hollow' (cf. RN 329–30, pol[2], pull, pyll), is commonest in the NW (Cu 487). (*a*) *Polgauer*, *Pottragon*, *Powburgh*, Pow Beck, Pow Maugham Cu. (*b*) Pow Cu; Crimple Beck YW, Wampool Cu.

polle ME, 'the head, the top of the head', used topographically of something resembling it. (*b*) Pauls Fm K. [Origin obscure.]

polled ME adj., 'polled, cut off, pollarded'. (*a*) Polefields K (feld), Poulter's Corner Sx (trēow). [~ polle, -ed.]

pollr ON, 'a pool', might enter into some p.ns. mentioned s.v. poll, but there is no other evidence for its use in England.

***polra** OE, 'marshy land', cognate with MLG *polre* 'low-lying land reclaimed from the sea', freq. in Netherlands p.ns. as *Polder*, etc., a word which was borrowed later in English as *polder* (NED s.v.); cf. Mawer, Problems 51, Sx 561, D 502, K 500. In p.ns. the ME forms generally have *Polre-*, but *Poldre-* with an intrusive *-d-* (perhaps influenced by the Du loan-word *polder*) is found occasionally. (*a*) Powderham D (hām), Pulverbatch Sa (bece). (*b*) As a simplex p.n. Poldhurst K, Pollard YE 41, Pools L, Poulders K. [~ pōl.]

ponde ME, 'a pond, an artificial or natural pool', first evidenced about 1300, in p.ns. somewhat earlier, as in *Eliasponde* C 341 from 1225, *Elepond* t. Hy 3 Hrt 258 (cf. also Mx 203, W 444). An alternative form ME *pande* also exists as in Pann Mill Bk 205, Penlan Hall Ess 391, *la Pande* Bk (described as a fish-pond). (*b*) Pond Fm Bk, Hampstead Pond Mx. [This el. is probably best derived from an OE **pand*, related by ablaut to *pund*, the sense being 'place where water is impounded by a dam or in an artificial hollow'; it has been taken as a phonetic variant of *pund*, cf. NED s.v. *pond*.]

pont[1], **pount** OFr, 'a bridge'. (*a*) Pomparles Bridge (in Glastonbury) So ('bridge perilous'), Pontefract YW (earlier *Pontfreyt*, OFr *freit*, Lat *fractus* 'broken'). (*b*) Grampound Co (**grant**). [Lat *pons, pontem*.]

pont[2], **pons** Corn, **pont** Welsh, 'a bridge'. (*b*) Penpont, Tolponds Co. [Lat *pons, pontem*.]

popel OE, 'a pebble', recorded only in OE *popelstanas*, a gloss to Lat *lapillulos, parvos lapides* (NED s.v. *pebble-stone*); it may also be the first el. of OE *to populfinige* KCD 652 (**fīn, ēg**). (*a*) Pope's Hall Hrt (**halh**), Poppleford D 592 (**ford**), Poppleton (OE *popeltun*, **tūn**), Popplewell (**wella**) YW. [~**papol**.]

popig OE, 'a poppy'. (*a*) Pophills Wa (**hyll**).

poplier OFr, **popler** ME, 'a poplar-tree'. (*b*) Poplar Mx. [~Lat *pōpulus* 'poplar'.]

porcus Lat, 'a pig'. (*c*) Toller Porcorum Do.

port[1] OE, 'a haven, a harbour', is also used of 'a town having a harbour' as in OE *to þam porte þe is nemned Cwæntwic* (OEBede iv, 1), and in that respect might be confused with **port**[2]. In p.ns. it is difficult sometimes to distinguish this *port* from others, but it may be assumed in many examples round the coast. (*a*) Porchester (**ceaster**), Portsdown (**dūn**), Portsea (**sǣ**), Portsmouth (**mūða**) Ha (all named from *Port*, which was probably the old name of Portsmouth Harbour, known as *Portum Adurni* in *Notitia Dignitatum*), Porlock So (**loca**), Portbury, Portishead So (**burh, hēafod**), Portslade Sx (**gelād**). (*b*) Portland Do (OE *Port*). [~Lat *portus* 'a harbour'.]

port[2] OE, 'a town, a market town, a market'.

(1) In OE it occurs as an alternative to **burh** as a gloss to Lat *civitas* (*Lindisfarne Gospels*, Matt. xxxi. 40); it also glosses Lat *castellum* (WW 144.24, etc.), which suggests that it could also mean 'fortification, fortified town', a sense required by Alport La 34 (**ald**), near the site of the old Roman fort of *Mamucio* (Manchester), as well as Portfield La 77, also near the site of a Roman camp.

(2) Mostly, however, it denotes in p.ns. 'a town with market rights'; this is the usual meaning in ME when many towns so named came into existence or were granted charters. Newport Pagnell Bk was already a borough in DB, Milborne Port So got its affix *Port* after it had become a borough in 1225; the el. is also often

rendered by Anglo-Lat *burgus* 'borough' (*v.* burh) in the Lat versions of p.ns. like Newport Sa (*novo burgo*).

(3) The allusion in some p.ns. containing *port* is sometimes to outlying possessions, fields and the like, belonging to nearby towns or townspeople; thus Portswood Ha was a wood belonging to the town of Southampton, and this use is well exemplified in ME f.ns. (as C 341, W 444, etc.).

(4) In some p.ns. like Gosport ('goose'), Langport ('long'), the first el. suggests that the significance of *port* was here 'a market place', as does its use as a st.n., as in Newport (Lincoln) L; *v.* Ekwall, Studies[2] 180ff.

(5) (*a*) Portfields Bk 22 (in Newport Pagnell Bk), Portisham Do (hamm probably belonging to the town of Abbotsbury), *Portsmouth* Wo 217 (gemōt, alluding to part of the town of Pershore belonging to Westminster), Port Street Wo (strǣt), Portswood Ha (wudu).

(*b*) Alport Db, La (ald), Bridport Do (Bredy Do), Doggaport D 95 (þocere), Gosport Ha (gōs), Holyport Brk (horig), Lamport Bk, Nth, Sx, Langport K, So (lang), Newport Bk, Co, Ess, L, Sa, Wt (nīwe), Taddiport D (tādige).

(*c*) Milborne Port So.

[From Lat *portus* 'harbour' (*v.* port[1]) or *porta* 'gateway' (*v.* port[3]); *v.* NED s.v. *port* sb. 2.]

port[3] OE, porte OFr, ME, 'a gate, the entrance to a walled town', in OE glossing Lat *porta* (*Psalter* lxviii. 12) and *porticus* (*Rushw. Gospel*, John x. 23); it is equivalent to duru and geat (*Lindisf. Gosp.* Matt. vii. 13). The OE word is thought to have become obsolete, and the word was then reintroduced in ME through OFr. It is rare in p.ns. (*a*) Portgate Nb (geat, alluding to the gap by which Watling Street passed through the Roman wall). (*b*) Langport K 483 (on the east of Lydd). [~Lat *porta* 'gateway'.]

port-cwēn(e) OE, 'a prostitute'. (*a*) Portinscale Cu (skáli). [port, cwēn, cwene.]

porth Corn, Welsh, 'a harbour, an estuary; a gate'. (*a*) Pelistry Co. (*b*) Porth; Porthgwarra, Porthleven, Porthpean Co. [Lat *portus*, *porta*, cf. port[1], port[3].]

port-weg OE, 'a road leading to a town'. (*b*) Portway Wo 4, Port Way D, etc. [port[2], weg.]

post OE, 'a post, a pillar', in allusion to posts used in building or as marks. (*a*) Posbury D 406, Postlebury So (burh, probably a stockade), Postern Db (ærn, built of posts), Postgate YN (gata, marked by posts); cf. also ME minor names in C 341, Ess 587, W 444.

pot(t) late OE, 'a pot', may occur in some p.ns., but the usual word for 'pot' in OE was crocc, and the early history of *pot* itself is obscure; it may be of continental origin, for neither *pott* nor the derivative pottere is independently evidenced before the 12th century (NED s.v.), though *pot* appears in OE p.ns. such as *Pottaford* BCS 1269 Sf. Where it occurs in p.ns. it may refer to places where pots were made or even where ancient pottery had been discovered. It is scarcely distinguishable from potte. (*a*) Podberry K (burh), Potcote Nth (cot), Potterne Do, W (ærn), Potton Bd (*Pottun* c. 960, tūn), Potworthy D 470 (worðig). (*b*) Pothill Sx 187. [Origin unknown; cf. potte.]

potte ME, 'a deep hole, a pit, a deep hole in a river-bed, a natural deep hole, esp. in the mountain limestone', is found in texts, p.ns. and dials. in the NCy, which suggests that the word may be of ON origin and related to Swed dial. *putt*, *pott* 'a water-hole, the abyss'. If this is so, the examples of *pot* in SCy p.ns. should be referred to OE pott. (*a*) Potlock Db (lacu), Pott Beck (bekkr), Potto (haugr) YN. (*b*) Pott Hall YN 234; Bishopspot Cu, Crackpot YN (kráka); *Petepottes* Cu (pete), Sandpot YN (sand), Stonepot Cu (stān), referring to materials, and Drakepits YW (draca), Thirlspot Cu (þyrs) to monsters. [An unmutated variety of pytt; on formal grounds *potte* could be OE or ON, and it is not impossible that pott 'a pot' is a sense-variant of the same origin.]

pottere OE, 'a pot-maker', evidenced in OE only in the p.n. *on potteres lege* 11th BCS 890 (cf. Fransson 184, Tengvik 266). (*a*) Pottergate (Lincoln) L (gata), Potterkeld YN (kelda), Potter Street Ess (hyll), Potterton YW (tūn), Pottosy Nth (halh). (*c*) Potters Marston Lei (from 1043), Potterspury Nth, and *Potter* prefixed to Brompton YE, Heigham Nf, Newton YW. [pott, -ere, also reinforced by OFr *potier* 'potter'.]

pourpris(e) OFr, ME, 'a precinct, an enclosure, a close'. (*b*) Purprise YW, Purps D.

pras Corn, 'a meadow'. (*b*) Praze, Penpraze Co. [~pre, Lat *pratum*.]

***prā(w)** OE, 'a look-out'. (*a*) Prawle D (hyll). [~OE *beprīwan* 'to wink', ME *prien* 'to look closely, to spy, to pry'.]

pre, pree OFr, **prey, pre** ME, 'a meadow', is common in ME f.ns.

(as C 341, Ha, Hrt, Sr, etc.) and is sometimes rendered by Lat *pratum*. (*a*) Pray Heath, Primemeads Sr 158. (*b*) The Prae Hrt, Sr, Delapre Nth 148, Catsprey, Sudprey Sr. [~Lat *prātum*.]

* prēon OE, 'a brooch, a pin', used in some undetermined way, but perhaps like pagol or pinn, in (*b*) Preen Sa. [~MLG *pren*(*e*) 'a pin, a spike'.]

prēost (prēosta gen.pl.) OE, 'a priest'. It is often difficult to decide whether the el. is used in the sg. or pl. in p.ns.; in names like Prescot it may be sg. and refer to a cottage occupied by a priest, whilst in Presteigne it is certainly collective; in many of the Prestons (OE *prēosta-tūn*) it may denote places set aside for the endowment of priests or monks. (*a*) Prescot(t) Gl, La, O, Sa, Prustacott Co (cot), Prestleigh So (belonging to the Bishop of Wells), Priestley Bd (lēah), Presteigne Sa (hǣmed 'household'), Preston Bk, Ch, Cu, Do *et passim*, Purston Nth, YW (tūn), Prestwich La, Prestwick Nb (wīc), Prestwold La (wald), Prestwood St (wudu), Priestgill Cu (gil), (*c*) As an affix in Priest Weston Sa (*preostes*), Candover Preston Ha, Preston Crowmarsh O (*prestene*, a new ME wk. gen.pl., cf. -ena).

pres, prys Welsh, *pres, *pris Corn, 'brushwood, a covert'. (*a*) Preesall La (hǫfuð), Presincoll Co; Priston So (OE *Prisctun*) is from a derivative OWelsh **prisc*, Welsh *prysg* 'brushwood, copse'. (*b*) Prees Sa, Preese La, Preeze Co. [Ultimately related to hrīs.]

prey ME, 'a meadow', *v.* pre.

pric(c)a OE, 'a prick, a prickle', used to form plant- and tree-names, as in *prick-willow* in (*b*) Prickwillow Bridge C (from 1250) and possibly used elsewhere, as in Prickley Green Wo.

pridd Welsh, 'earth, soil'. (*a*) Priddy So (tig).

prince OFr, ME, 'a prince'. (*c*) Princes Risborough Bk 70.

prior OFr, late OE, ME, 'a prior (of a religious house)'. (*a*) Prior Howe Cu (haugr). (*c*) Cleve Prior Wo, Priors Dean Ha.

*prisc OWelsh, 'brushwood', *v.* pres.

*pritol OE adj., 'prattling, babbling', probably as a reduplicated variant in *prittle-prattle*, may be an old word (cf. MLG *pratelen* 'to chatter'); (OE *pritigian*, which has been suggested as a parallel, is merely a misreading of OE *writigian* 'to chirp' and is not relevant, cf. writol). (*a*) Prittlewell Ess 190 (wella).

prūme OE, 'a plum', corresponding to OSax *prūme*, OHG *pfrūma*. (*a*) Broomhyll Sx 529 (hyll). [~Lat *prunus*, plūme.]

* *pryfet OE, 'a privet (copse)'; *privet*, with its variant *privy*, is not found independently before the 16th century, but may well be much older (DEPN 357). (*a*) Prewley D (lēah). (*b*) Privett Ha (OE *æt pryfetes flodan* ASC 755), Privett Fm W 397 (from 1268). [Origin unknown; cf. -et.]

prysg Welsh, 'brushwood', *v.* pres.

pūca OE, 'a goblin', surviving as *puck*, *pook*. (*a*) Parkwalls Co (wall), Pock Field C (feld), Poppets Sx (pytt), Puckeridge Hrt (ric), Puckshot Sr 206 (scydd), Purbrook Ha (brōc); it is found also in ME minor names (D 691, Ess 587, Sx 562, W 444).

pūcel OE, 'a goblin'. (*a*) Popple Drove C (drāf), Putshole D (hol), Puxton Wo (tūn). [pūca, -el.]

*puddel OE, podel ME, 'a pond or pit full of water, a small shallow dirty pool, a puddle', is rare, but it is found in later p.ns. (*a*) Puddle Dock Ess, Sx, Puddlewart Ess. [~OE *pudd* 'a ditch, a furrow', -el; cf. G dial. *pudel* 'a puddle'; Welsh *pwdel* 'a puddle, a pool' is a loan from ME *podel*.]

puer Lat, 'a boy, a youth'. (*c*) Ashby Puerorum L (in allusion to the choir-boys of Lincoln). Cf. LatAdd 339.

*pull OE, 'a pool, a creek', recorded only in OE p.ns., interchanges with and often replaces pōl; it may be original in (*a*) Poulton Gl (OE *Pultun*), La (tūn), Pulford Ch (ford, DB *Pul-*), Pulham Nf (hām). (*b*) Poolfields Wo (OE *Pull*). [~pyll. The relationship with Welsh *pwll*, etc., is obscure, but *pull*, it may be noted, occurs mostly in the WMidl.]

*pund OE, pund ME, 'a pound, an enclosure into which stray cattle were put', is not recorded independently before the 15th century, except in p.ns. and the compounds pund-fald, early ME *pundbreche* (*v.* NED s.v. *pound-breach*), and the related pynd-(fald), which are older. In some dials. the word appears to be used of 'a pond, a pool', and this use no doubt is due to some confusion with the related ponde. The word is first found in p.ns. in DB, but mostly it occurs first in the 13th century, as might be expected with minor p.ns. (cf. also Mx 203, W 444). (*a*) Poundstock Co (stoc), Punda YE (haga). (*b*) Pound Fm, etc., K, Sr, Sx, W *et freq.* [~pynd; this and the related words occur in no other Germ language.]

*pundere OE, 'a pinder', first evidenced independently from the 17th century (NED), and as a surname from the 12th century (Fransson). (*a*) Poundisford So (ford). [pund, -ere.]

*pund-fald OE, 'a pinfold, a pound', recorded only in OE *on hacan pundfald* BCS 1080, 1144, appears later as *punfold* and *pinfold*, the latter (ultimately from pynd) not being found till the 15th century; it occurs chiefly in f.ns. and minor names (as C 341, Cu 487, Ess 587, W 445, etc.). (*b*) Pinfold Nb, Poundfield Sx. [pund, fald.]

*pur OE, 'a bittern' or 'a snipe' (cf. NED s.v. *purre*). (*a*) Purbeck Do (bīc), Purleigh, -ley Ess 222, Brk (lēah).

purceynt OFr, purseynt ME, 'a precinct, an enclosure'. (*a*) Postland L (land).

*putta OE, 'a hawk, a kite' (cf. Ekwall, Studies[2] 91 ff), is difficult to distinguish from a postulated OE pers.n. *Putta*; either the word or the pers.n. may occur in some p.ns. such as (*a*) Pitton (tūn), Puthall (halh, OE *puttan ealh*) W, Putford D (ford), Putley He (lēah), Puttenham Sr (hām). [~ puttoc, pyttel.]

*puttoc OE, 'a kite', not evidenced till 1400, is found earlier in p.ns., possibly used sometimes as a pers.n. (*a*) Pittescombe (cumb, from 1238), Pudsham D (hām). [putta, -uc.]

pwll Welsh, 'a pool', *v.* poll, pull.

pyll OE, 'a tidal creek, a pool in a river', is established by OE charter p.ns.; it is for the most part found in the SW, esp. in the Severn Estuary (cf. NED s.v. *pill* sb. 3), and in ME minor names in Sx 561, W 444. It survives as So dial. *pill* 'a small stream'. (*a*) Pilton D (tūn). (*b*) Pyle So (near Pilton So); Crockern Pill (croccere), Huntspill (pers.n.) So, Lamphill Co (lām), Uphill So (upp). [~ pull.]

pynd OE, pend (Kt), 'an enclosure, a pound', an *i*-mutated variant of pund; it occurs in OE in *Frodeshammespend, flothamespynd* BCS 335, 336 K. It is also used of 'a pool, a pond' in *Westpende* (a mill-pond) Sx; *pynd* also may have this sense in the OE *Riming Poem* 49; cf. also OE *pynding* 'a dam'. (*b*) Pean, Penn K, Pendell Court Sr, Pen Hill, Penland, Pinland Sx, Piend D, Pin Green Hrt (all originally simplex); Gumping, Well Penn K, Monkyn Pin Sx; cf. also ME minor names in C 341, Sr 364.

*pynd-fald OE, 'a pinfold', is found in ME and later f.ns. in C 340, Ess 587, Nt 288. [~ pynd, pund-fald.]

pytt OE (Angl, WSax), pett (Kt), 'a pit, a natural hollow, an excavated hole, esp. one where minerals or other materials are got, a grave, a hole in the ground serving as a trap for animals', found also in ME f.ns. (as Bd 295, C 341, *et passim*). (*a*) Petlands K (land). (*b*) Pett

K, Pitt Ha; *Fulepet* Ess 327 (fūl), Bumpitt K (bān), Cockpit Co (cocc), Colpitts Nb (col), Grimpits Wo (Grīm), Houndapit Co (hund), Sandpits YN (sand), Stonepits K (stān); *v.* also **wulf-pytt**. [~Lat *puteus* 'well, pit', ~**potte**.]

pyttel OE, 'a hawk, a mousehawk' (cf. Ekwall, Studies[2] 91), possibly used sometimes as a by-name as in Pittleworth Ha, Pudleston He. (*a*) Pickledean W 306 (**denu**), Pitshanger Mx (**hangra**). [~**putta**, **-el**.]

Q

quabbe ME, 'a bog', *v.* **cwabba**.

quarrelle ME, 'a quarry', a variant of **quarriere**, surviving as NCy dial. *quarrel*, *wharrel* (cf. Cu 488). (*a*) Wharrels Hill Cu. (*b*) Quarle Co.

quarriere OFr, **quarrere** ME, 'a quarry', occurs as *quarre* in f.ns. (C 342, W 445). (*b*) Quarr Do, Wt.

queche ME, 'a thicket', dial. *queach*, is found in a few ME p.ns. such as *le Queche* Wo 392, *Quethelake* (*sic*) Mx 203, *Thirsqueche* Nth 268 (**þyrs**), cf. also Hrt 258. (*a*) Cotchford Sx 366 (**ford**). [Possibly from an OE **cwǣc*, related by ablaut to **cwic**.]

quike ME, 'couch-grass', *v.* **cwic**.

quiken ME, 'a mountain-ash', *v.* **cwicen**.

R

* rā[1] (rān gen.sg., rāna gen.pl.) OE, rá ON, 'roe, a roe-buck'; in the Danelaw it is difficult to keep the OE and ON words apart and to distinguish them from rá[2]. The earlier OE form was rāha, which survives in compounds like *rāh-dēor* 'roe-deer', rāh-hege and other OE charter forms (Mdf 106), and this form may occur in Roe Beck Cu (olim *Raghe*, ēa); cf. also the nearby Raughton. (*a*) Rae Burn Cu (burna), Rayhead YW (hēafod), Rodden So (denu), Roecombe Do (cumb), Roel Gl (hyll), Roe Wood Nt (wudu), Rogate Sx (geat); the gen.sg. or gen.pl. occurs in Rancombe, Renham Wt, Renhold Bd; Raskelf YN (skjalf), Rowland Db (lúndr) have ON els. [~ rǣge.]

rá[2] ON, 'a land-mark, a boundary', as in OSwed and Dan *raa*, cf. Lindkvist 188 and the p.ns. Swed *Råby*, Dan *Raaby*; it is difficult to distinguish from rā[1]. (*a*) Raby Ch, Cu, Du, Roby La (bý).

-ra OE noun-suffix, used to form concrete nouns, such as hangra (related to OE *hangian* 'to hang'), polra (related to pōl); cf. also -er, -or.

* racu OE, 'a hollow, a stream, the bed of a stream', occurs in OE only in the compounds *on ða ealdan ea race* BCS 549 and *strēam-racu* which glosses both Lat *alveus* 'a hollow' as an alternative to strēam (WW 178.5, 345.22) and Lat *flumen* (*Psalter* lxx, 8); a sense such as 'river-bed' is required by the context in *Andreas* 1580, *Him þurh streamræce stræt wæs arymed*. The topography of Langrick L and Long Drax YW suggests that it also had the meaning 'reach, the straight stretch of a river'. This word is difficult to distinguish from hraca and rák. (*a*) Rackenford D (ærne, ford), Rackheath Nf (hȳð), Ragden La (denu).

rād OE, 'the act of riding on horseback', probably also 'suitable for riding on' in compounds with ford and weg. This el. with the modern sense 'road', not evidenced before Shakespeare, is probably much older, as it is found with this meaning in an affix from the 13th century. An adjectival form *rǣde, found in the compound *rǣde-here* 'cavalry', is possible in some p.ns. like Radford but it cannot be distinguished from rēad. (*a*) Radford O (ford), Radway Wa, Roadway D, Rodway So (weg), St Rhadegund's Path Wt (gang). (*c*) Radstock So (on the Fosse Way). [~ OE *rīdan* 'to ride', ride.]

*rǣc OE, 'a reach', is certainly used in p.ns. of 'a strip of land, a stretch of water, a road or path through the fens'; it is not evidenced independently before the 16th century, but it is found in p.ns. from the 11th. (*b*) Reach Bd 125 ('a fenland road'), C 136 ('a straight stretch of water'), D 384, The Reaches Nth 234; Langary Gate Road L (lang). [~OE *rǣcan* 'to reach', related either to ON *reika* 'to walk about, to go' and ric or to rák, possibly racu.]

ræcc OE, 'a hunting dog'. (*a*) Rochford Ess, Wo 69 (ford).

ræced OE, 'a building', *v.* reced.

*rǣde OE adj., 'suitable for riding on', *v.* rād.

rǣden OE, 'rule, government', probably in the sense 'administrative district'. (*b*) Walreddon D 248 (walh). [OE *rǣd* 'advice, plan, rule', -en.]

rǣdere OE, 'a counsellor, a councillor'. (*c*) Rothersthorpe Nth (also rendered by Lat *advocati* 1220, þorp). [OE *rǣd* 'advice', -ere.]

ræfter OE, 'a rafter, a beam', in allusion to a place where they were obtained. (*a*) Raddicombe D 508 (cumb).

rǣge OE, 'a roe, a female roe-deer'. (*a*) Read La (hēafod), Roeburn La (burna), Reigate Sr (geat).

rægu OE, 'moss', *v.* ragu.

*ræsc OE 'a rush', *v.* risc.

ræsn OE, 'a plank', probably in the sense 'a plank-bridge', and later in the builders' usage 'a wall-plate'. (*b*) Market Rasen L.

ræt OE (Angl, WSax), *ret (Kt, Merc), 'a rat'. (*a*) Ratsborough Ess (probably 'a deserted rat-infested burh'), Rushcroft Sr (croft).

*rætten OE adj., 'infested with rats'. (*a*) Rattenbury Co (burh, probably 'a deserted camp'), Rettendon Ess (dūn). [ræt, -en.]

rǣw OE, 'a row, a row of houses'; some of the compounds in the OE charters, such as *hæsel ræwe* BCS 1282, *hegeræwe* ib. 327 (*et freq*), *ðorn ræwe* ib. 1282, *wiðig ræwe* ib. 1103, associate the word particularly with trees, hence 'a row of trees, a hedgerow'. (*b*) Rew D, Wt, Merrow Sr (gemǣre), Woodrow Wo (wudu); cf. also ME *le Rewe, le Stanrewe* W 445. [~rāw.]

ragge ME, 'rough stone' may occur as in Rag Hill, etc. Sr 364, but in some p.ns. such as Ragley Wa 196 there is nothing in local topography to fit this use and Ekwall suggests that there may have been an OE **ragge*, a secondary form of ragu 'moss, lichen'; *rag* in the latter sense is evidenced from 1758 (NED s.v.). [~OE *raggig* 'shaggy, rough', ME *rag* 'a rag, a tatter', ON *rǫgg* 'rough hair'; *ragge* 'rough stone' and **ragge* 'moss' may well be the same word with different sense developments. Cf. *Rock Terms* 92–3.]

ragu, rægu OE, 'moss, lichen'. (*a*) Raywell YE (**wella**). Cf. **ragge**.

rāha OE, 'a roe', *v.* **rā**[1].

rāh-hege OE, 'a deer-fence', found only in p.ns. in BCS 246, etc. (Mdf 106). (*b*) Roffey Sx. [~**rā, hege**.]

rák ON, 'a stripe', has been proposed as the source of ME *rake* 'a rough path over a hill, a narrow path up a ravine' (cf. NED s.v. *rake* sb. 3) and of the common f.n. *Rake* (Cu 488, Db, etc.), but these names are more likely to be from **hraca** in view of the length of the vowel in ON *rák* which should have given ME *roke* in the Midl. [~**rǣc**.]

rake ME, 'a narrow path up a hill', *v.* **hraca** and **rák**.

ramm OE, 'a ram', is difficult to distinguish from **hramsa** and **hrafn**. (*a*) Ramhurst K (**hyrst**), Rampside La (**hēafod**), Rampton C, Nt (**tūn**), Ramsbottom La (**botm**), Ramshorn St (**horn**).

***rān** OE, 'a boundary strip, a balk', is used in that sense in ME f.ns. (cf. YN 329); as a first el. in OE charter names such as *to rancumb* BCS 724, *ofer randune* ib. 390, and p.ns. like Ranell Bk, Roncombe D, it is difficult to distinguish from *rān*, gen.sg. of **rā**, though the OE examples are of course boundary points. (*a*) Ranmore Sr (**mōr**, on a parish boundary), Rhon Hill Bk 55 (**hyll**). [~**reinn**, OHG *rain* 'boundary strip'.]

*__rand__ OE, 'edge, border, a brink, a shore', is found only in OE poetry, commonly meaning 'shield', but in *Beowulf* 231, etc., also 'a bank, a shore'; it occurs in OE charters as *wið westan randes æsc* BCS 603, where it seems to mean 'boundary'; it also has a topographical sense 'border, edge, bank' in the ME phrases *rawez and randez* (*Alliterative Poems*) and *bi a strothe rande* (*Sir Gawayn* 1710), and in dials. *rand*, *rond* of 'a border' such as 'the untilled edge of a field', 'the border of land on a river-bank' (NED s.v. *rand*). (*a*) Randworth Nf (**worð**). (*b*) Rand L, YN, Raunds Nth. [~**rinde**.]

rann[1] ON, 'a house', is possible in (*b*) Cowran La (**kýr**). [~**ærn**.]

rann[2] OIr, 'a lot, a share'. (*a*) Ravenglass Cu 245 (pers.n.).

rāp OE, 'a rope', used also in the sense 'an administrative district' as in OHG *reiffa*, Du *reep*, probably in allusion to the marking off of the open-air court of a district with stakes and ropes; it is found as a term for a large administrative district in the Rapes of Sx (*v.* Sx 8–9). (*a*) Roper Lane K (land). (*b*) Rope Ch; Styrrup Nt 98 (stīg, possibly OE *stīg-rāp* 'stirrup', from the fancied resemblance of some local feature to a stirrup).

rás ON, 'a rush of water, a water-channel', occurs in late minor names, esp. in *Mill Race*. (*b*) Gipsey Race YE.

raton OFr, **ratoun** ME, 'a rat', surviving as NCy dial. *ratton*. (*a*) Ratten, -on Row Cu, Nb, Rotten Row L (rāw). [~ræt.]

***raun** (*raunar gen.sg.) ON, 'a rowan, a mountain ash' (cf. Norw *raun*, Swed *rönn*, Icel *reynir*). (*a*) Roundthwaite We (þveit).

rauðr ON adj., 'red', usually in allusion to the colour of the soil; the meaning, however, is not always clear from the topography and Ekwall has suggested that in stream-names there might have been an ON *rauði* 'the red one' denoting a trout or the like (as the derivative ON *reyðr* did). In some p.ns. which have OE els. it may have replaced rēad. (*a*) Rathmell YW (melr), Rawcliffe La, YN 15, 146 (OE *readeclif*), YW, Rockcliffe Cu, Roecliffe YW (clif, klif), Rawmarsh YW (mersc), R. Rawthey YW, We, R. Rothay We (á), Roppa YN (pæð). [~rēad.]

rāw OE, 'a row', esp. 'a row of houses', from which developed the meanings 'a street lined with a row of houses' and 'a hamlet'. Later it is confused in form and probably also in meaning with the related rǣw. (*b*) Baggrow Cu, Bagraw Nb (probably from ME *bagge* in the sense 'beggar'), Milnrow La (myln), Ratten, -on Row Cu, Nb, Rotten Row L (a contemptuous name for a street, 'rat-infested', *v.* raton), Ulcat Row Cu (ūle, cot), Woodrow W (wudu), cf. also *Thornrow* Nt 289. It is very common in st.ns. such as Baxter's Row (Carlisle), Bishop's Row (Penrith) Cu, Butcher Row (Beverley) YE, Long Row, Smithy Row (Nottingham) Nt, *et passim*; cf. also Mx 203. [~rǣw.]

rēad (readan wk. obl.) OE adj., 'red', in allusion to the colour of rocks (esp. the Red Sandstone), soil, water (esp. peat-stained water), or foliage. It is sometimes replaced by ON rauðr and is difficult to distinguish from hrēod. (*a*) Radcliffe La, Lei, Mx, Nt (the latter from its red clay), Radclive Bk, Redcliff So (olim *rubeam rupem*, from its red sandstone), all from clif, Radford Nt, Wa, Retford Nt (ford), Radley Brk (lēah), Radnage Bk (āc), Rattery D (trēow), Redhills Du (hyll), Redleaf K (lēaf), Redmile Lei, Rodmell Sx (mylde). [~rauðr.]

reced, ræced OE, 'a building, a house, a hall', is possible in (*a*) Rochdale La 55 (olim hām), though it may be from a Brit r.n. (R. Roch, olim *Rached*, DEPN).

*reden OE (Kt), 'a clearing', *v.* ryden.

(ge)rēfa OE, 'a reeve, a bailiff', sometimes 'an official in charge of a royal estate or of a town', reve ME, 'a reeve, a bailiff' (cf. also scīrgerēfa), is sometimes difficult to distinguish from hrēof. (*a*) Raveley Ha, Reaveley Nb (lēah), Rayton Nt, Reve-, Rif-, Riva-, Riverton D (tūn), Reepham L (hām).

refr ON, 'a fox'. (*a*) Reagill We (gil), Riffa YW (haugr).

reinn ON, 'a boundary strip', surviving as dial. *rean* 'a strip, a boundary'. (*a*) Rains Brook Wa 5 (brōc, on the county boundary), Rainworth Nt (vað, on the wapentake boundary). [~rān.]

*rend OE, 'an edge, a border', *v.* rind(e).

renn OE, 'a house', *v.* ærn.

*rēod OE, 'a clearing', has been proposed for some p.ns. such as Coldred K, Rede Sf, and as the ultimate base of OE rȳd; but this word, if it existed, would be difficult to distinguish from hrēod and sometimes from rȳd itself and some other els. It is formally possible, however, in OE *reod-*, *rydmædwan* BCS 183 and *reod lea* ib. 987. *v.* rȳd.

repaire OFr, 'a place of retreat, a retreat'. (*b*) Baripper Co, Bear Park Du, Beaupre Hu, Belper Db, Beaurepaire Ha, Bewper K (bel).

*res Corn, 'a ford', *v.* rid.

resc OE (Kt), 'a rush', *v.* risc.

*rescett OE (Kt), 'a rush bed', *v.* riscett.

rex (regis gen.sg.) Lat, 'a king', used in affixes in much the same way as cyning (with which it interchanges) and roial. (*c*) *Regis* suffixed to Bere, Lyme Do, Milton K, Rowley St, Stanford He. This suffix is not found in the NCy or NMidl (cf. Dickins, Lat Add 340).

rhiw Welsh, 'a hill'. (*a*) Ruardean Gl (worðign). (*b*) Cumrew Cu, Ganarew He (Welsh *genau* 'the opening of a valley').

rhos Welsh, 'a moor', *v.* ros.

rhyd Welsh, 'a ford' (from **ritu-* Brit, which occurs in OE *Andred* from *Anderitum*). (*a*) Redmain Cu, Tretire He, possibly Ridware St (ware). (*b*) Rhydd Wo, Penrith Cu. [~rid.]

ribbe OE, 'ribwort, hound's tongue'. (*a*) Ribbesford Wo (bedd, ford), Ribton Cu (tūn).

*ric OE, 'a narrow strip', is not recorded in independent use, but is fairly common in p.ns. as far back as DB (cf. Escrick YE 267, etc.). The word is related by ablaut to rǣc, ON *reik* 'parting (of the hair)', *reika* 'to go, walk', Norw, Swed dial. *reik*, *rek* 'stripe, furrow' and is cognate with MHG *ric* 'a narrow road'. The OE word would appear from local topography or its combinations with other els. to denote (i) 'a strip of land' (esp. one growing with trees), (ii) 'a stream or ditch' (esp. one used as a sewer, as in Skitterick, Glynde Reach), and (iii) probably also 'a narrow road'. The NCy forms with *rik* are due to ON influence, and the el. is sometimes replaced by the more common hrycg or hryggr.

(*a*) Reighton YE (tūn, cf. also a lost p.n. in this par. *Strop*, from OE *strop* 'a strap, a band' used also of 'a strip' here), Riccall YE (halh), *Richeham* Ess 238 (hām), Richey C (ēg).

(*b*) Riche L, Glynde Reach Sx 353; in compounds it is found with (i) tree-names, as Askrigg YN (askr), Escrick YE 267 (eski), Lendrick YW, Lindrick Nt, YW, Lindridge Db (lind); (ii) other significant words, as Chatteris C (cēto-), Langrick YE (land), Lostrigg Beck Cu (hlōse), Moulderidge Db (molde), Puckeridge Hrt (pūca), Rastrick YW (rǫst), Skitterick YN, YW (scite), Wheldrake YE (cweld); (iii) pers.ns., as Cookridge YW. [*v.* RN 370.]

rid,*res Corn, 'a ford'. (*a*) Reddavallon, Reterth, Rice Co. [~rhyd.]

*ride OE, 'riding, a place suitable for riding', possibly in the sense 'bridle-path' or the like. (*b*) Leatherhead Sr 78 (OE *æt Leodridan*, *v.* lēode). [~rād.]

*rīed OE (WSax), 'a clearing', *v.* rȳd.

riht[1] OE, 'right, duty', in allusion to 'land held by right', occurs in land-riht.

riht[2] OE adj., 'straight'. (*a*) Rightadown D (dūn).

rima OE, 'a rim, an edge, a border', in allusion to 'the edge of a river, a hill, etc., a shore' or to 'a boundary'. (*a*) Rimington YW (ing², tūn), Rimpton So (tūn, on the Do boundary), Rimside Nb (sīde). (*b*) Ryme Do (on So boundary).

*rimuc OE, 'an edge, a border', perhaps in the sense 'boundary'. (*a*) Ringwood Ha (OE *to rimuc wude* BCS 917, wudu). [~rima, -uc.]

*rind(e) OE, 'a hill, a ridge', has been proposed by Ekwall (DEPN 362) for some p.ns. It would be cognate with Norw *rinde* 'ridge', Crimean Gothic *rintsch* 'a hill' and related by ablaut to rand. The el. occurs in OE p.ns. in *rindburna* BCS 187 Gl, *on rinda crundel* ib. 1022 Brk, *rindgesella* ib. 377 Ha, as well as in ME in *Morte Arthur* (NED s.v. *rind* sb. 4). It is possible in (*a*) Randwick Gl (wīc) and some other p.ns. like Roundway W, etc., which have been derived from rȳmed; most of these names have spellings in *Rinde-*, a few in *Rende-* and practically none in *Runde-*. As with Randwick Gl, an OE **rend* 'edge, border' (an *i*-mutated form of rand in ablaut relation to *rinde*) would probably explain most of them, and would best account for the spellings *Rende-*, which later become *Rinde-*.

*rip(p) OE, 'a strip, an edge, a shore, a slope' or the like, occurs in some OE charter p.ns. such as *suð fealcing rip oð sæ* 'south *fealcing rip* to the sea' BCS 813 and in *ad silbam qui apellatur ripp et ad terminos Suthsaxoniæ* 'to the wood called *Ripp* and to the bounds of Sussex' (OET 429), both of which suggest some such meaning as 'edge, border (of forest or sea)'. It is related to ripel, LG *riep* 'shore, slope', EFris *ripe* 'edge', and ON *rípr* 'crag', and survives as late ME and K, Sx dial. *ripe* 'shore, bank' (NED s.v. *ripe* sb. 2). (*a*) Ripton Ha, Hu 218–9 (tūn). (*b*) Ripe Sx 404. [~rāp, ModE *rip* 'to tear, cut', OE *rīpan* 'to reap', etc., the root meaning being something like 'tear, cut off sharply'.]

*ripel, *rippel OE, 'a strip of land', found in OE only in p.n. forms, such as *andlang riple* BCS 1218, *myntleage riple* ib. 624, *be repple* KCD 752, and those of several surviving p.ns. It is cognate with Norw *ripel*, 'strip' (as in *skógar-ripel* 'strip of wood') and survives as dial. *ripple* 'a coppice, a thicket' and occasionally in f.ns. (Nt 289). (*a*) Ripley Db, Ha, Sr (lēah). (*b*) Ripple K (3), So, Wo 158. [~rip, -el.]

*ripsett OE, 'place overgrown with brushwood', *v.* rispett.

* risc, rix, rysc OE (Angl, WSax), resc Kt, 'a rush (Juncus)'.

(1) OE *risc* is the better established form (with *rix* as a metathesized variant), and this could well be the source of later spellings with *rush*, which arose from the well-attested influence of *r* and *sh* in such words. There are in fact no examples of the spelling *rysc* in contemporary OE documents; but there is the possible Kt variant *resc* in the gloss *juncus uel scyrpus*, *resce* in a list of words which is not otherwise Kentish (WW 324.2); *rysc healas* occurs in a late and spurious charter (BCS 124), ME (SE) *resse* in the *Ayenbite* and ME (SW) *rosshe-* in Rushmore W, all of which point to an

OE *rysc*. Forms with *rusch* occur in MLG, MHG, etc. (cf. NED s.v. *rush* sb. 1), but they are usually late. A NCy variant *rash* (probably from an OE **ræsc*) is found in f.ns. (Cu 489).

(2) The plant is the common rush, which had some importance in thatching and basket-making. As a first el. it is frequent with words denoting 'water'. As a final el. this word (like **hrēod**) may have had a collective sense 'rush bed'.

(3) (*a*) Rhiston Sa, Rishton La, Ruishton So, Rushton Ch, Do, Nth, St (**tūn**), Rishworth YW (**worð**), Ruislip Mx (**slǣp**), Rushall St (**halh**), Rushbourne K (**burna**), Rushbrooke Sf (**brōc**), Rushford Nf, Rushyford (also *vadum cirporum*) Du (**ford**), Rushmere Sf (**mere**).

(*b*) Rusholme La (dat.pl.); Langrish Ha (**lang**).

riscen OE adj., 'growing with rushes, rushy', perhaps also 'thatched with rushes'. (*a*) *Riskington* L (**tūn**, with ON *-sk-*), Rushden Hrt, Nth (**denu**), Rushingwells Hrt (**wella**). [**risc, -en.**]

***riscett**, ***ryscett** OE (Angl, WSax), ***rescett** (Kt), 'a rush-bed, a place growing with rushes'. (*b*) *Reschett* Ess (14), Rushett(s) K, Sr, Sx. [**risc, -et.**]

***riscuc**, ***rixuc** OE, 'a rushy place, a rush-bed'. (*b*) Rushock, Rushwick Wo (OE *Rixuc*). [**risc, -uc.**]

***rispe** OE, 'undergrowth, brushwood', surviving as dial. *risp* 'sedge' (Scots), 'a bush, a twig, a branch' (EAngl), and cognate with OHG *rispahi*, MLG *rispe* 'brushwood', G *rispe* 'cluster, shrubs, briars' (cf. Mawer, Problems 45). (*a*) Resphill YW (**hyll**), Respholm Cu 269 (**holmr**), Reston We (**tūn**), Ribsdon Sr 154 (**dūn**), Ripsley Sx 45 (**lēah**). (*b*) The Rips Sr. [The original form is probably *rips-* and is related to **ripp**, in the sense 'that which rips or tears'; if the correct OE form is *hrispe*, it would be related to **hrīs**, but this is not certain.]

***rispett**, ***ripsett** OE, 'a place overgrown with brushwood'. (*b*) Ripsette Sr. [**rispe, -et.**]

rið OE, 'a stream', thought to be the source of Ha and Sx dial. *rithe*, *ride* 'a small stream'. It is difficult on the available evidence to say whether the OE form is *rið* or *rīð* (cf. RN 342); the history of the name Reeth YN 273 points very definitely to an OE *rið* (dat.sg. *riðe* with ME lengthening of short *-i-* to *-ē-* in the open syllable); Ryde Wt 193 and dial. *rithe* point to a long vowel (which may recur in MLG *ride*), but these may well be old spelling pronunciations of the kind paralleled by *chine* from OE **cinu** (cf. Wt xcvi, and *v.* also **hlið**[1]).

(*a*) Ritton Nb (**tūn**).

(*b*) Reeth YN, Ryde Sr, Wt. In compounds it is found with (i) animal- and bird-names, as Hendreth Brk (**henn**), Rawreth Ess (**hrāgra**), Shepreth C (**scēap**); (ii) other significant words, as Coldrey Ha (**col**), Meldreth C (**myln**), Shottery Wa (**Scott**), Tingrith Bd (**þing**); (iii) words denoting people and pers.ns., as Sawtrey Hu (**saltere**), Chaureth, Fingrith Ess, Childrey Brk.

* **riðig** OE, 'a small stream', evidenced in OE only in charter forms, chiefly also in p.ns. in the SMidl., as well as in f.ns. (as Bd 295, Sr 365, *et freq*). (*b*) Cropredy O (**cropp**), Efferiddy Bd (pers.n.), Fulready Wa (**fūl**). [**rīð**, **-ig**.]

***riveling** ME, 'a rivulet', first independently evidenced in the 17th century, and in p.ns. from the 12th. (*a*) Rivelindale YW (**denu**). (*b*) Revelin Moss Cu, Rivelin YW, *Tackriveling* YN 7. [~OE *rifelung* 'wrinkle', *v.* RN 343.]

rivere OFr, ME, 'a river'. (*b*) River K.

rix OE, 'a rush', *v.* **risc**.

***rixuc** OE, 'a rush-bed', *v.* **riscuc**.

rocc OE, 'a rock', *v.* **roke**.

roche[1] OFr, ME, 'a rock, a cliff'. (*b*) Roach D, YW, Roche Co. [~**roke**.]

roche[2] OFr, ME, 'a roach'. (*a*) Roachburn Cu (**burna**).

***rod**[1], ***rodu** OE, 'a clearing', may occur in OE in charter names like *andlang rode* BCS 208, *andlang ðære bradan rode* ib. 1129 (where the preposition *andlang* 'alongside' shows that they cannot be for **rōd**[2] 'cross'), *on æsc stede rode* ib. 1319, *on norðan sylfa roda oð ða east roda* ib. 419, *to rodleage* ib. 1067, *innon rodstubban* KCD 1310 but in some of these examples we may have OE *rōd* in the sense 'rood of land'. The word is not found in independent use except in La and YW dial. *royd* 'a clearing in a wood', though there are examples of its use for 'an assart' in ME f.ns. (La 16); it is also found elsewhere as a ME f.n. el. (Bk 259, Hu 295, C 342, Ess 588, Nth 268, Wa 332, YN 330). The La and YW dial. *royd* presupposes an OE *rodu*. The el. is very common in La and YW and is evidenced in p.ns. from the time of DB. (*b*) Road(e) D, Nth, Rhode D, Rhodes, Royd(s) YW, Rhodecourt K, Rodd He, Rode Ch, So; Roddam Nb (dat.pl.). In compounds it is found usually with significant words, Blackrod, Coptroyd, Heyroyd, Langroyd, Standroyd La, Ackroyd, Ellenroyd, Greenroyd, Mytholmroyd, Oakroyd YW, Oxroad K, Pepper Wood Wo; rarely with pers.ns., as Ormerod La, Woodroyd YW. [~ **roð**, **ryd**, G *rod*, *rot*, MLG *rod* (from the pa.part. grade); cf. NGN ii, 32–78, Jellinghaus 112.]

rōd[2] OE, 'a rood, a cross', used of 'a cross for executing criminals' in **wearg-rōd** and 'the holy cross, a crucifix' in **rōd-stān**. (*a*) Rooden La (**dūn**), Rood Street Ess (**strǣt**). (*b*) Rhude Cross Co; *Halyrode* K, Holyrood St (**hālig**). (*c*) Rood Ashton W, Ampney Crucis Gl (olim *Sancte Crucis*, *Holirode*). The use of this el. for 'a measure of land' is of doubtful occurrence in OE (being indistinguishable from **rod**[1]), but it is certainly found in ME f.ns. (cf. C 342). [The original meaning was 'rod' which remains in OE *segl-rōd* 'sail-yard'; ~ **rodd**.]

rodd(e) OE, 'a rod, a switch, a slender shoot', cognate with Norw *rodda* 'a stake', is possible in (*a*) Rodborough Gl (**beorg**). [~ **rōd**.]

***rōd-stān** OE, 'a stone cross, a rood-stone', as in *rodestan* BCS 1127. (*b*) Radstone Nth, *Rodestane* Nb, Rudston YE. [**rōd**, **stān**.]

rodu OE, 'a clearing', *v.* **rod**[1].

***rogge** OE, 'rye', cognate with OHG, OSax *roggo*, MLG *rogge* 'rye', and related to **rȳge** in the same way as **twigge** is to **twig**, **ragge** to **ragu**, etc. (*b*) Rugward Ess 171, Rugwood Ess 184 (**wereð**).

roial OFr, **real** AN, adj., 'royal' (cf. **cyning**, **rex**). (*a*) Rewley O (**lieu**). (*b*) Vale Royal Ch (**val**). (*c*) Easton Royal W.

roke OFr, **rocc** OE, **rokke** ME, 'a rock, a peak'; OE *rocc* (found in glosses in the compound *stān-rocc* WW 458.1) is thought to be an early loan from OFr *roke*, but probably had no continuous history; in p.ns. the el. appears to be mostly of post-Conquest origin. (*b*) Rock D, Rocks Nb, Sr, Sx; Starrock Sr (**stān**). [~ **roche**.]

rond OFr, **round** OFr, ME adj., 'round'. (*a*) Roundhay Nt, YW (**gehæg**). (*c*) Acton Round Sa.

rondel OFr, **roundele** ME, 'a circle, anything circular'. (*b*) Randall Wood K, Rendlestone D, Rundle Beck Nt. [~ **rond**.]

ros OWelsh, **rhos** Welsh, 'a moor, a heath', **ros** Corn, 'a hill, a heath, a headland' (cf. Ir *ros* 'a promontory, a wood' and *v.* Gover, LMS i, 249–64). The word may well have been borrowed in OE as an appellative, as it appears to survive as dial. *ross* 'marsh', *rossland* 'moorland'. (*a*) Rossendale La (**dæl**). (*b*) Roos YE 56, Roose Co,

La 202, Ross He, Nb; Moccas He (Welsh *moch* 'swine'), Penrose (penno-), Trerose (tref) Co.

rǫst (rastar gen.sg.) ON, 'a resting-place, the distance between two resting-places'. (*a*) Rastrick YW (ric).

rōt OE adj., 'cheerful'. (*a*) Ratley Wa (lēah), Roothill Sr (helde).

*roth ODan, 'a clearing', evidenced in Dan *Roager*, etc., indistinguishable from its cognate OE roð. (*b*) Rot Hole YE 265.

rotinn ON, roten ME adj., 'rotten', used of 'soft yielding ground'. (*a*) Redford Du (ford), Rudmoor YN (mýrr).

*roð OE, 'a clearing', evidenced only in OE *Roðe* BCS 737 (Roe Green Hrt 165), cognate with OFris *rothe*, OHG *rod*. (*a*) Rodley YW, Rothley Hrt (lēah), Roestock Hrt 65 (stoc), Rosway Hrt (weg), Rothwell L, Nth 118–19, YW (wella). (*b*) Roe End, Roe Green Hrt 95, 165, Rothend Ess (cf. also C 342, Ess 588 for f.ns.). [~rod, roth, ryd(d).]

*roðer OE, 'a clearing'. (*b*) Fenrother Nb. [roð, -er.]

rouge OFr adj., 'red'. (*a*) Ridgmont Bd, Rougemont YW (mont).

round ME adj., 'round', *v.* rond.

roundele ME, 'a circle', *v.* rondel.

rūde OE, the shrub 'rue'. (*a*) Roudham Nf (hām), Rudyard St (geard).

rudig OE adj., 'ruddy, red'. (*a*) Roddimore Bk (mōr). [OE *rudu* 'redness', -ig.]

ruelle OFr, 'a small road, a path'. (*b*) Rewell Sx. [OFr *rue* 'street' and the diminutive suffix *-elle*.]

rúgr ON, 'rye', sometimes difficult to distinguish from rūh. (*a*) Roughton L, Nf (tūn), Ruckcroft Cu (croft). [~rȳge.]

rūh (rūgan wk. obl.) OE adj., 'rough'; the strong form *rūh* usually becomes *Rough-*, *Ru-* and the weak form *rūga*(*n*) becomes *Row*(*n*)-. (*a*) Rawden, -don YW, Rowden He (dūn), Roborough D, Ru-, Rowberrow So, Rowborough Wt (beorg), Rougham Nf, Sf (hām), Roughley Nb, Rowley D, Du, St, YE, YW (lēah), Roughside Du, Nb (sīde), Rowhill K (hyll), Rownall St (halh), Rowner Ha (ōra), Rowney Hrt (gehæg), Rowthorn Db (þorn), Rowton Sa, YE (tūn), Ruchester Nb (ceaster), Rufford La, Nt, Rufforth YW (ford), Rusper Sx (spearr).

*rūhet OE, 'a place overgrown with brushwood, a piece of rough ground'. (*b*) Ruffet(t) Sr, Sx. [rūh, -et.]

rūm[1] OE, rúm ON, 'room, space, an open space, a clearing', sometimes difficult to distinguish from runnr, also found in f.ns. (as La 16). The OE word does not appear to have been used in a topographical sense and since examples in p.ns. are mostly from the NCy the usage may well be from ON. (*b*) Boldron YN (**boli**), Dendron (**denu**), Dertren (**drit**) La.

rūm[2] (**rūman** wk. obl.) OE adj., 'roomy, spacious'. (*a*) Romford Ess (**ford**), Romiley Ch (**lēah**), Roomwood Nt (**wudu**), Rumbridge Ess (**brycg**), Rumstead K (**stede**), Rumworth La (**worð**), Runcorn Ch (**cofa**).

rūn OE, 'a secret, a mystery, a council'. (*a*) Rumwell So, Runwell Ess (**wella**, probably 'a wishing well'), Runnymede Sr (**ēg**, **mǣd**, 'isle where a council was held').

runnr ON, 'a brake, a thicket' (*v.* Ekwall, ScandsCelts 93 ff). (*a*) Ronhead La. (*b*) Bowerham La 174 (**bula**, **boli**), Tickering YW (**ticcen**), Tymparon Cu 188 (Ir *tiompan* 'a standing stone').

rust OE, 'rust, rust-colour', difficult to distinguish from a pers.n. *Rust* as in Rushall W 323. (*a*) Rusthall K (**wella**).

ruð ON, 'a clearing', common in Norw p.ns. (cf. NGIndl 71–2), is rare. (*a*) Ruffhams YE (**holmr**). [~**roth**, **roð**, **ryð**.]

***rȳd**, ***rīed** OE (WSax), ***rēod** (Angl, Kt), ***ryde** (Angl, WSax), ***rede** (Kt), 'a clearing'.

(1) This el., whose original form is difficult to determine, is found in the SE counties from K to Wt and there are two examples of its use as Rhydd in Wo 212, 252; the distribution raises a suspicion as to the identity of the Wo names with this el., esp. as the ME spellings are *ride* (*rude* or *rede* are the forms to be expected in Wo); they may well be from Welsh **rhyd**. The el. is therefore probably a SE one.

(2) The word is not evidenced in OE with any certainty, except perhaps in Coldred K (OE *Colredinga gemercan* BCS 797). In ME the forms are *red*(*e*) in C 342, Ess 588 (rarely *rude*), K, Sx, Ha, and *rud*(*e*) in other parts, Sr 364 (occasionally *rede*), Ha, Wt, West Sx. In so far as they are not to be confused with other els. (such as **hrēod**), these spellings would represent a late OE *ryd*(*e*), which would be from either (i) an original OE *ryd*(*e*), Kt *red*(*e*) (from WGerm **rudi-*), or (ii) an original Angl, Kt *rēod*, WSax *rīed* (from WGerm **riudi-*). An original *ryd*(*d*) masc., neut. *ja*-stem or *ryde* masc., neut. *i*-stem could have existed on formal grounds, but probably *rydd* should be ruled out, as there are no traces anywhere

of ME spellings like *rudde* or *redde*, nor could the modern forms with a long vowel such as Rede, Reed arise from it. An OE (WSax) *ryde* (Kt *rede*) or an OE (WSax) *rīed* (Kt *rēod*) would in fact account for all the variant spellings, including OE *Colred-*, which is from a late transcript with other post-Conquest spellings.

(3) On purely formal grounds both *ryde* and *rīed* (*rēod*) are likely forms; *ryde* is from the pa.t.pl. grade, PrGerm **rud-*, which also appears in OE **ryddan* (*v.* gerydd, rydding), ON *ryðja* 'to clear', ruð; and *rīed*, *rēod* is from the pa.t.sg. grade, PrGerm **riuð-*, which appears in rēod, OHG *riuti* 'a clearing', ON *hrjóða* 'to strip', *rjóðr* 'clearing'. The choice between WSax *ryde* and *rīed* cannot be made on the available evidence, but in view of OHG *riuti* and ON *rjóðr*, WSax *rīed* (Kt *rēod*) is perhaps to be favoured; *rȳd* would then be a late WSax form of *rīed*.

(4) These various words concerning the clearing or ridding of land of wild vegetation for the purposes of cultivation are ultimately related to Lat *ruo* in the sense 'scrape, rake up, dig up' (cf. Walde 664–5) and the rare and occasional spellings with *hr-* (as in OE *hryding* for rydding, ON *hryðja* for *ryðja*, *hrjóða* for *rjóða*) are therefore errors.

(5) (*b*) Rede K, Sx, Reed C 101, Rhode Ha; Brandred K (brand), Colred K (col), Inchreed Sx 378 (pers.n.), Languard Wt (lang), Stonereed K (stānig); also in f.ns. in Ess 588, Sr 364–5, Sx 561.

(ge)ryd(d) OE pa.part. used as adj., 'cleared (of trees)' (cf. BTSuppl), is common in f.ns. esp. in Sx 547. (*a*) Redland Gl (lang), Ridley Ch, Nb (lēah). [~ryd. An OE vb. *ryddan* 'to rid, to clear' is not recorded, though evidence for it is found in *gerydd* itself and in OE *ā-ryddan* 'to strip, to plunder'; it is probably the source of ME *ruden*, *rydde* 'to clear woodland' rather than the cognate ON *ryðja* which has been suggested.]

*rydding OE, 'a clearing', is probably identical with the once recorded OE *hryding* which glosses Lat *subcisiua* 'a small piece of land cut off, what is cut off'; the spelling with *hr-* is probably an error for *r-* (cf. rȳd § 4). The el. is not otherwise evidenced in independent use, but it is common in p.ns. and in ME and later f.ns. (as C 342, Cu 479, D 690, Ess 582, Hrt 256, Mx 203, Nt 289, YE 325, YN 328, *et passim*), where it usually denotes 'an assart' or is equivalent to Lat *incrementum* 'land taken into an estate from waste' (cf. Nb 165). (*b*) Reading K, Reddings Wo, Redding Wood Hrt, Riding Lee Bk, Nb, Riddings Cu, Db, Nt, Rudding Cu, Ryding Nb; Armetridding, Row Ridding La, Nunriding Nb, Woodridings Hrt. [Probably originally a verbal sb. from OE **ryddan* (*v.* gerydd), -ing[1].]

*ryden OE (Angl, WSax), *reden (Kt), 'a clearing', is evidenced only in p.ns. from ME and in f.ns. (C 342, Ess 588, Sr 364). (*b*) Reading, Redden Ess, Reedings, Riddens Sx, Rydens Sr; Kingsridden, Woodridden Ess. [~OE **ryddan* 'to clear' (*v.* gerydd), -en.]

rȳge OE, 'rye'. (*a*) Riby L (bý), Royton La, Ruyton Sa, Ryton Du, Sa, Wa (tūn, the compound may have had something of the sense of bere-tūn), Roydon Nf (dūn), Royley La (lēah), Ryal, Ryle Nb, Ryhill YE, YW (hyll), Ryarsh K (ersc). [~rogge, rúgr.]

rȳgen OE adj., 'growing with rye'. (*a*) Ray-, Reydon Sf, Roydon Ess, Sf (dūn), Renacres La (æcer). [rȳge, -en.]

*rȳhð OE, 'a rough piece of ground'. (*b*) Reed Hrt. [~rūh, -ð(e).]

rȳmed (rȳmdan wk. obl.) OE pa.part., 'cleared', has been suggested for some p.ns. but in the form it takes in these p.ns. it is indistinguishable from rinde (or *rende*) which does in fact offer a better explanation of the usual ME spellings *Rinde-*, *Rende-*, the only ones found for Rendlie, Renhurst, Roundhurst Sx, Roundhay W, Runley Bd 159. [~rūm.]

rynel OE, 'a small stream, a runnel' (cf. Dalby Brook Nt), rare in p.ns. It is possible in (*a*) Runland D 82 (land).

rysc OE, 'a rush', *v.* risc.

*ryscett OE, 'a rush bed', *v.* riscett.

ryt OE, 'underwood, rubbish for burning'. (*a*) Ratling K (hlinc). (*b*) Rat Wt, Rutt D; Collard D. [~rȳd or rūh, -et.]

ryð (rytz gen.sg.) OEScand, 'a clearing', as in OSwed (cf. Hellquist, *Svenska Ortnamnen på -by* 24 and NK 105, 151). (*a*) Risby YE (bý). [~ruð, rjóðr, cf. rȳd.]

*ryðer OE, 'a clearing'. (*b*) Ryther YW. [~roð, -er, roðer.]

S

-s[1], **-es** OE noun-suffix, possibly used with a collective function as in hens, but it is obscure; another form *-es* (PrGerm *-usjō-*, *-isjō-*, cf. Kluge § 85) occurs as a concrete suffix in words like OE *byres* 'boring tool, graver', *ides* 'a woman'; cf. also *bors, fyrs, hramsa, hyles, rispe (from *ripse*), all plant-names.

-s[2] ON gen.sg. ending, usually replaced by OE -es, frequently remains, esp. with pers.ns. It is represented by a variety of spellings in ME; the usual spellings indicating this include (i) ON *-ds* spelled *z*, *ze*, *ce*, *sce*, *tse*, as in Brandsby YN 28, Bransby L (*Branz-*, *Brance-*, for ON *Brands-bý*), Haceby L (*Haze-*, *Hasce-*, *Hatse-*, for ON *Hadds-bý*), Winceby L (*Winze-*, *Wince-*, for ON *Vinds-bý*); (ii) ON, *-fs* spelled *fse*, *se* as in Laceby L (*Laifse-*, *Leyse-* for ON *Leifs-bý*); (iii) ON *-ks* spelled *x*(*e*), *cse*, *cs*, *xse*, as in Baxby YN (*Baxe-*, *Baxse-* for ON *Baks-bý*), Claxby L (*Cleax-*, *Clacse-*, *Clax*(*e*)- for ON *Klaks-bý*); (iv) ON *-ts* spelled *ze*, *ce*, *sce*, *ts*, as in Faceby YN 176 (*Feiz-*, *Fayce-* for ON *Feits-bý*), Foston YE 91 (*Fots-*, *Fosce-*, *Fods-*, *Fos-* for ON *Fóts-tún*); (v) ON *-ðs* spelled *ze*, *sce*, *ce*, *tse*, as in Roxby YN 139 (*Roze-*, *Rosce-*, *Roce-*, *Rotse-* for ON *Rauðs-bý*). There are also examples of uninflected genitives, as in Asselby YE 248 (*Áskel-bý*), Conington Hu 182 (kunung, tūn), Haldenby YW (*Halfdan-bý*), Kettleby L, Lei (*Ketil-bý*), etc.

***sā** OE (EAngl), 'sea', *v.* sǣ.

***sabrinā** Brit, of unknown meaning. Cf. ṚN 360 and on the forms *v.* Jackson 82, 271, 516–19, etc. (*a*) Savernake W. (*b*) R. Severn Gl, etc.

***Sachson** PrWelsh, 'the Saxons', *v.* Saxones.

***sacu-mann** OE, 'a litigious person', corresponding to ON *sakamaðr*. (*a*) Seckington, Secmarton D 358, 493 (tūn). [OE *sacu* 'lawsuit', mann.]

sadol OE, 'a saddle', used of something resembling a saddle in shape or appearance, such as a ridge; it occurs several times in OE charter names, such as *sædeles sceat* BCS 982, *sædeles steort* ib. 1319, *sadol hongran* ib. 1282 (Mdf 109); cf. Tengstrand 273 ff. ON *sǫðull* is similarly used in Norw p.ns. of 'a saddle-shaped dip in the hills' (NGIndl 81). (*a*) Saddlesborough (burh), Saddlestone (stān), Saddle Tor (torr) D, Saddlescombe Sx 286 (cumb), Saddleworth YW (worð).

sǣ OE, ***sā** (EAngl), **sǽr** ON, 'a sea, a lake'.

(1) This OE word is used in p.ns. in a variety of senses, the chief of which include (i) 'the ocean' in coastal p.ns. such as Seaford Sx, Seascale Cu, Seaton Cu, D, Du, etc.; (ii) 'an inland lake', as in Hornsea, Withernsea, Seaton YE; (iii) possibly also 'a marsh' (as in the cognate Goth *saiws* 'marsh, sea', OHG *gesig* 'ponds, marshes', cf. also **sǣge**), esp. in the names of some inland places where the lake, if ever there was one, has long disappeared, as at Seacroft YW, and in compounds with **mere** (such as Seamer YN), where its use in the sense 'lake' would be tautological.

(2) There is little evidence to show that ON *sǽr* was used except perhaps in one or two p.ns. with ON els. such as Seascale Cu. In Scandinavia the el. was used only of 'the ocean' or 'a very large inland lake'.

(3) OE *sǣ* is found in p.ns. all round the coast, but it is particularly common in YE. An OE unmutated form *sā* occurs in some EAngl counties in such p.ns. as Saham Nf, Soham Sf, and it has replaced the related **sǣge** in Soham C.

(4) (*a*) Saham Nf, Seaham Du, Soham Sf (**hām**), Seacroft YW (**croft**), Seaford Sx (**ford**), Seamer YN (2), Semer Nf, Sf, Semerwater YN (**mere**), Seasalter K (**salt**, **ærn**), Seascale Cu (**skáli**) Seathwaite Cu (**þveit**), Seaton Cu, D, Du, Nb, YE (2) (**tūn**), Sea Wood La (**wudu**), Silloth Cu (**hlaða**).

(*b*) Bursea YE (**bȳre**), Haddlesey YW (**haðel**), Hornsea (**horn**), Kilnsea (**cyln**), Meaux (**melr**), Sicey (**sīd**), Skipsea (**skip**), etc. YE.

(*c*) As an affix (sometimes rendered by Lat *super mare* as in Weston super Mare So), in Newton by the Sea Nb, Sutton on Sea L.

[PrGerm **saiwiz*, Goth *saiwis*, **sǣge**.]

***sǣge** OE, 'a swamp, a marsh, a lake', ***sǣge** OE adj., 'swampy, slow-moving (of water)', may be found in some p.ns. The words are cognate with G dial. *saig* (Bavaria), *sege*, *söga* (Tyrol) 'a swamp' and there are various related words such as OHG *gesig* 'ponds, marshes', OE *sīgan* 'to sink, descend', *sǣgan* 'to cause to sink', MLG *sege* 'dripping, bleary eyed'. It is also related to **sǣ**, and as a noun may have had much the same significance, 'marsh, lake'. The adj. form may be thought preferable in stream-names. (*a*) Seabrook Bk 98, D 455 (**brōc**), Sealodes C 200 (**gelād**), Sellake D 550 (**lacu**), Soham C 195 (**hām**, in allusion to a former pond). (*b*) *Medeseye* Mx 5 (**mǣd**). [PrGerm **saigiz*, ~ **sǣ**.]

*sælte OE (Merc), 'a salt-pit', *v.* selte.
*sænde OE, 'a sandy place', *v.* sende.
*sængel OE, 'a tuft, a bundle', *v.* sengel.
*sænget OE, 'a clearing', *v.* senget.
sæpig OE adj., 'sappy, juicy', possibly used as a r.n. in (*b*) Sapey He, Wo (OE *æt Sapian*), both on Sapey Brook.
sæppe OE, 'a fir-tree'. (*a*) Sabden La, So (denu), Sapley Hu 208 (lēah).
sǽr ON, 'sea, a lake', *v.* sǣ.
Saeson Welsh, 'the Saxons', *v.* Saxones.
sæt OE, 'a lurking place, a lair, a trap', probably surviving in dial. *sett* 'a badger's earth'. (*b*) Merstham Sr 300 (OE *mearsætham*, from mearð, hām). [~OE *sittan* 'to sit', *sǣtian* 'to ambush', by ablaut.]
sǣte[1] (sǣtan nom.pl., sǣtna gen.pl., sǣtum dat.pl.) OE pl., 'settlers, dwellers', was used in the formation of the names of the inhabitants of a region (cf. Schram, ZONF iii, 200ff). Such names are formed from (i) older p.ns. and r.ns., esp. those of Brit origin, as Dorset (from *Durnovaria*), Grantchester C 76 (R. Granta), *Stursett* Hundred K (R. Stour), Tempsiter Sa (R. Teme), OE *Magon sætum* (from Maund He), *Peacsætna* (from The Peak Db), *Tomsetan* Wa xvii (R. Tame); (ii) significant words, as in OE *Dūnsǣte* 'the Welsh' (i.e. the hill-dwellers, dūn), *Merset* Hundred Sa (gemǣre, the boundary along the Welsh border and Offa's Dyke) and possibly Elmsett Sf (elm); (iii) elliptical forms of older p.ns., as in Somerset (OE *Sumersetum*, from Somerton So), OE *Wilsætan* (from Wilton W 348); other examples of elliptical formations occur in OE charters, as in *Beansetum* ('the inhabitants of Beanhall' Wo), *Beonetsetena gemære* (Bentley Wo), *Bradsetena gemære* (Broadwas, Broadway Wo), *Elmesetene gemære* (Elmley Wo), etc. Folk-names of this type also occur as the first els. of p.ns., as in Bilston St (OE *Bilsetenatun*), Phepson Wo 137 (*Fepsetnatun*), Poston He. These uses of *sǣte* are paralleled by those of hǣme and ware. In ME the el. is difficult to distinguish from others. It does not appear to have been used in the NCy. [~OE *sittan* 'to sit', by ablaut.]
sǣte[2] OE, possibly 'a house', is evidenced only in OE *on Beornwoldes sætan, of sætan* BCS 1282; it may occur in Guist Nf (OE *Gæssæte*), but it is difficult to distinguish from other commoner els. like sǣte[1], sǽtr, set, etc.

sǣtere OE, 'a robber'. (*a*) Satterleigh D (lēah). [~sæt, OE *sǣtian* 'to ambush', -ere.]

Sætern-dæg OE, 'Saturday'. (*a*) Saturday Bridge L, Saturday Market YE. Cf. Sr 411.

*sǣti ON, sǣte late OE, sete ME, 'a seat, a residence' (cf. NED s.v. *seat* sb.), has been suggested for certain p.ns. in NbDu 237, such as Allerside, Causey, Earlside, Tarsett, which may however be equally well from the better-evidenced sǣtr or set. The word is also used of 'a lofty place', as in Arthur's Seat (Edinburgh), Kingsett D 201. *v.* sǣtr.

sǣtr (sǣtri dat.sg.) ON, 'a mountain pasture, a shieling'.

(1) This word is a common el. in Scandinavia, but there it is often difficult to distinguish from ON *setr* (gen.sg. *setrs*) 'a house, a permanent residence' (cf. NGIndl 74, NK 153). It is, as Ekwall La 16–17 shows, clearly *sǽtr* and not *setr* or sǣti which enters into most English examples, partly because ME spellings in *sat*(*e*) as well as *set*(*e*) could hardly be from *setr* and partly because the lofty situation of many of the places on mountains is more likely to favour the meaning 'shieling' which *sǽtr* has than 'permanent residence' which *setr* or *sǽti* has, for in the mountainous regions of the NW (Cu, We, YN, YW, La), though to a much smaller degree than in Norway or Iceland, livestock found its keep progressively up the mountain sides as the summer advanced, and when the distances had become too great huts were built on the lofty pastures for temporary summer use; it is such a hut or shieling which is called a *sǽtr*; it is equated with erg.

(2) The one difficulty is the loss of final *-r*; in *sǽtr* and *setr* this final *-r* was part of the stem and not the ON nom.sg. ending *-r* (which was lost in ON loanwords in English); Ekwall thinks that there might have been an alternative form *sǽt* (which is likely enough in ON with a PrGerm *-s-* stem) or it may simply be that in English usage *-r* was regarded as a nom.sg. ending and was then lost; in one or two names *-r* remains in the spelling *Satter-*.

(3) (*a*) Satterhowe, -thwaite La (haugr, þveit); Seatoller Cu (alor), Sedbusk YN (busk), Setmabanning, Setmurthy Cu (pers.ns. in inversion compounds).

(*b*) In combination it is found with (i) significant words, as Appersett (æppel-trēow), Forcett (fors), Swineside (svín) YN, Greenside (grēne), Stubbside (stubb), Swinside (svín) Cu, Rayside

We (rá), Selside We (sel), YW (selja), Summerseat La (sumor); (ii) words for people, as Lord's Seat Cu (hlāford), Earlside Nb, Yarlside La (jarl); (iii) pers.ns., as Annaside, Fornside, Oughterside Cu, Arkleside, Gunnerside YN, Arnside, Hawkshead, Swainshead La, Corsenside Nb. It is possible in other p.ns. such as Allerside Nb (alor), Causey Du (cald), Gibside Du, Simonside Du, Nb (pers.ns.), but set is also possible.

[~ON *sitja* 'to sit', sæt, sǽti; *setr* is from a different root, ON *setja* 'to set, settle'; *v.* also F. Hedblom, *De svenska ortnamn på säter* (Lund 1945).]

salceie, saucie OFr, 'a willow-copse'. (*b*) Salcey Forest Nth.

*salegn OE, 'a willow-tree, a willow copse', is in ME difficult to distinguish from *saline.* (*b*) Sallings Wo 42. [salh, -ign.]

salh OE (Angl), sealh (Kt, WSax) (sale, seale, dat.sg., salas, sealas nom.pl., sala, seala gen.pl.), salig OE, 'a willow, a sallow'. The various modern forms are due partly to the different OE case forms (*salh* giving *Saugh-*, *salig* giving *Saigh-*, *sale* giving *Sale*, and *sala* giving *Sal*(*e*)-, *Saw-*) and partly to differences in OE dials., WSax forms becoming *Sel-* and *Zeal.* (*a*) Saighton Ch, Salton YN (tūn), Salehurst Sx (hyrst), Sale Wheel La (wǣl), Salford Bd, La, Wo (ford), Salph End Bd (hōh), Saughall Ch (halh), Sawcliffe L (clif), Sawley Db (hlāw), YW (lēah), Selwood So (wudu). (*b*) Sale Ch, Saleway Wo, Saul Gl, Zeals W; Salome Hu (dat.pl.). [~sele^2, selja.]

*saliht, -uht OE adj., 'growing with willows'. (*a*) Saltley Wa (lēah). [salh, -iht.]

saline ME, 'a salt-pit, a brine-pit', as in *le ssalin* YE 254.

salr ON, 'a dwelling, a hall'. (*b*) Upsall YN (2) (upp, cf. Swed *Uppsala*, etc.), Upsland YN (upp, lúndr). [~sele^1.]

salt^1 OE (Angl), sealt (Kt, WSax), 'salt', possibly also 'brine pit, salt-pan', is found in p.ns. usually in allusion to the manufacture, transport, storage or sale of common salt; on the importance of salt production and salt-ways *v.* Wo 4ff, Wa 10–11. (*a*) Salcombe Regis D (cumb), Salcott Ess (cot), Salford O, Wa, Saltford So (ford), Salter Cu (erg), Salthouse Nf (hūs), Salthrop W (hearpe) Saltwick Nb (wīc, cf. *in wico emptorio salis quem nos saltwich vocamus* BCS 138). (*b*) Salts House YE (also Lat *salinis*). (*c*) Saltash Co.

salt^2 (saltan wk. obl.) OE (Angl), sealt (Kt, WSax), adj., 'salty, brackish', mostly applied to 'water' or 'marshland' near the ocean, but occasionally used of inland salt-deposits. (*a*) Saltburn YN (**burna**), Saltfleet L (**flēot**), Saltmarshe Gl, He, YE, Saltney L (**ēg**), Saltwell Du (**wella**). [~**salt**[1].]

salt-ærn, -ern OE, 'a building where salt was made or sold'. (*a*) Saltings D. (*b*) Salterton D 583, Saltren's Cottages D 101; Seasalter K (**sǣ**). [**salt, ærn**.]

saltere OE (Angl), **sealtere** (Kt, WSax), 'a salter, a salt-worker, a salt-merchant', mostly in the names of fords and roads, etc., connected with the distribution of salt. (*a*) Salterford Nt, -forth YW, Saltisford Wa (**ford**), Saltergate L, YN, YW (**gata**), Salter Lee YW (**lēah**), Salter's Bridge St (**brycg**), Salterton D 602, W (**tūn**), Saltram D (**hām**), Sawtry Hu (**hȳð**). [**salt, -ere**.]

salu (**salwan** wk. obl.) OE adj., 'sallow, dark, dark-coloured'. (*a*) R. Salwarpe Wo 306 (**wearp**).

sand OE, **sandr** ON, 'sand', in p.ns. in allusion to sand deposits like the Greensand in Sandy Bd, to 'a sandy shore, the shore of a sea or lake' as in Sandsend YN, Wassand YE, to a sand bank or sandy soil generally as in Sandford. (*a*) Sambourn Wa (**burna**), Sambrook Sa (**brōc**), Sandford Brk, D, Do, O, Sa, We (**ford**), Sandal (**halh**), Sandbeck (**bekkr**) YW, Sandbach Ch (**bece**), Sandgate K (**geat**), Sandhurst Brk, Gl, K (**hyrst**), Sandon Brk, Ess, Hrt, Sandown Sr (**dūn**), Sandtoft L (**topt**), Sandwich K (**wīc**), Sandwith Cu (**vað**), Santon L, Nf (**tūn**), Saundby Nt (**bý**). (*b*) Sand So, Sands Sx, W; Chicksands Bd (pers.n.), Cockersand La (R. Cocker), Wassand YE (**vað**). (*c*) Burgh by Sands Cu, Sandringham Nf. [~**sende**.]

***sanden** OE adj., 'sandy'. (*a*) Sanderstead Sr 53 (**stede**). [**sand, -en**.]

sandig OE adj., 'sandy'. (*a*) Sandhills Wt (**hyll**), Sandiacre Db (**æcer**). [**sand, -ig**.]

***sangel** OE, 'a tuft, a bundle', *v.* **sengel**.

***sāpere** OE, **sopere** ME, 'a soap-maker, a soap-dealer', first recorded (as a surname) in 1195 (Fransson). (*a*) Sapcott Wo (**cot**), Sapperton Db, Gl, L, Sx (**tūn**). [OE *sāp* 'soap', **-ere**.]

saurr (**saurar** nom.pl.) ON, 'mud, dirt, sour ground', as in Icel *Saurbœr*, the name of a farm built by Steinulfr and so called 'because the ground there was very swampy' (*Landnámabók*, cf. Lindkvist 162). (*a*) Sogill La, Sosgill Cu (**skáli**), Southwaite We (**þveit**), Sowerby Cu, La (2), We (2), YN (2), YW (**bý**). (*b*) Sawrey La (nom.pl.).

sauðr (sauðar gen.sg.) ON, 'a sheep'. (*a*) Southwaite (þveit), *Sautheberch* (berg) Cu 379.

sawn, zawn Corn, 'a cleft, a chine' (cf. Welsh *safn* 'mouth'). (*a*) Zawn Reeth, Zawn-a-Bal Co.

*Saxones Brit, *Sachson PrWelsh, Saeson Welsh, 'the Saxons'. (*b*) Pensax Wo (penno-); cf. also Glensax and Pennersax in Dumfriesshire. [Jackson 539. ~ Seaxe.]

scǣð OE, 'a boundary', *v.* scēað.

scēacere OE, 'a robber'. (*a*) Sha(c)kerley La (lēah), Shackerdale Nt 223 (dæl), Shackerstone Lei (tūn), Shootersway Hrt 49, Sugar Hill W (originally weg), Sugarswell Wa (wella).

sceacol, scacol OE, 'a shackle', more precisely 'an iron ring to constrain a prisoner', enters into several p.ns., but the exact application is difficult to determine. Two series of words and meanings have been adduced to illustrate this word, (i) words closely related to *sceacol* in meaning, such as ON *skǫkull* 'the pole of a cart' (that is, one to which horses were harnessed), in Iceland also with the sense 'horse-yard' (that is, a yard in which horses were shackled or tied up); (ii) words with a topographical meaning, such as OHG *scahho* 'a strip or tongue of land', ON skekill as in *útskekill* 'the outskirts of a field' and NCy dial. *sheckle* 'a circular depression in the limestone caused by a subsidence'; dial. *shackle* 'stubble, quaking grass' (from 1824) and the vb. *shackle* 'to trample down growing corn' (from 1670) may be old, going back to the root *shake*, but this is probably another root. The second group may not be relevant, and it is not improbable that ON *skekill* is an assimilated form of **skenkill* (from **skank-* 'shank, long leg', cf. also ODan **skænkil* in the Dan p.n. *Scenkilsio*, APhS xxi, 110). Of the various parallels only two are likely in p.ns.; the root sense of OE *sceacol* 'a shackle' is probable in most, esp. in the sense of 'a place where animals are tied up or shackled' (as with ON *skǫkull* 'horse-yard'), which is certainly that demanded by Snook Bank Nb (olim *Schackelȝerdesnoke*, *v.* geard) and probably also by Shacklecross, Shalcross Db ('cross with shackles for tethering horses, etc.'); some other p.ns. such as OE *scacalwic* BCS 834, *scaceluuic* ib. 1125 (wīc), Shackleton La (tūn), may also be farms with 'shackle-yards'. In other p.ns. which are originally topographical, such as Shackleford Sr (2) (ford), Shackleton YN (denu), Shackleton YW (tūn, named from a lost *Schakelhull* 1219, *v.* hyll), Shacklewell Mx (wella), we may have *sceacol* in one of its derivative applications (which is not improbable) or a much older form of the dial. word *shackle* 'quaking grass', but no decision is possible, and there is nothing in the topography of these places to make any connexion with other meanings likely.

scēad OE, 'separation', used in the sense 'boundary', suggested by Ekwall for OE *sceadwellan* BCS 1282 and (*a*) Shadwell Nf, O, YW, possibly Shadingfield Sf (denu, feld, near Hundred River, on the hundred boundary). (*b*) R. Shode K (RN 361). [~scēað.]

sceadu, scadu OE, 'a shadow, shade, a shady place, a shelter', difficult to distinguish from scēad, is possible in (*a*) Shadwell Nf, YW (wella); Shadow Brook Wa.

sceaft OE, 'a shaft, a pole', probably used of a pole acting as a landmark or a boundary post. (*a*) Shaftoe Nb (hōh), Shafton YW (tūn), Shebbear D (bearu, where shafts were obtained).

sceaga, scaga OE, 'a small wood, a copse, a strip of undergrowth or wood'.

(1) Like NFris *skage* 'the edge of cultivated land' (NED s.v. *shaw*), dial. *shaw* means 'a strip of undergrowth surrounding a field' and the vb. *shaw* 'to border a field with a fence of low trees'. This use may be old, as OE *sceaga* is equated with Lat *mariscem* 'marsh' (BCS 227) and is compounded in p.ns. with such words as alor in OE *of alrscaga*, *on arlscagan* BCS 1331, brēmel in *on bremeles sceagan* ib. 677; cf. also *in hæðleage sceagan ðær he ðynnest is* 'in *sceaga* of *Hǣð-lēah* where it is thinnest' ib. 455. On the other hand it is not found in the OE charters combined with tree-names like āc, etc., which would indicate a wood of the usual kind.

(2) Usually OE *sceaga* becomes *shaw*, but occasionally *shay* in YW (which arises from *scaga* in the same way as *haigh* comes from haga). The el. is commonest in La and YW, but it is less common in the Midl and SCy. It is found in ME minor names in many counties.

(3) (*a*) Shawsbury Sa (burh), Shawdon Nb (denu).

(*b*) Shaugh D, Shaw Brk, La, W, YW, Shay YW. In compounds it occurs with (i) tree-names, as Aldershaw St (alor), Birkenshaw YW, Birtenshaw La (bircen), Helshaw Sa (hæsel), Nutshaw La (hnutu), Oakenshaw YW (ācen), Wishaw La (wīðig); (ii) animal- and bird-names, as Bagshaw Db (bagga), Cranshaw, Cronkshaw (cranuc), Dunkenshaw (dunnoc) La, Evershaw (eofor), Hogshaw (hogg) Bk, Ickornshaw YW (ikorni), Ottershaw Sr (oter), Ramshaw Du (ramm), Stagshaw Nb (stagga); (iii) other significant words, as Bradshaw La, YW (brād), Frenchay Gl (R. Frome), Fulshaw Ch, La (fūl), Lightshaw La (leoht), Sansaw Sa (sand); (iv) rarely pers.ns., as Audenshaw La, Ellishaw Nb.

[~ skógr by ablaut.]

sc(e)alc OE, 'a servant, a soldier', as in OE *scealcesburna*, *-hom* BCS 144, 702, possibly used as a pers.n. (*a*) Chalkham Sx (-ingahām).

* *sc(e)ald OE adj., 'shallow' (esp. of water), is not evidenced before the 14th century (NED) except in p.ns. with OE forms. The root idea seems to be 'a thin layer' as in related words like scelet, *shale*, *shell*, etc. (*a*) Salden Bk, Shalden Ha (denu), Scaldwell Nth (wella), Scalford Lei (ford), both with ON *sk-*, Shadfen Nb (fenn), Shadforth Du, Shalford Ess, Sr, Shallowford St (ford), Shadwell Mx (wella), Shalbourne W (burna), Shalcombe Wt (cumb), Shaldfleet Wt (flēot). In ME it is also used as a sb. 'a shallow', as in The Shoals C 175. [~ scelde.]

sc(e)alfor OE, 'a diver-bird'. (*a*) Chalderbeach Hu 188 (mere, bece).

*sc(e)alu (*scealwan wk. obl.) OE adj., 'shallow', not recorded independently before the 14th century (cf. NED s.v. *shallow*). (*a*) Shallowford D (2) (ford). [~ sceald.]

* sceamol, scamol, scomol OE, 'a shamble, a bench, a stall for displaying goods for sale' and in ME 'one for the sale of meat'. This latter sense is found in st.ns. such as The Shambles Cu, Nt, YE, Yk, etc., which are often from older forms like *Fleshamels*, *Fleschameles* (Lat *seldæ carnificium*) or *Butcher Shambles*. The word would, however, appear to have had some topographical extension of meaning similar to that of G *sand-schemel* 'a sand shelf' (Mdf 110), and a sense like 'shelf of land, a ledge (as on a river-bank)' is probable in p.ns., including OE *to þane* (*þam*) *scamelan* BCS 629, 691, and in ME f.ns. in Ess 588. (*a*) Samblesbury La 69 (burh), Shalmsford K (ford), Shamblehurst Ha (hyrst), Shamblers Copse Wt 121 (ord), Shamley Sr 256 (lēah). (*b*) Shamwell Hundred K; Plashams Sr (pleg, cf. Löfvenberg 153).

scēap OE (WSax), scēp (Angl, Kt, late WSax), scīp (ONb), *scȳp, *scī(e)p (WSax), 'a sheep'.

(1) The forms *scēap*, *scēp*, *scīp* occur in texts and are phonologically correct for the different OE dialects (cf. Bülbring §§ 153–6); in addition, *scȳp* is found in the WSax of the OE charters,

as in *on scypacumb* BCS 936, *scypeladæs pyll* ib. 959 (now Shiplade So), and this may well be an *i*-mutated variety **scīep*, later *scȳp*, corresponding in formation to celf for calf.

(2) The later p.n. forms are derived from one or another of the OE dial. forms, the commonest *Sheep-*, *Shep-* being from WSax *scēap*, Angl, Kt *scēp*; the forms *Sap-*, *Shap-*, *Shop-* are from WSax *scēap* with the stress shifted to the second el. of the diphthong. Also in the WSax area later forms with *Ship-* (as well as *Shup-*) are very common and these are from WSax *scīep* or *scȳp*. The NCy *Ship-* or *Skibe-*, *Skip-* (with ON *sk-*) are the regular forms in p.ns. from ONb *scīp*. ME and later spellings with *S-* for *Sh-* are AN.

(3) (*a*) Sapcote Lei (cot), Shapwick Do, So, Shopwyke Sr (wīc), Sheepscar YW (kjarr), Sheffield Sx (feld), Shefford Bd, Brk, Shifford O (ford), Shepeau Stow L (ēa), Shephall Hrt (halh), Shepley YW, Shipley Db, Du, Nb, Sa, Sx, YW (lēah), Sheppey K (ēg), Shepreth C (rið), Shepshed La (hēafod), Shepton So, Shipton Bk, Do, Gl (2), Ha, O (2), Sa (tūn), Shipbourne K (burna), Shipden Nf (denu), Shipham So (hām), Shiplade So (gelād), Shiplake O (lacu), Shipway K (weg), and with ON *sk-*, Skibeden YW (denu), Skiprigg Cu (hryggr), Skipton YN, YW (tūn), Skipwith YE (originally wīc).

*scēapde, *scīpde OE, 'a flock of sheep'. (*a*) Shipdham Nf (hām). [~ scēap, -de.]

scēap-hirde OE, 'a shepherd', is possible in (*a*) Shepperton Mx 17 (tūn) and later minor p.ns. like Shepherds Bush Mx. [scēap, hirde.]

scēap-wæsce OE, 'a place for dipping sheep, a sheep-wash'. (*a*) Shipston on Stour Wo (tūn). (*b*) Sheepwash D (2), Nb, Sx. [scēap, wæsce.]

sceard, scard OE, 'a cleft, a gap (as in a fence)', also adj., 'notched, mutilated'; it is freq. in f.ns. (as C 343, Nt 269, W 445). (*a*) Scarcliff (clif, with ON *sk-*), Shardlow (hlāw) Db, Sharstone Ch (stān), Shardley La (lēah). (*b*) Red Shore W (rēad, with *sceard* replacing geat), Shepherds Shard W (both at gaps in the Wansdyke). [~ scearu, skarð.]

scearn, scarn OE, 'dung, muck', frequent with words for 'stream', etc. (*a*) Scarle Nt (lēah, with ON *sk-*), Sharnal K (wella), Sharnbrook Bd (brōc), Sharnford Lei (ford), Sharrington Nf, Sherrington W (tūn), Shernborne Nf (burna), Shernden K (denn), Shernick Co (wīc), Shorncote W (cot).

*sc(e)arnig OE adj., 'dirty, mucky'. (*a*) Scarrington Nt (tūn, with ON *sk-*). [scearn, -ig.]

scearp, scarp (scearpan wk. obl.) OE adj., 'sharp, pointed', perhaps also 'steep'. (*a*) Sharpenhoe Bd (hōh), Sharperton Nb (beorg, tūn), Sharp Ness K, Sharpness Gl (næss), Sharpway Wo (weg).

*scearpol, *scerpel OE, 'a place characterized by some pointed feature, a pointed hill', is possible in (*b*) Sharples La 47–8. [scearp, -ol, -el.]

scearu, scaru OE, 'a share', occurs uncompounded in such senses as 'shearing', 'groin', but it is found in p.ns. with such meanings as 'share, share of land, a share of the common land' (as in OSax *scara* 'a share of the common-field'), 'district' (as in OE *folc-scearu* 'a province, a nation', *lēod-scearu* 'a tribe'), and 'boundary', that is, 'something which cuts off' (as in land-scearu). (*a*) Sharoe La, Sharow YW (either 'boundary hōh' or 'hōh where the district met'). (*b*) Esher Sr 95 (æsc), Waldershare K (wald, ware, 'share of land or district of the wold-dwellers'). [~ OE *scieran*, *sceran* 'to cut, shear'.]

scēat, scēata OE, 'a corner of land, an angle, a projecting piece of land'.

(1) The root idea of this el. is clearly 'that which shoots forth, that which projects', and in p.ns. as in the literary language it developed more precise meanings such as 'angle', 'corner of a building', and 'a corner of land'; this sense is found also in the related *nook-shotten* (a field with many angles, cf. nōk). In the *Orosius*, for example, Sicily is described as being *þryscyte, on ælces sceatan ende sindon beorgas*, 'Sicily is three-cornered, at the end of each *sceata* or corner are hills' (cf. ON *þri-skeyta* 'triangle' and OE *on ðone þryscytan crundel* BCS 693 which refers to a three-cornered chalk-pit); cf. also the derivative sciete. In p.ns. *scēat* is often combined with vegetation names and it may well denote 'an angle of overgrown or cultivated land projecting into a different type of countryside' or 'a projecting angle of woodland', as in OE *upp bætweonæ ða twægen bromfeldas andlang ðæs alarsceatæs* 'up between the two broom-covered open lands along the alder-grown strip', where the *alarsceat* clearly projects forward between two pieces of open country (BCS 393). In later f.ns. it seems to have developed the meaning 'a strip of land, a share of a field' (cf. NED s.v. *shot* sb. 1, § 25, Sr 365).

* (2) This el., which should appear as ME *shete*, *shate*, *shote*, is difficult to distinguish in ME from scīete (ME *shute*, *shete*) and sceot (ME *shot*), and there has undoubtedly been some confusion amongst these els. in the ME spellings of many p.ns., so that the ultimate source is hard to determine.

(3) The greatest concentration of p.ns. with *scēat* is in the adjacent parts of Sr and Ha, but there are a few sporadic examples elsewhere, as in Cu, Db, Do, Sx as well as in f.ns. in C 343, Cu 489, Ess 588, Hrt 259, Hu 295, Mx 203, Nt 269. In some cases, however, alternative explanations may be preferable (as with Eshott Nb, which may be from æsc with the suffix -et).

(4) (*a*) Possibly Shatton Cu, Db (tūn).

(*b*) Sheet Ha, Sheet's Heath Sr, Shot Ess. In compounds it is found with (i) vegetation names, as Aldershot (alor), Bramshott (brēmel), Ewshott (īw), Grayshott (grāf), Spurshot (pirige) Ha, Exceat (āc), Heyshott (hǣð) Sx; (ii) other els., as Bagshot Sr (bagga), Blackshots Ess (blæc), Empshott Ha (imbe), Mytchett Sr (micel); (iii) pers.ns., as Badshot, Bagshot, Oxshott Sr.

[PrGerm **skaut-*, ~OE *scēotan* 'to shoot', scēot(a), scīete, by ablaut.]

scēað, scǣð, scēð OE, 'a sheath', belongs to a root **skaiþ-* whose original meaning was 'separate, divide', as in OE *scēadan* 'to separate, divide, part', OHG *skeida* 'boundary' and also 'cross-roads'; in the senses 'that which divides, that is, a boundary', or 'cross-roads' it is found in r.ns. and p.ns. (cf. RN 360–1). (*a*) Shadwell Lei (wella). (*b*) R. Sheaf YW (forming the Y, Db boundary, also in Sheffield YW), Seed K 275 (in the sense 'cross-roads'), *Haveringe-sheth* Ess 8. [~scēad.]

sceaða, scaða OE, 'a thief, a criminal' (in poetry also 'a warrior') (*a*) Scadbury K (burh).

*scedd OE (Kt), 'a shed', *v.* scydd.

*scegel OE (Angl), 'a small wood'. (*b*) Seal Db. [~sceaga, -el.]

*scēla OE (Angl), sciale, shale, schele ME (NCy), 'a temporary hut, esp. a shepherd's hut on the summer pastures, a summer pasturage, a hovel', is not found in vernacular sources before 1400, but it is found earlier in p.ns. It is confined to the NCy and Scotland, esp. to Nb and Du (cf. also Cu 490). It has precisely the same meanings as the cognate ON skáli (cf. Ekwall, Studies[2] 57, Lindkvist 190). The derivative OE **scēling*, ME *scheling*, NCy dial. *shieling* occurs in Shelley Nb (lēah). (*b*) North and South Shields, Shiel Hall Nb. In compounds it is found in Axwell (āc), Espershields (ēast, brende), Linsheeles Nb (lynn), Winter Shields Cu (winter), and with pers.ns. (post-Conquest), as in Abshields, Agarshill, Old Shield Nb, Allenshiel, Carp Shield Du. (*c*) Sheldon Db (olim *Schele-Haddon*). [It is doubtful whether this el. or the cognate ON skáli is related to ON *skjól* 'shelter'.]

sceld OE (Angl, Kt), scield, scyld (WSax), 'a shield, protection', probably used in p.ns. of 'a shelter' of some kind (cf. hōd). (*a*) Sheldwick K, Shelwick He (wīc).

***sceldu** OE (Angl, Kt), *scieldu, *scyldu (WSax), 'a shallow place, a piece of shallow water, a shallow stream', evidenced in OE only in p.ns. like *Sceldmere* BCS 523, *scyldmere* ib. 633, 682, and in names referring to 'water'. It may be confused with sceld and an OE pers.n. *Sceld*. (*a*) Shelford C, Nt, Shilford Nb (ford), Shell C (strengr). [~sceald.]

***scelet** OE (Angl, Kt), *scielet (WSax), 'shale, clay slate', surviving as dial. *shillet*, *shilt* 'clay slate', is possible in (*a*) Sheltwood Wo 364. [~sceald, -et.]

scelf OE (Angl, Kt), sci(e)lf, scylf, scylp (WSax), scylfe (Angl, WSax), 'a rock, a ledge, a shelving terrain, a turret, a pinnacle'.

(1) This el., which may be the source of ModE *shelf*, *shelp*, esp. in the sense 'a submerged ledge of rock, an oyster bed' (NED s.v.), is found in OE with two principal applications.

(i) 'a crag, a rock', glossing Lat *scopulus* 'a projecting point of rock, a cliff, a crag, a ledge of rock in the sea'; *sticule scylpas* glosses Lat *scabri murices* 'rough pointed rocks' (BTSuppl s.v. *scylf*), *stanscylf* Lat *scrupea uel aspera saxa* 'rugged or rough rocks', *on sandigum stanscilfum* Lat *de arenosis sablonibus* 'sandy shores', and the adj. *scylpige* glosses Lat *scopulosus* 'rocky, craggy'.

(ii) 'a turret, a pinnacle', in glosses of Lat *macio*, *pinna* 'pinnacle, battlement'; cf. also the allusion to the Temple in *uppan ðam scylfe ðæs heagan temples*, etc., in the *Homilies* and to 'the turrets and *scylfas*' borne on an elephant's back (BT s.v.).

(2) The word WSax *scylf* is also found in OE p.ns. such as *scylf hrycg* BCS 547, *scylf weg* 937 (now Shell Wo 138), *scylfes wille* 197, *to byrnan scylfe* 1282, *hnæfes scylf* 1307, *succan scylf* 1071, and non-WSax *scelf* occurs in *scelfdun* BCS 264, *scelfleah* 1289.

(3) OE *scylfe*, a weak noun, is found once in OE in *Genesis* 1306,

gescype scylfan on scipe bosme 'make *scylfan* in the bosom of the ship (that is, the Ark)', but it is difficult to know whether this means 'compartments' or 'decks', though the Biblical text would suggest that the former is meant; there is nothing in fact to suggest that its meaning was 'shelf, ledge', or that its basic form was *scilfe* as is sometimes supposed. This word *scylfe* does not occur elsewhere in OE, nor is it found in OE charter p.ns. Indeed, the chief reason for assuming its occurrence in p.ns. is the existence of ME spellings like -*shulf* in the NWMidl and *shilve*- as in Shildon Du, which can only be from an original OE *scylf*(*e*), as well as *Shilve*- as a first el. in Shilstone D 280, 433 (ME *Silve*-, *Shilvestan*, etc.)—the strong noun *scilf*, *scylf* normally appears as ME *Shilf*- as in Shilton Brk (ME *Shilfton*)—but *Shilve*- may be from a gen.pl. *scilfa*, *scylfa* and too much reliance, therefore, need not be placed on this differentiation between *Shilve*- and *shilf*-; Shelley Sf for example is OE *Scelfleage* BCS 1289 but *Sceueleia* in DB. The main point is that in the Midl and NCy *shilve*- and *shulve*- could only be from an original OE *scylf*(*e*) or *scilf*(*e*) and not from *scelf*.

(4) The chief varieties of spelling of these els. are represented by ME *shelf*, *shilf* and *shulf*; *shelf* is commonly found all over the NCy, Midl, WMidl, EAngl and SE with little variation; *shilf* occurs chiefly in the SWMidl and the extreme SW; *shulf* (apart from the special case mentioned in § 3 *supra*) is found as an occasional variant to *shelf* in a few p.ns. like Bramshall St (mostly -*selle*, occasionally -*schulf*), Gomshall Sr 248 (mostly -*s*(*h*)*elve*, with a few instances of -*shulf*), Oxhill Wa 283 (where -*shulve* occurs as often as -*shelve*), etc.

(5) The best explanation of the variants mentioned and their provenance is to assume that the base of the word was PrGerm **skelf*- (which is evident from the related ON *skjalf*); this would regularly appear as Angl and Kt *scelf* but would become WSax *scielf* through the influence of the initial palatal, later WSax *scilf*, *scylf*. We also have to assume that there was an ablaut variant PrGerm **skulf*-, which with *i*-mutation would become Angl, WSax *scylf*-, Kt *scelf*. Theoretically only Angl dialects would make a distinction between these words as *scelf* and *scylf*, for in Kt they would fall together as *scelf* and in late WSax they would fall together as *scylf*, *scilf*. They are to be distinguished as:

(i) Angl, Kt *scelf*, WSax *sci*(*e*)*lf*, *scylf*, a masc. or neut. *a*-stem

(PrGerm *skelfaz), denoting 'a rock, a ledge, a shelving terrain', becoming *shelf* in all parts of the NCy, WMidl, EMidl, EAngl, and the SE, and *shulf* or *shilf* in the SW.

(ii) Angl, WSax *scylfe*, Kt *scelfe*, a weak *-jan*-stem (PrGerm **skulf-jan-*), of doubtful meaning, but possibly 'shelf' as well as the doubtfully evidenced sense 'compartment' or the like, and clearly later confused with *scelf*; it gives *shilve* in the NCy and EMidl, *shulve* in the WMidl and SW, *shilve* in the extreme SW and *shelve* in the SE. Of these two words *scelf* is very common, whilst *scylfe* is very rare.

* (6) The meanings in p.ns. are of fairly wide range (cf. also § 1 *supra*). The sense 'rock, crag, pointed rock' is certain in Shilstone D 433 (stān), which is named from a well-known cromlech, and is possible in others. Mostly, however, it denotes 'a ledge of land, a shelving terrain, a plateau' and occasionally 'the ledge of land on a river-bank'. The sense 'sandbank' (cf. § 1 *supra*) is found in ME minor names in Ess 589. There is no evidence of the meaning 'turret, pinnacle' in p.ns.

(7) Most of the variant spellings have been dealt with in §§ 3–5 *supra*, but other common variants are initial ME *s-* for *sh-* (due to AN influence) and *sk-* for *sh-* (which may be due to the substitution of ON *sk-*, if such names are not from ON skjalf itself).

(8) (*a*) From *scelf*, Salden Bk (dūn), Shelfanger Nf (hangra), Shelfield St, Wa (hyll), Shelland Sf (land), Shelley Ess, Sf, YW, Shelleys K (lēah), Shilstone D 280, 433 (stān), Shelton Sf, St (tūn). From *scylfe*, Shildon Du 177 (dūn).

(*b*) From *scelf*, Shelf YW, Shell Wo, Shelve K, Sa; Bashall YW (bæc), Bramshall St (brōm), Litchfield Ha (hlif), mostly with pers.ns., as Basil Co, Gomshall Sr, Hunshelf, Tanshelf YW, Tibshelf, Wadshelf Db. Probably from *scylfe*, Shareshill St (scræf), Minshull Ch, Moxhull, Oxhill Wa (pers.ns.).

*scēling OE, 'a shieling', *v.* scēla.

scenc OE, 'a drink, a draught', possibly as a r.n. in (*a*) Shanklin Wt. (*b*) R. Sence Lei.

scēne (scēnan wk. obl.) OE (Angl, Kt), scīene (WSax), adj., 'bright, beautiful'. (*a*) Sheinton Sa, Shenington O (tūn), Shenfield Ess (feld), Shenley Bd, Bk, Hrt (lēah), Shenstone St (stān). [~OE *scēawian* 'to look'.]

*scēo (scēon nom.pl.) OE, 'a shelter', probably related to Norw *skjaa* 'shed, kiln' or ON *skjól* 'shelter' (cf. Ekwall, Studies² 56). (*a*) Shoebury Ess (burh), Shoeland Mx (land). (*b*) Sheen Sr, St.

sceolh (sceolwan wk. obl.) OE adj., 'twisted, awry', evidenced in a gloss and in *sceolh-ege* (Ælfric) where it means 'squinting' (as does the cognate ON *skjalgr*). It probably also meant 'oblique, twisted'; this is a sense developed by the ON *skjalgr* in NCy dial. *skellow* 'warp, twist' which lies behind Scorce Bridge YE 265; OHG *scelah* meant 'oblique' and G *scheel* 'sloping, slanting'. The el. is possible in (*a*) Shoulton Wo 133 (tūn), Showley La 70 (lēah).

sc(e)oppa OE, 'a shop, a booth, a shed', found in OE only in allusion to the treasury of the Temple (Luke xxi. 1). In ME its chief use is of 'a building for the manufacture or sale of goods'. Its relation with scypen and its use in f.ns. would suggest that its primary meaning was 'shed'. (*a*) Shopland Ess 200 (-ing-, land). (*b*) Shoebury Shop Ess.

*sc(e)orf, *scrof OE, 'a cutting, an incision', probably in the sense of 'a hollow, the side of a hollow', which would appear to be topographically appropriate, and which is a sense development from the root of OE *scearfian* 'to cut, shred', *sceorfan* 'to scarify, scrape' and scræf 'a cave, a hollow'. The cognate words MHG *schorf*, *schroff(e)*, G dial. *schroffe* mean 'cliff, bluff', and G *schroff* has the sense 'abrupt' from the idea of something 'cut off abruptly', rather than just 'steep'. (*a*) Sharcott W 351 (cot), Shawstead K (KPN 121–3, stede). (*b*) Hoadsherf, Hodshrove Sx 263, 309 (hāð).

sc(e)ort (sceortan wk. obl.) OE adj., 'short'. (*a*) Shortflatt Nb (flat), Shortgrove Ess (grāfa), Shorthampton O (hām-tūn).

sc(e)ot¹ OE, 'shooting', is possible in (*a*) Shushions St (stān), and perhaps some other p.ns. like Shotley Nb, Sf (lēah), but cf. sc(e)ote. [~scēat.]

(ge)sc(e)ot² OE, 'a chancel, an inner room' (cf Ekwall, NoB xli, 169 n.), which is used to render Lat *sacrarium* (Gregory's *Dialogues*) and *propitiatorium* and *sanctum sanctorum* (Ælfric's *Grammar*) and is cognate with MHG *geschoz* 'a floor, a story', ON *skot* 'a narrow passage on the side of a hall'. It is also found in the compound *sele-(ge)scot* rendering Lat *tabernaculum* (itself often glossed by *eardung(stow)* 'dwelling'). On the available evidence the uncompounded *(ge)scot* scarcely means 'building' but only 'part of a building partitioned off'. It is difficult to separate from scēot, Scott, etc., but has been suggested for (*a*) Shotley Nb 179, Sf (lēah), possibly Shotton Du (tūn), Shottery Wa 240 (rīð).

*scēot[3] OE, 'a steep slope', has been suggested by Ekwall, Studies[2] 147, to explain certain p.ns. in *Shot-*, which would be difficult to interpret satisfactorily if the first el. were sceot[1] or (ge)sceot[2]. It is cognate with MHG *sciez* 'steep slope, abyss' and topographically it is appropriate. (*a*) Shotover O (ōfer), Shottle Db (hyll), Shotwick Ch (wīc), possibly Shotton Du (tūn). [PrGerm **skeut-*, ~ scēat, scyte, also ODan **skiūt* found in the Dan p.n. *Skydebjerg*.]

sc(e)ota OE, 'a trout', difficult to distinguish from an OE pers.n. *Scēot*, is possible in (*a*) Shottesbrook Brk (brōc), Shotwell Mill Nth (wella). [~ sceot[1] in the sense 'rapid movement, a darting movement'.]

*sc(e)ote OE, 'a pigeon', found only in the compound cūscote, may, according to Ekwall (DEPN), enter into some p.ns. in *Shot-* like Shotley Nb, Sf; cf. sceot[1].

*scēotere, *scȳtere OE, sheter, shoter ME, 'a shooter, an archer', is not recorded independently in OE. (*a*) Shooter's Green Hu, Shooter's Hill K, Nth 177, Wa. [~ OE *scēotan* 'to shoot', -ere.]

scēp OE (Angl, Kt), 'a sheep', *v.* scēap.

*scerde OE (Angl, Kt), *scierde, *scyrde (WSax), 'a gap, a cleft, a pass', is possible in (*a*) Shurdington Gl. (*b*) Sheard's Copse Wt 222 (which may however be from sceard). [~ sceard, -e.]

*scerpel OE, 'a pointed hill', *v.* scearpol.

*scerte OE (Angl, Kt), *scierte, *scyrte (WSax), 'a piece of land cut off, a short piece of land', so far found only in K. (*a*) Crowhurst (crāwe), Flighshot (cf. K 192), Hartsheath (heorot) K. (*b*) Shoart K 498. [~ sceort, -e.]

schele ME, 'a shed, a cottage', *v.* scēla.

scheling ME, 'a shieling', *v.* scēla.

schingled ME adj., 'having a shingle roof', *v.* shingel[1].

* scid OE, 'a split piece of wood, a block, a beam', possibly used also of 'a foot-bridge'. (*a*) Shedfield Ha (feld), (*b*) Shide Wt 179 (also called *Schidhambrigge*). [~ OE *scēadan* 'to divide', scēad.]

scield OE (WSax), 'a shield, a shelter', *v.* sceld.

scīene OE (WSax) adj., 'beautiful', *v.* scēne.

*scīete, *scȳte OE (WSax), 'a corner or nook, a strip of land', is used in much the same way as scēat, of which it is an *i*-mutated variety (cf. Zachrisson, ZONF ii, 146, Wo 180–1). It is found chiefly in the SCy and SWMidl. The primary meaning is 'that which shoots forth' and in a great many cases it is used of the land in the angle or corner of a parish-boundary; in cocc-scīete it has a special sense and in Water Shoot D 104 it refers to a spring. In ME the common form is *shute*. (*a*) Shootlands Sr (land), Shutelake (lacu), Shuteley (lēah), Shuthanger (hangra), Shuttaford (ford) D. (*b*) Shate, Sheat Wt, Sheetland Sx, Shewte D, Shute D (*freq*), W; Evershot Do (eofor), Hardingshute Wt (horte). [~ scēat, -e.]

scilf OE (WSax), 'a shelving terrain', *v.* scelf.

scilling OE, 'a shilling', is possible in some p.ns. in allusion to the rent paid, but it may be difficult to distinguish from a pers.n. *Scilling* as in Shillingford D. (*a*) Shillingham Co (hamm).

*scingol OE, 'a roofing tile', *v.* shingel[1].

scinn(a) OE, 'a phantom, a spectre'. (*a*) Shincliffe Du (clif), Skinburness Cu 294 (with ON *sk-*, burh interchanging with burgæsn). Cf. Dickins 157.

scinnere OE, 'a magician', perhaps used as a pers.n. (*a*) Shearston D (tūn). [scinna, -ere.]

scīp OE (ONb), 'a sheep', *v.* scēap.

*-scipe OE noun-suffix, used to form abstract nouns (from PrGerm *-skip-*, Kluge § 138), some of which came to be used in a concrete sense, as in (ge)burscipe, (ge)mǣnscipe, wæter-scipe, OE *burgscipe* 'a township', *tūnscipe* 'the inhabitants of a tūn, a township' (cf. a similar use of -nes).

scipen OE, 'a cow-shed', *v.* scypen.

scīr[1] OE, 'a shire, a jurisdiction, an administrative district, a county'.

(1) This el. is largely used in p.ns. to denote a large administrative district made up of a group of hundreds or wapentakes and supervised by an alderman and later a sheriff (*v.* aldormann, scīr-gerēfa), its affairs being managed in the shire-moot (*v.* scīr-gemōt). It is usually combined with the names of the principal town in the area, as in Bedfordshire, Buckinghamshire, Cheshire, Hampshire, Lancashire, Wiltshire, Yorkshire; some counties which do not incorporate the el. *scīr*, like Kent or Surrey, are old district-names, and others like Cumberland, Northumberland, Westmorland, Norfolk, Suffolk, Essex, Sussex, Cornwall, Dorset, Somerset (*v.* land, folc, Seaxe, sǣte), are derived from old folk-names. On the origin of these divisions, *v.* F. M. Stenton, *Anglo-Saxon England* 289–90, 322–4.

(2) The term *scīr* was also used of smaller districts and administrative units than the county, which vary much in extent. The actual significance of *scīr* in these names depends upon local conditions; it is sometimes used of hundreds or wapentakes, as in the older forms of Allerton and Hang Wapentakes YN 204, 208, *Borgscire* YW, Powder (earlier *Pourdreschire*), Wivelshire Co, Salford Hundred La. But in most cases it denotes the district comprised in an honour or liberty, that is, a district or estate which had a separate jurisdiction from the county in which it stood; thus the wapentakes of Howdenshire YE 243 and Islandshire Nb 123 were Liberties of the Bishop of Durham, the Honour of Richmond YN 218 was called Richmondshire and the Liberty of Ripon YW was called *Ripeshire* (probably going back to OE as the tribal name is here in the gen.pl., *v.* **Hrype**); Upshire Ess 31 was the higher part of the Liberty of Waltham.

(3) There are also cases where the el. *scīr* is used of still smaller divisions, as in Hallamshire, Sowerbyshire and Kirkby Malzeard (olim *Kirkbyshire*) YW, Mashamshire YN 230, Wilpshire La 72, Pinnock Gl (olim *Pinnocschire*), all corresponding to parishes or townships; these may well be small districts with independent privileges and jurisdiction. York was divided into six shires (including Marketshire YE 293), whilst Foghamshire W 90 was a street or district of Chippenham.

(4) In Nb and Du the term *shire* was also used of a small district, not always within definite limits; sometimes it denoted an outlying part of the palatinate of Durham (as in Bedlingtonshire, Norhamshire), but it was also closely associated in other names with ecclesiastical jurisdiction; Hexhamshire denoted the land with which St Wilfrid endowed the bishopric of Hexham, Wirralshire was a district granted to the monks of Durham in 1093 and Tynemouthshire was a district in which the same monks had certain rights.

(5) In p.ns. the el. denotes either an actual district of the types discussed or it refers to land, woodland, etc. generally available for the men of the shire, to meeting-places of the shire-court, or to places and objects on the boundaries of a shire. As a first el. it is difficult to distinguish from **scīr**[2], and with initial *sk-* (through ON influence) from **skírr**.

(6) (*a*) Sherland K 113 (**land**), Sherwood Forest Nt 10 (**wudu**, probably a wood for the use of the whole shire), Shiremark Sr, Sx,

(mearc, both places being on the county boundary), Shireoaks Nt (āc, on the county boundary), Shireshead La (hēafod, near the upper boundary of Amounderness), Shirland Db (lúndr), Shirlet Sa (hlet), Skirwith Cu 242 (viðr), Skyrack YW (āc, eik, with ON *sk-*, the wapentake meeting-place); it is also possible in Shirley He (lēah) which stands on the county boundary, and Skirlaugh YE 49 may well be compound of *scīr* (with ON *sk-*) and lǫgr, forming a parallel compound to býjar-lǫg. *v.* also scīr-mann, scīr-gemōt, scīr-gerēfa.

(*b*) In compounds, *scīr* is usually found with (i) an older p.n., as in Bedfordshire, Buckinghamshire and many other counties, Howdenshire YE, Richmondshire YN, Sowerbyshire YW, etc.; (ii) an older district name, as in Berkshire, Pinnock Gl, Powder, Wivelshire Co; (iii) an old folk-name, as in Devonshire, Ripon Liberty YW; (iv) a significant word, as in Marketshire Yk (market), Upshire Ess 31, K 116 (upp).

scīr[2] (scīran wk. obl.) OE adj., 'bright, gleaming', in wood-names probably also denoting 'thinly grown, sparsely wooded' (a sense paralleled by dial. *shire* applied to 'thin scanty crops'), in names of plots of ground 'clear of weeds, clean', and in stream-names 'clear'. It is sometimes difficult to distinguish from scīr[1] and (with ON *sk-*) from the cognate ON skírr. (*a*) Sheerness K (næss), Sherborne Do, Gl, Ha, Wa, R. Sherbourne Wa, Sherburn Du, YE, YW (often with ON *sk-*) (burna), *Sherbarrow* YW (bearu), Shereford Nf, Sherford D, So (ford), Sherfield Ha (feld), Shirley Db, Ha, Sr, Wa (lēah), Shirwell D (wella). (*b*) Used as a sb. 'the bright one' in old r.ns., as Shere Sr, R. Rother Sx (olim *Scir*, *Shire*). [~skírr.]

scīr-man OE, 'a sheriff, a steward', used also as a by-name (Tengvik 268), is evidenced earlier in OE than scīr-(ge)rēfa, for which it was sometimes an alternative term; it was also used of 'an inhabitant of a shire'. (*a*) Shermansbury Sx 212 (burh). [scīr[1], mann.]

scīr-(ge)mōt OE, 'a shire-moot, the meeting-place of a shire'. (*b*) Skirmett Bk 180 (with ON *sk-*). [scīr[1], (ge)mōt.]

scīr-(ge)rēfa OE, 'a sheriff, the king's chief executive' (cf. Stenton 540–2), is rarely recorded in OE except as a title (as in *Ælfnoð scirgerefa* ASC 1056, *on Æðelwines scirgerefan gewitnesse* ib., etc., *v.* Tengvik 267). It occurs once as a gloss to Lat *præses* 'chief, president', once in the phrase *Cristen scirgerefa* for 'a bishop'. (*a*) Cherry Orchard Wo (orceard), Shears Green K (grēne),

Shrewton W, Shroton Do, Shurton So (tūn). (*c*) *Sheriff*(*s*) prefixed to Hales Sa, Hutton YN, Lench Wo. [scīr[1], (ge)rēfa.]

scite OE, 'dung'. (*a*) Shutwell Wa (wella), Skidbrook L (brōc, with initial ON *sk-* or from ON skítr). [~ skítr.]

scitel OE, scytel (WSax), 'dung', may occur in some p.ns. like Shuttleton D 618 (dūn), but it is difficult to distinguish from scyt(t)els, esp. when the latter word lost its suffixal *-s*. [scite, -el.]

*scitere OE, possibly 'a sewer, a channel or stream used as an open sewer', a freq. r.n., formed as *nomen agentis* from scite 'dung'. It occurs in OE in *rivulus qui Scitere dicitur* BCS 476 So (alternately called *sciteres stream* BCS 729, and surviving as the first el. of Sharford So). It is difficult to decide whether *skitter* in Danelaw p.ns. is from *scitere* with ON initial *sk-* or from an ON r.n. such as that found in Norw *Skytteren*, *Skytra* (NG ii, 285) from the same root as scyte 'shoot', but in view of its particular use of ducts, sewers and the like it is probably the former. As a first el. it is sometimes difficult to separate from scytere. (*a*) Kipperlynn Nb 128, Shatterford Wo 32, Shiter So, Shetterton Do (olim *Scetre*), Shutterton D 493 (on a stream called *sciterlacu* in 1044); with ON *sk-*, Bitter Beck Cu 4, Skitterick YN, YW, *Skiterik* YW, Skitterness L. (*b*) The Shooter La 28; with ON *sk-*, Skitter, Ulceby Skitter L. [scite, -ere.]

sclate ME, 'slate', *v.* slate.

scofl OE, 'a shovel', appears to be used in p.ns. but with some meaning not fully determined; it may denote 'something resembling the hollow blade of a shovel' in Sholden K (dūn), or 'something the width of a shovel' in Shulbrede Sx, Shoebroad Db, *Scovelbrede*, *-brode* Db, Nt, Y (brǣdu), that is, 'a narrow strip', a sense paralleled by that of furh 'furrow' in ME furbrede, furlang, etc., cf. Wa 322.

scole-house ME, 'a school house', first evidenced from 1401, in p.ns. earlier. (*b*) Skills Fm Ess (Hy 3).

scoppa OE, 'a shop', *v.* sceoppa.

*scor(a) OE, 'the shore of the sea or a lake, a river-bank, a precipitous slope', is not recorded in OE except in p.n. spellings, but it is cognate with MLG, MDu *schore* 'shore', OHG *scorro* 'a steep slope', OE *scorian* 'to jut out', and *scoren* 'precipitous'; the word is well-evidenced in ME alliterative poems of the NW (*v.* NED s.v. *shore*). The form may be *scora* as in OE *Waldmeres scora* BCS

381 and *Scorranstan* ib. 574 (beside *Sceorstan* ASC 1015E, now Sherston W), but p.ns. with a gen.sg. *Shores*- suggest that a strong form *scor* was also current. (*a*) Sharland Ha (hlinc), Sherston W (stān, probably 'precipitous rock'), Shoreditch Mx (dīc, olim *Schores*-), Shoreham K (OE *scorham*, hām), Shoresworth La, Nb (worð), Shorwell Wt (wella). (*b*) Shore La, YW, Helmshore La (helm). [~scoren[1], [2], scoru.]

*scoren[1] OE, 'a steep precipitous place'. (*b*) Shorne K. [scor(a), -en.]

scoren[2] OE pa.part., 'cut, shorn', hence 'sharply cut off, precipitous, abrupt'. (*a*) Shorncliffe K (clif). [~OE *scieran* 'to cut', scor(a), scoru.]

scoru OE, 'a score, a mark', perhaps also 'a boundary mark' (cf. NED s.v. *score* sb. § 2), is possible in (*a*) Scorsham Co (hām), Compton Scorpion Wa 305 (olim *Scorefen*, fenn). (*b*) Score, Scur D. [~scoren[2].]

scot ME, 'a tax, a payment'. (*a*) Scotland D 212, Wt 158; cf. also Ess 589. [~OE *sceot* 'payment' with ON *sk*-, OFr *escot*.]

Scot(t) (Scottes gen.sg., Scotta gen.pl.) OE, 'a Scot', Skottar (Skotta gen.pl.) ON, 'the Scots'. The OE word denoted the inhabitants of Ireland and the Irish colony in Argyllshire up to the 9th century and thereafter the inhabitants of Scotland; the ON word was also used of the inhabitants of both Ireland and Scotland. In p.ns. the word usually denotes people from Scotland. Ekwall in an important note on this el. in NoB xli, 168ff, calls attention to the difficulty of distinguishing it from other els. and suggests that it occurs (with the initial palatal *Sh*- preserved) in (*a*) Shottery Wa (rīð). The form *Scot* (with initial *Sk*- from ON *Skotar* or from the Lat spelling *Scotti*) is possible in (*a*) Scotby Cu 163 (bý), Scotforth La (ford), Scothern (þorn), Scotter (trēow) L, Scotton L, YN, YW (tūn), Scottow Nf (hōh).

scræf OE, 'a cavern, a hollow', had two principal senses in OE:

(i) 'a cave, a cavern, a hole in the ground', as is evident from its use in glossing Lat *antrum*, *spelunca* and *concavas petras* (BT s.v.); this use in p.ns. is established by Salford Bridge Wo (olim *Scraford*) which was in the vicinity of a *Scrave medwe* (mǣd) and *Dwarfeholys* 'dwarf holes' (*v.* YN xlv); cf. also scræfen.

(ii) 'a hovel, a hut, a poor dwelling', found in glosses to Lat *domicilium* 'a dwelling' and *gurgustium* 'a mean poor dwelling'; in the *Blickling Homilies* the phrase *ge min hus doþ sceaðum to scrafum* is a free rendering of the Gospel Matt. xxi. 13 (in the WSax version *ge worhtun ðæt to þeofa cota* 'ye have made it a hut of thieves', *v.* cot), and it is equated with hulc 'hovel' in Ælfric's *Homilies* (ed. Thorpe i, 544).

The el. is sometimes difficult to distinguish in ME from scīr-gerēfa, as in Shrewley Wa. In some p.ns. a metathesized form *scærf* is possible. (*a*) Salford Wo (ford), Scrafton YN (with ON *sk*-, tūn); Shareshill St (hyll), Sharlston YW (tūn), both with metathesis, Shrawardine Sa (worðign), Shrawley Wo 78 (lēah), Shrofield K (feld). [~sc(e)orf.]

*scræfen, *screfen OE, 'a hollow place, a place with caves or pits'. (*b*) Scriven YW (where there are old gravel pits and quarries). [scræf, -en.]

scrætte OE, 'a harlot', *v.* scratta.

*scratta OE, 'a hermaphrodite', possibly also later 'the devil' (cf. skratti). OE *scratta* is not recorded, but is proposed as an emendation for *scritta* which occurs in glosses (cf. NED s.v. *scrat*); *scratta* may well be a secondary form of OE *scrætte* 'a harlot, a prostitute'. Either word would be appropriate in (*a*) Scratchbury Hill D (an old camp, with the dial. form *Scratch* 'the devil').

scrēawa (scrēawan gen.sg., scrēawena gen.pl.) OE, 'a shrew-mouse'; the later ME meaning 'a wicked man, a rascal' may be old, since OHG *scrawa* is used of 'a dwarf, a goblin' and MHG *schröuwel* of 'a devil', and in some such sense it may be found in some p.ns. (*a*) Scrainwood Nb (wudu), Scray K (hop), Shrawnell Wo (hyll), Shrewsnest C 289 (nest), Shroner Ha (ōra).

*screfen OE (Merc), 'a place of pits', *v.* scræfen.

scrīc OE, 'a shrike, a missel-thrush'. (*a*) Shrigley Ch (lēah).

scrifen OE pa.part., 'allotted'. (*a*) Shrivenham Brk (hamm). [~OE *scrīfan* 'to allot, assign'.]

*scrippa OE, 'something sharp or rough', perhaps in allusion to 'a point or spit of land, rough ground' or the like, found in OE only in *on þone midmestan scrippan* BCS 390, is possible in (*a*) Shripney Sx 91 (OE *Scrippan eg*). [~OE *screpan* 'to scrape', *screpu* 'a curry-comb'.]

*scrof OE, 'a hollow, the side of a hollow', *v.* sc(e)orf.

* scrogge, shrogge ME, NCy dial., 'a bush, brushwood', also occurs in f.ns. (Cu 490, Nt 289, YW). (*b*) Scrog, Shrogg YW, Clipstone Shroggs Nt 74. [Origin unknown.]

***scrubb, scrybb** OE, ***screbb** (Kt), 'a shrub, brushwood, a place overgrown with brushwood'; ME p.n. spellings with *shrib* and *shreb* from the OE mutated form *scrybb* (only once attested in OE in ASWills 40.25) are very rare; the spelling *shrub* in most parts of the country would therefore point rather to an OE *scrubb* corresponding to Dan dial. *skrub* 'brushwood', NFris *skrobb* 'brook, brushwood'. (*a*) Scrubcut K (**cot**), Shrubs Hill Sr 124, Shrubland Sf (**lúndr**). (*b*) Shrub Fm, etc., Ess, Nth, Sx, The Shrubs Sx 42; Bushrubs Nth (**busc**), Wormwood Scrubs Mx.

scrūd-land OE, 'land given for the provision of clothing', survives in *Scrudlande* (13th century) Ess 589.

scucca, sceocca OE, 'an evil spirit, a demon', as in OE *scuccan hlau* BCS 264 (now Warren Fm Bk). (*a*) Shacklow Db (**hlāw**), Shobrooke D (**brōc**), Shocklach Ch (**læcc**), Shuckborough St (**burh**), Shuckburgh Wa (**beorg**), Shucknall He (**hyll**); cf. Dickins 157.

***sculd** OE, 'an obligation, a debt, a liability', an unmutated form of OE *scyld* 'debt', is suggested (DEPN) for (*a*) Shouldham Nf (**hām**).

***scydd** OE (Angl, WSax), ***scedd** (Kt), 'a hovel, a shed', **schudde** ME 'a hovel, a pig-sty', is recorded in OE only in charter p.ns. such as *hudelinga scydd* BCS 702 (a swine-pasture), *stepacnolles scydd* ib. 216, and in ME only as *ssed* in the Kentish *Ayenbite* and *schudde* in *Prompt. Parv.* where it is rendered '*hovel or swine-kote*'. It survives as dial. *shud* 'shed' in EAngl, Db, Y, Gl, He; ModE *shed* is probably from the Kt form. The expected EMidl, NCy *shid* appears only occasionally in p.n. spellings, whilst *shudde* and *shedde* are usual and often interchange; *v.* Mawer, Problems 18. It is found also in ME f.ns. (Ess 589). (*a*) Sheddon Ess 344 (**hōh**), Shedyard Db (**geard**), Sidbury W (**burh**). (*b*) Bowshots Sx 185 (**burh**), Denshott Sr (**dūn**), Gunshot Sx 132, *Palshuddes* Sx 117 (the p.n. Poling Sx), Paulshott, Puckshot Sr 206 (**pūca**), Rumstead K 66 (**rūm**). (*c*) Shudy Camps C 103. [~PrGerm **skeuð*-, **skuð*- 'cover', represented by OE **scēod* 'shood, pod', ON *skjóða* 'a bag'.]

scylf(e), scylp OE, 'a shelf', *v.* **scelf.**

***scȳp** OE (WSax), 'a sheep', *v.* **scēap.**

scypen, scipen OE, 'a cow-shed', surviving in f.ns. (C 343, Ess 589, W 446) and as dial. *shippen*. (*b*) Shippen YW, Shippon Brk, Skiplam YN (dat.pl., with ON *sk*-). [~**sc(e)oppa, -en.**]

scyrte OE (WSax), 'a piece of land cut off', *v.* **scerte.**

scyte OE, 'shooting', probably used like dial. *shute* 'a shoot, a steep hill' of 'a steep slope'; cf. OE *scyte-heald* 'precipitous' and the related scēot. It is also used later of 'a steep channel of water, a mill-shoot'. (*b*) Shute Shelve So (a hill), Shut Mill Wo (a mill-shoot). [PrGerm **skutiz*, ~scēat.]

scytel[1] OE (WSax), 'dung', *v.* scitel.

*scytel[2] OE adj., 'unstable', *v.* scyttels.

*scytere OE, 'a shooter', *v.* scēotere.

scyt(t)els, scyt(t)el OE, 'a bolt, a bar', also 'a dart, an arrow', surviving as dial. *shuttle* 'the horizontal bar of a gate, a flood-gate', in p.ns. probably denoting 'something that can be barred or bolted'; but it is difficult to tell whether p.ns. have this word or scitel or an OE **scytel* adj., 'inconstant, wavering' used either as a pers.n. or of 'something shaky or unstable' (cf. NED s.v. *shittle* adj.). (*a*) Chesters Nb (olim *Scytlescester*, from ceaster), Sheepsbyre (bearu), Sheepstor (torr) D, Shutford O (ford), Shuttleworth Db, La 63, YW (worð). [PrGerm **skutisl-*, ~scēat, -els.]

sealh OE (Kt, WSax), 'a willow', *v.* salh.

sealt(-) OE (Kt, WSax), 'salt', *v.* salt(-).

sēar OE adj., 'dry, barren'. (*a*) Saredon St (dūn). (*b*) As a sb. in Seer Green Bk.

sēað OE, 'a pit, a hole', sometimes difficult to distinguish as a final el. from hǣð, is fairly common in OE charter p.ns. (Mdf 116). (*b*) Horseheath C (horu), Orsett Ess (ōra[2]), Odsey C, Roxeth Mx (pers.ns.), also in f.ns. (Bd 295).

*seax OE, 'a stone, a rock', has been suggested for some p.ns. but it cannot be distinguished from Seaxe; except where topography is decisive for *seax*, *Seaxe* is preferable. [~Lat *saxum* 'a large lump of rock'.]

Seaxe (Seaxna gen.pl.) OE, 'the Saxons', the Germanic settlers of much of southern England, in p.ns. usually denoting isolated settlements of Saxons amongst other tribes; it sometimes appears in an uninflected form *Seax-* (cf. Swǣfe), and so could formally be confused with seax. (*a*) Exton Ha (*æt East Seaxnatune* BCS 758), Saxton C, YW (tūn), *Saxhale* YW (halh, near Saxton), Saxham S (hām), Saxondale Nt 241 (dæl, originally denu); cf. also a lost *Saxedale* L. (*b*) In district names (originally folk-names), Essex (ēast), Middlesex (middel), Sussex (sūð), Wessex (west), the last being a name revived by antiquarians. [*v.* Ekwall, NoB xli, 135 ff. ~Saxones.]

secg[1] OE, 'sedge, a reed, a rush'. (*a*) Sedgebrook L (**brōc**), Sedgemoor So (**mōr**), Sedgewick Sx (**wīc**), Setchel Fen C (**haga**). (*b*) *Breithsegges* (f.n.) L. [*v.* Tengstrand 257ff, NoB xxxvi, 26.]

secg[2] OE, 'a warrior', difficult to distinguish from **secg**[1] and an OE pers.n. *Secg*, is possible in (*a*) Seckloe Bk (**hlāw**), Sedgeberrow Wo (**bearu**), Sedgley St (**lēah**).

secrestein, segrestein OFr, ME, 'a sacristan, a sexton'. (*a*) Sacriston Heugh Du 171 (**hōh**, named from the sacristan of Durham).

sedl OE, 'an abode', *v.* **setl**.

sef ON, 'sedge, a rush', surviving as dial. *seave*, *seavy* (esp. in minor names and f.ns.). (*a*) Seathwaite Cu (**þveit**), Seavy Carr YE (**kjarr**), Sefton La 118 (**tūn**), Soffham YE (**holmr**). (*b*) Possibly R. Seph YN.

sege OFr, ME, 'a seat', used also of 'ground on which a ship lies', as in ModE *sedge* (cf. NED s.v. *siege* sb.). (*b*) Sedge D 455.

sel ON, 'a mountain hut, a shed', difficult to distinguish from **selja** as in Selside We, YW. (*a*) Sella La 223 (**haugr**). (*b*) Brunshaw Cu (**brúnn**). [~ **salr, sele.**]

seld OE, 'an abode', *v.* **setl**.

sele[1] OE, 'a dwelling, a house, a hall', chiefly found in OE poetry; it is often difficult to distinguish from **(ge)sell**, as in Lawshall Sf (**hlāw**), and **halh**, as in Markshall Ess 396, Ringshall Sf (**hring**). (*a*) Seldon D (**dūn**), Selhurst Sx (**hyrst**), Silbury W (**burh**). (*b*) Seal(e) K, Sr, Sele Sx, South Zeal D; Lindsell Ess (**linde**), Newsells Hrt (**nīwe**). [~ **salr.**]

***sele**[2] OE (Angl, Kt), ***siele**, ***syle** (WSax), 'a willow copse', difficult to distinguish from **sele**[1] and **syle**, may be found in some p.ns. (*a*) Selborne Ha (**burna**), Selham Sx (**hām**), Selworthy So (**worðig**), Silchester Ha (**ceaster**), Silton Do (**tūn**). [~ **salh, -e.**]

***sele**[3] OE (Kt), 'a bog', *v.* **syle**.

***selet** OE (Angl, Kt), ***sielet**, **sylet** (WSax), 'a willow copse'. (*a*) Selaby Du (**bý**), and alternating with **sele**[2] in Selham Sx (**hām**). [~ **salh, -et.**]

selja (**selju** gen.sg.) ON, 'a willow'. (*a*) Salem Bridge L (**holmr**), Selby YW (**bý**), Selker Cu (**kjarr**), Selside We, YW (**sǽtr**), Silecroft (**croft**), Sillerea (**vrá**) Cu. [~ **salh.**]

(ge)sell (**selle** dat.sg., **sella** nom.pl.) OE, 'a shed, a shelter for animals, a herdsman's hut', is recorded in OE only in charter p.ns., chiefly from K and Sx, where it may well be associated with swine pastures.

The meaning 'collection of sheds' is implied in the use of the prefix *ge-*. It is sometimes confused in form with **hyll** (Kt **hell**), as in Hamsell Sx 378, and with **sele**; *v.* Ekwall, Studies[2] 44ff. (*b*) It is usually combined with significant words, as in Bemzells Sx (**bēam**), Boarzell K (**bār**), Breadsell Sx (**bred**), Buxshall Sx 340 (**bōc**[1]), Horsell Sr (**horu**), Nizel's Heath K (**nīge**), Spilsill K (**speld**), Stradishall Sf (**strǣt**), Wormshill K (**weorn**); occasionally with words denoting people, as in Drigsell Sx (**drihten**), Yorkshire Sx (pers.n.). [~ **sele**.]

***selte** OE (Angl, Kt), ***sielte** (WSax), ***sælte** (Merc), 'a salt-pit, a salt-working'. ME *selte* (Angl, Kt) and *salte* (Merc) interchange. (*b*) Salt St 129 (replacing Welsh *Halen* 'salt', from DB). [~ **salt, -e.**]

***sende** (earlier ***sænde**) OE, 'a sandy place', found only in p.ns.; cf. Norw dial. *senda* 'sandy bottom'. (*a*) Saintbridge Gl (**brycg**). (*b*) Scene K, Send Sr 50; Seend W 131 and Zine So may be from *sende* but are more likely to be Brit p.ns. from a root **sento-*, whence Welsh *hynt* 'a path'. [~ **sand, -e.**]

***sengel** (earlier ***sængel**) OE, 'a bundle, a tuft' or the like, is found in OE only in *Sængelpicos* BCS 144 (in the neighbouring parish to Singleton Sx) and in some p.ns. in *Single-*; it may survive as NCy dial. *single* 'a small bundle of gleanings'. An unmutated form *sangel* seems to lie behind WCy dial. *sangle, songle* 'a small sheaf, a handful of corn, gleanings', which is certainly cognate with G dial. *sangel, sängel*, LG *sangele* 'a tuft, a bundle' (Jellinghaus s.v.). The exact meaning of *sengel* cannot be determined; Mawer, Problems 16, suggests something like 'brushwood', but this is doubtful; probably 'tufts of grass, gleanings' is nearer the recorded senses. (*a*) Singleton Sx 53 (**tūn**); *Songlefield* Gl (**feld**) is from the unmutated *sangel*. (*b*) Sengle Sx 17. [~ OHG *sanga* 'a bundle of gleanings', **-el.**]

***senget** (earlier ***sænget**, also ESax) OE, 'a place cleared by burning, a clearing', occurs in OE in *sænget þorn* BCS 629 and in the OE spellings of other p.ns. (*a*) St Chloe, Saintlow Gl, Syntley Wo 3[illegible] (**lēah**), St Ives Sx (**tēag**), Saint Hill D, Sx (**hyll**), Saintofts YE (**topt**), Saynden (**denn**), Sundridge (**hrycg**) K. (*b*) Signet O. [~ OE *sengan* 'to singe, to burn', **-et.**]

***senk** ON, 'a hollow where water collects' (as in Swed dial. *säkk*, Norw dial. *senk, søkk* 'a hollow, a small valley'). (*a*) Sinkfall La 20 (**fall**).

seofon OE num., 'seven', is of frequent occurrence in p.ns., mostly denoting the actual number of objects (such as trees), but in some p.ns. such as Seavington So, Sevenhampton Gl, W, Wo, Sevington Ha, Ekwall has suggested that *Seven-* is an elliptical form of some older name such as *seven-wells* or the like, which is not improbable with **hǣma-tūn**; in Wo 35–6, however, attention is called to the significance of *seven* as the number of manors for which a much higher relief was paid to the king. These p.ns. may well recall some such custom. The number *seven* had other significance too, for a breach of the peace by seven or more men constituted an act of war and was not an act of private violence. There may also be forgotten elements of folk-lore in the choice of *seven* in some of the compounds with *wella*, or such names may recall 'the seven years of plenty' and 'the seven years of dearth' of Genesis xli, 47 ff. (*a*) Besides the p.ns. mentioned, *seofon* is combined chiefly with (i) tree-names, as Seabatch Sx (**bēce**), Sevenash D (**æsc**), Sevenoaks K (**āc**); (ii) words for 'stones', 'mounds', etc., as Seaborough D, Do, Ess (**beorg**), Sewborwens Cu (**burgæsn**), Soussons D (**stān**), Hallsenna Cu (**haugr**, an inversion compound); (iii) words for 'spring', as Seawell Nth, Sewell Bd, O, Sowell D (**wella**).

seohtre OE, 'a drain, a ditch'. (*b*) Sefter Sx 95, cf. also Sx 561. [~ **sēoluc**.]

seolfor OE, **silfr** ON, 'silver', may in some examples of the common street-name Silver Street refer to silver-smiths. But in p.ns. this concrete meaning is unlikely. For the most part *silver* may well be an elliptical form of some older plant-name, though apart from Sellers L (a compound of *seolfor* and **hrīs**), such plant-names as *silver-thistle* and the like are not evidenced before the 16th century and most are much later. In some p.ns. and stream-names it might allude to the colour or appearance, and in f.ns. and some p.ns. there might be a jocular reference to the richness of the ground or an allusion to the rent paid. (*a*) Silver Beck Cu (**bekkr**), Silverdale La 189 (**dæl**, from the grey limestone), Silver Ley Ess 627, Silverley C (**lēah**). (*b*) Monksilver So (perhaps an old r.n.). [The form *silver* in p.ns. is late and usually replaces the ME *seluer* of the p.n. spellings through the influence of StdE *silver*.]

seolh (**seoles** gen.sg.) OE, 'a seal'. (*a*) Selsey Sx 82 (**ēg**, rendered by Bede *insula vituli marini* 'island of the sea-calf').

***sēoluc, *sīoluc, *sīluc** OE, 'a gulley, a small drain', found in OE only in *siolucham(m)* KCD 673; this word is suggested by Ekwall (DEPN 402) to explain certain p.ns. in *Selk-*, *Silk-*; it would be a derivative of a word OE **sēol* (from **sihul*) which corresponds to MLG *sīl* 'drain, canal' and is related to seohtre as well as OE *sēon* 'to filter, to ooze'. (*a*) Selkley W, *Silkley* Ha (lēah, cf. *Selkleg* Sf), Silkmore St (mōr), Silkstead Ha (stede, near a lost *Silkeley* Ha).

*sēret OE (Angl, Kt), *sīeret (WSax), 'a dry barren place', is difficult to distinguish from serret. (*b*) Sarratt Hrt 102. [~ sēar, -et.]

serret OFr, 'an enclosure', is not well-evidenced in England: it has been suggested by Skeat for Sarratt Hrt (but cf. sērett).

(ge)set (setu nom.pl.) OE, 'a dwelling, a camp, a place for animals, a stable, a fold', is usually found in the pl. setu in literary documents, sometimes appearing as *seotu*, *seota* with back-mutation; there is therefore no need to explain, as Wallenberg KPN 80 does, such OE p.ns. as *hafing seota*, *bobingseata* BCS 289, *hiredes seota* ib. 539, by postulating an OE **seta*, **seota* (said to mean 'a pasture in open country'). At the same time, *(ge)set* is very difficult to separate from sǣte; according to Ekwall (DEPN), *(ge)set* appears to be very common in East Anglia, but Schram (ZONF iii, 200ff) takes many of the p.ns. to be from sǣte[1]; on formal grounds either would suit the forms of most p.ns., but some compounded p.ns. would favour *(ge)set*. It would also be more likely in parts of the NCy in preference to ON sǽtr (which has a limited provenance) and to sǣte[1] (which does not appear to be used at all there). (*b*) It is compounded mostly with (i) significant words, as in Brenzett K (brende), Cadishead La (an old p.n.), Coxett K (cocc), Dassett Wa (dēor), Hessett Sf (hecg), Hethersett Nf (hǣddre), Lissett YE (lǣs), Stradsett Nf (strǣt), Thornsett Db (þorn), Warser Gate Nt (wall), Winsetts YE (wind), Wintersett (winter), Woodsetts (wudu) YW, (ii) pers.ns. occasionally, as in Adsett Gl, Forncett Nf, Ossett YW, Tarsett Nb, Tattersett Nf, Wetheringsett Sf (from *Wederingas*, that is 'the people of Wetherden Sf', an elliptical formation with -ingas). Cf. also set-copp. [~ OE *settan* 'to settle'.]

set-berg ON, 'a flat-topped hill', as in the Icel and Norw p.ns. *Setberg* (Cleasby-Vigf s.v., NG xi, 32). In ME *set-* often becomes *sed-* by assimilation of *t* to the following *b*. (*b*) Sadberge Du, Sedbergh YW, Sedbury YN. [ON *set* 'a seat', berg.]

*set-copp OE, 'a hill with a fold', possibly also 'a seat-shaped hill', that is, 'a flat-topped hill', corresponding to ON set-berg. (*b*)

Sidcup K 18, and ME f.ns. *Settecoppe*, etc., C 343, Ess 589, Hrt 259, Nt 289. [OE set in the sense 'fold, dwelling' or in that of 'seat' (as in OE *set-hrægl* 'a seat cloth'), copp.]

seten OE, 'a plantation', glossing Lat *plantaria* and found in OE compounds like *feld-seten* which glosses Lat *campus* 'a field' (cf. BT s.v.) and *land-seten* which probably means 'cultivated land', the sense that *seten* itself has in Laws (Ine 68); such a meaning would be appropriate in p.ns. (cf. Mawer, Problems 19 and Sx 561). (*b*) Seaton Boughton K, Oxteddle Sx 355 (an old earthwork which was probably adapted as an enclosure for oxen). [(ge)set, -en.]

setl, seld, sedl, *seðl OE, 'a seat, an abode, a dwelling', occurs a few times in the OE charters, as in *on setl ðorn* BCS 702, *on prestes setel* ib. 769, *to hafocys setle* KCD 1332 (cf. Mdf 115). The variant forms are to be explained in the same way as those of bōðl. In a few cases the meaning is 'seat', probably used to indicate a lofty situation, as in Warshill, etc. (cf. Fägersten, Do 29). (*a*) Sedlescombe Sx 524 (cumb). (*b*) Seattle La 199, Settle YW; Kingsettle Do, So (cyning), Kingslow Sa (cyne), *v.* ān-setl, weard-setl. [(ge)set, -el.]

seðl OE, 'an abode', *v.* setl.

sex, seox, six OE, siex (WSax), num., 'six'. (*a*) Sixhills L, Six Hills Hrt (hyll), possibly Sexhowe YN (haugr).

shingel[1] ME, 'a shingle, a wooden roofing tile', schingled, shingelede, ME adj., 'roofed with shingles', from *scingol OE, 'a shingle', a WGerm adaptation of Lat *scindula* 'a roofing tile' (cf. also OE *scindol* also from Lat *scindula*); for its use cf. also spánn. This word *shingel* is not evidenced in English before 1200 (NED s.v.). It is difficult to distinguish from sengel and shingle[2]. (*a*) *Shingeldhall* K 480, Shingle Hall Ess, Hrt (hall), Shinglewell K (wella), Singlecross Sx (crūc[3]), both referring to a well or a cross covered with a shingled roof; probably also Singleton La 154 (tūn).

*shingel[2], *chingel ME, 'shingle, pebbles', is not recorded before 1578 (NED s.v. *shingle* sb. 2) and is of obscure origin and form. Some spellings point to an original OE **cingel*, others to **singel*; the latter may be correct, as possible parallels noted by NED include Norw *singl* 'small stones' and NFris *singel* 'large gravel'. It is difficult to distinguish from shingel[1]. (*a*) Chingford Ess (OE *cinge-*, ME *Chingel-*, ford), Singleborough Bk 69 (mostly *singel-*, beorg).

shrogge ME, 'a bush', *v.* scrogge.

sīc OE, 'a small stream, esp. one in flat marshland', sík ON, 'a ditch, a trench'; cf. dial. *sike*, *sitch*. In p.ns. sīc was often used of a stream that formed a boundary (cf. examples in Tengstrand 269ff) and so came to denote 'a field, a piece of meadow along a stream', a sense found in ME and later f.ns. (as in Bd 295, C 343, Cu 490, Nt 289, Nth 269, Wa 332, YE 327, etc.). (*a*) Sykehouse YW. (*b*) Sykes YW; Eel Sike Cu (ǣl), Gorsuch La (an old p.n. *Gosford* 'goose ford'), Gussage Do (gyse), Kelsick Cu (kelda), Midsyke YN (midd). [~sīcel.]

sicca Lat adj., 'dry' (cf. drȳge). (*c*) Marston Sicca Gl.

*sīcel OE, 'a small stream'. (*a*) Sicklebrook, Strickle Brook Db. (brōc). [sīc, -el.]

sīd (sīdan wk. obl.) OE adj., 'large, spacious, extensive, long' (esp. in contrast to wīd 'broad' in the phrase *wide and side*). (*a*) Sednor K (ōra), Sicey YE (sǣ), Siddal La, Siddells Nt (halh), Sidebeet La (byht), Sidestrand Nf (strand), Sydling Do (hlinc), Syston L (stān). (*b*) R. Sid D (used as a sb.). [~sīde.]

sīde OE, 'a side, the long part or view of an object', in p.ns. 'the long side of a slope or hill, a hill-side', and in ME 'the land extending alongside a river or lake, the edge of a wood or village'. It is common in the NCy. (*a*) Sidcot So (cot). (*b*) Syde Gl; Birkenside Du (bircen), Edderside Cu (ēdre), Facit La, Fawcett We (fāg), Garside La (garðr), Langsett (lang), Whernside (cweorn) YW. [sīd, -e.]

*sīdling OE, ME, 'a strip of land lying alongside a stream or some other piece of land', is found in f.ns. in C 343, Wo 392. [sīde, -ing[1].]

*siele OE (WSax), 'a willow copse', *v.* sele[2].

*siel(l)ing OE (WSax), 'a willow copse', may lie, according to Ekwall (DEPN), behind (*a*) Sullington (tūn) and (*b*) a lost nearby *atte Sulling* Sx 179. [~salh, -ing[1].]

*sīerett OE, 'a dry barren place', *v.* sēret.

sifeða OE, 'siftings, tares'. (*a*) Seething Lane Ln, Siddle YN (hyll). [OE *sife* 'sieve', -ðe.]

sík ON, 'a ditch', *v.* sīc.

silfr ON, 'silver', *v.* seolfor.

sin- OE prefix, 'huge, great', as in OE *sin-here* 'a host', *sin-snǣd* 'a large piece', OHG *sinfluot* 'flood', and the OE p.n. *sinnleah* BCS 499. (*a*) Syndale K 226 (denu).

sinder OE, 'cinder, slag', probably in allusion to places where cinders were dumped. (*a*) Cinderford Gl (ford, either one across which slag and waste-products of smelting were carried or one with its track built up of cinders or slag, cf. also *Sinderford* BCS 887 also Gl), Cinder Hill K (hyll), Synderborough D (burh), Syndercombe So (cumb).

***sīoluc** OE, 'a drain', *v.* **sēoluc.**

(ge)sīð OE, 'a comrade, a noble, a leader', is possible in (*a*) Sidewood Sr 130 (**wudu**).

six OE num., 'six', *v.* **sex.**

sjón (**sjónar** gen.sg.) ON, 'a view', perhaps used in the sense 'look-out'. (*a*) Shunner Howe YN (**haugr**).

skál ON, 'a bowl, a hollow' (cf. NGIndl 74), difficult to distinguish from **skáli**, is probable in (*a*) Scawton YN 56 (**tūn**), describing a short steep-sided valley.

skáli OWScand, 'a temporary hut or shed', is found in that sense in NCy p.ns. and survives as the rare ME *scale*, Cu dial. *scale*, *skell*, 'a hut' (*v.* NED s.v. *scale* sb. 4). It is an OWScand word and is to be associated with the Norwegian rather than the Danish settlement in England. Although it is found chiefly in the NW (Cu, We, La, YN, YW) and also in ME f.ns. (Cu 490, La 248ff, YN 330), it also occurs, though rarely, in ME in YE 327 and L (as in *Scalehyll*, *Skalesgate* L) and also in Nf, Nth 269. (*a*) Scaleby Cu 106 (**bý**, olim *villa de Scales*), Scalescough Cu (**skógr**), Scalthwaiterigg We (**þveit**, **hryggr**), Scholar Green Ch (**halh**), Skell Gill YN (**geil**); Scarrowmanwick, *Skalmannok* Cu (inversion compounds with OIr pers.ns.). (*b*) Scales Cu, La, YN, Scholes La, YW, Scole Nf. In compounds it is combined with (i) significant words, as in Brinscall (**brende**), Feniscowles (**fennig**) La, Gatesgill Cu (**geit**), Landskill La, Longscales YW (**lang**), Laskill YN (**lágr**), Seascale (**sǽr**), Summersgill (**sumarr**), Winscales, Winskill (**wind**) Cu, and (ii) pers.ns., as in Brianscholes YW, Elliscales La, Gammersgill YN, Simonscales Cu. [~**scēla.**]

***skāling** ME, 'a shieling, a hut, a shed'; the exact significance of this derivative cannot be determined; it is probably an adaptation of **skáli** based on **scheling**. (*a*) Scale Foot YN (**þveit**). (*b*) Scaling YN, Skelling Cu. [**skáli**, **-ing**[1].]

skalli ON, 'a bald head', used of 'a bare hill' (cf. NGIndl 75 and a similar use of **calu**). (*a*) Sca Fell (**fjall**), Scallow (**haugr**) Cu.

skammr ON adj., 'short', probably used also as a by-name in Scampston YE. (*a*) Scampton L (**tūn**).

skarn ON, 'dung'. (*a*) Scarndale YE (dalr), Scarah YW (vað). [~scearn.]

skarð ON, 'an opening, an open place in the edge of something, a gap, a mountain pass'. (*a*) Scarf Hill YN, Scartho L (haugr). (*b*) Scarth Hill La; Aysgarth YN (eik), Ayton Scarth YN (p.n.), Wainscarre Nt 69, Wainscarth Cu 343 (wægn, 'a gap for the passage of a wagon'); cf. also Nt 290, YN 330. [~sceard.]

*skeið ON, 'a course, a track, a race, esp. a race-course'. The root meaning is somewhat obscure but the el. is related to scid, and its other uses in ON such as 'a swift sailing vessel', 'the slay of a loom', *ríða á skeið* 'to ride at full speed', would suggest 'race'; the meaning 'race-course', clearly evidenced in some p.ns., may be a later one. A further meaning 'boundary road' and then 'boundary' is also probable in view of its use in Norw p.ns. of 'a track between fields' (NGIndl 75) and ODan *skede* 'a boundary' (cf. Whitehall, *Essays and Studies in English*, Michigan 1935, 73 ff). (*a*) Scaitcliffe La (clif), Skygates YE 171 (gata, cf. the nearby Race Dale). (*b*) *Brunskaith* Cu 127, Brunstock Cu 109 (bruni), Hesket(h) Cu, La, YN (hestr), Wickham Skeith Sf.

skekill ONorw, skækel OEScand, 'a point, something projecting, a corner'; for its use in p.ns. cf. Norw *Skjekle* (NG i, 115, etc.), Swed *Skäkla* (Modéer, *Småländska Skärgårdsnamn* 72), Dan *Skikkild* (DaSN (Sj) iii, 78). (*a*) Skeckling YE 34 (possibly a derivative **skekling*, *v.* -ing[1]). [*v.* sceacol.]

sker ON, 'a rock, a scar, a reef, a skerry', cf. dial. *scar* 'a rocky cliff, a bed of rough gravel'. (*a*) Skerton La (tūn). (*b*) Scare Cu; Dove Scar (dúfa), Green Scar (grēne), Killing Nab Scar (p.n.), Ravenscar (hrafn) YN, Stonestar (stān), Seawood Scar (p.n.) La.

*skerpin(g) ON, 'a dried-up stream, dried-up barren land', from ON *skarpr* 'dried up', a derivative of this being common in Norw p.ns. such as *Skjerpen* NG iii, 4, *Skjerpa* ib. 293, which denote 'barren land'. (*a*) Skirpenbeck YE 150 (bekkr).

skial ODan, 'a boundary' (cf. DaSN (Sj) iii, 78). (*a*) Skeldike L (dīc), Skelfleet YE 11 (flēot). It may also be thought of in some other p.ns. like Skelton, but cf. scelf, skjalf. [~ON *skilja* 'to divide, separate', skil.]

skil ON, scyl late OE, 'a boundary', an early loan in English or an adaptation of ON *skilja* 'to divide', which was itself borrowed already as OE *scylian* in the sense 'to pay off' (ASC 1049 C), has been suggested for (*a*) Skilgate So and late OE *scylget* BCS 970 Do (geat). [~skel.]

skinnari ON, scynnere ME, 'a skinner'. (*a*) Skinners Well Mx (wella), Skinnerthorpe YW (þorp), Skinningrove YN (gryfja).

skip ON, 'a ship'. (*a*) Skippool La (pōl), Skipsea YE (sǣ).

skirn ON, 'the bright one', used in Norw r.ns. (cf. RN 367); the word is recorded only in the sense 'baptism'. (*b*) Skerne (Beck) YE, R. Skerne Du. [~skírr, ON *skirna* 'to become clear'.]

skírr ON adj., 'clear, bright, pure', applied to streams (cf. skirn), may sometimes have replaced the cognate OE scīr². (*a*) Skirbeck L, Skyer Beck YN (bekkr), R. Skirfare YW (far).

skítr ON, 'dung' (or possibly OE scite with ON *sk*-). (*a*) Skitham La (holmr), Skitwath Cu 27 (vað). [~scite.]

skíð ON, 'fire-wood, a billet of wood, a ski, a snow-shoe', skiða ON 'a stick', are possible in (*a*) Skiddaw Cu 319 (haugr) on phonological grounds (but cf. skýti); *v*. skið-garðr. [~scid.]

skið-garðr ON, 'a wooden fence, an enclosure made with palings'. (*b*) *Skidgarth* Cu 318. [skíd, garðr.]

skjaldari ON, 'a shield-maker'. (*a*) Skeldergate Yk (gata).

skjálf ON, 'a shelf, a seat', recorded only in *hlið-skjálf* 'a seat', a name for the god Oðin's seat, may be found in some p.ns., but in view of its rarity elsewhere these p.ns. may in fact contain a Scandinavianized form of OE scelf, as in (*a*) Skelton Cu, YE, YN (3) (tūn). (*b*) Raskelf YN (rā), Ranskill Nt (hrafn); Hinderskelfe, Skutterskelfe YN, Ulleskelfe YW (pers.ns.). [~scelf.]

skjallr ON adj., 'resounding', probably sometimes used substantivally of 'something resounding' such as a rapid stream or a waterfall; it is difficult to keep apart from scelf and skel. (*a*) Skeldale, Skelden YW (dalr, denu), Skelwith La (vað, near a waterfall), Skill Beck Cu (bekkr). (*b*) R. Skell YW.

skjól ON, 'a shelter', may be thought for some p.ns. like Skelton, etc., but it cannot easily be distinguished from other els. such as skel, skjalf or skjallr.

skjǫldr ON, 'a shield', perhaps in allusion to some topographical feature resembling the boss of a shield. (*a*) Skelda Cu 347 (haugr).

skógr (skógs, skógar gen.sg., skógar nom.pl.) ON, 'a wood', preserved occasionally in NCy ME texts (*v*. NED s.v. *scogh*). (*a*) Skewkirk YW (kirkja), Skewsby YN 30 (gen.sg. *skógs*, bý), Scorborough YE (gen.sg. *skógar*, búð). (*b*) Scaws, Sceugh, Schoose Cu.

In compounds it is found with (i) tree-names, as Aiskew YN (**eik**), Aldersceugh Cu (**alor**), Briscoe, Busco YN (**birki**), Ellershaw Cu (**elri**), Thrunscoe L, Thurnscoe YW (**þyrnir**); (ii) other significant words, as Burscough (**burh**), Greenscoe (**grēne**) La, Lambsceugh Cu (**lamb**), Loskay YN (**lopt, í**), Loscoe YW (**lopt**), Roscoe La (**rá**), Swinscoe St (**swīn**); (iii) words for people, as Briscoe Cu (**Brettas**), Haddiscoe Nf, Scalderscew Cu, Skelderskew YN, Tarlscough La (pers.ns.); cf. also Nt 290, Nth 269, YE 327, YN 330. [~**sceaga**, by ablaut.]

skor, skora ON, 'a cut, a notch, a rift in a rock or precipice', used also in ME of 'a cut, a ditch' as in the *fosse Syrithescore* YE 328. (*a*) Scorton La 164, YN 278 (**tūn**). [~**scora, scoru.**]

skot ON, 'a projecting piece of land, a projecting hill', also used in Norw p.ns. of 'a lumber shoot' (NG v, 288, xiii, 135). (*b*) Scoat Fell Cu 441. [~ON *skjóta* 'to shoot'.]

skøyti ON, 'a shaft, a missile', used figuratively of a rapid stream. (*a*) Skate Beck YN (**bekkr**, cf. also *Scaitebec* YW). [~ON *skaut* 'nook, bend', **skot.**]

skratti ON, 'a goblin, a monster', surviving as NCy dial. *Awd Scrat* 'the Devil'. (*a*) Scarthing Moor, Scratta Nf, Scrathawe Nth (**hagi**), *Scratgate* Cu (**gata**), Scrathowes YN, Scratters YE (**haugr**). [~**scratta**, OHG *scrato*, MHG *schrate* 'a demon, a goblin'.]

skreið ON, 'a land-slide'. (*a*) Scrafield La (**feld**, cf. the local f.n. *Shifting Close*), *Scraithegil* Cu 411 (**gil**). [~**skrið**, by ablaut.]

skrið, skriða ON, 'a land-slide', cf. dial. *scree*. (*a*) Scrithwaite La (**þveit**). (*b*) Scrath YN, The Screes Cu. [~**skreið.**]

skuggi ON, 'a shadow'. (*a*) Scugdale YN (2) (**dæl**).

skurðr ON, 'a cutting, a canal', **skyrþ** OSwed, 'a cut, a cutting', **skyrdh** ODan, 'a stream' (cf. Knudsen, NoB xxiii, 79ff), surviving as ModE dial. *skirth* 'a fen drain, a dike'; both the unmutated and the mutated forms occur. (*b*) Scurth Dike YE 10, Skerth Drain L, Skurff Hall YW. [~**skor, -ð(e).**]

skúti ON, 'a projecting cliff, an overhanging rock', found as ME *scowte* (as in *Sir Gawayn* 2167), dial. *scout* 'a lofty overhanging rock'. (*b*) Scout Moor La, Kinder Scout Db. [~ON *skúta* 'to project', **skýti.**]

skyrþ OSwed, 'a cut', *v.* **skurðr.**

***skýti** ON, 'a crag', has been suggested for (*a*) Skiddaw Cu (**haugr**), but cf. **skíð.** [~**skúti.**]

slā OE, 'a sloe', *v.* **slāh.**

slæd OE (Angl, WSax), **sled** (Kt, Merc), 'a valley'. This el. is very common in OE charter p.ns. (cf. Mdf 117–18) and in ME minor names in some counties (as Bd 295, Bk 259, etc.). In OE it is found but once in independent use in a passage in the OE *Orosius* (II, iv, 76) where the phrase *on an micel slæd* 'into a great *slæd*' loosely renders the Lat *inter montes* 'between the hills'; this would suggest the meaning 'valley', as do some ME contexts (cf. NED s.v. *slade* sb. 1); dial. *slad* (from the OE nom.sg. *slæd*) and *slade* (from OE oblique cases *slæde*, etc.) have a variety of meanings including 'low flat marshy ground, a valley', 'a breadth of greensward in ploughed land, a broad strip of greensward between two woods, generally in a valley'; the latter meaning may well be found in ME minor names (C 343, Nt 290, W 446, *et passim*). Some cognates, such as Norw dial. *slad*(*e*) 'a slope, a hollow', Dan dial. *slade* 'a piece of level ground' and Westphalian dial. *slade* 'a dell, a ravine', seem to have a common idea 'valley', a meaning which is confirmed by the topography of some p.ns. Its combination with *dæl* 'valley', however, would indicate that there was some more particular application which has not yet been determined. (*a*) Sladdacott Co (**cot**), Sleddale We (2), YN (2) (**dæl**), Sledmere YE (**mere**). (*b*) Slade La, Slede K; in compounds, Bagslate La (**bagga**), Castlett Gl (**catt**), Walderslade K (**wald**), Weedslade Nb (**wīðig**).

***slæf** OE, 'mud', cognate with Dan *slaf* 'mud' and related to ON *slafa* 'to slaver', ModE dial. *slab* 'a muddy place, a puddle, sludge'. (*a*) Sladen La 58 (**denu**), Slaley Nb (**lēah**). [~ **slefa**.]

***slæget, *sleget** OE, 'a sheep pasture', recorded only in OE *on ðæt slæget* KCD 1318 Do and surviving as dial. *slait* (cf. Löfvenberg, *Studier i Mod. Språkvetenskap* xvii, 87–94 for a full discussion). (*b*) Slait, Slate(s), Sleight(s) Do, Gl, Ha, W.

***slǣp** OE, 'a slippery muddy place', possibly also 'a slip-way or portage, a slope', is cognate with OHG *sleifa* 'a mire' (that is, 'a slippery place') and **slǣpe**. In OE it is recorded only in p.n. spellings (cf. BT s.v. and Ekwall, Studies[2] 186ff). (*a*) Slapton Bk 100, D (**tūn**). (*b*) Slape Do, Sleap Sa, *Slepe* (now St Ives) Hu; in compounds, Hanslope (pers.n.), Islip Nth (R. Ise, possibly here 'a portage'), Postlip Gl (**pott**), Ruislip Mx (**risc**). [~ OE *slipig* 'slimy', *slipor* 'filthy, slippery', **slipa**, **slifu**, from a root **slip* in ablaut relation to **slaip*, from which *slǣp*, *slǣpe*, **sleipr** are derived; the root idea is 'slip, slide'.]

***slǣpe** OE adj., 'slippery, muddy'. (*a*) Sleep Hill YW (**hyll**). [~**slǣp, sleipr.**]

***slaggi** ME adj., 'muddy', from **slag** ME, 'slippery with mud' first evidenced in 1440 (NED s.v.). (*a*) Slaggyford Nb (**ford**).

slāh, slā (**slān** gen.sg.) OE, 'a sloe, the fruit of the blackthorn'. (*a*) Slaithwaite YW (**þveit**), Slaugham Sx (**hām**), Slocum Wt (**cumb**), Sloley Nf, Wa (**lēah**).

***slāhett** OE, 'a sloe thicket'. (*a*) Sloswick Nt 109 (**wīc**). [**slāh, -et.**]

***slāh-trēow** OE, 'a sloe tree, the blackthorn', not found in OE, but evidenced in ME (NED). (*a*) Slaughterford Sx 177 (**ford**). (*b*) Slaughter(s) Sx 150, 160. [**slāh, trēow.**]

slāh-þorn OE, 'a sloe thorn, the blackthorn', well evidenced in OE, is generally reduced to ME *slaghter*, *sloghter* and would then be indistinguishable from **slāh-trēow** 'sloe-tree' and later from **slōhtre.** Each is possible in (*a*) Slaughterford W (**ford**), Slaughterwicks Sr 288 (**wīc**). [**slāh, þorn.**]

slakki OWScand, 'a small shallow valley, a hollow in the ground', the OWScand assimilated form of an older **slanke* which survives as Dan *slank* 'a hollow'. It is found sometimes in ME minor names (as Cu 491, Nt 290, YE 328, YN 330) and occasionally in p.ns. (*b*) Slack La, YW; Castle Slack Cu (**castel**), Hainslack La (**hegn**), Hazelslack We (**hesli**), Nettleslack La (**netele**), Painslack YE (**pers.n.**).

slate, sclate ME, 'slate', is possible in (*a*) Scaitcliffe La 59 (**clif**), but *v.* **skeið.** [OFr *esclate.*]

***slēa** OE, 'a grassy slope' or the like, cognate with Norw *slaa* 'a grass-grown slope'. (*b*) Slay Down W 329.

slecg OE, 'a hammer'. (*a*) Sletchcot D (**cot**, probably a workshop).

slefa ON, 'saliva', probably also 'mud, sludge'; cf. Norw *Slævdal* (DEPN 406). (*a*) Sleagill We (**gil**). [~**slæf.**]

slege OE, 'slaying, slaughter', probably used in p.ns. in much the same way as **morð.** (*a*) Slayhills K (**hyll**).

***sleget** OE, 'a sheep pasture', *v.* **slæget.**

sleipr ON adj., 'slippery', the source of NCy dial. *slape* 'slippery, smooth'. (*a*) Slapestones Cu 404, 419 (**stān, steinn**), Slapewath YN (**vað**). [~**slǣp(e).**]

***slēt** OE (Angl), ***slīet** (WSax), 'sleet', probably used in p.ns. with the meaning 'mud, sludge', which some cognates have; cf. Löfvenberg 191. (*a*) Slathurst Sx 30 (**hyrst**), Sluts Sx 229 (**land**).

slétta ON, 'a smooth, level field', assimilated from an earlier ON *sleht-* which survives in ModE dial. *sleet, slight*; it is found also in ME f.ns. (Nt 290, YE 328). (*b*) Slates L, Sleights YN (2); Bracelet La (breiðr), Deerslet La (dēor), Mislet We (pers.n.). [~ sléttr, slicu.]

sléttr ON adj., 'smooth, level', found as ME *sliȝt* 'smooth, glossy' (*a*) Sleet Beck Cu (bekkr), Sleightholme (Dale) Cu, YN (holmr). [~ slétta.]

*slicu OE, slyke ME adj., 'smooth, glossy', related to the OE pa.part. *nig-slycod* 'made smooth, polished' and OE *slic* 'a mallet, a hammer (for beating)'. (*a*) Sleekburn Nb (burna). [Related by ablaut to OE **slīc*, ME *sliche* 'mud, slime', ModE *slick* 'pounded ore', etc.].

*slīet OE (WSax), 'sleet, mud', *v.* slēt.

*slif(u) OE, 'a slippery place', probably lies behind certain p.ns. Sleeve Co has normal lengthening of short *-i-* in an open syllable to ME *-ē-*, whilst others have developed spelling pronunciations (like *chine* from OE cinu). The sense is difficult to determine, but a connexion with the root *slip* (cf. slǣp) offers a most likely interpretation; there are phonological difficulties in associating the el. with OE (WSax) *slīef*, *slȳf* 'a sleeve'. (*a*) Slifehurst Sx 107, Slithehurst Sr 241 (hyrst), Slyfield Sr 100 (feld). (*b*) Sleeve Co. [~ slǣp(e).]

slīm OE, 'slime, mud'. (*a*) Slimbridge Gl (brycg), Slimeford Co, D (ford), Slymlakes D (lacu).

*slind OE, 'a slope, the side of a hill', cognate with OSwed *slind* 'side'. (*a*) Slinfold Sx 159 (fald). (*b*) *Slinde* Sx. [~ slinu.]

*slinu OE, 'a slope', related to Norw *slein* 'a gentle slope', Goth *hlains* 'a hill', and slind. (*a*) Slindon St, Sx 96 (dūn), Slynehead La (hēafod). (*b*) Slyne La 185.

slipa, slypa, slyppe OE, 'a soft semi-liquid, a paste, slime, mud', first recorded in the OE *Leechdoms* and then in 1440 (NED s.v. *slip* sb. 1). (*a*) Slipton Nth 187 (tūn). [~ slǣp, Norw *slip*(*a*) 'slime' (as on a fish).]

slipe, slippe ME, 'a slip, a narrow strip of land', as in dial. *slip*, *slipe* and ME f.ns. in Ess 590, Hrt 259, Mx 204. (*b*) Slipe Fm Nth, Sx 280. [~ MLG *slippe* 'a strip'.]

slōh (slōge, slō(e) dat.sg.) OE, 'a slough, a mire'. (*a*) Sloe House Ess (hūs). (*b*) Slough Bd, Bk, Sx, Slow Lane Sr; Dadsley Wo, Pinslow D (pers.ns.), Polsloe D (pōl), Rassler Bk, Ratsloe D (rēad); cf. also ME f.ns. in C 343, Ess 590, Mx 204, Sr 365.

*slōhtre OE, 'a slough, a mire, a muddy place', cognate with LG *slochter* 'ditch', OHG *sluhter* 'slough'; it is found in p.ns. in OE. (*a*) Slaughterford Gl (ford), near (*b*) Slaughter Gl. [~slōh.]

slypa, slyppa OE, 'slime, mud', *v.* slipa.

smæl (smalan wk. obl.) OE adj., 'narrow, thin', smal(r) ON adj. prefix (rare), 'small'. (*a*) Smallburgh Nf (probably from an old r.n. *Smale* 'the narrow one', burh), Smallcombe So (cumb), Smalley Db (lēah), Small Hythe K (hȳð), Smalllands Ess (land), Smallwood Ch (wudu), Smawith YW (viðr). (*b*) As a sb. used of a stream, Smales Nb.

smá(r) ON adj., 'small, little'. (*a*) Smaithwaite Cu (þveit), Smaws YW (hūs).

*smēagel OE, 'a hole, a burrow' (cf. Mawer, Problems 18), recorded in OE only in the p.n. *smeagelhyrst* BCS 1114 and in a mutated form OE *smȳgels* 'a burrow'. (*b*) *Smeghel*, Brooksmarle, Broxmead Sx 262 (brocc). [~smugge, OE *smūgan* 'to creep', -el; *smȳgels* has the suffix -els.]

smeoru OE, 'fat, grease, lard', smjǫr ON, 'grease, butter', usually in allusion to rich pasturage or to places where fat (lard or butter) was produced. The usual meaning in OE is 'fat, grease', but the precise sense 'butter' is sometimes deduced from the evidence of OE *smeoru-mangestre que mangonant in caseo et butiro* 'one who deals in cheese and butter'. (*a*) St Martin's Down Wt, Smeardon D (dūn), Smarber YN (beorg), Smardale We (dæl), Smarden K (denn), Smercote Wa (cot), Smerrill Db (hyll), Smersole K (sol), Smylet YE (hlið).

smēðe[1] (smēðan wk. obl.) OE adj., 'smooth, level', is in late ME sometimes difficult to distinguish from smið. (*a*) Smeathalls YW (halh), Smedmore Do (mōr), Smeetham Ess 418 (tūn), Smestow St (stall), Smithdown La (dūn), Smithfield Mx (feld), Smithills La (hyll).

smeðe[2] OE, 'a smithy', *v.* smiððe.

*smēðett OE, 'a smooth level place'. (*b*) *Smethatte* Sr 359, Smithwick W 247. [smēðe[1], -et.]

*smīte OE, 'a dirty stream', a derivative of OE *smītan* 'to pollute, soil, daub'. (*b*) R. Smite Lei, Nt, Smite Wo 140, Smite Brook Wa.

smið (smiðes gen.sg., smiða, *smeoða gen.pl.) OE, smiðr (smiðs gen.sg.) ON, 'a smith, a worker in metal' (cf. gold-smið), is sometimes difficult to distinguish from smēðe, esp. when it has the Angl back-mutated gen.pl. *smeoða*, as is likely in Smethwick St, or in late

ME when *smithe* became *smethe* through lengthening of short *-i-* to *-ē-* in the open syllable. It is mostly found in the gen.pl. in p.ns. (*a*) Smeaton Co, YN, YW, Smeeton Lei (tūn), Smethcote, -cott Ha, St (cot), Smethwick Ch, St, *Smithwick* Sx (wīc), Smiddales YN (dæl), Smisby Db (bý), Smith's Hall K (hyll).

smiððe, smeðe (smiðan wk. obl.) OE, 'a smithy, a metal worker's shop'. (*b*) Smeeth K, Smitha D 386 (also called *la Forge*), Smithaleigh D; Brownsmith Sx 529, Hammersmith Mx 109 (hamor), Wayland Smith's Cave Brk (OE *Weland*, the smith of Germanic literature), Whitesmith Sx 403. [~smið.]

smjǫr ON, 'grease, butter', *v.* smeoru.

*smol(e) OE, 'a crumb, a small piece', related to OSwed *smula*, Norw *smola* 'crumb', Norw *smol* 'a fragment'; for the sense cf. cruma, crymel. (*b*) Smoles Sx 515.

*smugge OE, 'a small secret place, a hiding place'; cf. Dan *i smug*, Du *ter smuig* adv. 'secretly', OE *smūgan* 'to creep, crawl'. (*a*) Smug Oak Hrt 98. [~smēagel.]

*smȳgels OE, 'a burrow', *v.* smēagel.

*snabbe ME, 'a steep place, a projecting part of a hill or rock, a rugged point', occurs several times in f.ns. in Cu 491; ModE *snab* is not evidenced before 1797. (*a*) Snabdhaugh Nb (halh, from 1325). (*b*) Snab, Snab Murris Cu. [Origin obscure, but cf. Flem *snabbe* 'beak, point of land', ON *snapa* 'to snuffle', snap.]

snād OE, 'something cut off, a detached piece of land or woodland' recorded only in OE charter p.ns. (Mdf 119), except for a single explanatory note in BCS 442, *unus singularis silva ... quem nos theod[is]ce snad nominamus* 'a single wood ... which in the vernacular we call a *snad*'; this suggests the meaning 'a piece of woodland'. As with hāð beside hǣð, the unmutated *snād* appears to belong chiefly to the SE; cf. also C 344. (*a*) Snathurst Sx, Snodhurst K (hyrst), Snodbeam K (bēam). (*b*) Snoad Fm, Snoad's Hole K. [~snǣd.]

snǣd OE (Angl, WSax), snēd (Kt), 'something cut off, a fragment, a detached piece of ground'. (*a*) Snedham Gl (hām). (*b*) Snead Wo, The Sneyd St; Halsnead La 108 (half), Pensnett St, Whipsnade Bd. [~OE *snīðan* 'to cut' by ablaut; snād, sneið.]

snægl, snegl OE, 'a snail', possibly used sometimes as a by-name. (*a*) Snailcroft C (croft), Snailham Sx (hām), Snailslinch Sr (hlinc), Snailwell C (wella). [~snigill.]

✱ *snæp OE, probably 'a boggy piece of land', is recorded only once in OE in the rather ambiguous phrase *andlang dun and snæp* BCS 1124 Sx and later as a Latinized appellative in *unam snappam terre* (Sx 28); it survives as SW dial. *snape* 'a swampy place in a field'; it is found also in f.ns. (as W 446). Topographically 'a boggy patch of ground' appears suitable in most SCy p.ns. But it is very difficult to separate this word from **snap** in the Midl and NCy, esp. in f.ns. (as Bd 297, Nt 290). (*a*) Snapdown D (**dūn**), Snapelands Sx 28 (**land**). (*b*) Snap Sx, W, Snape D, Sf, Sx, W, Snapper D, Snipe End Wt; Barnsnape Sx. [~Swed dial. *snape* (cf. Löfvenberg 192ff), Swed p.ns. *Snapås, Snapen*, Norw *Snapa* (cf. A. Janzén, *Ortnamnen i Göteborgs och Bohus län* ix, 35). Löfvenberg 193 assumes an OE **sneppe* to explain Sneps Sx 510, but this could well be from *snæp*.].

***snafa** OE, 'a spit or strip of land', is possible in (*b*) Snaves K. [~Norw *snav* 'spit of land', OHG *snabul*, MLG *snavel* 'beak, spit of land', **snabbe**, **snap**.]

snap Icel, 'a patch of scanty grass for sheep to nibble at in snow-covered fields, poor pasturage', is not recorded in early Scandinavian (La 17). It would appear to be the source of the rare ME *snape* as in the phrase (*As blaȝt ere þaire wedis*) *as any snyppand snawe þat in þe snape liȝtis* 'as any cutting snow that settles in the *snape*' (*Alexander* 1560). This and the NCy p.n. el. may well be identical, with the meaning 'poor pasture'; but formally it cannot be distinguished from **snæp**. It is probable in (*b*) Snape La, Nt, YN, YW, Snapes YE; Black-, Bulsnape, Boysnope (**boli**), Kidsnape La (**kide**). [Possibly related to ON *snapa* 'to snuffle', *snafðr* 'sharp-scented', **snabbe**, or to **snæp**.]

✱ ***snār** OE, 'brushwood', cognate with Norw *snaar*, Swed *snår* 'brushwood', has been suggested for some p.ns., but the original form of some of them is difficult to determine. (*a*) Snower Hill Sr 284, Snow Hill Ln, Sr (**hyll**), possibly Snoreham Ess 217 (**hām**).

snāw OE, 'snow', used esp. of hills where the snow lies long. (*a*) Snowden YW, Snowdon D, Snow End Hrt (**dūn**), Snowford Wa (**ford**), Snowhope Du (**hop**), Snowshill Gl (**hyll**).

sneare OE, **snara** ON, 'a snare, a trap'. (*a*) Snargate K (**geat**).

snēd OE (Kt), 'a detached piece of ground', *v.* **snǣd**.

sneis ON, 'a twig'. (*b*) Snaizeholme YN 267 (dat.pl.).

sneið ON, 'a slice, a piece cut off, something cut on the slant', used in Scandinavia in a somewhat different way from the cognate OE snǣd; cf. ODan **sneth* (in p.ns.), Norw *sneide* 'a slope', Norw *sneid*, Swed dial. *sned* '(the top of) a gable'. In England it appears to be used, like snād and snǣd, of 'a detached piece of land', a sense which may well be OE in origin. (*b*) Snaith YW (a small part of Snaith parish across the R. Aire in another wapentake); *v*. also sneiðing. [~ON *sníða* 'to cut, slice' and Dan dial. *sned* 'slope' from ODan **snith*, by ablaut.]

*sneiðing ME, 'a detached piece of land', used in p.ns. in the same way as sneið (cf. Lindkvist 81). (*b*) Snaith Ings YW (in Snaith), *Snaythinges* L, *Snaidhinges* Db. [sneið, -ing[1].]

snid(e) OE, 'a cut, cutting, slaughter'. (*a*) Snydles D (lēah). [~OE *snīdan* 'to cut', by ablaut.]

snigill ON, 'a snail', possibly used as a by-name. (*a*) Snilesworth YN (vað). [~snægl.]

snīte (snītan gen.sg., snītena gen.pl.) OE, 'a snipe'. (*a*) Snitterfield Wa (feld), Snydale La (hyll), YW (halh).

*snōc(a) OE, 'a point, a projection' (cf. E & S iv, 67, NED s.v. *snook* sb. 1). (*a*) Possibly Snorescomb Nth 21 (cumb). (*b*) Blyth Nb (olim *Blythesnuke*), *Ravenelesnok* Hu 296, Snook Bank Nb.

snōte ME, probably 'a piece of dry land', occurs in (*b*) Snoots C 262 and a good many f.ns. in C 344, describing points of dry land on the edge of the fens. The ME forms are usually *snote*; it has been connected with ME *snūte* 'snout', in the sense 'projecting point of land' which is first recorded in 1536 (NED), but there are obvious phonological difficulties.

soc OE, 'suck, sucking', in p.ns. probably with the much later recorded meaning of 'sock, moisture collecting in the soil, the drainage of a dunghill' or the like; it may well have had some such sense as 'drain, drainage' in OE in *þas soces seað* 'sock pit' BCS 691. (*a*) Sockbridge We (bred), Soppit Nb (pæð). (*b*) Sock, Old Sock So. [~socen.]

socen OE pa.part., 'wet, saturated'. (*a*) Socknersh Sx 472 (ersc), Sokenholes Sx 123 (hol). [~OE *sūcan* 'to suck', soc.]

sōc-mann OE, 'a soke-man, a man holding land in socage, a man under a lord's jurisdiction but of some personal and economic independence' (cf. Stenton 470, 508). (*a*) Socken Wood YE. [sōcn, mann.]

sōcn OE, soke ME, 'the exercise of judicial power, jurisdiction, the district over which a right of jurisdiction was exercised, an estate'. (*b*) Soke Ha, North Clay Nt 25 (olim *Oswardesbeksokene*, a division of a wapentake), Parkbury Hrt (olim *Parksokne*), Soke of Peterborough Nth, Walsoken Nf (wall). (*c*) Eaton Socon Bd, Kirby le Soken, Thorpe le Soken Ess.

sōfte OE adj., 'soft, yielding, agreeable'. (*a*) Softley Du (hlāw), Nb (lēah).

*sogh, swough ME, 'a bog, a swamp', surviving as dial. *sough* 'a bog, a marsh'. (*b*) Sough La 75. [~sugga; cf. Löfvenberg 194.]

soke ME, 'an estate', *v.* sōcn.

sol[1] (solwe dat.sg.) OE, 'mud, slough, a wallowing place', is fairly common in OE charters; in BCS 282 *ceabban solo* is the name of a *stagnum* or pond, and in later dial. the word denotes 'a dirty pond'. (*a*) Solefield (feld), Sole Street (strǣt), Solton (tūn) K, Sollom La (hegn), Soyland YW (land). (*b*) Soles K, Sollom Cu (dat.pl.); Brasole K (brād), Blakeshall Wo (blæc), Culversole K (culfre), Grazeley Brk (grǣg), Rodsell Sr (rēad), Smersole K (smeoru). [~OE *solian* 'to soil'.]

sól[2] ON, 'the sun', in p.ns. in allusion to sunny hills, as in Norw *Solberg* (NG i, 11, etc., *Ortnamnen i Göteborgs och Bohus län* xx, 83ff). (*a*) Sowber YN, Sulber YW (berg).

*solig OE adj., 'muddy', *v.* sylig.

sompe ME, 'a swamp', *v.* sumpe.

soror (sororum gen.pl.) Lat, 'a sister, a religious sister' (used in p.ns. in much the same way as myncen, nunne); cf. LatAdd 340. (*c*) Buckland Sororum So.

sōt OE, 'soot', possibly in allusion to charcoal burning or the like or to the colour of the soil. (*a*) Soothill YE (hyll).

spǣc[1] OE (WSax), 'speech', *v.* spēc[1].

spǣc[2] OE (WSax), 'a small branch', *v.* spēc[2].

*spǣg OE, 'brushwood', *v.* sprǣg.

*spær OE, 'a spar', *v.* spearr.

spæren OE adj., 'made of chalk or plaster'. (*a*) Spernall Wa (ōfer). [OE *spær(stān)* 'gypsum, plaster', -en.]

spǣtl OE, 'spittle, spit'. (*a*) Spittle Brook Wa (brōc). [~spald.]

*spald OE, 'spittle, spit' (with the variant *spǣtl*) may denote a river or stream, and *spald OE, 'a ditch, a trench', cognate with OHG *spalt*, 'a ditch, a trench'; the sense 'ditch' would seem the most likely in p.ns. The two words are indistinguishable; cf. also

Spaldas. On the relationship of *spald* and *spǣtl* cf. bōðl. (*a*) Poles Pitch Sx (pīc), Spaldwick Hu 247 (wīc), Spalford Nt 207 (ford); Ekwall, NoB xli, 147, may well be right in taking the latter to be from the tribal name Spaldas.

Spaldas OE, an Anglian tribe, settled chiefly in the fenlands of L and YE. (*a*) Spalding L (from OE *Spalda* of the Tribal Hidage, BCS 297, cf. ingas), Spalding Moor, Spaldington YE 234, 241 (-ingas, mōr, tūn); it may occur in one or two other names but it is difficult to distinguish from spald. [~spald, probably in the sense 'ditch'.]

spang OE, 'a clasp, a buckle', probably used in some topographical sense such as that of dial. *spong* 'a long narrow strip of ground'. (*b*) Spong Fm K 423. [~spen.]

spann[1] OE, 'a hand's breadth, a span', is related to spang and spenn, and, as with those els., it is difficult to determine its meaning in p.ns. It may denote something narrow, such as 'a strip of land' or something which joins or links two things, such as 'a foot-bridge', 'a strip of woodland' or the like; *v.* YE 332. This el. is commonest in the WMidl. In early spellings it seems to interchange occasionally with *spenn*. (*a*) Spunhill Sa (hyll). (*b*) Span Wt, Spon End Wa 167, Spon Fm (Flint), Spon Lane St. [~spenn.]

spánn[2] ON, 'a chip, a wooden shingle tile'. (*a*) Spanby L (bý), Spaunton YN (tūn). [~spōn.]

*spearca OE, probably 'brushwood' or 'a shrub' of some kind; it survives as 16th-century *spirk* 'a sprout, a shoot' (cf. NED s.v.). The el. is cognate with OE *sprǣc* 'a shoot, a twig' (*v.* spēc[2]), *spracen* 'a species of alder', ON *sprek* 'a dry twig' and Norw dial. *sprake* 'juniper'. (*a*) Spare Bridge Ess (brycg), Sparket Cu (hēafod), Sparkford Ha, So (ford), Sparkhayne (haga), Sparkwell (wella) D.

*spearr, *spær OE, sperre ME, 'a spar, a shaft, a rafter', is found in OE charter p.ns., mostly in woodland areas (Mdf 121), as in *Wynburgespær*, *-spear* BCS 834, 1125. Its cognates OHG, OLG *sparro* and ON *sparri* denote 'a rafter, a beam', which is no doubt often its sense as a first el. in p.ns. As a final el. it has been suggested to mean 'an enclosure' of some kind, but evidence for this is in fact lacking. (*a*) Sparham Nf (hām), Sparsholt Brk, Ha (holt), Sporle Nf (lēah). (*b*) Holtspar Bk (holt), Rusper Sx (rūh).

spearwa OE, 'a sparrow'. (*a*) Sparrow Fields Wo, Sparrow Herne Hrt.

spēc[1] OE (Angl, Kt), **spǣc** (WSax), from **sprǣc** earlier OE, 'speech', used in p.ns. to denote 'a place where speeches were made at an assembly, a meeting place'. For its use in p.ns. cf. **spell**. It is not always easy to distinguish from **spēc**[2]. On the loss of *-r-* cf. Brunner § 180; the *-r-* still remains in the DB form of Speeton. (*a*) Speeton YE 104 (**tūn**), Spetchley Wo 165 (**lēah**, a hundred meeting-place).

spēc[2] OE (Angl, Kt), **spǣc** (WSax), 'a small branch, a twig, a tendril', used also perhaps like OHG *spah*, *spahho* of 'dry brushwood'; cf. also MHG *spāken* pl. 'dry twigs'. The el. may well be a variant of OE *sprǣc* 'a shoot' with loss of *-r-* as in **spēc**[1] and be related to ON *sprek* 'a dry twig' and to **spearca**. (*a*) Possibly Speccott Barton D (**cot**), Speckington So (**tūn**). (*b*) Speke La 110. [Possibly also related to OE *spāca* 'a spoke'.]

spēd OE, 'success, wealth, abundance', in allusion to land highly productive. (*a*) Spitlye Sx 383 (**lēah**).

speld OE, 'a chip, a splinter', as in ME, is recorded in OE only in the sense 'ember, torch'. (*a*) Speldridge Sx 410 (**ersc**), Speldhurst (**hyrst**), Spilsill (**gesell**) K.

spell OE, 'speech, discourse', is used in p.ns. esp. of places where speeches were made in assemblies and frequently denotes a hundred- or other meeting-place; it is found often with words for 'hill'; cf. also **spell-stōw**. (*a*) Spelhoe Nth (a hundred), Spella Nth (near the point where the boundaries of Nth, O and Wa meet), Speller Hill Nth, Spellow L, Nth (wapentake and hundred meeting places), Spillers Cu (**hōh**), Spellbrook Hrt (**brōc**), Spell Howe YE (**haugr**), Spellow La (**hlāw**), Spelsbury W, Spilsbury Wo (**burh**), Spelthorne Hundred Mx (**þorn**), *Spelverden* C (**ford, denu**), Sperberry Hrt (**beorg**, cf. also *Spelbeorhge* Ess 530).

spell-stōw OE, 'a place where people assembled for speech-making, a meeting-place', as in OE *spelstow* BCS 165, 882. (*b*) *Spelestowe* Wa. [**spell, stōw**.]

***spenn(e)** OE, **spenni** ON, **spenne** ME, 'a clasp, a buckle', developed topographical meanings from the original sense of 'that which spans or joins' (cf. **spann**[1]) but it is difficult to determine these meanings in either p.ns. or literary contexts. In the *Wars of Alexander* 462 it is stated that after the camp of the army was destroyed by a storm *þan ferd þai forth fra fild to fild & freschly assemblis All was sperpolid on þe spene & spilt with þe blastis*, 'then they went forth from field to field and freshly gather together all that had been scattered on the *spene* and ruined by the blasts'; here some general sense like 'area or strip of land' would seem appropriate, and a similar but even wider connotation is implied in the adverbial tag *in spenne* in *Sir Gawayn* 1074 where it means 'there, in that place' and is equivalent to *in stedde*. In *Sir Gawayn* also there are two other uses of the word for which the contexts suggest some such meaning as 'fence, hurdle, hedge' or the like; in line 1709 the hunted fox doubles through groves and listens at hedges and *At þe last bi a littel dich he lepeȝ ouer a spenne, steleȝ out ful stilly by a strothe rande, Went haf wylt of þe wode*, 'at last by a little ditch he leaps over a *spenne*, steals out quietly by the edge of a plantation, he intended to have escaped from the wood'; in line 1896 Gawayn's host has long pursued the fox and *he sprent ouer a spenne to spye þe schrewe*, 'he jumped over a *spenne* to espy the wretch'. In YE 330ff the possible uses and cognates are fully discussed but p.ns. are no more decisive than the literary references. On the whole, some meaning like 'fence, hurdle' and then 'a piece of land enclosed with a fence', seems most appropriate; *v.* also spenning. (*b*) Spen Du, *Spen* La, Spen, Speng Lands, Spen Carr YE, Spen Fm (olim *Munkehaithespen*), Spen Valley YW, *Braithwaitspen* YW. [~ spang, spann.]

*spenning OE, ON, probably 'a hedge, a fence, an enclosure', is evidenced only in p.ns. and presents the same difficulties of interpretation as spenne. There is a Norw word *spenning* in the compound *vidje-spenning* 'a rope made of twisted fibres' and in the p.ns. *Spenningsby* and *Spenningen* (NG ii, 293, 301), where it is thought to have the meaning 'circle of willows which form an enclosure' (cf. YE 331–2). (*a*) Spennithorne YN (þorn), Spennymoor Du (mōr). [spenne, -ing[1].]

*speoht, *speht OE, 'the green wood-pecker', surviving in Scots dial. as *specht* (recorded from c. 1450 NED s.v. *speight*) and cognate with OHG *speht*, MLG *specht*. (*a*) Spettisbury Do (burh), Spexhall Sf (halh).

spere OE, 'a spear, a spear-shaft', used in p.ns. in allusion to woods where such shafts were obtained. (*a*) Sparcells Fm W, Sparsholt Brk, Ha (holt), Sparhanger D (hangra).

*sperte OE, 'a shoot', *v.* spyrt.

spic[1] OE, 'fat bacon'. (*a*) Spitchwick D (wīc).

*spic[2] OE, 'brushwood' or the like, cognate with LG *spike* 'brushwood, an enclosure made of brushwood, a causeway made of brushwood', Du *spik* 'a bridge made of brushwood', Westphalian *spik* 'a fish-weir'; cf. NGN vii, 45 and Mawer, Problems 18. This el. is found chiefly in K, Sr and Sx, as in the f.ns. *le Heth voc' Spytche, Heyrespeche, Thornespych* Sr, *Spicheford* Sx, *Spiche, Cildan spic* (KCD 688), *holanspic* (BCS 175), etc., K. (*b*) Speach Meadow Sr, Busbridge Sr 383, Fastbridge Sr 222 (fearn), Mispies Sx 487 (mōr), Poles Pitch Sx 190, possibly Wansbeck Nb. [Origin obscure, but possibly connected with Lat *spīca* 'spike, an ear of corn, the spike of a plant'.]

*spil OE, spile ME, 'sport, play', related to OE *spilian* 'to play' and cognate with OHG, OSax, OFris *spil* 'sport'. (*a*) Spilcombe D 627 (cumb).

spinele OE, 'a spindle', used in p.ns. of something resembling a spindle in shape. (*a*) Spindlestone Nb (stān), *Spyndelrudene* Sx 265 (ryden).

spinney ME, 'a copse, a small plantation, a spinney', not independently evidenced before 1600 (NED), but found occasionally in ME p.ns. such as *Burthonspynay* (Lat *spineto de Burton*) YE from the 13th century and as a surname *de Spineto* L from the 12th (YE 331 n.); it is common in late minor names. (*a*) Spinney Oak Sr 114. (*b*) Spinney C, Spinney Wood Ess 525. [~OFr *espinei.*]

spīr OE, 'a spike, the blade of a plant', surviving as dial. *spire* 'reeds, rushes', which may also be the meaning in p.ns. (*a*) Spear's Fm (land), Spirewell D (wella).

spirt ModE, 'a jet of liquid', *v.* spyrt.

spitel ME, 'a hospital, a religious house, a house of the Knights Hospitallers', often rendered by Lat *hospitale.* (*a*) Spital Bridge Nth 227, Spitalfields Mx, Spital Moor YN, Spittle Beck YE. (*b*) Spital Cu, L, Nt, Spital le Street L, Spitlar Cross D, Spittal Co, Spittle D, YE, Blyth Spital Nt. (*c*) Spittal Hardwick YW. [~OFr *hospitale.*]

spitu OE, 'a spit or tongue of land', also 'a cooking spit'; the root meaning is 'something pointed'. (*a*) Spithead Ha, Spithope Nb (from 1324).

split ME, 'a split, an opening, a gap', not found before the 16th century (NED). (*a*) Spithurst Sx 314 (hyrst, from 1296). [Origin obscure, but cf. LG *splitt.*]

splott OE, 'a plot of land, a small patch of ground', as in OE *on clænan splott* BCS 1103, still used in this sense in SW dial., cf. also f.ns. in D 691, W 446. (*b*) Plot D 303, Splatt D 137, The Splatts O. [~ **spot.**]

spōn OE, 'a chip, a shaving of wood', perhaps also used like the cognate ON *spánn* of 'a wooden shingle tile'; in p.ns. the sense in compounds is not clear, as in OE *Sponford* BCS 1066 (**ford**), *Sponwælle* ib. 356 (**wella**), or such ME f.ns. as *Sponstrate, Spanfeld* Ess 590. (*a*) Spondon Db (**dūn**), Spoonlets K, Spoonley Gl, Sa (**lēah**). [~ **spánn.**]

spor OE, 'a spoor, a track', may also have had some such meaning as 'inquiry, investigation' in p.ns. which are associated with meeting-places; cf. OE *spyrian* 'to track, investigate', *spyrung* 'investigation'. (*a*) Spurstow Ch (**stōw**). (*b*) Goldspur Hundred Sx.

spora OE, 'a spur', possibly in its later sense of 'a spur of land, a projecting ridge' (which is not recorded independently before 1652, NED), cannot be distinguished from **spor**, but it has been suggested on topographical grounds for (*a*) Spurham D (**hām**), (*b*) Gasper W 181. [~ **spurn.**]

sporier ME, 'a spur-maker'. (*a*) Spurriergate Yk. [~ **spora, -ere.**]

***spot** OE, **spotti** ON, 'a small piece, a bit', used as in Norw *spott* of 'a piece of ground' (cf. *Spot* NG xvi, 329); ME *spotte* 'a small plot of ground' is found chiefly in the NCy and Scotland as in Spott (Scotl), *a spot of erthe* (*York Plays*). (*a*) Spodden Brook La (**brōc**), Spofforth YW (**ford**), Spotland La (**land**). (*b*) Spout House K 223, *Londespott* YW (**land**), Whisperdale YN (**hwīt**). [Ekwall may be right in regarding ME *spotte* in some of these p.ns. as a variant of **splott** (*v.* RN 376), but *spot* itself is fairly well-evidenced in other Germ languages; cf. NED s.v. *spot.*]

spoute ME, 'a spout, a gutter, the mouth of a water-pipe', chiefly in NCy p.ns., esp. in combination with **kelda** in Cu f.ns. (such as *Sputekelde* Cu 87, 407). (*b*) Spout House Cu. [Possibly from an ON *spúta*; cf. MSwed *eld-spūta* 'a flame-thrower', ON *spýta* 'to spit, to spurt'.]

spræ̆c[1] OE, 'speech', *v.* **spēc**[1].

spræ̆c[2] (**sprāca** gen.pl.) OE, 'a shoot, a tendril, a twig'. (*a*) Spreakley Sr (**lēah**). [~ **spēc**[2].]

***spræ̆g**, ***spæ̆g** OE, **spraye** ME, 'brushwood, twigs' possibly used also of 'shoots, a young plantation', with loss of *-r-* as in **spēc**[1].

(*a*) Prehayle Co (halh), Spreacombe (cumb), Sprecott (cot), Spreyton (tūn) D. (*b*) Spray(s) Brk, W, Sprytown D, Hamspray W (all simplex originally), Oaksberry (āc), Ratsbury (rēad) D. [~ spræ̆c².]

sprēot OE, 'a pole, a spear, a spar'. (*a*) Spratton Nth (tūn), Spritsland Co (land).

spring, spryng OE, 'a spring, a well, the source of a stream', found chiefly in such compounds as OE *ǣ-spring*, *wyll-spring* (cf. ēa, wella). In ME the second meaning is first found of 'a young shoot, a small branch', hence 'a young plantation, a copse'; some p.ns. suggest that the latter sense may be older. Both meanings are found in ME f.ns. (Hrt 259, Nt 290). (*a*) Springfield (feld), Spring Hill (hyll) Ess, Springham Sx (hamm), Springthorpe C (þorp), mostly denoting 'copse', Springthorpe L (þorp, a water-spring). (*b*) Derwent Head YN (olim *Springes*, R. Derwent), Hazelspring Cu (hæsel), Woodspring So (wōr), both meaning 'copse'; *v.* orspring. [~ OE *springan* 'to burst forth'; spryng is an *i*-mutated form of the pa.part. grade *sprung-*.]

sprota, sprott OE, 'a sprout, a shoot, a twig'. (*a*) Splatford D (ford), Sproatley YE (lēah), Sprotborough YW (burh). [~ OE *-sprūtan* 'to sprout', spyrt.]

***spurn** ME, 'a spur, a projection, a projecting piece of land'. (*a*) Spurn Head YE (from 1399, replacing oddr). [~ spora, -en.]

spúta ON, 'a spout', *v.* spoute.

***spyrt** OE, spirt NE, 'a spirt, a jet of liquid', may be used in stream-names. It is not evidenced independently before the 16th century, but p.ns. carry its use back several centuries, possibly to OE if any reliance can be put on the spellings of Spirthill W 88. In some later p.ns., esp. in wood-names, it may denote 'a sprout, a young shoot'; *spirt* is recorded in this sense from 1634 (NED) and it is a cognate of sprota. There is also an OE *spyrte*, *sperte* (said to be a Germ loan from Lat *sporta* 'a plaited basket') which is in fact on record and means 'wicker-basket'; Ekwall suggests that this occurs in Spargrove So (grāfa, 'a copse where osiers were cut for basket-making'). All these uses seem to be different sense-developments of the original notion of 'that which bursts forth'. (*a*) Sparkey Wood Ess (gehæg), Sparklie Wood Sr 47, Spartylea, -well Nb (lēah, wella), Sparkmead Ess (mǣd), Spirthill W (hyll), Spurtham D (hamm). (*b*) *Sperte* Wo 392, Spirt Lane Mx, Spurt Street Bk 158. [~ sprota.]

staca OE, 'a stake', may be used in some specific sense in p.ns., such as 'boundary post'; ME *stake* denoted 'a stake used in execution by burning' and OE *stacung* 'the piercing of an effigy in witchcraft'. (*a*) Stagsden Bd (denu), Stakehill La (hyll), Stathern La (þyrne). (*b*) *Thieve Stake* Wa (þēof).

*stacing OE, 'something marked out or enclosed with stakes', probably 'a fishing enclosure' in *Stakynge juxta Temede*, *Stakynbroke* Wo, possibly also (*a*) Stakenford Bridge Wo 150 (ford). [~staca, -ing.]

staddle ME, 'a foundation', *v.* staðol.

stæf (stafa gen.pl.) OE, stafr ON, 'a staff, a stave, a rod', in p.ns. usually in allusion to places where staves were obtained or where they were used as marks. Forms with *Staf-* are from the nom.sg., those with *Stave-* from the gen.pl. (*a*) Staffhurst Sr (hyrst), Staffield Cu 248 (hóll), Stalybridge Ch, Staveley Db, La, YW (lēah), Stowford D 41. (ford).

*stæfer OE, 'a pole, a stake', cognate with ON stafir (cf. Ritter 125–6). (*a*) Stareton Wa 184, Staverton Sf (tūn). (*b*) Quickstavers YW (cwicu). [stæf, -er.]

*stæfren OE adj., 'made of staves'. (*a*) Staverton Gl (tūn). [stæfer, -en.]

stǣgel OE adj., 'steep', also a noun, 'a steep place' (though not recorded as such), surviving as Scots dial. *steel* 'a ridge projecting from a hill, a precipice'. (*b*) Steel Nb 188. [From a root **staig-* (cf. *stāg*, pa.t. of *stīgan*), -el; ~stīg, stigel by ablaut.]

stǣger OE, 'a stair'. (*b*) Steer's Common Sx 107, Broadstairs K (brād). [From the root **staig-* (cf. stǣgel) and -er.]

stæll OE (Merc), 'a fishing enclosure', *v.* stell.

*stǣne OE, 'a stony place'. (*b*) Staines Sr, Stains Sx, Steane Nth, Stein Sx 48, 292, Steyne Wt. [~stān, -e.]

stǣnen OE adj., 'made of stone, stony'. (*a*) Steanbow So (boga, originally brycg), Stenbury Wt (burh), Stenhall, Stenhill, Stiniel D (hall). [~stān, -en.]

stǣner OE, 'stony, rocky ground'. (*a*) Standerwick So (wīc), Sterndale Db (dæl). [~stān, -er.]

*stǣnig OE adj., 'stony, rocky'. (*a*) Stanlake D (lacu), Stonyford Co (ford). [~stān, -ig; ~stānig.]

stǣniht OE adj., 'stony, rocky'. (*a*) Stanmer Ess (mere), Stantyway D (weg), Stentaford (ford), Stentwood (wudu) D. (*b*) As a sb. in Stant Fm Hrt. [~stān, -iht; ~stāniht.]

stæpe OE (Angl, WSax), **stepe** (Kt, Merc), **steppa** (Merc) 'a step', used of stepping-stones; cf. also *bridge called Steppe* W 446. (*b*) Stepps Co (hēah), Plym Steps D 239.

stær(e) OE, 'a starling'. (*a*) Starraton D (tūn).

stæð OE, 'the bank of a river, a shore'; the sense 'landing-place' is not evidenced till the 14th century (NED s.v. *staithe*) and may be due to the influence of the cognate ON stǫð. (*a*) Stafford St (ford). (*b*) Stathe So; it is found also in ME minor names (C 344, Nt 290, YE 328).

***stafir** ON, 'a stake', found as OSwed, Dan *staver*. (*a*) Starbottom YW (botn). [~ stæfer.]

stafn ON, 'a stock, a pole', also 'a gable'. (*a*) Stephney Cu (erg). [~ stafr.]

stafr ON, 'a staff', *v.* stæf.

stagga (staggan gen.sg., staggena gen.pl.) OE, 'a stag'. (*a*) Stagenhoe Hrt (hōh), Stagshaw Nb (sceaga).

stall OE (Angl), **steall** (Kt, WSax), 'a place'. The principal connotations in OE include:

(i) 'a standing-place, a stall for cattle' and the like, glossing Lat *stabulum* (WW 48.10), as in OE *nytena steall* 'cattle stall' (BT), *scypsteal* 'a sheep stall' (BCS 1085); this sense is possible in (*a*) Stalisfeld K (feld, cf. also OE *steallesfeld* BCS 197 Sx), and in ME f.ns. like *Scepestal* C 343, Nt 289 (scēap).

(ii) 'a place, a site, esp. the site of a building or other object', a sense demanded by many OE compounds cited in BT (s.v. *steall*), such as borg-steall, burh-stall, hām-stall, hege-stall, tūn-stall and OE p.ns. like *andlang ðæs aldan geard stealles* 'along the site of the old enclosure' (BCS 428), *mylansteall* (ib. 692); cf. also *sealternsteall* (ib. 507). In some cases like *aldan geard steall* or burh-stall its use may imply that the building or object no longer existed. The sense 'site or place where an object stood' is the one needed in such p.ns. as (*b*) Costal Sr (cot), Finstall Wo 360 (fīn, 'a place for heaping firewood'), Kirkstall YW (kirkja).

(iii) 'a place for catching fish, a fishing pool', a meaning which is probably not original but one which would appear to have been taken over from the *i*-mutated stell. It is probable in (*a*) Stalham Nf (hām), (*b*) Dernestall Lock L (derne), Pickhill Bridge L (pīc 'pike'), Trouts Dale YN (truht 'trout'). [The word is widespread in Germ, as ON *stallr* 'stable', OFris, OHG *stal* 'cattle-stall, a cattle standing', and like other els. such as **stōw** is ultimately related to *stand*, Lat *stāre*, etc.]

stalun ME, 'a stallion'. (*a*) Stalling Busk YN (**buskr**). [~OFr *estalon*.]

stān OE, 'a stone, stone, rock', has a variety of applications in p.ns.

(1) Its common meanings include (i) 'rock, stone' in allusion to the character of the ground, esp. when used as a first el. (almost with the adj. function 'stony, rocky') in the names of streams (such as Stainburn YW), valleys (as Standen Brk), hills and slopes (as Stanage He, Standon Hrt, Stonor O), enclosures, clearings and plots of ground (as Stainland, Stanley YW, Staward Nb, Stonial St and perhaps some cases of Stanton), as well as some ford-names. (ii) 'rock', in allusion to places where it was obtained (as Standhill O, *v.* also **bæc-stān, hwet-stān**). (iii) 'stone paving', esp. in road-names (as Stanway Gl) and perhaps some names in **ford**. (iv) 'a monolith' or other standing-stone(s) (as in Stonehenge W, Stanton Drew So and esp. when it is a final el.); in Hurstingstone Hundred Hu 203 it refers to a large square stone (now called Abbot's Chair) used as a seat at the hundred meeting-place; *v.* also **bug-stān, feoðer-**. (v) 'a boundary stone', as in Fourstones, etc. (vi) 'stone-built', esp. with names denoting bridges, buildings and barrows, with a good many names in **tūn** and perhaps some with **wella**. (vii) possibly 'a stone-built dwelling, a stone building', esp. when combined with a pers.n. (as in Boston L), a meaning which ON **steinn** had developed.

(2) The more usual ME and later spellings of *stān* include *stan-* (with earlier ME shortening in compounds) and *Staun-* (which is an AN spelling of *Stan-*); *Ston-* is a later ME shortening of Midl and SCy *Stone*, the latter being chiefly found in p.ns. of late origin. In the Danelaw there are a good many examples of the replacement of *stān* by ON *steinn*, as in Stainburn (OE *stanburna*), Stainland (DB *Stān-*), Stainley (OE *Stanleh*) YW, and it may be presumed in other p.ns. like Stainforth YW which have OE final els. In a number of Midl and SW p.ns. *stān* undergoes loss of *-n-* before labial consonants, as in Stowey So, Stafford Do, Stoford So, Stowford D, W (cf. Ekwall, *Klaeber Miscellany* 21–7). In final positions it usually appears as *-stone* but sometimes it has been confused with **tūn**; in fact it is sometimes difficult without 12th century or earlier spellings to decide whether the el. is *tūn* or *stān*, except in the NCy where

stān regularly remains until recent times, when StdE *stone* tends to replace it. The modern form *Stain* which appears in some Midl and SCy p.ns. like Staine C 129, Staines Mx 19 (which are apparently from *stān* and not *stǣne*) has not been satisfactorily explained; it may be a spelling-pronunciation based upon the very early spelling *stane* which for one reason or another became the traditional one.

(3) (*a*) As a first el. *stān* is very frequent in one or another of the senses already mentioned: Stafford Do, Stainforth YW; Stamford L, Mx, Nb, YE, Stanford Bd, Brk, Ess, He, K, Nf, Nt, Nth, Wo, Stoford So, Stowford D, W (**ford**), Stainborough YW (**burh**), Stainburn YW, Stambourne Ess (**burna**), Stainland YW (**land**), Stainley YW, Stanley Db, Du, Gl, St, W, YW (**lēah**), Stambridge Ess, Stanbridge Bd, Ha (**brycg**), Stanage He (**ecg**), Standen Brk, La, W (**denu**), Standen Wt, Standon Hrt, St, Stondon Bd, Ess (**dūn**), Standhill O (**gedelf**), Standish Gl (**edisc**), Stanfield Nf (**feld**), Stanion Nth (**ærn**), Stanmore Mx (**mere**), Stanste(a)d Ess, Hrt, K, Sf, Sx (**stede**), Stanton C, D, Db, Gl *et passim*, Staunton Gl, He, Lei, Nt, So, W (**tūn**, mostly with the sense 'stone-built', but in Stanton Drew So 'megalith'), Stanwardine Sa (**worðign**), Stanway Ess, Gl, He, Sa, Stowey So (**weg**, sometimes referring to Roman roads or other ancient tracks), Stanwick Lei (**wicga** 'logan-stone'), Staward Nb (**worð**), Stoborough Do, Stow Barrow So (**beorg**), Stonal St (**halh**), Stoneham Ha (**hām**), Stonehenge W (**hencgen**), Stonehouse Gl (**hūs**), Stonepit K (**pytt**), Stonor O (**ōra**), Stowell Gl, So, W (**wella**).

(*b*) As a simplex p.n., Staine Hundred C, Staines Mx, Stone Bk, Gl, Ha, K, So, St, Wo.

In compounds, it is found as a final el. chiefly with the following categories of first els.:

(i) Descriptive adjs., as Cold Stones YW (**cald**), Kingston Nt 252 (**cyne**), Shenstone St (**scēne**), Syston L (**sīd**).

(ii) Colour adjs., as Blackstone Edge La (**blæc**), Redstone Wo (**rēad**), Whiston La, YW, Whitestone D, So (the latter is a stone at the hundred meeting-place), Whitstone Co (**hwīt**), mostly in allusion to monoliths.

(iii) Words denoting some type of standing-stone or some stone of unusual shape, as Belstone D (**belle**), Copplestone D (**copel**), Featherstone St, YW (**feoðer-**), Froxton Co ('forked'), Holstone

Du (hol), Mainstone He, Sa (mægen, maen), Spindlestone Nb (spinele), Teston K (tær), Wigston Lei (wicga).

(iv) Words indicating boundaries and other land-marks or meeting places, as Folkestone K (folc or a pers.n.), Fourstones (feower), Harston Lei, Hoarstone Wo, Horston Db, Warstone St (hār), Mottistone Wt (mōtere).

(v) Words suggesting religious associations, as Holystone Nb (hālig), rōd-stān.

(vi) Topographical terms, as Dunstan Nb (dūn), Humberstone L (R. Humber), Sherston W (scora), Shilstone D (scelf).

(vii) Words denoting people, as Kingstone So (cyning), Maidstone K (mægd).

(viii) Pers.ns., as Allerston YN, Axton K, Aylstone He, Brixton Sr, Cuddlestone St, Keystone Hu, Tilston Ch, etc.; saints' names sometimes appear as in Boston L (St Botolph), Guthlaxton Lei (St Guthlac);

(ix) Folk-names, as in Chiddingstone K, Lillingstone Bk (-ingas), Ribstone YW (Hrype).

(*c*) As an affix in Thorpe under Stone YN.

[~steinn, stǣne, etc.]

stanche ME, 'a pond', *v.* stank.

*stand OE, 'a stand, a standing-place', and in later use 'a hunter's stand, a station from which to shoot game'. (*b*) High Stand Cu, King's Stand Nt. [~OE *standan* 'to stand'; OE *stand* is recorded but only in the sense 'delay'.]

standard ME, 'the standing stump of a tree', is found in ME f.ns. such as *le Standard* C 344, *Standerdbusk* Nt 277 (both 13th century).

standing ME, 'a standing place, a hunter's stand from which to shoot game' (cf. O. G. S. Crawford, *Archaeol. Journal* lxxviii, 33–5). (*b*) King's Standing Nth, Sx, Kingstanding Wa. [stand, -ing[1].]

stānig OE adj., 'stony, rocky, made of stone'. (*a*) Stanystreet La (strǣt, a Roman road), Stonehill (hyll), Stonereed (rȳd) K, Stoneywell St (wella), Stonydelph Wa (gedelf), Stonyhurst La (hyrst). (*c*) Stone Easton So, Stone Acton Sa, Stoney Stratton So, Stony Stratford Bk. [stān, -ig, ~stǣnig.]

stāniht OE adj., 'stony, rocky' (as distinct from stān in the sense 'paved with stone'). (*a*) Stantway Gl (weg). [stān, -iht, ~stǣniht.]

*stāning OE, 'a stony place', may occur in (*a*) Stannington Nb (tūn), but it is impossible to decide whether this is an appellative (-ing)[1], or an old sg. p.n. in -ing[2], or a pers.n. *Stān* (*v.* -ing[4]). [stān, -ing.]

stank ME, 'a pond, a pool'. (*b*) (The) Stank He, La, YN. A variant *stanche* is found in (*b*) The Staunch Ess. [OFr *estanc*, *estanche*.]

stapel ME, 'a staple, a market, a town or a body of merchants with exclusive trading privileges'. (*b*) Barnet Hrt (olim *la Barnet Staple* 1326). [OFr *estaple*, ultimately from MLG *stapel*, ~ **stapol**.]

***stapled** ME adj., 'stapled, built with pillars'. (*a*) Staple Inn Mx 116 (hall, from 1333). [**stapol**, **-ed**.]

***stapol** OE, 'a post, a pillar (of wood, stone, etc.)'.

(1) This el. is fairly common. (i) As far as its precise use can be determined a *stapol* was a post or pillar of wood or stone (cf. OE *on ðone stenenan stapol* 'to the stone pillar' BCS 391) erected as a landmark to indicate a boundary, a meeting-place, the position of a ford, or the like, for the el. is common in OE charter boundaries (Mdf 123–4); it is found in hundred-names and it is often combined with **ford**. (ii) In wood-names it may well denote places where such posts were obtained. (iii) In compounds with **tūn** or **brycg** its use may sometimes recall the OE meaning 'foundation, platform', for *stapol* glosses Lat *batis* (an error for *basis*, WW 361.3) and the meaning 'raised platform' (that is, 'a platform erected on pillars') seems to be required by *Beowulf* 926; it is also found as a gloss to Lat *patronus* (for *petronus* 'a short staircase leading up to a house') in a list of parts of a common dwelling-house (WW 126.3); the allusion generally is to buildings erected above ground level on a raised platform on a number of supporting posts (cf. also **stapled**).

(2) (*a*) Stalbridge Do (**brycg**), Stapeley, -ly Ch, Ha (**lēah**), Stapenhill Wo 100 (**hyll**), Stapleford C, Ch, Ess, Hrt, L, Lei, Nt, W (**ford**), Staplegrove So (**grāf**), Staplers Wt, Staplehurst K (**hyrst**), Stapleton Cu, Gl, Lei, So, YN, YW (**tūn**), Staploe Bd, Staploe Hundred C (**hōh**).

(b) Staple K, So, Staple Hill Wo, Staple Hundred Sx, W; in compounds Barnstaple D, Barstable Hundred Ess (**beard**), Hextable K (**hēah**), Whitstable K (**wita**), sometimes with pers.ns., as Chipstaple So, Dunstable Bd, Thurstable Hundred Ess (**Þunor**).

[On the cognates in other Germ languages, *v.* NED s.v. *staple* sb. 1; the root meaning seems to be 'that which supports'; *v.* **-ol**.]

star ODan, 'sedge', *v.* **stǫrr**.

staðol OE, **staddle**, **steddle** ME, 'a foundation, base, support', is used later in dial. *staddle* of 'a supporting framework, a framework on which ricks are built', and some similar meaning such as 'platform, supporting framework on which buildings and the like are erected, platform for people to stand on' would be appropriate in p.ns.; cf. also ME minor p.ns. in C 344, Sr 365. (*a*) Staddle Bridge YN (**brycg**), Staddlethorpe YE (**þorp**). (*b*) Costell's Wood Sx 341 (**cot**, cf. also *Cotstedele* in Dorking Sr), *Hundredsteddle* Sx 79, 214 (**hundred**, perhaps in allusion to some platform used at the hundred meetings for the speakers to stand on). [Ultimately related to **stand**, **stede**, **-ol**.]

staðr (**staðir** nom.pl.) ON, 'a place, a site', common in Scandinavia in both the sg. and the pl. forms (cf., for example, NGIndl 76–8), is rare in England and cannot in any case be distinguished from **stæð** and **stǫð**, which would account satisfactorily for most p.ns. (*b*) *Burstath* La 151 (cf. **býjar-staðr**), Ganstead YE (**gagn-staðr**). [~**stede**.]

staup ON, 'a steep declivity, a precipice'. (*b*) Stoupe Brow YN [~**stēap**.]

stēap (**stēapan** wk. obl.) OE adj., 'steep, precipitous'. (*a*) Stapenhill St (**hyll**), Steep Holme So (**holm**). [~**stēpe**.]

stearc OE adj., 'stiff, hard'. (*a*) Startley W (**lēah**).

stearn OE, 'a tern, a sea-swallow'. (*a*) Starnash Sx 441 (**ersc**), *Sternekelde* YE 326 (**kelda**).

stēda OE, 'a steed, a stallion'. (*a*) Studhayes D 641 (**gehæg**); cf. also *Stedefold* Nt 281 (**fald**). [~**stōd**.]

***stedda** OE, 'a horse', has been suggested, used possibly as a pers.n., for (*a*) Stedham Sx (**hām**). [~**stēda**, ON *stedda* 'a mare'.]

steddle ME, 'a foundation', *v.* **staðol**.

stede, **styde** OE, 'a place, a site, a locality'.

(1) This el. presents many difficult problems of interpretation and in many p.ns. it is not possible to define its meaning more closely than 'place, site'. It is ultimately connected with words like Lat *status* 'state', *statio* 'station', *stāre* 'to stand' as well as **stand**, **staðol**, **staðr**, etc., and its root meaning would appear to be something like 'standing place'. There is, of course, no doubt about its generalized meaning in English. In OE it glosses Lat *locus* 'place, spot, locality' and *situs* 'site, the place occupied by a person or thing'. In ME, the meanings 'site of a building', 'a hamlet, village or town or other inhabited place' and in the NCy 'an

estate, a farm' are well attested in literary documents. In p.ns. these meanings also occur. It is used of

(i) 'the site of a building', esp. in the compounds hall-stede, hām-stede and with other appellatives for structures of any kind. From this more precise meanings developed, as

(ii) 'a deserted site', which is possible in some examples of tūn-stede (cf. also burh-stede and a similar use of stall), and

(iii) 'a religious house or foundation', as in Stidd La 144 (a chapelry), Newstead L (a Gilbertine priory), Nt (a priory),

(iv) in other p.ns. which recall some activity, the implication may well be 'a place of communal activity', as in Chipstead K (cēap) or Market Place in Ripon YW (olim *Merketstede*), Flamstead Hrt (flēam), Guildsted K (geld), *Spychestede* Hu 296 (spēc[1]).

(v) 'a farm, a dairy-farm, an estate', chiefly in the NCy, esp. in later p.ns. such as Abbeystead La (*vaccary del Abbey* 1323), Stead YW, etc.,

(vi) in compounds with plant- and animal-names it is impossible to define its use less generally than as 'a place (that is, a pasture, piece of land, building) where such animals or vegetation were habitually found'.

(2) It is difficult to find any sort of semantic connexion between these various meanings, but senses (iii) and (iv) at least suggest that a *stede* was 'a place where groups of things or folk were found together', perhaps applied to a greater variety of objects, creatures and people than with stōw which had a similar but more strictly limited range of application. The numerous examples with tree-names cited below, for example, certainly suggest 'a clump of trees' and in many other names the idea of 'a group of buildings', 'a group of homesteads', 'a place where creatures congregated' and the like is feasible. And it may be for this reason that the el. is rarely compounded with pers.ns. or other personal designations, except where, as in the case of Winestead YE (wīf), it alludes to a group of people.

(3) The el. is comparatively rare in the NCy, except in later p.ns. where it usually denotes 'a farm or estate'; it is also rare in the WMidl and the SW. It is commonest in the counties south-east of a line from the Wash to the Isle of Wight, that is in EAngl, Ess, Hrt, K, Sr, Sx, Ha and Wt. It also occurs in ME minor p.ns. in some counties (as C 344, Ess 590, Hrt 259, Hu 296, Sr 365, etc.).

(4) The common form of this el. is *stede*, but an OE secondary form *styd(e)* is also found in WSax and Angl (cf. hǣm-styde) and this survives as *Stidd* or *Stude*, but in final positions it has usually been replaced by *ste(a)d*.

(5) (*a*) The el. does not occur as a first el. (*b*) Stidd La, Stead YW, The Stude Wa.

In compounds, it is combined with:

(i) Adjs., as Brasted K (brād), Fairstead (fæger), Greenstead (grēne) Ess, Highstead K (hēah), Newstead L, Nb, Nt, YN (nīwe), Twinstead Ess (twinn).

(ii) Words for buildings or other artificial objects, as Fenstead Sf (fīn), Halstead L, La (hall), Hursted W (hūs), Kirkstead L (kirkja), Ringstead Do, Nf, Nth (hring, hringe), Wherstead Sf (hwearf), Worstead Nf (worð); *v.* also burh-stede, hām-stede, hǣm-styde, tūn-stede, and cf. minor p.ns. like *Cotestede* Hu (cot), *Garthsted* L (garðr), *Hulkestede* Hu (hulc), etc. In many of these the meaning is 'site'.

(iii) Words denoting animals and birds, as Cranstead (cran), Henstead Sf (henn), Horste(a)d K, Nf, Sx (hors), Tisted Ha (ticcen), Wrinstead K (wrǣna), all with the meaning 'place where such creatures gathered'.

(iv) Words denoting trees, as Alderstead Sr (alor), Ashtead Sr (æsc), Boxted Sf, Buxted Sx (box), Elmstead Ess, K (elm), Lynsted K (lind), Maplestead Ess (mapuldor), Nurstead K (hnutu), Oxted Sr (āc), Pastead K (peru), Plumstead K, Nf (plūme), Prinsted Sx (peren), probably with the sense 'a clump of trees'.

(v) Words denoting crops and other vegetation, as Binstead Wt (bēan), Whetstead K (hwǣten), Bensted K (beonet), Brumstead Nf (brōm), Hempstead Nf (henep), Nettlestead K, Sf (netele).

(vi) Topographical terms and words descriptive of the ground, as Bastead K (beorg), Felstead Ess (feld), Halstead Ess, K, Lei, Hawstead Sf (hald), Helstead K (hyll), Medstead (mǣd), Morestead (mōr) Ha, Polstead Sf (pōl); cf. also Maxted K (meox), Stanste(a)d Ess, Hrt, K, Sf, Sx (stān), Wanstead Ess, Ha (wenn);

(vii) Words denoting function, as Chipstead (cēap), Guildsted (geld) K.

(viii) Words denoting people, as Winestead YE (wīf), and pers.ns. (rare), as Cowstead K, Harkstead Sf.

stefna ON, 'a meeting', hence 'an administrative district, a meeting place' (cf. Ekwall, PN -ing 83, 181). (*a*) Steyning L (-ing[1], [2]). (*b*) *Crakestevene* (kraka), Kesteven (cēto-) L.

stein-bogi ON, 'a stone arch, a stone bridge'. (*b*) Stonebow Yk. [steinn, bogi.]

steinn (steinar nom.pl.) ON, 'stone, rock', is used in p.ns. in much the same way as stān. As a first el. it denotes the stone of which things are made or which characterizes the ground, or boulders from which some feature is named. As a final el. it generally denotes particular stones or boulders; it was also used in ON of a stone building. In the Danelaw it frequently replaces *stān* and may have done so in p.ns. like Stainfield L (feld) which have *Stain-* exclusively in early spellings but which have OE final els.; it is often itself replaced in later times by *stan-* and *stone*. (*a*) Stainburn Cu (burna), Staincross YW (cros), Staindale YN (dalr), Stainmore We (mōr), Stainton Cu, Du, La, L, We, YN, YW (tūn), Stanhowe YN (haugr), Stanwick YN (ancient rock entrenchments), Stanwix Cu (Hadrian's wall) (both from veggr 'wall'), Stenwith L (vað), Stonegrave YN (gryfja). (*b*) Stain L (a mound of boulder clay), Stainer YW (nom.pl.); *Divlinstones* Yk (ON *Dyflinn* 'Dublin'), Ravenstonedale We (hrafn), Whitestones YN (hvítr). [~stān.]

stell OE (Angl, Kt), stiell (WSax), stæll (Merc), 'an enclosure', as in dial. *stell* 'an enclosure giving shelter to cattle or sheep', in p.ns. usually 'a place for catching fish'; cf. OE *stællo* glossing Lat *captura* (*Lindisf.Gosp*. Luke v. 4) and OE *wæter-steal* and for which the WSax gospel has *fisc-wer* 'fish weir'; apart from *stællo* and one or two p.ns. like OE *Bykenstill* BCS 715, *stiell* is recorded only in the sense 'leap'. The Merc form *stæll* cannot be distinguished in ME from stall and in p.ns. like Stalmine, *piscaria de Depestale* and Smestow St (smēðe), the forms could be from either word, though the context suggests *stæll* in the sense 'fishing pool'. [This el. may be connected with MDu *stel* 'a trap'; though it might be an *i*-mutated form of stall, the semantic connexion is obscure.]

***stelling** OE (Angl), 'a place for standing, a cattle shelter' or the like, surviving as dial. *stelling* 'a cattle fold, a shelter for cattle from the sun'. (*a*) Stella Du (lēah). (*b*) Stelling Nb. [stall, -ing[1].]

steng OE, 'a pole, a staff', as in OE *stenges healh* BCS 890. (*b*) Sting Head Nb. [~stǫng.]

stēor OE, 'a steer, a young bullock'. (*a*) Stafford Sx (ford), Stourbridge C (brycg), Sturgate L (geard).

***steorf** OE, 'poor pasture' or the like, as in OE *biddan stiorf* BCS 502, *to siferþinge steorfan* ib. 208. It occurs chiefly in K and Sx (*v.* Mawer, Problems 16). (*b*) Denstroude K (KPN 207), Dixter, Purster Sx 523. [~ OE *steorfan* 'to die', *steorfa* 'pestilence'.]

steort OE, 'a tail', used in p.ns. of 'a tail or tongue of land, the end of a piece of land, a projecting piece of land' (cf. a similar use of **tægl**); it occurs in OE charter p.ns. (Mdf 125) and ME f.ns. (C 345, D 691, Ess 590, Sr 365, Sx 561, etc.). (*a*) Stirtloe Hu (**hlāw**), Sturthill Do (**hyll**). (*b*) Start Co, D, Start Point D, Stert So, W, Sterts Gl, Storth Oaks K, Sturt Wo; Gastard W (**gāt**), Hunstrete So (**hund**), Woodstreet Do (**wind**).

***stēpe**[1] OE (Angl, Kt), ***stīepe**, ***stȳpe** (WSax), 'a steep place, a declivity'. (*b*) Bucksteep, Hucksteep Sx, Pastheap K (**peru**) (from Kt *stēpe*); Steep Ha, Stype, *la Blakestype* W (from WSax *stȳpe*). [~ **stēap, -e**; cf. **staup**, OHG *stouf* 'cliff'.]

stepe[2], **steppa** OE (Merc), 'a step', *v.* **stæpe**.

stēpel OE (Angl, Kt), **stīepel**, **stȳpel** (WSax), 'a steeple, a tower', is common in that sense as an affix, esp. in allusion to church steeples; it may have been used also of buildings with watch-towers or the like. But in some older p.ns., both simplex and compound, such a meaning is less probable and it may well be that it simply denoted 'a steep place, a declivity', which is of course its root meaning. (*a*) Stepleton He, Sa, Steepleton Do (**tūn**). (*b*) Steephill Wt, Steeple Do, Ess 226. (*c*) As an affix *Steeple* is usually prefixed as in Steeple Ashton W, Aston O, Bumpstead Ess, Claydon Bk, Gidding Hu, Langford W, Morden C; Ainderby Steeple YN. [~ **stēap, -el**.]

***sterne** OE, possibly a metathesized form of **(ge)strēon** 'property', has been suggested by Ekwall for certain p.ns. including (*b*) Sewstern Lei, Syderstone Sf, Tansterne YE (DEPN s.n.); some of these could equally well be from **tjǫrn**, whilst Sternfield Sf (**feld**) may well contain a pers.n.

stewe, stuwe ME, 'a pond or tank for keeping fish till needed for the table', is found in ME minor names such as *les Stues*, etc. Ess 590. [OFr *estui*.]

sticca OE, 'a stick, a rod, a twig, a branch', may enter into some p.ns., but it is difficult to distinguish from **sticce** and **stycce**. It is possible in (*a*) Stickwick D (**wīc**).

sticce[1] OE, of doubtful origin and meaning, has been suggested (W 447) to explain a series of f.ns. in W which invariably appear with ME *stic(c)he*, the earliest example being *clenan sticche* BCS 1127. ModE dial. *stitch* 'a ridge or balk of land' may be associated with this el., but the earlier forms of that word are rather *steche* (NED s.v. *stitch* sb. 3) and it seems to be an EAngl term. In view of the absence of ME *stucche* spellings (which would be expected if this el. were from the common f.n. el. stycce), it seems best to regard *sticce* as the source.

sticce[2] OE adj., 'sticky', is possible in (*a*) Stechford Wo (ford).

*sticel(e) OE, 'a steep place, a declivity'. (*b*) Stittenham YN (dat.pl.). [~ sticol, -el.]

sticol OE adj., 'steep'. (*a*) Sticklepath D (pæð), *Stickleton* Mx (dūn), Winterbourne Stickland Do (lane). (*c*) Stickleball Hill So (ball). [~ stīg, by ablaut, -ol.]

stiell OE (WSax), 'a leap, a fishing enclosure', *v.* stell.

*stīepe OE (WSax), 'a steep place', *v.* stēpe.

stīepel OE (WSax), 'a steeple, a declivity', *v.* stēpel.

*stīg OE, stígr ON, 'a path, a narrow road', glosses Lat *callis* 'a narrow footpath, a mountain track, a cattle track' and Lat *semita* 'a narrow way, a footpath', and this meaning is reflected in the compounds ān-stiga and ein-stigi as well as such phrases as *nearwe stige* 'narrow path' (OE *Riddle* 16.24), *stige nearwe, enge anpaðas* 'the narrow paths, narrow footpaths (*Beowulf* 1409), but it was probably used also more loosely of a road, since it stands in apposition to strǣt in *stræt wæs stan-fah, stig wisode* 'the road was stone-paved, it indicated the way' (*Beowulf* 320). The original root of this and other related words like stigel, sticol, etc., implies a sense 'ascending path'. It is almost impossible to distinguish this el. formally from stigu and some examples may belong to the latter word. (*a*) Stifford Ess, Styford Nb (ford). (*b*) Bransty Cu (brant), Bringsty He (brinca), Gresty Ch (grǣg), Winnowsty L (wægn, wella); Corpusty Nf, Hardisty YW, Ravensty La, Spruisty YW, Thorfinsty La, *Wolmersty* L (all with pers.ns.). [~ OE *stīgan* 'to go, to ascend', stǣgel, stǣger, sticol, stigel, etc.]

stigel, -ol OE, 'a stile, a place devised for climbing over a fence', probably also on topographical grounds 'a steep ascent'; it occurs in ME minor names (C 345, Ess 590, Hrt 259, W 447). (*a*) Stilton Hu 199 (tūn). (*b*) Steel(e) Nb, Sa, Stile Cu; Hamsteels Du (hām), Henstill D (henn), Huntstile So (pers.n.). [~ stīg (by ablaut), -el.]

stīg-rāp OE, 'a stirrup', used in some undetermined sense, possibly from a fancied resemblance (as with geoc, sadol). (*b*) Styrrup Nt 98. [stīg 'step', rāp 'rope'.]

stigu, stig OE, 'a sty, a pen', is almost impossible to distinguish from stīg even in OE, and it is only the context in a compound that is decisive. (*a*) Styal Ch (halh). (*b*) Housty, Houxty Nb (hogg).

stīg-weard OE, stiward ME, 'a steward'. (*c*) Thornton Steward YN. [stīg, weard.]

*stint (*stintes gen.sg.) OE, 'a sand-piper, a dunlin', first evidenced independently in the 15th century, but found in p.ns. in OE (Mdf 126), cf. Ekwall, Studies[2] 92. It cannot easily be separated from stynt. (*a*) Stinchcombe Gl (cumb), Stinsford Do (ford, cf. also *Stintesford* BCS 567, 699 W).

stinting ME, 'a portion of common meadow set apart for one man's use', as in ModE dial., is found in ME f.ns. such as *Stynting* L. It is probably from an ODan **stynting*. [~ stynt, ON *stuttr* adj. 'short'.]

stīpere OE, 'a prop, a post', only recorded in a gloss, has been suggested for (*a*) Stipershill Wa l, 22 (hyll), *le Styperesdon* Hrt (dūn).

stīrc, stīorc, stȳric, stȳrc OE, 'a stirk, a young bullock or heifer'. (*a*) Stirchley Sa (lēah), Storthwaite YN (þveit), Stretton Ch (tūn), Strickland We (land). [~ stēor, -ic.]

stīð (stīðan wk. obl.) OE adj., 'stiff, hard, strong', difficult to distinguish from stīðe. (*a*) Stevenage Hrt (hæcc).

stīðe OE, 'lamb's cress, nettle', is possible in (*a*) Stisted Ess 460 (stede), but it could equally well be from stīð.

*stobb OE, 'a tree-stump', *v.* stubb.

stoc (stoces gen.sg., stoce dat.sg., *stocu nom.pl.) OE, 'a place, a religious place, a secondary settlement'. This el. has been carefully investigated in great detail by Ekwall, Studies[2] 11–43.

(1) The word *stoc* is rare in literary documents. In OE it is once used as a parallel to mynster (Gregory's *Dialogues* 12) and once to render Lat *cella* in the phrase *in Cassinum þæt stoc* 'the monastery of Monte Cassino', with variant readings *þære stowe* (*v.* stōw) and *þam stocwic* (*op. cit.* 172); it is also found in the compounds *stoclif* glossing Lat *oppidum* 'a town' and *stocweard* for Lat *oppidanus* 'townsman'. In ME it occurs only in the *Ormulum* in a general context 'place, stead' (NED s.v. *stoke* sb. 1), and Symeon of Durham (ii, 267) translates Woodstock O as Lat *silvarum locus* 'place of the woods'. It is also worth noting here that in the old

name for Langley Bk 241, *Laverkestoke* sometimes alternates with *Laverkestou*, an interchange of *stoc* and *stōw* already noted above. From these few references it is quite clear that the word had a religious connotation (similar to *stōw*) and meant 'monastery' and the like, in addition to the more general use 'place'.

(2) This religious association of *stoc* is also well attested in p.ns. like Bindon Abbey Do (which was called *Bindonestok* in the 13th century) and Halstock Do (hālig); at Bradenstoke W, Stoke by Nayland Sf and Tavistock D there were monasteries; and the names of several other places have at one time or another incorporated saints' names with *stoc*, as Stockwood Do (olim *Stokes sancti Edwoldi*), Stoke D (St Nectan), Stoke St Milborough Sa (St Milburg, earlier *Godestoch* from god); lastly, Stockland D, Gl belonged to Milton Abbey and Bath Priory respectively, and North and South Stoke So also belonged to Bath Priory.

(3) The root meaning of *stoc*, which is ultimately related to stede, stōw, stand, etc., was probably 'standing place', and in OE, as Ekwall suggests, the *stoc* may have been a place where cattle stood for milking in outlying pastures. Hence it came to mean something like 'cattle farm, dairy farm, esp. an outlying one' as it became necessary with the further exploitation of peripheral lands to erect buildings, huts and dwellings. It then developed the meaning of 'secondary settlement from an older one'. The evidence for the meaning 'dairy farm' is slight (a few p.ns. like *Hurdestoke*, now Stockenham D, from heord or hirde, and Poundstock Co from pund, point to this), but it is a necessary stage in the sense development to 'secondary settlement'.

(4) The meaning 'secondary settlement' or 'outlying farmstead' can be established and the most significant evidence is provided by the combination of *stoc* with the name of some neighbouring place as in Basingstoke Ha from Basing (cf. § 8 *infra*). It is noteworthy too that the majority of examples were originally simplex p.ns. to which distinguishing els. were added later, often after the Conquest, and this fact suggests that a *stoc* was not a place with more than very local importance and that it was dependent on some neighbouring village.

(5) The el. *stoc* also appears in the names of hundreds such as Redbornstoke Bd, but it is not certain whether it could have the meaning 'assembly place', as *stōw* did.

(6) The forms of the word in p.ns. are now usually *Stock* (not common) from the OE nom.sg. *stoc*; *Stoke* from the OE dat.sg. *stoce* or the unrecorded nom.pl.**stocu*; in ME a new pl. *Stokes* developed. The el. is sometimes difficult to distinguish from stocc, esp. as a first el., but usually the context is decisive.

(7) The el. is found in all parts of the country, and it is esp. common in the WMidl and the SW.

(8) (*a*) As a first el., Staughton Bd, Stockton Ch, Du, He, Nf, Sa, W, Wo, YN, Stoughton Lei, Sr, Sx (tūn), Stockland D, Gl (land), Stockport Ch (port), Stocksfield Nb (feld), Stockwood So (near a *Stoctūn*), Stokesby Nf (bý), Stokesley YN (lēah); Stockbury K (olim *Stochingeberye*, 'the burh of the people of a *stoc*').

(*b*) As an original simplex p.n. (often with affixes and sometimes originally in the plural *Stokes*), Stocklinch So, Stockwood Do, Stoke Bk, Ch, D, *et passim*; Stokeinteignhead, Stokenham D, Stokes Ha; Stokeham Nth (dat.pl.).

In compounds, it is found with the following categories of first el., some of which are or may be later additions to an older simplex *stoc*:

(i) Older p.ns., r.ns. and folk-names which had probably become p.ns., as Basingstoke Ha (Basing), Bradenstoke W (Braydon), Calstock Do (Callington), Chardstock D (Chard), Chew Stoke So (Chew or R. Chew), Costock Nth (olim *Cortingestoches*, *v.* ingas), Greystoke Cu (R. Cray), Meonstoke Ha (Meon or R. Meon), Navestock Ess (Nazcing), Severn Stoke Wo (R. Severn), Tavistock D (R. Tavy), Tawstock D (R. Taw), Winterbourne Stoke W.

(ii) Topographical words, as Brigstock Nth (brycg), Poolstock La (pōl), Woodstock O (wudu).

(iii) Words associated with husbandry, as Linstock Cu (līn), Lostock La (hlōse), Poundstock Co (pund), Stockenham Sf (olim *Hurdestoke*, heord or hirde), Winterstoke So (winter, 'a *stoc* used in winter').

(iv) Bird-names, as Crastock Sr (crāwe), Larkstoke Gl, Laverstock W, Laverstoke Bk 241 n., Ha (lāwerce), Stoke Canon D (olim *Hrocastoc*, hrōc).

(v) Words indicating religious association and saints' names, as Halstock Do (hālig), Hinstock Sa (hīwan, possibly in the sense 'religious household'), Kewstoke So (St Kew), Stockwood D (*Stokes sancti Edwoldi*), Stoke D (St Nectan), Stoke St Milborough Sa (St Milburg, olim *Godestoch*, *v.* god); there are also examples with later affixes, as Stoke Abbott D (from the Abbot of Sherborne), Stoke Bishop Gl (the Bishop of Worcester), Stoke Canon D (the canons of Exeter), Stoke Prior He (the Prior of Leominster), Wo (the Prior of Worcester), as well as other church dedications as in Stoke St Gregory, Stoke St Mary, Stoke St Michael So.

(vi) Pers.ns., as Adstock Bk, Bostock Ch, Edstock So, Frithelstock D, Hadstock Ess, Maxstoke Wa; Redbornstoke Bd (fem. pers.n.).

stocc OE, **stokkr** ON, 'a tree-trunk, esp. one left standing, a stump, a log of wood, a stock', used in p.ns. in these senses (esp. in boundary marks) and also in p.ns. that denote structures made of logs. It is sometimes difficult to distinguish from stoc, esp. in some of the Stocktons (which may mean either 'a tūn belonging to a stoc' or 'an enclosure or farm made of stocks') and Stockleigh, -ley D, Du, Sf (which denotes either 'a lēah belonging to a stoc' or 'stump clearing'). ME spellings for *stocc*, however, are usually *stokk*(*e*), *stock*(*e*), and the combination with particular els. is often decisive. No distinction can be made between *stocc* and ON *stokkr*; the latter had also a variety of applications as in compounds like *stokk-land* 'land cleared of trees', etc. (*a*) Stockbridge Do, Ha, YW (brycg), Stockeld YW (helde), Stockerston Lei (fæsten), Stockett Sa (geat), Stockholm YE (holmr), Stockholt Bk (holt), Stockwell Gl, He, Sr (wella), Stockwith L, Nt (hȳð). (*b*) Stock Bk, K, Wo; Stockham Ch (dat.pl.); Burn Stocks YE (brende), Calfstock K (calu), Hurstock Co, Warstock Wo (hār).

stoccen OE adj., 'made of logs', is assumed from OE *to ðære ealde stoccene sancte andreas cyricean* (BCS 1048 Mx) 'to the old wooden St Andrew's Church', and from the reference to 'the wooden chapel of St Mary, in English called *Stockkin* (emended from *Stocklim*)' beside 'the stone chapel of St Nicholas in English called *Stonin* (that is, the stone one', cf. stǣnen)' in BCS 461. (*a*) Stockbridge Sx, Stockenbridge D (brycg), Stokenchurch Bk (cirice). (*c*) Stocking Pelham Hrt, Stoke Newington Mx. [stocc, -en.]

✱***stoccett** OE, 'a place with tree-stumps'. (*b*) Stockhurst Sr, *Stockett* Ess 578. [stocc, -et.]

***stoccing** OE, **stocking** ME, 'a clearing of stumps, a piece of ground cleared of stumps', first recorded as a verbal sb. in the 15th century, is fairly common in ME f.ns. (as Bd 296, C 345, Ess 590, Hrt 259, Mx 204, Nt 290, YE 328, etc.). (*a*) Stockingford Wa (ford), Stottingway Do (weg). (*b*) Stocking He, St, YN, YW; Benstoken Wo. [stocc, -ing[1].]

stōd OE, 'a stud, a herd of horses'. (*a*) Stadhampton O (tūn is a late addition), Stidham So, Studham Bd (hām, hamm), Stoddah Cu (hōh), Stodday La, Studdah YN (haga), Stody Nf (gehæg), Stodmarsh K (mersc), Stoodleigh D, Studley O, W, Wa, YW (lēah), Studdal K (wald), Studland Do (land). [~ stēda.]

stōd-fald OE, 'a stud-fold, a horse-enclosure'; the word is often applied to ancient enclosures which the Anglo-Saxons used for horse-folds (*v.* IPN 150); OE *stodfald* KCD 736, for example, is the site of Borough Hill Camp Nth 11, *Stodfald* YE 112 is an old site now called Maiden's Grave. (*b*) *Stodfold* L, Stodfold Hundred Bk 40, Stotfold Bd, Du, Stuffle Co, Stutfall Castle K; it occurs in ME f.ns. in Nt 281, Nth 270, Wa 325, YE 328, YN 330. [stōd, fald.]

stofn OE, ON, 'a stem, a shoot from a tree, a tree-stump'. (*a*) Stonesby Lei (bý). (*b*) Stoven Sf.

stōl OE, 'a stool, a seat, a throne', probably in allusion to a seat or stone chair used at an assembly (cf. Abbots Chair Hu 203 and *v.* stān § 1). (*a*) Stoulton Wo 166 (tūn, near a hundred meeting-place).

stólpi ON, 'a stake, a stump, a post', recorded in English from the 15th century as *stulpe*, *stolpe*, occurs several times in ME f.ns. (as C 346, Ess 99, Hrt 261, L). (*b*) Stoop Bridge Ess, *Burnt Stulps* L (brende).

stǫng (stangar gen.sg., stangir nom.pl.) ON, 'a pole, a stave', also used as a standard of measure 'a pole', as in ME f.ns. such as *le Stongs*, *Scortstonges*, *Twelfstong* L (which appear to retain the ON *u*-mutated form *stǫng*). (*a*) Stanghowe YN (haugr), Stangrah Cu (*stangar* gen.sg., hǫfuð), Stank Top La (top). (*b*) Stanger Cu (nom.pl.); Garstang La (geiri), Kettlestang YW (pers.n.), Mallerstang We (moel, bre).

stoppa OE, 'a pail, a bucket', used in some topographical sense of something resembling a pail, 'a hollow', difficult to distinguish from an OE pers.n. **Stoppa*. (*a*) Stopham Sx (hām), Stopsley Bd (lēah); in *Stoppewell* O 16 (wella) it may mean simply 'pail'. (*b*) Stop W.

storc OE, 'a stork'. (*a*) Storrington Sx 161 (tūn).

*stork, *strok ON, probably 'dried-up or drained land', related to

ON *storkna* 'to stiffen' (surviving as ModE dial. *storken* 'to thrive') and by ablaut to stearc. (*b*) Storkhill YE lx, 200–1.

stórr[1] ON adj., 'big, great', is rare in p.ns. in Scandinavia and the Danelaw. (*a*) Storeton Ch (tūn).

stǫrr[2] ON, star ODan, 'sedge, bent-grass'. (*a*) Starbeck YW (bekkr), Star Carr YE (kjarr), Stargill Cu (gil), Star Lode L (fenn, gelād), Starnmire Cu (mýrr).

storð ON, 'a young wood, a plantation, land growing with brushwood', usually in the pl. (*a*) Storwood YE 236 (þveit). (*b*) Storiths YW, Storrs La, Storth We; Dalestorth Nt 125. [~strōd.]

* **stot** OE, 'a horse, an ox'. The exact meaning in OE is not certain; it is glossed *equi uiles* 'poor horses' (Napier, *OE Lexicog*. 56) and it is used in ME of 'an ox, a steer'; it is probably related to ON stūtr 'a bull'. (*a*) Statfold St (fald, cf. also *Stotfold* Nth 270, Wa 325), Stotfield Du (feld), Stottesdon Sa (dūn).

stǫð (stǫðvar nom.pl.) ON, 'a landing-place, a jetty', usually indistinguishable from the cognate stæð, but probable with other ON els. (*b*) Staithes YN; Statham Ch (dat.pl.); Abbot's Staithe YW, Brinstage Ch, Croxleth La (pers.ns.). (*c*) Burton upon Stather L nom.pl.).

stōw OE, 'a place, a place of assembly, a holy place'.

(1) This el., like stede, was certainly used in a general sense 'place' (glossing Lat *locus* 'place', WW 92.8, 334.33). There can, however, be little doubt that its precise meaning was 'a place where people assembled'. In an unusually informative gloss (WW 216.35), Lat *curia, i. domus consilii, conuentus* 'court, that is, council house, meeting' is glossed *gemothus*, that is, 'council house' (gemōt, hūs), with an alternative gloss *stow*, Lat *congregatio* 'a herding together, an assembly'. In origin, *stōw* belongs to the same root as stede, stand, etc., and its root meaning would appear to have been 'a standing place, a place where people stood together' (cf. also stede for a similar connotation). In many compound words it can have only the significance 'place where people assembled', as in OE *burn-stōw* 'bathing place' (burna), *dōm-stōw* 'judgement place', *holding-stōw* 'slaughter house', *leger-stōw* 'burial place', *ōret-stōw* 'wrestling place', *þing-stōw* 'council place', *wæl-stōw* 'battle-field' (lit. 'corpse place'); *v.* also cēap-stōw, cwalm-stōw, mōt-stōw, pleg-stōw, spell-stōw. In other compounds like OE *den-stōw* 'pasture place', *sceawung-stōw* 'observation place' (in allusion to

the hill of Sion), *sundor-stōw* 'special place' or *wīc-stōw*, the significance is not so clear. Some p.ns. clearly retain the meaning 'place where people gathered', as Bristol Gl (brycg), Spurstow Ch (spor), Westow YE (wīf), besides those mentioned (cēap-stōw, etc.). It also explains how *stōw* could come to be frequently used in hundred-names such as Alstoe R, Broxtow Nt, Bunsty Bk, Longstow C, Stow Sf.

(2) The word *stōw* also developed a religious signification through the idea of 'a place where people gathered for religious purposes'. In OE, for example, it is once used to translate Lat *tabernaculum* *(Numbers xii. 5), whilst *to halgum stowum* of BCS 478 corresponds to the Lat *sanctis ecclesiis* of BCS 477. It is frequent in OE literary contexts which refer to places where Christ was and esp. to the place of the Crucifixion (cf. BT s.v.). The Welsh forms of English p.ns. in He, Sa, etc. usually have OWelsh lann 'church' for *stōw*, as in Bridstow (Welsh *Lann san Bregit*, 'St Bridget's church'), Marstow (*Lann Martin*), etc. Other p.ns. incorporate saints' names or are combined with els. which point to a religious association, like cirice, Cristen, god, hālig (*v.* examples in § 5 (*b*) *infra*), as does the OE compound word *gebed-stōw* 'oratory'. In most of these p.ns., the commonest meaning is 'church dedicated to a particular saint', probably with no idea of the original sense 'place where people assembled for the practice of religion' remaining. But it could also denote other types of holy place, such as 'monastery' in Stow L and Bury St Edmunds Sf (olim *Sanctae Eadmundes stow* BCS 1288), 'hermitage' in Plemstall Ch (where Plegmund, Archbishop of Canterbury 890–923, is said to have lived as a hermit) and even 'burial place' in Hibaldstow L (where St Hygebald was buried).

(3) In ME there is evidence of other developments in meaning which are difficult to derive from the two older senses. The generalized meaning 'place' is possible in *Grendestow* D 111 which is combined with post-Conquest surname *Garand*, but this may be merely a feudal addition to an older simplex *stōw* (which would then belong to one of the older categories of meaning). On the other hand, in the 15th-century *Promptorium Parvul.* 478.1, *stowe* is defined as a 'streythe passage betwyx ij wallys or hedgys, *intercapedo*' and in L dial. it denotes 'a sheep-hurdle'; in some such sense it would appear to be found in early f.ns. in L (such as *Half-*

stowe, *Sondystowe*) and frequently in C 345–6 (as in *Hyrauuicstouue*, *cowstowe*, *les Stowes in le Fendykfelde*, and the common *stow-croft* and *stow-way*). The idea of a 'track' or 'passage' is also suggested by the C f.ns. *portas vocat' stowes*, *unum cartestowe*. It can only be supposed that a *stow-croft* was 'a croft enclosed with sheep-hurdles' or 'a croft where animals were herded', and that the meaning of *stow-way* as well as *stow* 'a streythe passage' or (when equated with Lat *porta*) 'a gate or passage (leading from one field to another)' was suggested by the use of sheep-hurdles to prevent animals from straying. The semantic development seems to have been first 'a place where animals were herded and restrained from straying', then 'such a place made of hurdles or the like' and lastly 'the hurdle itself'. This at least would bring these later uses more in line with the original meaning of 'place of assembly'.

(4) The distribution of this el. is not significant, but it is much more common in D and Co and the Welsh border counties, and no doubt its frequency there in the sense 'holy place, church' is closely bound up with Cornish and Welsh interest in hagiology in name-giving. Its later survival in a different sense (§ 3 *supra*) seems to be confined to counties round the Wash (L, C).

(5) (*a*) As a first el. *stōw* occurs only in later f.ns. (cf. § 3 *supra*).

(*b*) As a simplex p.n., Stow C, Ess, Gl, Hu, L, Nf, Sa, Sf, Stowe Bk, C, L, Nth, St, Stow Hundred Sf (named from Stowmarket).

In compounds the el. is found chiefly with the following categories of first els.:

(i) Significant words and adjs., as Bristol Gl (**brycg**), Burstow Sr (**burh**), Fulstow (**fugol**), Horkstow (**horc**) L, Longstow Hu, Longstow Hundred C (**lang**, both originally simplex), Merstow Wo 263 (**mǣre**, in allusion to Evesham Abbey), Spurstow Ch (**spor**); most of these would appear to mean 'place of assembly', whilst Fulstow and Horkstow L may anticipate the developments mentioned in § 3 *supra*.

(ii) Words denoting religious association, as Austy Wood Wa, Halstow D, K, Hastoe Hrt (**hālig**, **hālga**), Cheristow, Churchstow D (**cirice**), Christow D (**Cristen**), Godstow O (**god**, in allusion to the nunnery), Virginstow D (St Bridget the Virgin).

(iii) The names of saints, as Bridestow D, Bridstow He (OWelsh *Lann san Bregit*, St Bridget), Davidstow Co (St David), Edwinstowe Nt (St Eadwine), Felixstowe Sf (St Felix), Hibaldstow L (St

Hygebald's burial-place), Instow D (St John), Jacobstow(e) Co, D (St James), Kenelmstowe (St Kenelm), Marstow He (OWelsh *Lann Martin*, St Martin), Marystowe D (St Mary), Michaelstow Co, Ess (St Michael), Morwenstow Co (St Morwenna), Padstow Co (St Petroc), Peterstow He (OWelsh *Lann petyr*, St Peter), Petrockstow D (St Petroc), Plemstall Ch (Archbishop Plegmund's hermitage), Warbstow Co (St Wærburg), Wistanstow Sa (St Wigstan), Stow L (olim *Marianstowe*, St Mary's Abbey); in most cases these are church dedications.

(iv) Pers.ns., as in Alstoe Hundred R, Broxtow Hundred Nt, Bunsty Hundred Bk, *Eadbaldes stowe* Hundred Nth; such compounds are rare, and, since they are hundred-names, clearly denote 'places of assembly'.

(v) A few compounds occur which offer some difficulty, as Elstow Bd 70, Walthamstow Ess (which may be OE *wilcuma* 'a guest' or *Wilcume*, abbess and queen), Westoe Du 211, Westow YE 145 (which may both be from *wīf*, gen.pl. *wīfa* and denote 'places where women assembled').

strá ON, 'straw'. (*a*) Strellas La 179 (hlāw). [~ strēaw.]

*straca OE, 'a strip of land', first recorded in that sense in 1503 but in p.ns. from the 14th century; in the sense 'strip of iron' (on a wheel or plough) it is found also in the 14th century. An ablaut variant **streca* would best explain some later forms like *streak* but it is impossible to say whether *streak* (ME *streke*) is from this or from another unrelated word, OE *strica* 'a streak'; there has certainly been confusion between the two (cf. NED s.v. *strake*). Ekwall (*v.* Sx 153) has suggested still another original root, OE **strēac* with much the same meaning (cognate with Du *strook* 'stripe, a stroke of a lash'). (*b*) Streak's Gill Sx 454 and Sx f.ns., Homestreet Sx 153. [OE *straca*, *streca* are related by ablaut; ~ strecca.]

strǣl OE, 'an arrow', appears to have been used in some topographical sense such as 'a long narrow strip of land, a projecting piece of land' (cf. Mawer, Problems 18 and a similar development of meaning in the cognate OHG *strala* and gāra). (*b*) Streel(e) Sx 155 (3).

strǣt OE (WSax), strēt (Angl, Kt), 'a Roman road, a paved road, an urban road, a street'.

(1) This el. was used, as the archaeological evidence shows,

chiefly of 'a Roman road' and the use of *strǣt* in the description of the road to the hall Heorot as *stræt wæs stan-fah* 'the road was stone-paved' in *Beowulf* 320 may reflect the poet's acquaintance with such Roman remains. The word did, however, undoubtedly develop the meaning 'paved way' and was used of roads other than Roman (cf. Bd 296). Already in late OE it denotes an urban road, equivalent to Lat *platea*, and it is of course everywhere the commonest el. in major street-names in all urban areas (though gata is also common in the NCy). Still later in dial., it is used of 'a straggling village', as in Barrow Street, Hawk Street W.

(2) The forms *Strat-* and *Stret-* arise in compound p.ns. from the shortening of OE *strǣt* and *strēt* respectively, but the dialectal provenance of these two forms is somewhat obscured in OE by the widespread use of standard WSax spellings and in ME by the general use of traditional Chancery spellings irrespective of dialect. Many names in *Strat-* which should be from the WSax form are thus found outside the WSax area. Brandl's survey of OE dialects based on the distribution of *Strat-* and *Stret-* whilst in the main correct has therefore some anomalies for this reason. (Cf. Brandl, *Zur Geographie der altenglischen Dialekte*, 1915.) Other forms like *Start-* and *Sturt-* are metathesized chiefly from *Stret-*.

(3) (*a*) Startforth YN, Stratford Bd, Bk, Ess, Mx, Nth, Sf, W, Wa, Stretford He, La (ford), Stradishall Sf (gesell), Stradsett Nf (geset), Stratfield Brk, Ha (feld), Stratton Bd, Do, Gl, Ha, Nf, O, Sf, So, Sr, W, Stretton Ch, Db, He, Lei, R, Sa, St, Wa, Sturton L, Nb, Nt, YW (tūn), Streatham Sr (hām), Streatlam Du (lēah, dat.pl.), Streatley Bd, Brk, Streetly C, Wa, Strelley Nt (lēah), nearly all on Roman roads.

(*b*) Streat Sx, Street He, K, La, So, Wt, Strete D. In compounds, Akeman Street, Buckle Street, Ermine Street, Haven Street Wt (hǣðen), Port Street (port), Stanystreet La (stānig), Watling Street, all major Roman roads; *v.* Wo 2, Bd 1–5.

(*c*) As an affix *le Street* suffixed to Appleton, Thornton YN, Chester Du, Spital L, Wharram YE.

[A WGerm loan from Lat (*via*) *strata*, cf. strāt[2].]

strand OE, strǫnd ON, 'land at the edge of a piece of water, esp. the sea, a shore, a bank'. (*a*) Stranton Du (tūn). (*b*) Overstrand (ōfer), Sidestrand (sīd) Nf, Whitby Strand YN (a wapentake).

✱ strang OE adj., 'strong, arduous', has many applications; already in

OE it appears to describe 'firm, compact soil' and 'water with a powerful current'. It could also be used as a by-name. (*a*) Strangeways La 33 (gewæsc), Strangsty YW (stīg 'path'), possibly also Strangaton D (dūn), the last two probably denoting an arduous ascent.

strat[1] OWelsh, **ystrad** Welsh, ***strat** OCorn, 'a wide valley'. (*a*) Straddle He (dæl), Stratton Co (tūn).

***strāt**[2] OE, 'a Roman road', which may be a form of **strǣt**, possibly a pre-thirteenth century latinization of **strǣt**, appears in (*b*) Stroat Gl (which stands on a Roman road and was OE *Stræt* BCS 928).

straumr ON, 'a stream, a river, a current of water'. (*a*) Stroom Dyke Nt 8. [~ **strēam.**]

stray ME, 'a piece of unenclosed common pasture', found only in p.ns. till modern times. (*b*) The Stray (Harrogate) YW, Stray Marshes K, Straypark D. [~ OFr *estraier* 'to stray' (of an animal).]

***strēac** OE, 'a strip', *v.* **straca.**

strēam OE, 'a stream', is very rare; it is found in ME *Stremlake* C 334. [~ **straumr.**]

strēaw OE, 'straw', as in OE *strea wyll* BCS 1119, also used in late p.ns. as a term of contempt, as in (*b*) Straw Hall Nt. (*c*) Stratton Strawless Nf (lēas). [~ **strá.**]

strēaw-berige OE, 'a strawberry'. (*a*) Strawberryhill D, Mx, Nt (hyll), Strawberry How Cu (haugr).

***streca** OE, 'a strip', *v.* **straca.**

***strecca** OE, ***strecche** ME, 'a stretch (of land)', not recorded independently in any sense before the 16th century. (*a*) Strashleigh D 273 (lēah), Stretch Down D 396 (dūn), Stretchford D 521 (ford); cf. also Ess 590. [~ **straca.**]

strengr ON, 'a water-course'. (*b*) Ellingstring YN 231, Kettle Spring YW (pers.ns.), Shell C 200 (olim *Sheldesstreng*, sceldu).

(ge)strēon OE, 'property, treasure', difficult to distinguish as a first el. from the OE pers.n. *Strēon* as in OE *Streonæshalch* YN 126, (now Whitby), *Streoneshalh* KCD 1358 Wo, Strensall YN 13. A variant *(ge)streond* also occurs in OE. (*b*) Ingestre St. [~ **sterne.**]

strica OE, 'a streak', *v.* **straca.**

***strigel** OE, 'a curry comb', used in some undetermined way in f.ns. such as Strills W 447, 449. [~ Lat *strigilis.*]

strind ME, 'a stream', found in the *Owl and Nightingale* 242 (C-text) and as dial. *strine* 'a water channel'. (*b*) Strines Db (ME *Strindes*). [Probably related by ablaut to **strand**.]

***strīp** OE, 'a narrow tract of land' (a sense not recorded till the 19th century), 'a small stream' (recorded in Scots dial. from the 15th century). (*a*) Stripes Hill Wa. (*b*) Stripes Fm Wa.

strōd OE, 'marshy land overgrown with brushwood', found only in OE charter material (Mdf 128), cognate with OHG *struot* 'brushwood', etc. The correctly developed modern form is *Strood* [stru:d]; *strode* is clearly a pronunciation based on traditional spellings, and Stroud [straud] is probably a pronunciation based upon a confusion of older spellings in *stroud* which has been interpreted as from ME *strūd*. (*b*) Strode Do, So, Strood K, Stroud Gl, Stroudgreen Wt 117; Bulstrode Bk (**bula**), Langstrothdale YW, Long Strath Cu (**lang**), Waystrode K (**hwǣg**). It occurs also in ME f.ns. (C 346, Mx 204, Nth 270, Sr 365, W 447). [~ **storð**.]

***strōdett** OE, 'marshy ground, a place overgrown with brushwood'. (*b*) Strettit House K 166. [**strōd, -et**.]

***strōðer** OE, 'a place overgrown with brushwood'. (*b*) Strother Du, Coldstrother Nb (**cald**). [**strōd, -er**.]

***strump** OE, 'a stump', cognate with MHG, MLG *strump(f)* 'stump'. (*a*) Strumpshaw Nf (**sceaga**).

***strūt** OE, 'strife, struggle, dispute' (cf. **þrēap, beadu**, etc.). (*a*) Studborough Nth 29 (**beorg**), Sutton K 202 (**tūn**). [~ OE *strūtian* 'to struggle'.]

stubb, *stobb OE, 'a stub, a tree-stump'. The variant *stobb* (cf. NED s.v. *stub*) may occur in some p.ns. (*a*) Stobswood Nb (**wudu**), *Stubhill* Cu 54 (**hyll**), Stub House Du, YW (**hūs**), Stubsgill Cu (**skáli**), Stubton L (**tūn**). (*b*) Stobs House Du, Cridling Stubbs, Hampole Stubbs, Stubbs Walden YW, Stub Hall La; Stubham YW (dat.pl.); Elstob Du (**ellen**). The el. is found in ME minor names (C 346, Ess 590, Hrt 259, Nt 291, Sr 365). [~ **stybb**.]

***stubbig** OE adj., 'stumpy, stubby, abounding in tree-stumps'. (*a*) Stobbilee Du (**lēah**). [**stubb, -ig**.]

***stubbing** OE, 'a place where trees have been stubbed, a clearing', first evidenced in ME in p.ns. and f.ns. (C 346, Ess 590, Nt 291). (*b*) Stubbing Nt, YN, Stubbinghill Nt 133, Stubbins La. [**stubb, -ing**[1].]

***stum** Corn, 'a bend, a curve', cognate with Welsh *ystum*. (*a*) Tamsquite, Stencoose Co.

***stumbel** OE, 'a stump', cognate with OHG *stumbal* 'blunted', G *stummel* 'a stump', is found chiefly in K, Sr, Sx (cf. also Hrt 259). (*a*) Stumbleholm Sx 208, Stumbleholt Sr 273 (**hol**), Stumblewood Sx 353 (**wudu**), Stumpshill K 9, Tumbler's Green Ess (**tēag**). (*b*) West Humble Sr 82.

***stumblett** OE, 'a place of stumps'. (*b*) Stumlets Sx 375. [**stumbel, -et.**]

stump ME, 'a tree-stump', first recorded in this sense in the 15th century (NED). (*b*) Stumpwell Bk (**wella**). [~MLG **stump.**]

stūr (**stūre** obl.) OE, a common r.n. probably to be associated with Norw *stūr* 'gloomy', MLG *stūr* 'unfriendly', MDu *stūr* 'fierce, heavy'; this group of words is from a PrGerm root **stūr-*, which seems to have meant 'strong, stiff, fierce', but no English derivatives are known apart from the r.ns. For that reason Ekwall (RN 381–2) would prefer a Celtic source, though Jackson (195 note 1) points out that there is no known Celtic root which would provide an explanation. (*b*) R. Stour C-Ess, Ha-W, K, O-Wa, St-Wo, hence Stourbridge Wo (**brycg**), Stourmouth K (**mūða**), Sturry K (**gē**), Stourton St, Wa, W (**tūn**).

stūt[1] (**stūtes** gen.sg.) OE, 'a gnat', possibly used also as a pers.n., is difficult to distinguish from **stūt**[2] and **stútr**. (*a*) Stitchcombe W (**cumb**), Stuchbury Nth (**burh**), Stuston Sf (**tūn**).

***stūt**[2] OE, 'a stumpy hillock', related to ON **stútr** in the sense 'stumpy thing, the butt end of a horn' (cf. also Mdf 128–9). (*a*) South Hill D (**hyll**), probably Stowting K (**-ing**[2]). (*b*) Stout D (2), Stouthaies D, also in ME f.ns. Ess 591; Brimpts D 192 (**brēmel**), Winstout D (pers.n.). [~ODan **stȳting* in the Dan p.n. *Styding*, APhS xviii, 274.]

stútr ON, 'a bullock', is possible in (*a*) Stutton Sf (**tūn**). [~**stot.**]

stuwe ME, 'a fish pond', *v.* **stewe.**

stybb OE, 'a stub, a tree-stump'. (*a*) Stubhampton Do (**hām-tūn**). (*b*) Steep Green W, Stibb Co, Stibb Cross D; Stippadon D (**tūn**); cf. W 447. [~**stubb.**]

***stybbett** OE, 'a place with tree-stumps, a clearing'. (*b*) Stubbetts Sr. [**stybb, -et.**]

***stybbing** OE, 'a place with tree-stumps, a clearing', difficult to distinguish from **stubbing.** (*a*) Stibbington Hu (**tūn**); also in ME f.ns. Nth 270. [~**stybb, -ing**[1].]

stycce (**styccan** gen.sg.) OE, 'a bit, a piece', cannot easily be distinguished from **sticce**[1], except that *stycce* should give ME *stucche* in the SW counties; in the EMidl ME *sticche* could be from either *stycce* or *sticce*. It is probably used in p.ns. of a small plot or strip of ground as in the ME f.ns. *le Hornedestiche*, *Horstych* Hu 296, *le Thwerstich*, *Withenstich* Nt 290, cf. also C 346, Ess 591, Wo 392. It is possible in (*a*) Stickford (**ford**), Stickney (**ēg**) L, two miles apart on a narrow strip between streams (-*k*- is due to ON influence). (*b*) The Stitches C, Stychens Sr 310.

styde OE, 'a place', *v.* **stede**.

styfecing OE, 'a clearing', *v.* **styfic**.

***styfic** OE, 'a stump', related to OE *styfician* 'to root up, to stump up', is found in OE charter names and in the derivative **styfecing** in *þone norðran styfecing* BCS 542 (cf. Wo 392). (*a*) Steeton YW (2), Stewton L (**tūn**), Stetchworth C 119 (**worð**), Stewkley Bk 72, Stukeley Hu (**lēah**), Stiffkey Nf (**ēg**), Stivichall Wa (**halh**). [~ **stubb**.]

***styfiht** OE adj., 'stumpy, covered with tree-stumps'. (*a*) Steetley Nt (**lēah**). [~ **styfic**, **-iht**.]

***stynt** (**styntes** gen.sg.) OE, 'stint, limit', as a first el. difficult to distinguish from OE **stint** 'a dunlin'. (*b*) Stent Sx 524. [~ OE *styntan* 'to blunt, to cut short', **stinting**.]

***stȳpe** OE (late WSax), 'a steep place', *v.* **stēpe**.

stȳpel OE (late WSax), 'a steeple, a declivity', *v.* **stēpel**.

styrc OE, 'a stirk', *v.* **stirc**.

sub, **subtus** Lat prep., 'below, underneath', in affixes with hill- and forest-names (cf. Dickins LatAdd 340); it often replaces **under**, etc. in early spellings of such p.ns. as Stanton under Bardon Lei, Sutton in the Forest, Sutton under Whitestone Cliffe YN. (*c*) Aston and Weston Subedge Gl (**ecg**), Thorpe sub Montem YW (Lat *mons* 'hill'), Westbury sub Mendip So.

subtus Lat prep., 'below', *v.* **sub**.

***succa** OE, 'a sparrow', a possible variant of **sugge** found in ME *heysoke*, ModE dial. *haysuck* 'hedge-sparrow' (by the side of OE *hege-sugge*). It may occur in OE in *succanpyt* BCS 1234 and *succan scylf* ib. 1071. (*a*) Suckley Wo 81 (**lēah**).

***sugga**, ***suga** OE, 'a swamp, a marsh, a bog', related to ME **sogh** and surviving as dial. *sog*, *sugg* 'a swamp, a bog, muddy ground'. It is probably connected with OE *sūcan*, *sūgan* 'to suck' and OE **soc** 'sucking'. Southway So (**weg**) is described by John of Glastonbury (Hist., ed. Hearne i, 11) as *aquosam viam que Sugeweye, id est scrofe uia, dicitur*, 'a watery way which is called *sugeweye*, that is, sow's way', which of course shows confusion with **sugu**. (*a*) Sudbrooke L (brōc), Sugden Sa (dūn), YW (denu), Sugwas He (wæsse).

*sugge (suggan gen.sg.) OE, a bird, possibly 'a sparrow', as in OE *hege-sugge* glossing Lat *cicada, uicetula* and surviving as dial. *hay-suck* 'hedge-sparrow', has been suggested by Ekwall for some p.ns., but it is sometimes difficult to distinguish it from other els. such as sugga and sugu and from the OE pers.n. *Sucga.* (*a*) Sugham Sr (hām), Sugnall St (halh), Sugworthy D (worðig).

sugu OE, 'a sow'. (*a*) Sow Clough La 93 (clōh). [~OE *sūgan* 'to suck', sugga.]

súl ON, 'a post'. (*a*) Solway Firth Cu 39 (vað, the *súl* probably being the Lochmaben Stone). (*b*) Loups YN (hlaup).

sulh (sule obl., sylg, sylh gen.sg., dat.sg., nom.pl.) OE, 'a plough', also 'a ploughland', that is, the amount of land which can be cultivated with one plough, as also with the derivative OE *sulung.* It may also have denoted the furrow made by a plough, and some p.n. compounds such as OE *sulhford* BCS 166, 1331 (Mdf 129) and the topography of others such as Southstone Rock Wo or Souldrop Gap Bd 42 suggest an extension of meaning to 'gully, narrow channel'. ME and modern forms in *Sil-* go back to OE mutated oblique cases. (*a*) Sela Hyn Sa (tūn), Sookholme Nt 97 (hólmr), Soulbury Bk (burh), Souldern O (þorn), Souldrop Bd (þrop), Southstone Wo 79 (stān), Sulgrove Nth (grāf), Sulham (hām), Sulhampstead (hām-stede) Brk. (*b*) Silk Stream Mx (OE *Sulh*), Sillins Wo 320 (ME wk. pl. *sulhene*).

*sulh-mann OE, 'a ploughman'. (*a*) Salmonsbury Camp Gl (burh). [sulh, mann.]

*sulig[1] OE, 'a pigsty', cognate with the rare OHG *sulag* 'pigsty' and found in OE *sulig cumb* BCS 1282 and *sulig graf* ib. 1108, has been proposed by Ekwall for (*a*) Solihull Wa (but cf. sylig).

*sulig[2] OE adj., 'muddy', *v.* sylig.

sumor OE, sumarr ON, 'summer', in p.ns. usually in allusion to fords, roads, dwellings, farms, land, etc., which were used or could be used only in summer; in stream-names it may have reference to the seasonal flow and in a few cases there are allusions to summer festivals. It is more common than winter in p.ns. In a few cases it cannot always be distinguished from an OE pers.n. *Sumor*, ON *Sumarr* and ME *Somer*, *Sumer*, as in Somershall Db (halh), Somersham Hu, Sf (hām), Summer Row Sx, etc. (*a*) Somercotes

Db, L (cot), Somerden K, Summerdown Sx (denn), Somerford Ch, Gl, St, W (ford), Somerley Sx, Summerley Db (lēah), Somerton L, Nf, O, So (tūn), Summergangs YE (gang), Summer Leaze D, W, Summer Lesure C, L (lǣs), Summerscales YW (skáli), Summerseat La (sǽtr), Summertree Sx (a tree or pole decorated for May games). (*c*) Midsomer Norton So (from Midsummer Day, the festival of St John Baptist, the patron saint of the church).

sumor-hūs OE, 'a summer residence'. (*b*) Summerhouse Du. [sumor, hūs.]

sumpe, sompe ME, 'a swamp, a marsh', found in ME f.ns. (C 346). (*b*) The Sump Ess. [~MLG *sump* 'marsh', ModE *swamp*.]

*sumpt, *sunt OE, 'a marsh, a swamp, boggy ground', cognate with OHG *sunft*, MLG *sumpt* 'fen, marsh' and related to ModE *sump*, *swamp*; it occurs in a ME f.n. *Pyllesunt* which is an alternative to *Pillesmore* (mōr) in Somerford Keynes Gl (Nth xlvii, W 448); *v.* Mawer, Problems 18. The el. is found chiefly in Sr and Sx. (*a*) Sompting Sx 201 (-ingas), *Sunton* Cu 358 (tūn). (*b*) Sunt Sr, Sx 191, Sunt Copse W. [~sumpe, -t.]

sund OE, 'the sea, the ocean' (only in poetry in this sense), sound ME, 'a channel'. (*b*) Plymouth Sound D. [~OE *swimman* 'to swim', -d(e).]

sundor, synder OE adv., 'asunder, apart', used as a prefix to denote either 'land or property detached or separated from an estate' or 'land or property of a special kind, that is, private or privileged'. (*a*) Cindery Island Ess (ēg), Sundercombe D (cumb), Sundorne Sa (ærn), Sundridge K (ersc); Sinderleigh D is from *syndred*, pa.part. of *syndrian* 'to separate', lēah; *v.* also sundor-land and W 448. (*b*) Cinders Wo 84 (used as a sb.).

sundor-land OE, 'land set apart for some special purpose, private land, detached land', occurs in glosses to Lat *predium* 'property' and *prediolum* 'small farm' (WW 343.18, 466.24), and in the reference to Bede's place of birth in the lands of the monastery of Wearmouth and Jarrow, the OEBede renders *in territorio* by *on sundurlonde*. (*a*) Sunderlandwick YE (wīc). (*b*) Sinderland Ch, Sunderland Cu, Du, La, Wo, YW. [sundor, land.]

sundri ON adj., 'southern'. (*a*) Swinderby L (bý́).

Sunnan-dæg OE, 'Sunday'; for its use in p.ns. *v.* Sr 410. (*a*) Sunday Burn (burna), Sundaysight (hōh) Nb, Sunday Street K.

sunor OE, 'a herd of swine', may occur in some p.ns. like Sundorne

Sa, Sundridge K, but the early spellings suggest that they are from sundor.

*sunt OE, 'a bog', *v.* sumpt.

super Lat prep., 'on, above', in affixes with hill-, river-names, etc., often replacing on in early spellings of many p.ns. like Barton on the Wolds Lei, Newton on the Moor Nb, Newton on Ouse YN. (*c*) Weston super Mare So (mare 'sea').

superior Lat adj., 'higher, upper', supra Lat adv., 'above, higher up', *v.* infra. (*c*) Peover Superior Ch, Rickinghall Superior Nf.

sūr (sūran wk. obl.) OE adj., 'sour, damp, coarse' (of land). (*a*) Surfleet L (flēot), Surrendell W (denu); Appledore D (olim *Sureapeldor* 'sour appletree', apuldor).

sūre OE, 'sorrel'. (*b*) Sewer D 308.

sūtere OE, sútari ON, 'a shoe-maker', also used as a by-name. (*a*) Sutherland YN (lúndr), Sutherby (bý́), Sutterton (tūn) L. [Lat *sūtor*.]

sūð OE adj., adv., 'south, southern'; the adj. and adv. uses are difficult to separate in p.ns.

(1) The adj. use is the more common and is used of places or objects lying to the south of some other place or facing the south, as in (*a*) Sedrup Bk (þrop), Sidbury Sa, Sudbury Db, Mx, Sf (burh), Soberton Ha, Supperton K, Surbiton Sr (bere-tūn), Southam Gl, Wa (hām), Southchurch Ess (cirice), Southfleet K (flēot), Southwick Du, Gl, Ha, Nth, Sx, W (wīc), Sudbourne Sf (burna), Sudbrooke L (brōc), Sudeley Gl (lēah), Suffield Nf, YN (feld), Suffolk (folc), Sussex (Seaxe), Sustead Nf (stede), Sutton Brk, C, Ch, D *et passim* (tūn). (*c*) As an affix, it is very common, as in Southampton Ha, South Kirkby YW, etc.

(2) The adv. use is not so frequent, but there are several examples of the elliptical formation OE *sūð in tūne* 'place south in the village', as in Seddington Bd 109, Siddington Gl, Sindon's, Sinton, Sodington Wo 60–1, etc.

sūðan OE adv., 'south, southerly', used in p.ns. elliptically, '(place) south of', sometimes with the prep. bī (which rarely survives). (*a*) Sidbury Wo (burh), Siddington Ch (tūn), Sidney Sx, Southenay K (ēa), Southover Sx (ōfer), Sun Doles C (dāl).

sūðer (sūðra wk.) OE adj. 'south, southern', cognate with ON *súðr*, OFris *sūther*, OLG *sūthar-*, is difficult to distinguish from suðerra and some p.ns. cited there may have *suðer*. (*a*) Surrey Sr (gē).

sūðerne (**sūðerra** comp.) OE, **súðrœn** ON, adj., 'southern, southerly'; the comparative may occur in some p.ns. in *Souther-* but the distinction is not kept in ME (*v.* **sūðor**). (*a*) Southernby Cu 246 (**bý**); Sotherton Sf (**tūn**), Southerham Sx (**hām**), Southery Nf, Southrey L (**ēg**).

svartr ON adj., 'black', *v.* **sweart**.

sveinn (**sveina** gen.pl.) ON, 'a young man, a servant, an attendant', borrowed in that sense in ME; it is already found in OE in the compound *bāt-swegen* 'boatswain'. (*a*) Swainby YN (2) (**bý**). [~**swān**.]

svín ON, 'a swine', *v.* **swīn**.

sviri ON, 'a neck, a ridge', *v.* **swēora**.

sviða ON, 'burning', used in Norw of 'woodland cleared by burning'. (*a*) Swithland Lei (**lúndr**). [~ON *svíða* 'to burn'.]

***sviðinn** ON, 'land cleared by burning', surviving as dial. *swithen* 'a moor cleared by burning' (cf. YN 30). (*a*) *Swithenthwaite* Cu 371 (**þveit**). (*b*) Sweden We; Swinsow YN (**swīn**). [~**sviða**.]

sviðnungr ON, 'a place cleared by burning'. (*a*) Swinithwaite YN 256 (**þveit**). [~**sviðinn**, **-ing**[1].]

Swǣfe OE pl., 'the Swabians', as with **Seaxe**, found in p.ns. in an uninflected form. (*a*) Swaffham C, Nf (**hām**). [*v.* Ekwall, NoB xli, 150ff.]

swǣr, swār OE adj., 'heavy'. (*a*) Swarland Nb (**land**).

swæð, swaðu OE, 'a track, a pathway', used also in ME *swathe* of 'a strip of grassland' (probably from the extent of the sweep of a scythe), is cognate with MLG *swat* 'swathe, measure of land' and is found occasionally in ME f.ns. (as C 346, Hrt 259, Nt 291, Nth 270, Sr 366). (*a*) Swayfield Nf (**feld**), Swathling Ha (**-ing**[2]), Swatfield K (**ford**).

***swalg** OE (Angl), ***swealg** (Kt, WSax), 'a pit, a pool' or the like. (*b*) The Swallow YE 189. [~(**ge**)**swelg**, OE *swelgan* 'to swallow'.]

swalwe[1] OE (Angl), **swealwe** (Kt, WSax), 'a swallow'. (*a*) Swalcliffe O, Swallowcliffe W (olim *rupis irundinis* BCS 756) (**clif**), Swallowfield Brk (**feld**), Swallowhurst Cu (**hyrst**).

***swalwe**[2] OE (Angl), ***swealwe** (Kt, WSax), 'a whirlpool, rushing water' or the like, related to **swalg**, MHG *swalm* 'whirlpool', etc., may be the source of the r.ns. Swale Brk, K, YN, and Swallow L.

swan[1] OE, 'a swan', is difficult to distinguish from **swān**[2], but may be assumed in stream- and lake-names. (*a*) Swanbourne Brk (**burna**), Swanlake Co (**lacu**), Swanmore Ha (**mere**).

swān[2] (swāna gen.pl.) OE, 'a herdsman, a swine-herd, a peasant', is sometimes difficult to distinguish from swan[1] and an OE pers.n. **Swān*. (*a*) Santon Bd, Swanton K, Nf (3) (tūn), Swanage Do, Swanwick Ha (wīc), Swanborough Sx (beorg), Swancote Wo, Swannacott Co (cot), Swanley K (lēah), Swanscombe K (camp), Swanshurst Wo (hyrst), Swanthorpe Ha (þrop). [~sveinn.]

swār OE adj., 'heavy', *v.* swǣr.

swathe ME, 'a strip of grassland', *v.* swæð.

swaðu OE, 'a track', *v.* swæð.

*swealg OE (Kt, WSax), 'a pit', *v.* swalg.

swealwe OE (Kt, WSax), 'a swallow', *v.* swalwe.

sweart OE, svartr ON, adj., 'black, dark', usually in NCy p.ns. and often of ON origin. (*a*) Swarcliffe YW (clif), Swartha Brow We (hǫfuð), Swarthgill Cu (gil), Swarthmoor La (mōr).

(ge)swelg, swelh OE (Angl, Kt), *swi(e)lg, *swylg (WSax), 'a gulf, a pit, a whirlpool', is the source of ModE dial. *swilly* 'an eddy, a whirlpool, a gutter washed out of the soil'; it is probable in (*a*) Swillaton D 97 (tūn). (*b*) Swilly D 241. [An *i*-mutated form of swalg; ~swelgend.]

swelgend OE (Angl, Kt), swylgend (WSax), 'a whirlpool, a deep place, an abyss'. (*b*) Sullens Wt 23, Swelling Hill (Ropley) Ha (OE *to ðære swelgende* BCS 786). [~swalg, (ge)swelg.]

*swelle (*swellan obl.), (ge)swell OE, 'a swelling', with a topographical application in p.ns. of 'a rising piece of ground, a hill' (cf. Ekwall, Studies[2] 151); this application to a hill is found in ModE but not before the 18th century (cf. NED s.v. *swell* sb.). The weak form *swelle* is found in OE only in the p.n. *on þe suellen* BCS 300 So. When final, this el. is difficult to distinguish from wella. (*b*) Swell Gl; Bromeswell Sf (brōm). [~OE *swellan* 'to swell'.]

swēora OE, swīra, swȳra, swūra (late WSax), svíri ON, 'a neck', used in p.ns. and dial. *swire* of 'a neck of land, a col, a hollow on the top of a hill or ridge'; in OE *duna swioran* it glosses Lat *juga* in the sense ridges (WW 427.13), and it is also used of 'a narrow strip of water between two shores' (BT s.v.) ON *svíri* is also used of 'a ridge' in *Svíri* in Iceland. (*a*) Sourton D (tūn), Swerford O (ford), Sword Point Hu 190 (ord). (*b*) Swyre, Swyre Head Do; Boulsworth La 67 (buli). It occurs several times in ME minor names in W 448.

sweord OE, 'a sword', appears to be used in p.ns. in some undetermined sense, possibly 'a narrow strip of land of the shape of a sword, a headland', or in allusion to places where swords were found or made; it may sometimes be confused with the OE pers.n. *Sweord* as in Swardeston Nf. (*a*) Sorley D (*on sueordleage* BCS 451, lēah), Swaddicote D (cot), Swarling K (hlinc), Swasedale C (gedelf).

swēte (swētan wk. obl.) OE adj., 'sweet, pure, pleasant'. (*a*) Sutton D, Swetton YW (tūn), Sweethope Nb (hop), Sweetlands D (land), Swetnage W (haga), Sweethay D (gehæg).

sweynt ME pa.part., 'swinged, beaten'. (*a*) Sainthill D (hyll). [OE *geswenced*, pa.part. of *swencan* 'to harass'.]

swice OE, 'a trap, a snare'. (*b*) Sweech K 518, *Swike* C 347. [~OE *swīcan* 'to deceive'.]

*swi(e)lg OE (WSax), 'a pit', *v.* swelg.

*swille OE, swylle (late WSax), 'a sloppy mess, a liquid mess', probably the source of ModE *swill*; it is recorded in OE only in *swyllan healas* BCS 1036 (the name of a place on a stream). (*b*) Swale Bank Sx 353. [~OE *swillan, swilian* 'to swill, wash'.]

swīn[1] OE, svín ON, 'a swine, a pig', fairly common in p.ns. and used of the domestic pig. (*a*) Swilland Sf (land), Swinacle YN 63 (ekla), Swinburn Nb, Somborne Ha (burna), Swinbrook O (brōc), Swinden YW (denu), Swindon Gl, St, W (dūn), Swineford So, Swinford Brk, K, St, Wo (ford), Swineshead Bd (hēafod), Swinfen St (fenn), Swinhoe Nb (hōh), Swincoe St (skógr), Swinside Cu (sætr), Swinton La, YN, YW (tūn).

*swin[2] OE, 'a creek, a channel', probably recorded in *swyn* BCS 1282, is cognate with MDu, Flem *zwin* 'inlet, creek' (cf. Ekwall, Studies[1] 88ff), and is sometimes difficult to distinguish from swīn[1], as in Swineshead L (hēafod) near a lost *Swinefleet* L. (*a*) Swinefleet YW (flēot). (*b*) The Swin Ess, Swine YE 51, *Swine Haven* L.

swīra OE (late WSax), 'a ridge', *v.* swēora.

swite ME, of doubtful meaning and origin, but suggested to be possibly connected with ModE *switch* 'twig, shoot' (which is itself of obscure origin), is certain from p.ns. and f.ns. (*b*) Swite's Fm, Swite's Wood Sr 273, 332, 366.

swithen ME, 'a clearing', *v.* sviðinn.

swough ME, 'a bog', *v.* sogh.

*swylg OE (WSax), 'a pit', *v.* swelg.

swylgend OE (WSax), 'a whirlpool', *v.* swelgend.

syle[1], **sylu** OE (Angl, WSax), ***sele** (Kt), 'a bog, a miry place', sometimes difficult to distinguish from **sele**[2]. (*a*) Selgrave K 286 (**græf**), Syleham Sf (**hām**). (*b*) Bramsells K 83 (**brēmel**). [~**sol**, **-e**.]

syle[2] OE (WSax), 'a willow copse', *v.* **sele**[2].

***sylig**, ***solig**, ***sulig** OE adj., 'muddy', is possible in (*a*) Solihull Wa 67 (**hyll**) and a lost *Solydene* (*loc. cit.*). [~**sol**, **sylu**, **-ig**.]

T

-t, OE noun suffix, from an original *-þa*, *-þō* (Kluge § 117, etc.). related to the suffix -ð(e), but found mostly after *s* and labial and back consonants. It is used chiefly in forming abstract nouns such as OE *cræft* 'skill', *meaht* 'power', *þoht* 'thought', etc., but it is also found in a few p.n. els. where its function is of course concrete, as in byht, hǣst, sumpt, wiht, wrǣst. Cf. also ON gift, topt.

*tacca, *tacce OE, 'a teg, a young sheep', is cognate with OSwed *takka*, Swed *tacka* 'a ewe', and related to tagga (cf. Ekwall, Studies[2] 73ff), but it cannot be distinguished from an OE pers.n. *Tæcca*, *Tacca* (cf. Takeley Ess 535). (*a*) Acton Do (tūn, cf. æt), Tackbear D (bearu), Tackley O (lēah).

tadde OE, 'a toad', *v.* tādige.

* tāde OE, 'a toad', *v.* tādige.

tādige, tadde, *tāde (tāddan, tādan gen.sg.) OE, 'a toad', sometimes wrongly used of the frog since the 14th century. The forms *tādige* and *tadde* are both recorded in OE glosses, the latter being probably a hypocoristic form of the former; *tāde*, possibly evidenced in OE in p.n. spellings such as *Tadanleage* BCS 625 (Tadley Ha) and as ME *tade*, *tode* from the 12th century (NED s.v. *toad*), is also no doubt a shortened form of *tādige*. The el. is difficult to distinguish from the OE pers.n. *Tada* and later on from todde. (*a*) Arracott (cot), Addislade (slæd) D, Taddiford D, Ha (ford), Taddiport D 111 (port), Tadley Ha (lēah), Tadmarton O (mere, tūn), Tathwell L (wella), Toadhill YW (hyll).

*tǣcels OE, probably 'a boundary mark, a boundary'. (*a*) Tachbrook Wa 258 (*Tæcelesbroc* KCD 751, brōc, on the boundary of the old dioceses of Lichfield and Worcester); cf. also OE *Tæcles broc* BCS 1242 Wo. [~OE *tācn* 'sign, symbol', -els.]

*tǣcne OE, 'a beacon', a by-form of OE *tācn* 'a sign, a symbol, a token'. (*b*) Teeton Nth 88. [~tǣcels.]

tæfl(e), tefle OE, 'a chess-board', may, as DEPN 440 notes, have had some topographical application such as 'plateau' as in G *Zabelstein*, Du *Tafelberg*; it may also have denoted 'the flat stones forming the track of a ford'. In addition, it may be recalled that ME *tavele*, *tevele* 'to contend at dice, etc.' was also used in a more general sense 'to argue, strive' and some such application in p.ns.

to 'land in dispute' (cf. þrēap), as proposed in Sx 329, is not out of the question. The el. is in any case difficult to distinguish from the OE pers.n. *Theabul.* (*a*) Tablehurst Sx (hyrst), Tellisford So, possibly Thelsford Wa (ford). [~Lat *tabula* 'a board, a panel'.]

tægl OE, taile ME, 'a tail', used like steort in some topographical sense such as 'a tail of land, a piece of land projecting out from a larger piece' (as in Scots dial. *tail*), or 'the bottom end of a pool or stream'. (*b*) Tail So; Bartle La (bere), Croxdale Du (pers.n.), Pondtail Sr (pond); also in ME f.ns. (C 347, W 448).

(ge)tæl (-tælan wk. obl.) OE adj., 'quick, swift', used substantivally of a river. (*b*) R. Tale D (OE *on tælen*).

tǣnel OE, 'a wicker-basket', probably in allusion to a place where osiers were got for basket-making or where baskets were made. (*a*) Tanholt Nth 235 (holt). [~tān, -el.]

tæppa OE, 'a peg, a spigot', in allusion to a wood where wood for pegs was got. (*a*) Tapeley D (lēah).

tær, ter (tæran wk. obl.) OE adj., 'gaping, cleft, torn'. (*a*) Teston K (stān). [~OE *teran* 'to tear'.]

tǣse (tǣsan wk. obl.) OE adj., 'convenient, advantageous, useful' (*a*) *Tasworth* (worð), Tawsmead (mǣd), Teasley (lēah) W.

tǣsel OE, 'a teasel'. (*a*) Tasley Sa (lēah); an unmutated **tāsel* may be found in Tocil House Wa (hyll) and a derivative *taselere* 'teasler' in *Taseleresbrok* Ess (brōc). [~OE *tǣsan* 'to tear, comb, card', -el.]

*tagga, *tegga OE, 'a teg, a young sheep', not recorded in English before the 16th century, but found in p.ns. from the 13th. It survives as dial. *teg*, *tag*. (*a*) Tagg Barn Wo 238 (burna), Tagmore Hrt (lēah, mōr), Tagwell Wo (wella), Tegleaze Sx (lǣs). [~tacca.]

taile ME, 'a tail', *v.* tægl.

tal Welsh, Corn, 'forehead', used in the topographical sense 'end, brow of a hill, steep slope'. (*a*) Talkin Cu 88, Tolcarne, Tolmennor Co.

*tamo- Brit, sense dubious, occurs in r.ns. in different forms, due partly to different Brit suffixes such as *-ā* in Tame, Thame, Team, *-arā* in Tamar, *-ēssa* in Thames and *-etio-* in Teme, and partly to the lenition of Brit *m* in some r.ns. like Tavy (Brit **Tamios*); cf. RN 389ff, and esp. Jackson 486–8. (*b*) R. Tame La-YW, St-Wa, YN, R. Team Du, R. Teme Sa-Wo, Thame O, R. Thames Gl-Mx; R. Tavy D.

tān OE, 'a twig, a sprout, a shoot' (as in cognates like Goth *tains*), possibly also 'a stake' (as in Icel *teinn* 'a shoot, a stake'), a sense which is likely in the OE boundary marks *on ealda tan* KCD 750, *Mules tan* BCS 197. Du *teen* means 'osier' and the OE derivative tǣnel 'a wicker-basket'; in p.ns. a similar meaning of young shoots suitable for wicker-work is possible. In OE *tān* also denoted 'the twigs used for casting lots', but this is not found in p.ns. The el. is difficult to distinguish from an OE pers.n. *Tān* in p.ns. like Tansley Db (lēah). (*a*) Tanfield YN (feld), possibly Tansterne YE (sterne) and (*b*) possibly Dumbleton Gl (OE *Dumol(a)tan*, *-tun* BCS 667, *Dumeltan* ASWills, beside *Dumeltun* BCS 52, *Dumoltun* KCD 1295).

tang, tong OE, 'tong, forceps', **tangi** ON, 'a tang, a spit of land'.

(1) ON *tangi* is found with a topographical sense of 'a spit of land, a point of land projecting into the sea or a river' and no doubt occurs in some Danelaw p.ns. or may well have influenced the meaning of OE *tang* (which is found only in the sense 'tong, forceps'); it is paralleled in LG by EFris *tang*(*e*) 'a tongue of land, a long narrow sandy ridge'.

(2) OE *tang*, *tong* is sometimes difficult to distinguish in both sense and form from OE tungu 'tongue, tongue of land' and in form from OE þwang 'thong, strip of land'. There is an indication in the spellings of some p.ns. of an early form *twang*, and for that reason the el. has sometimes been regarded as an unmutated base of an OE *twengan* 'to pinch, to tweak'; in this sense *twengan* itself, however, is not recorded, for it is an emendation of OE *tringan* 'to press' (probably for *þringan*) in the *Arundel Psalter* (*Anglistische Forschungen* 30) 103. There is, however, another OE *twengan* (for *twencgan*), ME *twenge* 'to pinch, twinge', related to MHG *zwange* 'tongs'.

(3) In those p.ns. which have an occasional spelling *Twang*, Tongham Sr (*Tuangham*), Tong La (2) (*Tange*, *Twan*(*n*)*ge*), Tong YW (*Tvinc*, *Tange*), Tong Sa (OE *into Tweongan*, *æt Twongan* BCS 1317, KCD 1298, *Tvange* DB), we may often have an AN form of *þwang*. If, however, *twang* is original (and it appears to be in Tong Sa) we have to recognize two different roots for names in *tong*, (i) one (in p.ns. with ME *tang*) represented by OE *tang*, ON *tangi* in the sense 'spit of land', and (ii) the other (in p.ns. which have ME *twang*, *tong*) going back to *twang* (related to MHG *zwange* 'tongs' and OE *twengan* 'to pinch', where the root meaning is something like a pair of tongs or forceps) which may have been applied to 'the fork

of a river'; the OE word *tang* itself had this meaning, but it must have got it through confusion of its secondary form *tong* with *twang*. Loss of *w* in *twang* is paralleled by the later forms of **þwang**; cf. La 18.

(4) From *tang*, *tangi*, (*a*) Tangley Ha, Sr 256 (**lēah**), Tangmere Sx 97 (**mere**). (*b*) Tang YN 10, Tonge K 267 (ME *Tanges*, *Tonges* (*passim*) with a single *Twhonge* 1465), Tonge Wo 335. For examples of *twang* cf. § 3 *supra*.

***tāsel** OE, 'a teasel', *v*. **tǣsel**.

***tāselere** OE, 'a teasler', *v*. **tǣsel**.

tēafor OE, 'red lead, vermilion', surviving as dial. *tiver* 'raddle for marking sheep'. The use of this el. in p.ns. is not clear; it may refer to red-painted buildings or, as in *teaforgeapa* in *Ruin* 30 to a 'red-tiled' roof, but in OE *Tæafersceat* ASWills (cf. **scēat**) the allusion is obscure; the cognate ON *taufr* and OHG *zoubur* mean 'magic, sorcery', but that meaning is not evidenced in England. (*a*) Taverham Nf (**hām**), Tiverton Ch (**tūn**).

tēag OE, 'a close, a small enclosure', occurs in OE only in charter names, except for the phrase *clausulam quod Angli dicunt teage quæ pertinet ad prædictam mansionem* 'a small close (which the English call a *teage*) which belongs to the aforesaid dwelling' (BCS 402). It is found in f.ns. (Ess 591, Sr 366) and it survives as dial. *tye* 'a large common pasture' in Sf, Ess and K; in p.ns. it is commonest in K and Sx. (*a*) Tyehurst K (**hyrst**). (*b*) Teigh R, Barty (**burh**), Grafty (**gærs**), Olantigh (**holegn**) K, Bramblety (**brēmel**), *Lavertye* (**lāwerce**) Sx, Tilty Ess (**til**). [~**tīege**.]

***tegga** OE, 'a teg', *v*. **tagga**.

teld OE, 'a tent, a pavilion, a dwelling'. (*a*) Tiltridge Wo 174 (**hrycg**).

telga, ***telg** OE, 'a shoot, a twig, a sucker', surviving as dial. *tiller*, *tillow* 'a sapling' (cf. Mawer, Problems 52–3). (*a*) Tilden K (**denu**), Tilkhurst Sx 333 (**hyrst**), Tilley Sa (**lēah**). (*b*) Sweetwillowshaw Sx 401 (**swēte**). *v*. Löfvenberg 209.

***telgett** OE, 'a copse of saplings, a plantation'. (*b*) *Telwette* Sr. [**telga**, **-et**.]

tempel OE, **temple** ME, 'a temple', in p.ns. found only from ME and always in allusion to the properties of the Knights Templar. (*a*) Templeton Brk (olim *Templeton Templariorum*, **tūn**). (*b*) Temple Co. (*c*) *Temple* prefixed to Balsall Wa, Guiting Gl, Hirst, Newsam YW. [~Lat *templum*.]

tēn OE, tīn, tȳn, tīen (WSax), num., 'ten', usually with els. denoting a measure of land, trees, etc. (*a*) Tenacre K (æcer), Tinhead W, Stoketeignhead D (hīd), Tinick Bk (āc).

tenement ME, 'a tenement, a dwelling', is found occasionally in ME and later minor names (as Gl, W 448).

*tēo OE, 'a boundary', cognate with OFris *tia* 'a boundary' and related to OE *tēon* 'to draw'. (*a*) Teffont W 193 (funta, on the boundary of two hundreds), Tyburn Mx 6 (burna, the mouth of the stream in the Thames was called in OE *on merfleote*, *v.* (ge)mǣre, flēot).

*tēonde, *tēnde OE, tende ME, 'a tenth, a tithing', used of a small administrative district (cf. Mawer, Problems 17). (*b*) *Intendyng* Sx 215n. (the inner tithing of Henfield). [~OFris *tianda*, OSax *tehande*, ON *tíund* 'tenth'.]

tēoðung OE, 'a tenth, a tenth part, a tithing', used either of 'land set apart for the payment of tithes' as in OE *teoðungland* BCS 591 or of 'a small administrative district', as in Aston Court Wo 53 (olim *tethenga de Estone*) and some p.ns. in Gl and other counties. [~OE *tēoða* 'tenth', -ing[1]; cf. teonde.]

terfyn Welsh, 'a boundary'. (*b*) Tarvin Ch. [Lat *terminus*, with lenition of *m* to *v*, cf. Jackson 488.]

*tester OE adj., 'right-handed', hence 'southern', as in Du *Testerbant* (cf. DEPN 442). (*a*) Testerton Nf (tūn). [~Goth *taíhswa* 'right hand'.]

ti Corn, 'a house', *v.* chy, tig.

ticcen (ticcnes gen.sg.) OE, 'a kid, a young goat'; some p.ns. like Tichborne Ha (OE *ticceburnan* BCS 622, 731) point to a shorter form ticce (ticcan gen.sg.). In p.ns. with *Tick*(*en*)- instead of *Tich*(*en*)- the medial *k*- may be from an obl. case such as *ticcnes* gen.sg., where -*k*- would be the normal development. (*a*) Ticehurst Sx, Tickenhurst K (hyrst), Tichborne Ha (burna), Tickencote R (cot), Tickenham So (hām), Tickenhill Wo (hyll), Tickering YW (runnr), Tickford Bk (ford), Ticknall Db (halh), Tisted Ha (stede), Titchfield Ha (feld), Titchwell Nf (wella).

tīedre OE (WSax) adj., 'weak, fragile', probably applied to young growth. (*a*) Tytherleigh D 654, Tytherley Ha (lēah).

tīege OE (WSax), 'a close', an *i*-mutated form of tēag. (*b*) Great and Little Tey, Marks Tey Ess (OE *Tygan*). [~tēag, -e.]

tīen OE (WSax) num., 'ten', *v.* tēn.

tig[1] OWelsh, ty Welsh, 'a house'. (*b*) Mordiford He (mawr, ford), Priddy So (pridd). [~chy.]

tīg[2], tīh, tīge OE, 'a meeting-place, a court', is recorded in OE in the compounds *fore-tig* (*OEGospel*, Matt. xi. 16, for Lat *forum* 'market place') and *forð-tige*, *-tege* glossing Lat *foris* 'a gate, an entrance', *vestibulum* 'a porch', and *atrium* 'a room, a court' (BT s.v.); it is also found in OE *cyninges tuntih* BCS 326 (cf. KPN 106). Cognates in other languages include the ON legal term *tigi* 'a charge', OHG *zīg* 'a charge', and OHG *zich*, MHG *tig* 'a public meeting-place in a village'; the latter words render Lat *viculis* 'hamlets' and *conventionalibus* 'small assemblies' (cf. Nth lii). The word therefore, whatever its precise meaning, has something to do with 'a meeting-place, a court'. The related ON *teigr* denotes 'a close, a strip of meadowland' and MLG *ti*, *tig* 'a meadow' (cf. Mdf 134), but the semantic relationship is not obvious, unless it referred first to a close at the entrance to a house or where an assembly was held. It has been suggested for (*a*) Tiffield Nth 93 (feld) and OE *tigwellan* BCS 1023 (wella). It is also possible that Tew O 287 (OE *æt Tiwan*) is from *tīwe*, a weak noun and a variant of *tīg*, with the same interchange of *w* and *g* that appears in nīwe and nīge, hīwan and hīgan, Tīw and Tīg. On formal grounds this el. would be difficult to distinguish from WSax tīege.

Tīg[3] OE, a heathen god, *v.* Tīw.

*tige (*tigan gen.sg.) OE, 'a goat', cognate with OHG *ziga*, G *ziege* 'a goat' and related to ticcen. (*a*) Tyneham Do (hām).

tigel OE, 'a tile', usually in p.ns. in allusion to places where tiles were made, as in OE *to tiggæl beorgæ* BCS 758, *tigel hangra* ib. 596, etc. (Mdf 134), being common in the names of woods where fuel was at hand for the firing, and also to tile-roofed buildings (esp. in ME in the combination of *tiled* pa.part. 'tiled' with hūs). (*a*) Tilehurst Brk, Tyler's Hall Ess (hyrst), Tile Kiln Wood Nt (cyln), Tiley Do, Tyley Gl (lēah), Tyle Hall Ess (hall), Tyler's Green Ess, Tylers Grove Wa (hūs). [~Lat *tegula*.]

*tiglere OE, 'a tile-maker', also used later as a surname. (*a*) Tylerhill K (helde). [tigel, -ere.]

til (tilan wk. obl.) OE adj., 'useful, good', is indistinguishable from an OE pers.n. *Tila*. (*a*) Tilford Sr (ford), Tilletsmarsh Ess (wereð), Tiln Nt 32 (ēa), Tilney L, Nf (ēg), Tilton Lei (tūn), Tilty Ess (tēag); cf. also OE *Tillnoð* BCS 217 Gl (OE *nōð* 'boldness', a r.n.).

tilð, tilðe OE, 'tilth, crop, land under cultivation', found chiefly in the SE. (*b*) Tilt K, Sr 89, Tiltwood Sx 283; Backtilt (bæc), Baretilt (bere) K. [~OE *tilian* 'to till', -ð(e).]

timber OE, 'timber, trees', also 'a wooden building', **(ge)timbre** OE 'a building, a timber structure'; both occur in p.ns., the former more frequently as a first el. in the names of woods from which timber was got. (*a*) Timberden K, Timberdine Wo (denu), Timberland L (lúndr), Timberscombe So (cumb), Timberwood K (wudu), Timperleigh Ch (lēah), Timsbury Ha (burh), So (bearu). (*b*) Birchtimber Cu (birki), Newtimber, Nyetimber Sx (nīge).

tīn[1] OE (WSax) num., 'ten', *v.* tēn.

***tin**[2] Corn, Welsh, possibly 'a stronghold', may be found in (*a*) Tintagel Co, Tintern Mon. [Probably a provected form of *din* from dūno-.]

tind OE, 'a tine, a spike, a prong'. (*a*) Tineley Nb (lēah).

tining ME, 'an enclosure', *v.* tȳning.

Tīw, Tīg OE, a heathen Germanic God, corresponding to ON *Týr* and OHG *Ziu* and glossing Lat *Mars* in the Corpus Glosses (OET 77); it is preserved in the name of *Tuesday* and is the name of the rune for T (as it is in late Gothic for the letter T in the Salzburg manuscript, cf. C. L. Wrenn, MedÆv i, 24–34). The recorded forms of the name are *Tig* and *Tiw*, with *g* and *w* interchanging as in nīge and nīwe; *Tīg* may be the original nom. with *Tīw* introduced from the obl. cases; both occur in p.ns. A third form *Tīr* (*Runic Poem* 17) for the rune-name corresponds to ON *Týrr*, but is not apparently found in p.ns., but it may be reflected in later spellings of Tuesley Sr 200 (*Tewersle*, *Tuersle*, etc. from the 14th century). (*a*) Tewin Hrt (-ingas), Tuesley Sr (lēah), Tuesnoad K (snād), Twiscomb D (cumb), all from *Tīw*; Tysoe Wa (hōh), also *Tislea* KCD 739 Ha, *Tyesmere* BCS 455 Wo, from *Tīg*, etc.; cf. Dickins 155.

***tīwe** OE, 'a meeting-place, a court', *v.* tīg[2].

tjǫrn ON 'a tarn, a small lake'. (*a*) Tarn Beck Cu (bekkr), Tarn Flat La (flat). (*b*) Tarns, Blea Tarn (blár), Blind Tarn (blind) Cu, Malham Tarn YW, Tindale Tarn Cu (p.ns.).

***todd** OE, originally 'a bushy mass', developed two uses, (1) 'a bushy mass, esp. of ivy' (evidenced from the 16th century, NED s.v. *tod* sb. 2), ModE dial. *tod* 'a pollard tree' (that is, one which has been lopped and has grown a mass of new shoots at the top of the stump);

somewhat similar meanings have developed in EFris *todde* 'a bundle of hay, straw, etc.', Swed dial. *todd* 'a mass of wool', Icel *toddi* 'a small wood of brushwood', and the related OE **tydd** 'brushwood'. (2) 'a fox', no doubt from its brush (evidenced from the 12th century, NED s.v. *tod* sb. 1). The latter sense of 'fox' is probable in many NCy p.ns., but the sense 'brushwood, bushy growth' may be preferable in the SCy where the meaning 'fox' does not appear to be found. (*a*) Todber YW (**beorg**), Todburn Nb (**burna**), Toddell Cu, Todhill Nb (**hol**), Todridge Nb (**hrycg**) and *tod* and *tod-hole* 'fox's earth' in f.ns. (Cu 495), all with the sense 'fox'. *Todbroc* Hu (**brōc**), Todhurst Sx 108 (**hyrst**) probably have the meaning 'bushy growth, brushwood'.

***tōf** OE adj., 'slow, slow-moving', related to MLG *tōven*, MDu *toeven* 'to linger' and used as a sb. in (*b*) R. Tove Nth (hence Towcester Nth, **ceaster**).

toft ODan, late OE, 'a curtilage', *v.* **topt**.

tōh OE adj., 'tough, sticky, hard'. (*a*) Tovil K, possibly Nuffield O 133 (**feld**).

tol Corn, 'a hole' (cf. Welsh **twll**). (*a*) Tolven Co. (*b*) Chytoll Co.

toln, toll OE, **toll** ME 'a tax, a toll'. (*a*) Tone Nb (**land**), Tolpits Hrt (**pæð**).

tolnere, tollere OE, 'a tax-gatherer'. (*a*) Tollerton YN (**tūn**). [**toln, -ere**.]

***tong** OE, 'a spit of land', *v.* **tang**.

topp OE, 'top, the top of a bank or hill'. (*a*) Topcliffe YN 186 (**clif**). (*b*) Stank Top La 68 (**stǫng**). A later derivative **topping** ME, 'a hill-top, a hill', is found in ModE dial. and late p.ns. It occurs in ME in *Sir Gawayn* 191 in the sense 'mane, top hair'. (*a*) Toppinhill Cu (**hyll**), Toppin Rays La (**hreysi**). (*b*) Roseberry Topping YN.

topping ME, 'a hill-top', *v.* **topp, -ing**[1].

topt ON, **toft** ODan, late OE, 'a building site, a curtilage, a messuage'.

(1) The origin and significance of ON *topt* has been fully investigated by B. Holmberg, *Tomt och toft som appellativ och ortnamnselement* (Uppsala 1946). Holmberg has examined the use of *topt* and all its cognates in great detail and has related it (333 ff) to the archaeology of ancient dwelling sites. The Scandinavian forms generally point to an older **tumft-* (which, as regards its root, is related by ablaut to words like **timber**, etc.); this developed two principal varieties, namely OSwed *tomt* (in which the nasal

sound remained) and ODan *toft*, ON *topt* (with loss of the nasal); it is this latter denasalized form only which appears in England. Holmberg's main conclusion is that a *topt* was originally in the late Iron Age 'a plot of ground prepared for a single dwelling'. Other meanings are developments of this: in Iceland it came to denote 'a place marked out for a building', 'a rectangular piece of ground with walls but no roof' as well as 'a messuage, a homestead' and the like. It remained in use as a common p.n. el. during the Viking Age (NK 106ff), for it is well evidenced in all the centres of Viking colonization, in Iceland, the Faroes, the Orkneys, Shetlands and Hebrides, the Danelaw and Normandy (Holmberg 202–81).

(2) In England, a good many early instances occur of its use as an appellative, but of those cited by Holmberg 127ff, Lindkvist 208ff and in NED s.v. *toft* only some are decisive as to its meaning and use.

(i) The original meaning of 'a building plot, a curtilage' is implied in such uses as *cum tofto illo in quo aula sita est* 'with the *toft* in which the hall is situated' (*Chronica de Melsa* (Rolls) i, 224), *ceo qil apele touft cest le sit dun molyn et un estank sek* 'what he calls a *toft* is the site of a mill and a dry pond' (*Year Book Ed I* 337); the common legal phrase *toft and croft* (as in *on tofte and on crofte* KCD 705) denotes 'the land occupied by a building (the *toft*) and an attached small field (the *croft*)'.

(ii) The word came to be used also of a somewhat larger plot than the actual messuage occupied, 'a large curtilage', since one toft is described as containing 'one acre, three and three-quarter perches' (*Chron. de Melsa* i, 224) and another of very considerable extent is referred to in '40 acres of land out of a *toft* in *Crokesle*' (*Annales St Albani* (Rolls) i, 268). In *Promptorium Parvul.* it glosses Lat *campus*, and a passage in the *Register of Godstow Nunnery* (EETS) 315 which reads *iiij mesis liyng togedir . . . with the toftis liyng therto* also suggests that it could be used of the plot of land attached to a messuage.

(iii) In later usage, the term is largely historico-legal, but in dial it has apparently come to mean 'a hillock in flat country'; this is obviously closely connected with the original meaning of 'building site', for in the fenlands such hillocks especially would provide the best building locations. It is first recorded in some such sense in *Piers Plowman* Prol. A 14, *I saiȝ a tour on a toft triȝely Imakid*, *dep dale bineþe*, 'I saw a tower on a *toft* well made, a deep valley below'; other manuscripts have replaced *toft* by such words as *twist*, *cost*.

(iv) The meaning 'small grove of trees' (EDD) has no connexion with *toft* and is probably due to confusion with *tuft* (cf. tuffe).

The best evidenced meaning of *toft* in England is therefore 'curtilage, the plot of ground in which a dwelling stands'.

(3) The provenance of this el. in p.ns. is of interest. It is typically Scandinavian, for it has no cognates in the other Germ languages. In Scandinavia, as Holmberg shows (*v.* esp. map 14), *tomt* belongs to central Sweden; *toft* occurs chiefly in southern Sweden and Denmark and to a less extent in Norway and Iceland, as well as Orkney, Shetland and the Faroes. In England *toft* is found chiefly in Y, the EMidl and EAngl; it is infrequent in the NW (no example, for instance, being found in Cu). This distribution would suggest that so far as England is concerned p.ns. containing *toft* belong to Danish rather than Norwegian settlement. But since it remained in appellative use in ME in most parts of the country (chiefly because it was a legal term), many examples in ME f.ns. (as in Bd 296, Bk 259, C 347, Ess 591, L, Nt 291, Nth 270, Wa 333, YE 328, YN 331) have no relevance to its original distribution—many are names of ME origin.

(4) (*a*) As a first el. *topt* is rare, *Tofthouse* (hūs), Toftshaw (sceaga), Topcliffe (clif) YW, Toothill Nth (hyll).

(*b*) As a simplex p.n. it is very common, as Toft C, Hu, L, Nb, Nf, Sf, Wa, YW, Toftrees Nf, Tofts YE.

In compounds, it is found chiefly with (i) significant words, as Blacktoft YE (blæc), Bratoft L (breiðr), Bruntoft Du (brunnr), Burtis Wood, Burtoft L (búr), Eastoft YE (eski), Huttoft L (hōh), Langtoft L, YE (lang), Moortoft L (mōr), Nortoft Nth (norð), Saintoft(s) YE, YN (senget), Sandtoft L (sand), Thrintoft YN (þyrne), Wartop Lei (vǫr), Wigtoft L (vík), Willitoft YE (wilig); (ii) pers.ns., very frequently, esp. in ME f.ns., chiefly of ON origin, as Brothertoft L, Caltofts Nf, Goldentoft (fem.), Knaptoft L, Lowestoft Sf, Raventoft YW, Silbertoft Nth, Wibtoft L, also OE in Antofts YN, Yelvertoft Nth, and OFr in Allan Tops YN.

tord OE, 'ordure, dung'. (*a*) Terrible Down Sx 403 (hyll, dūn), Terwick Sx 42 (wīc).

torf ON, 'turf', in allusion to a turf-roofed building (such as were to be found in Iceland). (*a*) Torver La (erg). [~ turf.]

torr OE, 'a rock, a rocky outcrop, a rocky peak'.

(1) This el. is evidenced in OE only in charter p.n. forms such as *on ðone torr* BCS 451, etc., and in *Boethius* Metr. v, 17, where *of ðæm torre* corresponds to the prose version's *of þam heohan munte* 'from the high mount'. In ME and later it is found in contexts which suggest a close association with 'rocks, crags', as in *Alexander* 4863, *Clynter and torres, rochis and rogh stanes*. In p.ns. it refers to 'craggy hill-tops, rocky outcrops'.

(2) The word is commonest in p.ns. in the extreme SW, but it is found also in Sx, W and Gl, and in minor names (as D 691, W 448); it occurs in later appellative use in more northerly parts (La, Db, etc.) and in Db minor names; its presence in Db has been explained by a migration of Cornish miners there, for which there is some evidence from the 14th century (cf. Sx 37 n.). Because of its main concentration in the SW it has been suggested to be of Corn origin, cf. NED s.v. *tor*. The various Celtic words, Corn *tor* 'belly', Welsh *twrr* 'a heap, a pile' (also with a different suffix, OWelsh *torr* 'bulge, belly, boss'), and Gael *torr* 'bulging hill', all go back to a root which had the primary meaning of 'bulge, belly', and then, with a topographical extension, 'bulging hill'.

(3) (*a*) Tercrosset Cu 97, Torberry Sx 37 (**burh**).

(*b*) As an original simplex p.n., Tor Hill Gl (OE *to þæm torre* BCS 764), Torbryan D, Torr Co, W, *la Torr(e)* Sx, W (BCS 458).

In compounds it occurs with (i) significant words, as Bagtor (**bagga**), Haytor (**īfed**) D, Hounster Sx (**hund**), Notter (**hnott**), Rough Tor (**rūh**) Co, Sheepstor D (**scyttels**), Worminster So (**wyrm**), Yar Tor D (**heorot**), and (ii) pers.ns., as Benter, Dunster, Vobster So.

[*v.* Ekwall, ES liv, 108–10.]

***tōt, *tōte** OE, 'a look-out', **tote** ME, 'a look-out hill', as in Trevisa's *Polychronicon* (Rolls) iii, 85, *temples þat were on groues vppon hiȝe totes* 'temples that were in groves upon high hills', is related to OE *tōtian* 'to peep, peer, look out', and was used in p.ns. of buildings and sites which were good observation places. It occurs in most parts but esp. in the SCy. It is particularly common in the compound **tot-hyll**. The word may occur in some OE p.n. spellings such as *Totleie* BCS 59 A, *to totanlege* ib. 61, but in few cases can it be distinguished from the OE pers.n. *Tot(t)a*. (*a*) Tostock Sf (stoc), Totham Ess (OE *Totham*, hām), Totteridge Bk (hrycg), Totternhoe Bd 140, Totterton Sa (ærn, hōh, tūn). (*b*) Toat Sx 155, 161 *et freq*, Pentwood Sx (penn). (*c*) Toot Baldon O.

*tōt-hyll OE, 'a look-out hill', first evidenced as *tothulle* BCS 922 (cf. also NED s.v. *toot-hill*). (*b*) Toot Hill Nt, Toothill YW, Tothill L, Mx, *Tothill* Wt, Tuttle Hill Wa, and in many minor names. [tōt, hyll.]

towan, *tewen Corn, 'a sand-dune' (cf. Welsh *tywyn*). (*a*) Tewington, (*b*) Towan Co.

trade ME, 'a way, a path', *v.* trede.

træppe, treppe OE, 'a trap, a snare'. (*a*) Trafford Nth (ford). (*b*) Bawdrip So (bagga).

trani ON, 'a crane', also used as a by-name as in Tranby YE (bý) and perhaps some other p.ns. (*a*) Tarnacre La (æcer), Tranker Nt, Trencar YN (kjarr), Tranmere Ch (melr), Tranmoor YW (mōr), Tranwell Nb (wella), Trenholme YN (holmr). [~cran.]

trasche ME, 'broken twigs, cuttings', first recorded in this sense in the 16th century, surviving as dial. *trash* 'hedge-croppings, small wood from a copse', and ultimately related to Norw *tras* 'twig' (NED s.v.). (*b*) Trashurst Sr 273 (pl.).

tré[1] ON, 'a tree', *v.* trēow.

tre[2] Corn, Welsh, 'a farmstead', *v.* tref.

treath, trêth Corn, 'a shore, a beach'. (*b*) Treath, Pentreath Co. [~Welsh *traeth*, Lat *tractus*.]

trede OE adj., 'firm, fit to tread on'. (*a*) Tratford Co (ford). A variant trade ME, 'course, path, way' (cf. NED s.v. *trade* sb.), is possible in *Tradebrede* C 347 (brǣdu). [~OE *tredan* 'to tread'.]

tref, tre Welsh, trev, tre Corn, 'a farmstead, a homestead, a hamlet', is found chiefly in He and Co; it is of course very common in Wales. (*a*) Treales La (lis), Tregate (coed), Tretire (rhyd), Treville (Welsh *melin* 'mill') He, Triermain Cu; Tregair (cair), Tregavethan (pers.n.), Tremaine, Trematon (maen), Treneglos (eglos) Co. (*b*) Hendra Co (*freq*). [cf. þorp § 4.]

trenche OFr, ME, 'a cutting, a ditch', used also in English of 'a path cut through a wood'. (*b*) The Trench K, Trench Lane Wo 143; cf. also ME minor names in C 347, Ess 591, Nth 270, W 448.

trendel, trindel, tryndel OE, 'a circle, a ring', used in p.ns. to describe something of circular shape, such as a wood, a well, an earthwork, etc. It is found in ME minor names (D 691, Ess 591, Hrt 256,

Mx 200, Sr 366). (*a*) Trendwell (**wella**), Trentishoe (**hōh**, a circular hill) Trundlebeer (**bearu**, near a small circular hill) D, Trundle Mere Hu (**mere**), Trundlemoor D (**mōr**, in a circular valley). (*b*) Trendells Wood Bk 195, Trull So, The Trundle Sx, Rowtrundle D (**rūh**, from an ancient hut-circle). [The various ablaut grades are represented by OE *trand-* in *trandende* 'steep' (and with *i*-mutation *trend-* as in *trendel*, *v.* **-el**), OE **trind** (cf. also *trindel* in *trindel lea* BCS 959) and OE *trund-* (cf. **trun**), with *i*-mutation in *tryndel*.]

* **trēow, trēo** (**trēowu, trēow** nom.pl.) OE, **tré** ON, 'a tree', probably refer in most p.ns. to the living tree, but a secondary sense 'a large piece of wood, a post, a beam' (already found in OE) developed and is found in compounds like *rōd-trēow* 'the holy cross', **wearg-trēow** 'gallows', a meaning which ME *tree* itself also had. The OE form *trēow* sometimes remains in p.ns. as *trow*, but it is usually replaced by the more common *tree* (which seems to be commoner in the NCy where it was probably reinforced by ON *tré*). The el. is very common indeed, partly because noteworthy trees were convenient boundary marks, partly because of the religious associations and partly because trees often marked the site of meeting places of the hundreds. It is found occasionally in ME minor names (C 347, Hrt 260, Sr 366). For variations in the later forms *trow* and *tree*, through stress-shifting in the diphthong, cf. Jordan §109.2.

(*a*) Treborough So (**beorg**), Treeton YW (**tūn**), Trewick Nb (**wīc**), Treyford Sx (**fyrde**), Trimdon Du (**mǣl, dūn**), Trobridge D, Trowbridge W (**brycg**).

(*b*) Train, Trewyn D (ME wk. nom.pl.), Trehane Co (dat.pl.). In compounds, it is found occasionally with

(i) Words denoting use or association, as *Garden Tree* C, Gartree Wapentake L, Lei (possibly **geirr** 'spear' in some undetermined connexion), Hallatrow So, Hallytreeholme YE 72 (**hālig**, probably in allusion to a holy cross), Harptree So (**hearpe**), Picktree Du (**pīc**, cf. Nb dial. *pick-tree* 'tree abounding in pitch'); cf. also **wearg-trēow**.

(ii) Descriptive adjs., as Fairtree Sa (**fāg**), Fairtrough K (**fæger**), Greytree Hundred He (**grǣg**), Langtree D, La, Longtree Hundred Gl (**lang**), Rattery D (**rēad**).

(iii) Words denoting number, as Aintree La (**einn**), Manningtree Ess (**manig**).

(iv) Designations of people, as Bishopstrow W (**biscop**), Cholstrey He (**ceorl**).

(v) Pers.ns., frequently, esp. in the names of hundreds, as Austrey Wa, Aymestrey, Bartestree He, Coventry Wa, Culliford Tree Hundred Do, Doddingtree Hundred Wo, Earnstrey Sa, Elmestree Gl, Emstrey, Oswestry Sa, Toltingtrough Hundred K, Wanstrow So, Wixamtree Hundred Bd; these would appear to denote prominent trees and the pers.n. may be that of the local hundred-man or law-man of the assembly.

trēowen OE adj., 'wooden', is possible in (*a*) Troney Bridge D, *Trowenebregge* Sr 356 (**brycg**). [**trēow**, **-en**.]

***trēowiht** OE adj., 'growing with trees'. (*a*) Trevor Bd 35 (**ford**). [**trēow**, **-iht**.]

treppe OE, 'a snare', *v.* **træppe**.

trev Corn, 'a farmstead', *v.* **tref**.

***trind**, ***trynd** OE adj., 'circular', cognate with OE *trinde* 'a round lump', occurs chiefly with **lēah** (and is therefore difficult to distinguish from **trendel** and its secondary form *trindel*), as in OE *trind lea* BCS 595, 689, *on trindleaie* ib. 112; cf. also OE *trindhyrst* ib. 1295, *trindteaganhrucg* ib. 419. Tengstrand 285ff thinks there was an OE *trind* meaning 'a stake for fencing' and cognate with Swed dial. *trind*. (*a*) Trendhurst K (**hyrst**), Trenley K, Tirley Gl (**lēah**). [~**trendel**.]

trindel OE, 'a circle', *v.* **trendel**.

***trisantonā** Brit, a river-name of doubtful meaning; it is thought by Ekwall to be a compound of Brit **tri-* 'through' and **santon-* (as in the Gaulish tribal name *Santones*); on the phonological developments, cf. Jackson 502–3, 524–5. (*b*) R. Tarrant Do, Sx, R. Trent D, Nt-St. [*v.* RN 415–18, but also I. Williams in *Archaeologia* xciii, 45.]

trōg OE, 'a valley, a trough, a long narrow vessel for various purposes such as feeding animals, baking, brewing, etc.', is not independently recorded with a topographical meaning, except perhaps in *mylentrōg* 'a mill-stream or conduit', until the 16th century when it was used of 'a hollow or valley resembling a trough, the bed of a stream', which is the meaning required in most p.ns. In some such sense it is already found in OE in Trow W and possibly in *on þone sæ troh*, *of þæm troge* BCS 1066 and *on trohhrycg* ib. 1282; cf. also C 347. (*a*) Trafford Ch (**ford**), Trawden La (**denu**), Troughfoot Cu (fōt), Troughton La (tūn). (*b*) Trough La, YN, Trough of Bowland YW, Trow W (OE *to trogan* BCS 917), Trows Nb (hwīt).

troll ON, 'a troll, a supernatural being'. (*a*) Troughburn Nb (hop, from 1352).

trouse ME, 'brushwood', *v.* trūs.

truht OE, 'a trout'. (*a*) Troutal La (hylr), Trout Beck Cu, We (bekkr), Trouts Dale YN (stall in the sense 'pool'). [~Lat *tructus* 'trout'.]

***trun, *turn** OE adj., 'circular, round', usually describing some topographical feature or something which turns. (*a*) Trumfleet YW (flēot), Trunnah, Turnagh La 158 (haga), Turley YW (lēah), Turncole Ess lxi (cole), Turnden K (denn); Turnham (hām), Turnhead (hēafod), YE (both near a river-bend), Turnshaw YW (sceaga); Turn Bridge YW (brycg, olim *pontem turnatum* 'swing bridge'). [~trind; ME *turn* is usually derived from OFr (cf. NED s.v.), but *v.* La 158.]

trūs OE, 'brushwood', **trouse** ME, 'brushwood, hedge croppings'. (*a*) Truscott Co (cot), Trusley Db (lēah).

***trūsen** OE adj., 'overgrown with brushwood'. (*a*) Trussenhayes W 153 (gehæg). [trūs, -en.]

***trynd** OE adj., 'circular', *v.* trind.

tryndel OE, 'a circle', *v.* trendel.

tū OE, num.neut., 'two', *v.* twegen.

tuffe, tufte ME, 'a tuft, a cluster of trees or bushes'. (*a*) Tuffland D (land). (*b*) Toft D 183. [Origin obscure, but cf. þūf.]

tūkere ME, 'a fuller, a cloth-finisher'. (*a*) Tuckerton So (tūn).

tūn OE, 'an enclosure, a farmstead, an estate, a village', **tún** ON, 'an enclosure, a farmstead', is by far the commonest el. in English p.ns.

(1) The precise meanings of *tūn* at any one stage are not easy to determine, but there is an obvious semantic evolution that links its differing uses from the original Germ notion of 'fence' or 'hedge' to the present-day English *town*.

(2) The word *tūn* seems to have denoted 'fence, hedge' in PrGerm, and a few traces of this remain in the cognate OHG *zūn*, G *zaun* and in Du, LG *tuun* (the latter also meaning 'enclosure'), and in ON *tún* in the sense 'fenced plot in which a house is built', also in Iceland 'an enclosed in-field' and ON *tún-riða* 'a witch, a ghost' (lit. 'a hedge-rider'). In OE the derivative verb *tȳnan* 'to enclose, fence' (*v.* tȳned) also points to some such meaning as

'fence' as in the Laws, according to which 'a ceorl's enclosure (*worðig*) shall be *betyned* or fenced in summer and winter'; *v.* also **tȳning**. It is probable that OE *tuneweorð* BCS 994 and *tunlesweorð* ib. 820 mean 'hedge enclosure' and 'hedgeless enclosure' (probably one made with a ditch or the like), for **worð** is frequently associated with a *hege* or hedge. No other certain examples of this older meaning 'hedge, fence', however, occur in p.ns.

(3) The first important development in meaning in OE is to 'that which is fenced in, an enclosed piece of ground', a meaning which is well-attested in such early glosses as Lat *cors*, *choors* (for *cohors*) 'a yard, an enclosed space, a courtyard, a pen' (WW 14.41, 283.1, 370.4), and similarly several OE compounds like *cafor-tūn* 'courtyard', *cyric-tūn* 'church yard', **līc-tūn** 'burial ground', **æppel-tūn**, **dēor-tūn**, **gærs-tūn**, **lēac-tūn**, **wyrt-tūn**, retain the sense 'enclosed piece of ground'; **burh-tūn** and **hām-tūn** are ambiguous, but in both *tūn* may sometimes denote 'enclosure'—*burh-tūn* 'a fortified or stockaded enclosure' and *hām-tūn* 'the enclosure in which a homestead stands'. The more specific sense 'garden' is implied in the gloss *nasturcium*, *tuncress* 'garden cress' and in the phrase *Harewyrt lytelu oftest weaxeþ on tune* 'Colocasia often grows in the garden' (*Leechdoms* ii, 132), whilst that of 'burial ground' is inferred from the context of *His lic lið þær on tune* 'His body lies there in *tune*' (ASC 867). It is difficult to say how far the meaning 'enclosure' is to be sought in p.ns., apart from the special compounds already mentioned (cf. also § 12 (*b*) vi *infra*); it is not improbable when it is combined with the names of domestic animals (ib. xv) and likely with some words denoting crops (ib. xvii) and trees, esp. fruit-trees (ib. xix).

(4) Other meanings of *tūn* are evolved from the idea of 'an enclosed piece of ground' to 'an enclosure with a dwelling', and then 'a farmstead', 'a hamlet or village' as well as 'manor, estate', and one or another of these is to be sought in most p.ns. It is most often equated with Lat *villa*, which had an equally varied group of meanings, 'country house, farmstead, manor, vill'. For the most part these uses of *tūn* imply a community of people; already in the 7th-century Kentish Laws it is implied that a *tūn* could consist of a community of people, since a thief is to be cleared by the oaths of persons from the *tūn* to which he belongs. It is contrasted with *hām* in a passage in the OEBede (*v.* **hām** § 1) and the rendering

of Bede's *villa* as *tūn* and *civitas* as *hām* suggests that a *tūn* was a smaller unit than a *hām*.

(5) The meaning 'a single dwelling' occurs in the rendering by *tūn* of Lat *habitaculum* 'a dwelling' in the *Cura Pastoralis* 43; and in a passage in Gen. xxxix. 5 the OE has *ge on tunum ge on landum* for the Lat *in aedibus quam in agris* 'in dwellings as in fields'. It may well be that in the many instances where *tūn* glosses *villa* it meant no more than 'dwelling' or 'farmstead'. Certainly in the older period when p.ns. in *tūn* were being created they are not likely to have denoted more than this. The sense 'farmstead' remains in Scots dial. *town* and is the common signification of ON *tún*; cf. also tūn-stall, tūn-stede. Some names indicate that a *tūn* often originated as an outlying settlement or farm—bere-tūn, as well as Brinton Nf, Carrington L, Ovington Nb, Snainton Nt, Spaldington YE, Winterton L which were clearly secondary settlements belonging respectively to Brinningham Nf, Corringham L, Ovingham Nb, Nottingham Nt, Spaldingmoor YE and Wintringham L (all of which go back to very old folk-names in -ingas). The majority of p.ns. in *tūn* probably had this meaning 'farmstead' when they were established.

(6) The later development of meaning to 'hamlet, village' followed the growth of a village round its nucleus farmstead. In the majority of literary references in OE, *tūn* appears to mean 'village, a collection of houses', as may be seen in such passages as *þa forburnon ealle þara monna hus þe on þæm tune wæron* 'all the men's houses in the *tūn*' (*Martyrology* 92) or *ðæs cyninges tune . . . ðe he ðær hæfde ane cyricean and an resthus* 'the king's *tūn* (Lat *villa regia*) where he had a church and a resthouse' (OEBede iii, 17). Both these imply a larger collection of buildings than a single farmstead; cf. also *cyricean ðæs tunes* 'the church of the *tūn*' (Lat *villula*, ib. v, 12), where the meaning 'village' is also likely. In this sense, it is found in the glosses *tunas* for Lat *oppida* 'towns' (WW 462.17) and *tuun* as an alternative to *þrop* for Lat *competum* (OET 54, WW 365.24, *v.* þrop § 1). How far the meaning 'village' is to be sought in p.ns. cannot be determined; in literary contexts its widespread use is clear enough—it was the growth of the nucleus farmstead into a village that brought about the change of meaning. In p.ns. which have added *tūn* to older Brit and OE p.ns. (cf. § 12 (*b*) xi, xii *infra*) and in p.ns. of post-Conquest origin, the meaning

'village' is likely, as well as in the names of well-established places like Kingston upon Hull YE 209 (which was thus renamed in 1292) and in ME p.ns. of the type Townsend, Townfield, etc., in all of which *tūn* is applied to an already existing village or town.

(7) The meaning 'estate, manor, vill' arose through the extension of the area of exploited land around an original *tūn* and through the legal aspects of the development of larger estates centred on a village. This use of *tūn* is established by references in the OE charters to the extent of a *tūn*; BCS 1282, for example, gives the boundaries of *feower tuna* 'four *tūnas*' and those of the *tunlonds* that belonged to Pershore Wo and both are extensive territories. Besides this, *tūn* glosses Lat *pagus* 'country district' (WW 177.20) and more precisely Lat *praedium* and *prediolum* (BT) both meaning 'property, estate'; cf. also tūnincel. Again, it is not possible to say to what extent this use is reflected in p.ns. It is unlikely to occur often, but it may be found in many of the Kingstons and perhaps some other p.ns. of a similar type (cf. § 12 (*b*) xx, xxi).

(8) The current meaning of *town* as 'urban area, a large collection of dwellings and buildings' dates from ME (cf. NED s.v. *town*) and is rarely found in p.ns., except as a first el. in late minor names which refer to lands belonging to a town (such as Townfield), and in the names of later suburbs which are often named New Town, Church Town and the like.

(9) The period during which *tūn* was an active name-forming el. was very long, covering the whole of the OE period and continuing for some time after the Conquest. Ekwall (DEPN 459) has called attention to certain well-evidenced p.ns. in Normandy and the Pas de Calais in *tūn* and *-ingatūn*, such as *Baincthun*, *Todincthun*, *Wadenthun* etc. (earlier *Bagingatun*, *Totingetun*, *Wadingatun*); such names probably originated in a Saxon colonization in the 6th century recorded by Gregory of Tours and establish the use of *tūn* as a p.n. el. at a very early date amongst the Saxons. In England, certain features in its use suggest that it was not so common in the earliest OE period and that its development as the commonest of all habitative els. is to be associated with secondary colonization from established centres: (i) It is rarely combined with els. of great antiquity like *burna* and for the most part the els. with which it is found do not offer anything like the etymological problems that are presented by such very ancient els. as hām or -ingas. (ii) It is also

rare with folk-names in *-ingas* (*v.* -ing[4] § 3, -ingas § 7 (*a*), (*b*)). (iii) It is everywhere very common with well-known OE pers.ns. (cf. § 12 (*b*) xxiii ff *infra*), implying individual possession; in a fairly extensive sample just over 50% of *tūn* names are combined with pers.ns. (about 30% with *tūn* and about 20% with -ingtūn). (iv) It is found with group-names, esp. in -hǣme, -sǣte, ware, many of which give evidence of secondary colonization from an older place, and some like Exton Ha ('East-Saxons' *tūn*'), Conderton Wo ('Kent-dwellers' *tūn*') or Saxton C ('Saxons' *tūn*') point to the same thing; other tribal names as in Ireton, Normanton (*v.* § 12 (*b*) xxii *infra*) are obviously later since they arose in the Viking period. (v) There are many examples of Christian associations as in combinations with cirice 'church', cristel-mǣl 'holy cross', mynster 'church', abbud 'abbot', munuc 'monk', nunne 'nun', prēost 'priest' (§ 12 (*b*) vi, ix, xx, xxi *infra*), which are very rare with els. like hām. (vi) It is a frequent addition to older p.ns. in the so-called triple compounds of the type Harvington Wo 134 (OE *Hereford, Herefordtun*) (cf. § 12 (*b*) xii *infra*). (vii) Although it is common in all parts of the country it is extremely so in the WCy and the SW, where the number of topographical compounds of the type Marton, Morton and the like is very great (cf. § 12 (*b*) xiii *infra*). (viii) Some *-ingtūn* names contain the names of identified persons (cf. -ing[4] § 4 (*b*)). (ix) There are some 14 cases of p.ns in *tūn* in which the first el. is the name of the TRE holder (cf. Feilitzen 32 ff). These facts suggest that *tūn* was not a common p.n. el. in the earliest days of the English settlement, but it became common with the extension of areas in occupation and with the advance of colonization to the west; it became more common as hām fell into disuse. For its continued use after the Conquest *v.* § 11 *infra*.

(10) The Danelaw p.ns. in *tūn* present a special problem. In some parts, esp. in Lei and Nt, compounds with ON pers.ns. are numerous (§ 12 (*b*) xxvi, xxvii, *infra*). ON *tún* is, however, rare in East Scandinavian p.ns. It has therefore been suggested (Nt xviii–xix) that such *tūn* names in the EMidl are in fact OE settlements and that the names of the new Danish owners merely replace those of the dispossessed English owners. Such renaming of old established settlements is also suggested by the alternation of *tūn* and bý in names like Scofton Nt (DB *Scotebi*, ME *Scofton*) where the original OE *tūn* happened to prevail, with ON *Skopti*, the name of

its new Danish lord, replacing some OE pers.n. Apart from this group of names, the number of compounds with ON els. is small and even in some of these, like Ayton YN (á), Aikton Cu (eik), Brayton YW (breiðr), Coniston YW (kunung), Spaunton YN (spánn), Stainton YW (steinn), etc., the ON els. may merely replace the corresponding OE words, ēa, āc, brād, cyning, spōn, stān. Scampton L (skammr) and Storeton Ch (stórr) may well be ON, but may also equally well be hybrids. The evidence for the use of ON *tún* in English p.ns. is therefore slight.

(11) The post-Conquest use of *tūn* is particularly evident in the SW (cf. IPN 131), but it is not limited to that area; cf. § 12 (*b*) vi, xii, xxviii *infra*. In most of the examples the meaning is 'manor' and its persistence may be due as much to the modelling of new p.ns. on older p.ns. in *tūn* as to the survival of *tūn* as an appellative with the meaning 'manor'.

(12) The following examples of *tūn* are a representative selection only of the principal categories:

(*a*) As a first el. *tūn* is very rare, except in late names such as Townsend and the like, usually denoting something belonging to, enjoyed by or maintained by a nearby village or town, as Tonbridge K (brycg), Tonwell Hrt (wella), Towneley La (lēah belonging to the *tūn* of Burnley), Townworth La, Tunworth Ha (worð); in Tumby L (bý) it may denote 'fence'. *v.* also tūn-stall, tūn-stede.

(*b*) This el. never occurs as a simplex p.n., but as a final el. it is found with the following types of first el.:

(i) An adj. denoting location usually in relation to other places, as Aston, Easton, Eston *passim* (*v.* ēast), Heaton *passim*, Hinton Blewett So (hēah), Middleton, Milton *passim* (middel), Nareton K (neoðera), Norton *passim* (norð), Sutton *passim* (sūð), Testerton Nf (tester), Upton *passim* (upp), Weston *passim* (west); on the type *ēast in tūne* '(place) east in the village', *v.* ēast, norð, sūð, upp, west, and cf. similar elliptical types in Beesons (bī, ēastan), Burton (būfan) C; from ON, Melton Ross L (meðal).

(ii) An adj. descriptive of size or shape, as Broad Town W (brād), Langton K, L *et freq*, Longton St (lang), Littleton *freq* (lytel), Mickleton *freq*, Muggleton Wt (micel); from ON, Brayton YW (breiðr), Scampton L (skammr), Storeton Ch (stórr).

(iii) A descriptive adj., not common, as Rowton Sa, YE (rūh), Sheinton Sa, Shenington O (scēne), Skarrington Nt (scearnig).

(iv) An adj. denoting age, seasonal use, etc., as Alton Bd (ald), Naunton Gl, Newington, Newton *passim* (nīwe), Newtown Gl, Ha, Nb, Wt *et freq* (post-Conquest, sometimes rendered by Lat *nova villa*, *v.* nīwe); Somerton L, Nf, O, So (sumor), Winterton Nf (winter).

(v) A word relating to tenure or possession, etc., as Galton Do (gafol), Kenton Nb, Kineton Wa (cyne), Manaton D (gemæne), Pennington Ha, La (pening); cf. also xviii-xix *infra*.

(vi) Words denoting buildings, roads, dikes, and other structures, as Cheriton D, Ha, So, Churston D, Churton Ch (cirice), Elloughton YE 220 (elgr), Millington Ch, YE, Milton Nt (myln), Misterton Nt (mynster), Steepleton Do (stēpel); Deighton, Ditton *freq* (dīc), Stratton, Stretton *freq* (strǣt); in Bolton (bōðl-tūn), Burton (burh-tūn), Casterton R, We, Chesterton C, Gl, etc. (ceaster), Stockton *freq* (stoc), Weighton (wīc-tūn), we may have technical compounds, but the sense of *tūn* is ambiguous; *burh-tūn*, for example, may sometimes be 'fortified enclosure or farmstead' or 'farmstead near a fortification'; *dīc-tūn* may be 'enclosure made with a ditch' or 'farmstead near a dike' as it is in Fen Ditton C (near Fleam Dyke) or Woodditton C (near Devil's Dyke). Castleton Db, La, YN (castel), Templeton Brk, D (tempel) are of post-Conquest origin.

(vii) A word for enclosure, clearing, etc., as Crofton YW, etc. (croft), Fritton Nf, Sf (frið), Stibbington Hu (stybbing), Yorton Sa (geard).

(viii) A word denoting its use or products (not common), as Butterton St (butere), Honington Wa, Honiton D (hunig), Playton Co (plega); *v.* also xiii, xv *infra*.

(ix) A word for a post, beam, cross or the like (perhaps in allusion either to building material or to a sign-post of some kind), as Bampton Cu, O, We, Bempton YE (bēam, possibly also in the sense 'tree'), Christleton Ch (cristel-mǣl), Melton Nf, Sf (mǣl 'cross'), Ruston YN (hrōst), Shafton YW (sceaft), Spaunton YN (spánn ON, 'roofing tile'), Stapleton Cu, Gl, Lei, So, YN, YW (stapol), Staverton Nth, Sf (stæfer), Stockton *freq* (probably sometimes from stocc).

(x) A river-name, as Aveton D (R. Avon), Bitton Gl (R. Boyd), Bledington Gl (R. *Bladon*), Camerton (Cam Brook, olim *Camelar*), Chewton (R. Chew), Corston (Corston Brook, OE *Corse*) So, Crediton D (R. Creedy), Frampton Do, Gl (R. Frome), Irton Cu

(R. Irt), Luton Bd (R. Lea), Ryton YN (R. Rye), Stourton St (R. Stour), Tanton YN (R. Tame), Waverton Cu (R. Waver); cf. also -ing[4] § 7.

(xi) Older Celtic p.ns. and els. (esp. in the SW), as Bryaton Co (bre), Cannington So (Quantock), Catterton YW, Chadderton La (cadeir), Christon So (crūc-), Coulderton Cu (Welsh *culdir* 'strip of land'), Launceston Co (*Lan-Steven*), Minton Sa (*Long Mynd*), Pendleton La (penno-, hyll), Priston So (prisc).

(xii) An older English p.n., usually a topographical feature (esp. a ford), near which a *tūn* was established, as Ashburton D (æsc, burna), Brafferton YN (brād, ford), Burlton He (burh, hyll), Carhampton So (OE *æt Carrum* ASC 833, *Carumtun* BCS 553, carr), Clareton YW (Claro Wapentake), Hartington Nb (heorot, weg), Harvington Wo (heorot, ford), Lamerton D (lamb, burna), Peckforton Ch (pēac, ford), Shipston on Stour Wo (scēap-wæsce), Silverton D (sulh, ford), Staverton D (stān, ford), Tadmerton O (tāde, mere), Tiverton D, Twerton So (twī, ford); *tūn* is a post-Conquest addition in Royston Hrt (olim *Crux Roheis*, *Roiston*), Budleigh Salterton D (olim *Salterne*), Welltown Co (wella).

(xiii) A word for a nearby natural feature (very frequent), as Ayton YN (ON á), Brockton Sa (4), Brotton YN, Broughton Bk, Cu, Db, La *et freq* (brōc), Brunton Nb (2) (burna), Clifton *freq* (clif), Clotton Ch, Cloughton YN (clōh), Clutton Ch, So (clūd), Compton *passim* (cumb), Dalton We, YW (dæl), Denton Hu, etc. (denu), Downton He (dūn), Eaton He, Nt, Yeaton Sa (ēa), Fenton Nt, St, YW (fenn), Halloughton Nt, Haughton Sa, Great Houghton YW (halh), Glass Houghton YW, Hutton *passim* (hōh), Knipton Lei (ON gnípa), Knowlton K (cnoll), Lawton Ch, He (hlāw), Marston, Merston *freq* (mersc), Marten, Marton *freq* (mere), Mitton, Myton *freq* (gemȳðe), Morton *passim* (mōr), Moston Ch, La, Sa (mos), Necton Nf (hnecca), Poulton K (pōl), Shelton *freq* (scelf), Stanton Fitzwarren W 30 (stān, a large standing stone), Twisleton YW, Twiston La (twisla), Welton *freq* (wella), Wotton, Wootton *freq* (wudu). This type is esp. common in the WMidl.

(xiv) A word descriptive of the soil or ground, as Clayton La, St, YW (clæg), Girton Nt, Gretton Gl (grēot), Manton L (malm), Sancton YE, Santon Cu, L, Nf (sand), Stainton *freq* (ON steinn), Stanton, Staunton *passim* (stān).

(xv) The name of a domestic animal, as Boughton Nt, Buckton

Nb, YE (bucca), Calverton Nt, Cawton YN (calf), Cowton YN (cū), Hunton K (hund), Lambton Nb (lamb), Nocton L (hnoc), Oxton Ch, Nt, YW (oxa), Rampton C, Nt (ramm), Shepton So, Shipton Do *et freq*, Skipton YN, YW (scēap), Swinton La, YN, YW (swīn); this group is well represented in the EMidl and NCy.

(xvi) The name of a wild animal or bird (not common), as Darton YW (dēor), Everton Nt (eofor), Foxton C, Lei, YN (fox), Laverton Gl, So (lǣwerce), Thrushelton D (þryscele).

(xvii) The word for a crop, vegetable or the like, as Flaxton YN (fleax), Hayton Nt (hēg), Laughterton L, Leighterton Gl (leahtric), Linton He, YN, YW (līn), Royton La, Ryton Du, Sa, Wa (ryge); *v.* also bere-tūn, gærs-tūn, grǣd-tūn, lēac-tūn, wyrt-tūn.

(xviii) The name of a wild plant or other vegetation, as Brampton, Brompton *passim* (brōm), Brearton, Brereton *freq* (brēr), Farrington So (fearn), Houghton YE, Hoveton Nf (hōfe), Laverton So (lǣfer), Lemmington Nb (hleomuc), Nettleton L, W (netele), Reston L, Ryston Nf (hrīs), Ribton Cu (ribbe), Rhiston Sa, Rishton La, Rushton Ch, Nth (risc), Sefton La (ON sef), Shipton YE, YN (hēope), Spreyton D (sprǣg), Watton Hrt (wād), Wretton Nf (wrætt).

(xix) A tree-name (common), as Ackton YW, Acton K, Mx *et freq*, Aughton La, YE, YW (āc), Aikton Cu (ON eiki), Allerton *freq*, Ollerton Nt (alor), Ashton *passim* (æsc), Birchington K (birce), Boughton Ch, K (bōc), Ellerton *freq* (elri), Elmton Db (elm), Haslington Ch (hæslen), Maperton So, Mapperton Do (mapuldor), Mappleton Db, YE (mapul), Parton Gl, Pirton He, Wo, Purton Gl, St, W (peru, pirige), Plompton YW, Plumpton Cu, K, La, Nth, Sx (plūme), Thornton *passim*, Thorton Do (þorn), Willington Bd, Db, Willoughton L (wilig), Widdington Ess, YW (wīðig-n); *v.* also æppel-tūn.

(xx) A word descriptive of the style, status or occupation of an individual, as Abbotstone W (abbodisse), Abbotstone Ha, Abson Gl (abbud), Bedmonton K (bed-mann), Bemerton W (bēmere), Bishopston(e) *freq*, Bishton Sa (biscop), Chilson O, Chilston He, K (cild), Coniston YW (ON kunung), Crockerton W (croccere), Hornblotton So (horn-blāwere), Kingston *passim* (cyning), Lewson K (hlǣfdige), Rayton Nt (gerēfa), Sapperton Db, Gl, L, Sx (sāpere), Shrewton W, Shurton So, etc. (scīr-gerēfa), Tuckerton So (tūkere), Webton He (webba).

(xxi) The designation of a group of individuals, esp. ecclesiastics, servants, craftsmen and tradesmen, as Bickerton *freq* (bīcere), Charlton *freq* (ceorl), Hinton He (hīwan), Huntington He, Hunton K (hunta), Minchington Do (myncen), Monkton K, YW (munuc), Preston *freq* (prēost), Santon Bd, Swanton K (swān), Smeaton YN, YW, Smeeton Lei (smið); cf. also cild, cniht, eorl, cwene, karl, walh.

(xxii) A tribal or folk-name, as Bretton YW (Brettas), Canterton Ha, Conderton Wo (Cantware), Exton Ha (ēast, Seaxe), Ireton Db, Irton YN (Íri), Normanton Db, L, Lei, etc. (Norðman), Saxon C (Seaxe), Scotton L, YN, YW (Scottas), perhaps a few of the Waltons (walh); *v.* also hǣma-tūn, sǣte, ware, -ing[4] §§ 3, 8, -ingas.

(xxiii) An OE monothematic pers.n., as Abdon Sa (*Abba*), Alton St (*Ælfa*), W (*Ælla*), Barnston Ess (*Beorn*), Bayton Wo (*Bǣga*), Burton Sx (*Budeca*), Chadstone Nth (*Ceadd*), Collaton D (*Cole*, tenant TRE), Harston C (*Herele*), Lullingstone K (*Lulling*), Olveston Gl (*Ælf*), Swardeston Nf (*Sweord*), Whiston St (*Hwīt*). Such monothematic pers.ns. are much less frequent in ordinary genitival compounds with *tūn* than with -ingtūn; they are less common than dithematic names.

(xxiv) An OE dithematic pers.n., esp. common in the WMidl, as Adbaston St (*Ēadbald*), Alderstone W (*Aldred*, tenant TRE), Alderton Ess (*Ælfweard*), Alfriston Sx (*Ælfrīc*), Allaston Gl, Alstone St, Alverstone Wt (*Ælfrēd*), Alstone Gl (*Ælfsige*), Aystone R (*Æþelstān*), Brighthampton O, Brighton Sx (*Beorhthelm*), Darlaston St (*Dēorlāf*), Ebberston YN (*Ēadbriht*), Edgbaston Wa (*Ecgbald*), Goodneston K (*Godwine*), Hermeston Nt (*Heremōd*), Kilmeston Ha (*Cynehelm*), Kinvaston St (*Cynewald*), Osbaldeston La (*Ōsbald*), Osmaston Db, Osmondiston Nf (*Ōsmund*), Shearston So (*Sigerēd*), Wistaston Ch (*Wigstān*), Woolstone Bk (*Wulfsige*).

(xxv) An OE woman's name, as Afflington Do (*Ælfrūn*, tenant TRE), Bilsington K (*Bilswīð*, queen and abbess), Darlton Nt (*Dēorlufu*), Knayton YN, Kneeton Nt, Kniveton Db (*Cēngifu*), Walberton Sx (*Waldburg*), Warburton Ch (*Wǣrburg*), Wilburton C (*Wilburg*).

(xxvi) An ON pers.n. (cf. § 10 *supra*), as Aslockton Nt (*Áslákr*), Barkston YW (*Bǫrkr*), Flowton Sf (*Flóki*), Gamston Nt (*Gamall*), Grimston YE, YN, YW (*Grímr*), Gunton Nf (*Gunni*), Kedleston Db (*Ketill*), Kettlebaston Sf (*Ketilbjǫrn*), Nafferton Nb, YE (*Nátt-*

fari), Nawton YN (*Nagli*), Odstone Lei (*Oddr*), Rolleston Nt (*Hróaldr*), Rolston YE (*Hrólfr*) Scoulton Nf (*Skúli*), Slauston Lei (*Slagr*), Swarkeston Db (*Sverkir*), Throston Du (*Þori*), Thurcaston Lei (*Þurketill*), Thurgarton Nf, Nt (*Þorgeirr*), Thurlstone Sf, YW (*Þúrúlfr*), Wigston Lei (*Víkingr*).

(xxvii) An ODan pers.n., as Booton Nf (*Bō*), Claxton YN (*Klak*), Flixton Sf (*Flik*), Toton Nt, Towton YW (*Tove*), Urmston La (*Urm*).

(xxviii) A post-Conquest pers.n. (cf. § 11 *supra*) as Bryanston Do (*Brian* de Insula 1232), Cripstone Co (cf. Henry *Cryspyn* 1356), Filston K (OFr *Viel*), Flamston W 393 (cf. Walter *Flambard* 1202), Garnstone He (OFr *Gerner*), Gurston W (*Girardus*, tenant TRW), Marlston Brk (Galfridus *Martel* 1242), Muston Do (Ric. de *Musters* 1303), Patient End Hrt (*Payn*, tenant TRW), Puxton So (Robert *Pukerel* 1166), Quarlston Do 63 (William *Quarrel* 1232), Trienstone K (Robert *Trian* 13th century).

tunge OE, **tunga** ON, 'a tongue', used in p.ns. of 'a tongue of land'; it has this topographical use in ModE. In Iceland its chief meaning is 'the tongue of land formed at the confluence of two rivers'. Its provenance in England suggests that its topographical use might be of ON origin, for such a use is not found in OE or ME. It is liable to confusion with **tang**. (*b*) Tonge Lei, Tongs Wood Nt, Tongue Head, Bleng Tongue, Middle Tongue Cu 252, etc.; also in ME f.ns. (as Nt 291, Wa 333, YE 328).

tūnincel, ***tȳnincel** OE, 'a small estate', glossing Lat *villa*, *praediolum* (BT s.v.). (*a*) Tincleton D (**denu**). [**tūn**, **-incel**.]

tūn-mann OE, 'a villein, a countryman', **tunman** ME, 'a villager', (cf. **tūn** § 4), is found occasionally in ME minor names (C 348, Ess 592, Nt 292).

* ***tūn-stall** OE, 'the site of a farm, a farmstead', is not found in independent use, but it occurs in p.ns. as early as DB. It is found in most areas, but particularly in YW; it occurs in early minor names in C 348, Ess 592, Nt 292, Wa 332, YE 328. In ME initial *tun-* sometimes appears as *dun-*, *don-*. (*b*) Dunstal, Dunstall C, L, St, Tunstall Du, K, La, Nf, Sa, Sf, St (2), YE, YN (2); Cruttonstall (**crumb**), Heptonstall (**hēope**, as in the nearby Hebden) YW, Rawtenstall La, Rawtonstall YW (**rūh**), Saltonstall (**salh**), Shackleton (olim *Schakeltunestal*, **sceacol**) YW, Whittonstall Nb (**cwic**). [**tūn**, **stall**.]

tūn-stede OE, 'a farmstead', recorded once in OE as a gloss to Lat *pagus* 'country district' (WW 144.26). (*b*) Tunstead La (a vaccary in 1324), Nf, *Tunstead Leigh* Db. [tūn, stede.]

tup ME, 'a ram, a tup'. (*a*) Tupholme L (holmr), Tupton Db (tūn). [Origin obscure.]

turf OE, 'turf, greensward', as in OE *turfhaga* (*Elene* 830) 'a grass enclosure', *turfhlawan* (BCS 537) 'a turf-covered mound'. (*a*) Turf Carr YE (kjarr), *Turfleigh* Sx 425 (lēah), Turvey Bd 48 (ēg). [~ torf.]

*turn OE adj., 'circular', *v.* trun.

tuyere OFr, ME, 'a blast-pipe for a forge or furnace', first noted in 1350 (NED s.v.). (*b*) Twyers YE (12th century).

twā OE num., fem., neut., 'two', *v.* twēgen.

twǣm OE num.dat., 'two', *v.* twēgen.

*twang OE, 'a spit of land', *v.* tang.

twēgen (twā gen., neut., tū neut., twǣm dat.) OE num., 'two'. (*a*) Toyd W (*tū* neut., hīd); Twantry Nth (trēow), Twemlow Ch (hlāw), both dat. *twǣm*. [~ twī-.]

twī- OE prefix, 'double, two', as in Bede's *Adtuifyrdi, ad duplex vadum* 'at the double ford'; it is common with ford (*fyrde*) and denotes two fords close together; at Twerton So, for example, there are two weirs across the Avon where it would originally have been shallow enough for fords, and at Twyford Wo 265 the double-ford was probably one track across the Avon separated in the middle by an ait. (*a*) Tiverton D, Twerton So (*fyrde*, *v.* ford, tūn), Tuelldown D, Twywell Nth (wella), Twycross Lei (cros), Twydall K (dāl), Twyford Bk, Brk, Db, Ha, He, L, Lei, Mx, Nf, Nt, Wo, Wyvern Gl (*fyrde*, *v.* ford), Tythrop O (þrop). [~ twegen.]

twicen(e) OE, 'the fork of a road, cross-roads', surviving as dial. *twitchel* 'a narrow passage' (NED s.v.). (*a*) Turchington D (tūn). (*b*) Titching Co, Touchen End Brk, Twitchen D (*freq*), Tytchney Wo 272; Bentwitchen D (pers.n.); cf. also W 449. [~ twī-.]

twig OE, 'a twig, a shoot, a sapling', occurs in OE *on þæt twigbutme del* BCS 398; it is difficult to distinguish from twī- and may be found in one or two of the names given there.

*twigen OE adj., 'covered with twigs or shoots', has been suggested for (*a*) Twinstead Ess 465 (stede). [twig, -en.]

twigge OE, 'a twig, a young shoot', recorded in OE only in *Lindisf. Gosp.* Mark xi. 8, as an alternative gloss to telga. It is difficult to distinguish from the OE pers.n. *Twicga*. (*a*) Twigmoor L (mōr), Twigworth Gl (worð). [~twig.]

twinn OE adj., 'double, two-fold', used like **twī-** in p.ns., is possible in (*a*) Twinstead Ess (**stede**), but cf. **twigen**.

(ge)twis OE adj., lit. 'having the same parents', related to OE *getwisa* 'a twin' and **twisla**, probably has a topographical application like the latter, 'the fork of a river'. Ekwall notes its use as an appellative in the Cockersand Cartulary. (*b*) Twiss La 97.

twisla OE, 'the fork of a river, the junction of two streams', found chiefly in NCy p.ns. Its use is well illustrated in BCS 675, *of ðam mere on þan lace þær þa brocas twisliað þanne of ðæm twislan* 'from the pool to the water-course where the brooks fork, then from the fork'. It occurs in early minor names in Bk 259, C 348, Ess 593 (of a road), Sr 366, W 449 (of a road). (*a*) *Twislebrook* YN (**brōc**), Twistleton YW, Twiston L (**tūn**), Twizzlefoot Ess (**wereð**). (*b*) Twizel(l) Nb (2); Birtwisle La, Castweazel K, Entwisle, Extwisle La, Haltwhistle Nb, Oswaldtwistle La, Sinkertweazel K (mostly pers.ns. or doubtful). [~**getwis**, **-el**.]

* **twist** OE, ME, 'something twisted', is found in OE only in the compounds *mæst-twist* 'a mast rope' and *candel-twist* 'a pair of snuffers' (from being made in two parts hinged together). In ME it denotes 'the flat part of a hinge fixed to a door and working in the pintle' and also 'a twig, a branch'. The root idea is 'something made of two parts working together, something which forks' (cf. **twigge**, **getwis**, **twisla**), and some similar topographical meaning like 'fork' is also possible in p.ns. (*a*) Twisgates D 650 (**geat**, probably 'hinged' or 'swinging'), Twisly Sx 486 (**lēah**, probably with the sense 'twig, branch'). (*b*) Twist D (2), Sx 516.

* **twll** Welsh adj., 'holed, hollow'. (*a*) Tollard (**ardd**), Toller (**dubro-**) Do. [On *-o-* in these p.ns. cf. Jackson 274–5; ~**tol**.]

ty Welsh, 'a house', *v.* **tig**[1].

***tydd** OE, 'brushwood, shrubs', an *i*-mutated form of **todd** (cf. Zachrisson, SNPh v, 3). (*b*) Tydd C 283, L.

tȳn OE (WSax) num., 'ten', *v.* **tēn**.

tȳned OE pa.part., 'enclosed'. (*a*) Tineley Nb (**lēah**), Tinfield Wo (**feld**), Tingreave La 131 (**græf**). [~OE *tȳnan*, **tūn**.]

***tȳnincel** OE, 'a small estate', *v.* **tūnincel**.

* **tȳning** OE, **tining** ME, 'fencing, an enclosure', recorded only in *æcer-tyning* 'fencing' (BCS 928) and *gafol-tining* 'fencing wood

due as part of the rent' (BCS 594). (*a*) Timbold K 227 (fald); cf. also f.ns. in W 449, Wo 392. [~OE *tȳnan* 'to fence', tūn, -ing[1].]

tyri, tyrfi ON, 'a resinous wood for fire-making', in p.ns. perhaps a building material. (*a*) Tarsett Nb (sǽtr), Tirrill We (erg), Trewhitt Nb (wiht). [~**torf, turf.**]

***tyrl** OE, 'that which turns, rolls or trundles along', related to ME *trille* 'to turn, to whirl', EFris *trullen*, *trüllen* 'to roll, to turn round', may enter into some r.ns. (cf. Ekwall, RN 409). (*b*) Tirle Brook Gl (OE *Tyrl* BCS 236), Wo 15. [~**trun, -el.**]

Þ

þaca OE 'a roof, a covering (of thatch)'. (*a*) Thakeham Sx (**hām**). [~ **þæc**.]

þæc OE, 'thatch, material for thatching, a thatched roof', used in p.ns. of thatched buildings or places where thatching materials (reeds, etc.) were got. In the NCy it cannot be distinguished from **þak**. (*a*) Thatcham Brk (**hām**), Thaxted Ess 496 (**stede**). [~ **þaca**, **þak**.]

þak ON, 'thatch, a roof, thatching material', usually in p.ns. in allusion to marshes where thatching reeds were got. It is difficult to separate from **þaca** and **þæc**. (*a*) Thack Carr YE (**kjarr**), Thackmire Cu (**mýrr**), Du (**mere**), Thackray YW (**vrá**), Thack Sike (**sīc**), Thackthwaite (**þveit**) YN.

-ð(e), **-eð(a)** OE noun-suffix, originally used to form from nouns and verbs abstract nouns, some of which later became concrete. There were two PrGerm forms of the suffix, *-þan* which was not accompanied by *i*-mutation of the root-vowel and *-iþō-* which usually caused *i*-mutation (cf. Kluge §§ 118, 122–3). Examples in p.ns. include **brēmðe** (from **brōm**), **erð** (from *erian* 'to till'), **fernðe**, **fileðe**, **fyrhð(e)**, **hēhðu**, **hylcð**, **rȳhðe**, **sifeða**, **tilð(e)**.

þe, **the** (**þem**, **þen** masc., **þer** fem., dat.sg.) ME def.art., 'the', is found chiefly in ME minor p.ns., though in most documentary sources it is rendered by Fr **le**, **la**. Its use implies that the name was still significant and probably often an appellative rather than a formal p.n. It is found, for example, in the earlier spellings of Even Swindon W 277 (ME *Theveneswyndon*, from **efen**, Swindon), and it survives in Thurleigh Bd (ME *La Lega* for OE (*æt*) *þǣre leage*); cf. **æt**, **atten**, **atter**. The general loss of the article in p.ns. has also resulted in initial *th-* being wrongly dropped, as in Ede Way Bd (**þēod** ,**weg**), Evegate K (**þēof**, **geat**), Elbridge K (**þel**, **brycg**), Ramacre Ess (**þrēo**, **æcer**), etc.

þēaw-lēas OE adj., 'ill-mannered, indecent'. (*c*) Thorpe Thewles Du.

þefa OE, 'brushwood, bramble' or the like, recorded only in the OE compound *þefan-þorn*, which glosses Lat *rhamnus* 'bramble, blackberry', and as late ME *theve* which is equated with *brusch* (*Promptorium Parvul.* 490); *v.* NED s.v. *theve-thorn*. This el. is difficult to distinguish from **þēof** in ME and may occur in some p.ns. cited s.v. (*a*) Thievely La 84 (**lēah**). [~ **þefel**.]

*þefel OE, 'a bush, a thorn-bush', a derivative of þefa or identical with þȳfel and influenced by *þefa* (as in OE *wiðigþeuel* BCS 781). It probably lies behind (*a*) Thelsford Wa 250, where OE *þyfel* itself is proposed; the ME spellings of this name are *Theulis-*, *Theules-*, *Tefles-*, etc., and neither *þyfel* nor Ekwall's alternative suggestion of tæfl explains these satisfactorily. [þefa, -el.]

þegn (þegna gen.pl.) OE, 'a servant, a retainer, a nobleman with a wergild of 1200 shillings'; it occurs in OE *þegna dene* KCD 1368. (*a*) Thenford Nth (ford).

þel OE, 'a board, a plank'; probably when found uncombined in p.ns. it had some such meaning as 'plank bridge', suggested by compounds like *thelbrycg* BCS 50, *ðæl brycg* ib. 1119. (*a*) Elbridge K (OE *be þæl brycge* BCS 869), Ellbridge Co (brycg), Thelwall Ch (wella). (*b*) Theale Brk, So. (*c*) Thelnetham Sf.

þengel, fengel OE, 'a prince'; like ON *þengill* 'a prince', it is recorded only in poetry. The two forms are a very early example of *þ* becoming *f*. (*a*) Finglesham K (OE *Đengles-*, *Fengles-*, hām), possibly Dinglesden Sx (denu).

þēod OE, 'people, a tribe, a region', used in p.ns. in some such sense as 'public, general', as it was in OE compounds like *þēodbealu* 'public catastrophe', *þēod-feond* 'public enemy', *þēod-sceaða* 'criminal, public nuisance', etc. In p.ns. it is generally combined with words for 'way' or 'ford' and probably had the meaning 'public'. (*a*) Ede Way Bd 122 (*The*) *Edeway* Hrt (weg), Tetford L, Thetford C, Nf (ford).

þēoden OE, 'a chief, a prince', occurs in (*a*) *Theodningc torrens* (BCS 230) Gl. [þēod, -en[1].]

þēof OE, þjófr ON, 'a thief, a robber', as in OE *þeofa cumb* BCS 1319, *þeofa dene* ib. 356. (*a*) Dupath Co (pæð), Evegate K (geat), Thethwaite (þveit), Thiefside (hēafod) Cu, Thievesdale Nt (dæl), Thieves Dikes (dīc, ancient earthworks), Thieves Gill (gil) YN, *Thieve Stake* Wa 175 (staca, no doubt a place of execution), Thiverton D 162 (þring), Thuborough D (beorg).

þēote OE, 'a torrent, a fountain, a water conduit, a pipe'. (*a*) Thatto La (wella), Theddon Ha (denu). [~ OE *þēotan* 'to roar, resound'.]

þicce[1] OE, 'a thicket, dense undergrowth', recorded only as *þiccan* pl. in the *Vesp. Psalt.* xxviii. 9. (*a*) Thicket YE 264 (hēafod), Thicko Ess 504 (hōh). (*b*) Blackmore Thick Nth 206 (blæc, mere). [~ þicce[2].]

þicce[2] (þiccan wk. obl.) OE adj., 'thick, dense', esp. with the names of trees, undergrowth and the like. (*a*) R. Dikler Gl (lǣfer), *Tickenappletree* Wo 305 (æppel-trēow), Thickbroom St (brōm), Thickley Du (lēah), Thicknall Wo 280 (possibly alor), Thickney Hrt (gehæg), Thickthorn Bk, W 272 (þorn), Thickwood W (wudu).

þiccett OE, 'a thicket, dense bushes or undergrowth'. (*b*) Thicket Copse W 302. [þicce[1], -et.]

þille OE, 'a plank, a board, flooring', possibly in p.ns. of a platform used at an assembly (cf. staðol). (*b*) Dill Hundred, Thylle Sx 435.

þing OE, ON, 'an assembly, a council, a meeting'; the OE word, found also in derivatives and compounds like *þingere* 'advocate', *þingstede*, *þing-stow* 'meeting place', occurs in some SCy p.ns., but it is not as common as some other words like mōt in OE. It was the usual term in ON (cf. þing-haugr, þing-vǫllr). Both are usually associated with hundred and wapentake meeting places. (*a*) Dinghurst So, Fingest Bk 176 (hyrst), Thinghill He (hyll), Tingrith Bd 134 (rið), all probably OE. (*b*) Morthen YW (mōr, a district name, which may be OE or ON). In the sense 'possession' OE *þing* is found in ME f.ns. (Nth 270, Wa 333).

þing-haugr ON, 'an assembly mound or hill', usually associated with wapentake meeting-places. (*b*) Fingay Hill YN 213 (the Riding meeting-place), Finger Lei, Thingoe Hundred Sf, *Thinghowe* (now Hanger Hill) Nt 92, *Thing(h)ou* L, Lei. [þing, haugr.]

þing-vǫllr ON, 'a field where an assembly met, a meeting-place', usually of a wapentake; cf. *The Tynwald*, the court of the Isle of Man, or *Þingvellir*, the old meeting place of the Icelandic All-thing. (*b*) Thingwall Ch, La 112, *Thingwall* YN 128. [þing, vǫllr.]

þistel OE, 'a thistle', as in OE *on þistel leage* BCS 763, *on þistel beorh* ib. 1145. (*a*) Thistleton La (tūn), Thistlewood Cu (þveit).

***þoccere** OE, 'a vagabond, a tramp'. (*a*) Doggaport D 95 (port). [~OE *þocerian* 'to run about'.]

þōh, þō OE, 'clay, loam'. (*a*) Southwaite Cu (þveit).

þorn OE, ON, 'a thorn-tree, the hawthorn'; cf. also blæc-þorn, lūs-þorn. This is one of the commonest tree-names in p.ns., due in part to the use of thorns for quick-set hedging; in many p.ns. and esp. in those which denote enclosures *þorn* as a first el. clearly refers to such a thorn hedge, as also with those in haga, hege and some of the Thorntons. In others it refers either to a place overgrown with thorns or to the presence of some prominent thorn-tree. As a final el. it usually refers to a single thorn-tree and it is particularly common in the OE charters (Mdf 139); its frequency is due to thorn-trees being often boundary marks. It may well have such a reference when combined with pers.ns. It is not common with words for 'wood'. (*a*) Tarbock La (**brōc**), Tarleton Gl, Thorington Sf, Thornton Bk, Ch, Do, La, Y *et passim* (**tūn**), Thorley Hrt, Wt, Thornley Du (**lēah**), Thornborough Bk, YN (**beorg**), Thornbrough Nb, YW, Thornbury Gl, He (**burh**), Thornby Nth (**burh**, replaced by **bý**), Thorndon Sf (**dūn**), Thornford Do, Thorverton D (**ford**, **tūn**), Thorness Wt (**hege**), Thorney C, Mx, So, Sx (**ēg**), Thorney Nt, Thornhaugh Nth (**haga**), Thornham K, La, Nf, Sf (**hām**), Thornhill Db, Do, W, YW (**hyll**), Thornthwaite YW (**þveit**). (*b*) Thorne Co, K, So, YW. In compounds, it is found with (i) descriptive words, as Althorne Ess (OE *ǣled* 'burnt'), Cropthorne Wo (**cropp**), Langthorne YN (**lang**), Pickthorn Sa (**pīc** 'prickle'), Rowthorne Db (**rūh**), Thickthorne Bk, W (**þicce²**); (ii) other significant words, as Crathorne YN (**krá**), Craythorne K (**crāwe**), Owthorne YE (**ūt**), Souldern O (**sulh**); (iii) pers.ns. (very common), as Burston Bk, Eythorne K, Fretherne Gl, Kelstern L, Pitstone Bk, Rostherne Ch (ON), Scothern L, Sigglesthorne YE (ON), Tedstone He, Wilstone Hrt. [~ **þyrne**.]

***þornegn** OE, 'a thorn copse'. (*a*) Thornwood Ess (**wudu**), Thornycombe Ha (**cumb**). [**þorn**, **-ign**.]

***þornett** OE, 'a thorn copse'. (*b*) Thornets Sr. [**þorn**, **-et**, **þyrnett**.]

þornig (**þornigan** wk. obl.) OE adj., 'thorny, growing with thorns'. (*a*) Horndon Ess (**dūn**). [**þorn**, **-ig**.]

þorp OEScand, ON, 'a secondary settlement, a dependent outlying farmstead or hamlet', is one of the more common habitative els. in Danelaw p.ns.

(1) OEScand *þorp*, which should be considered with the cognate OE **þrop**, is a loan-word of East and West Germanic origin, for it is found as Goth *þaurp* 'a field' (translating Gk ἀγρός) and OHG *dorf*, OSax *thorp*, OFris *thorp*, *tharp* 'village' (also Fris *torp* 'village, village-mound') and OE *þrop*. According to the present theories, the word, which was a well-established p.n. el. in Germany by the time of the folk wanderings, spread to the north-west into what is now called Denmark, where it was in common use during the Viking period (NK 83), and thence during that period to Sweden where it came into common use in the Middle Ages (ib. 150). It is

also probable that in its progress from Germany to the north *þorp* had reached the Continental Saxons by the 5th century, as it was certainly introduced into Saxon England (*v.* þrop § 3); it had probably also reached Slesvig before the Northumbrian Angles had left (if we can rely on the evidence of a few p.ns. in Northumbria which seem to point to OE *þrop* rather than ON *þorp*), but by the 5th century it does not appear to have arrived in the more northerly area of Jutland, from which, according to Bede, the first Kentish settlers came, since the el. is unknown in English p.ns. of the SE.

(2) The spread of *þorp* therefore coincided in time with the Saxon and Anglian migrations and with the occupation of their abandoned territories in Slesvig and South Jutland by the Danes. This is in accordance with the evidence of Dan p.ns. in *-torp*. Steenstrup rightly held—and it has since been confirmed by Knudsen (cf. NK 84)—that the South Jutland *torp* names are much older in character than those elsewhere in Denmark, for some of them like *Bjerndrupper*, *Bjerndrup*, etc., had the ODan gen.sg. *-ar* whereas elsewhere in the Danish islands the corresponding p.ns. like *Bjørnstrup* have the later remodelled gen.sg. in *-s*; secondly, no *torp* names in the Jutland area embody Christian allusions; and thirdly, many of them are names of places which have become unusually important and should therefore be very old. In Denmark generally, *þorp* was most productive in the Viking period and it is to this fact that we owe the extensive use of the el. in Scandinavian England.

(3) The subsequent spread of *þorp* to the rest of Scandinavia also has importance for English p.ns. During and after the Viking period, it moved to Sweden through Skåne and East and West Götland as far as the Mälar Lake and up the west coast of Sweden to Bohuslän; in Sweden most examples appear to belong to the post-Viking period (cf. Sahlgren, NoB 1923, 69ff). From west Sweden *þorp* then penetrated to Norway, where its use is limited; there its greatest concentration is in Östfold which lies nearest to Bohuslän (NK 22), but it was not in use to any extent during the Viking period, since, apart from one isolated *þorp* (NK 65), it was never used as a p.n. el. in Iceland. In view of this, the majority, if not all, of the *þorp* names in the Danelaw must be of Danish rather than Norwegian origin (*v.* also § 8 *infra*). Cf. further K. Hald, *Vore Stednavne* 117 map. In a new study of *torp-* names in Sweden (appearing in NoB 1954, 106-186), L. Helberg suggests that, whilst

the great majority of Swed *torp*- names conform to the general pattern of spread, there are some p.ns. which apparently belong to an older period and he proposes to find in these another word **þorp** used as an appellative to describe some natural feature or other; the evidence at this stage does not appear to be unquestionable, and it would not affect the interpretation of this el. in the Danelaw.

(4) The original meaning of *þorp* is somewhat obscure and in any case allowance must be made for the possibility of some change of meaning in its transfer from WGerm to ODan. According to some scholars, PrGerm **þurpa*- is ultimately to be associated with Lat *turba* 'a tumult, a mob, a crowd' and according to others with Lat *trabs* 'a beam' or with *tribus* 'a tribe' and Welsh **tref** (cf. NED s.v. *thorp*, Walde s.v. *trabs*, *turba*, and esp. M. Eriksson, NoB 1943, 72ff). Of these the connexion with *turba* has much to commend it, since traces of the meaning 'crowd' are to be found in the Germ cognates: OHG *dorf* meant also 'a gathering of people', OIcel *þyrping* 'a crowd' and *þyrpast* 'to crowd, throng', whilst the ON *Skaldskaparmál* defines it in this way, *Maðr heitir einnhverr* . . . , *þorp ef þrír ero*, 'one single person is called a man . . . if there are three they are called a *þorp*'; in OE too *þrop* is an alternative gloss to *þing-stōw* (*v.* **þrop** § 1). The semantic development from 'a crowd, gathering of people' to 'a place where folk lived together' and then to the well-established general meanings like 'farmstead, hamlet, village' found already in OHG is straightforward. In Denmark and Sweden, however, *þorp* acquired a very particularized sense of 'secondary settlement' probably because of the type of settlement that was being created at the time of its introduction and because other words like *bȳ* which would once have been appropriate had now a different use; places called *bý*, although originally secondary settlements (cf. **bý** § 2), had during the spread of the word *þorp* themselves become centres from which further secondary colonization could start, and a new term to describe this type of settlement was necessary; the word *þorp* seems to have provided it. The meanings which *þorp* had in Denmark and later in Sweden were 'a secondary settlement, an outlying farm' and the evidence for this, as Knudsen (NK 83) points out, is: (i) the word *þorp* became a legal term for such a settlement to distinguish it from the *adalby* from which it was

colonized; (ii) in both Denmark and Sweden, a good many examples of *torp* have the name of the parent village as a first el., as in Dan *Karrebækstorp* (from *Karrebæk*) or Swed *Bregardstorp*, *Ekebytorp*; (iii) many *torp* names are combined with significant words, esp. those denoting natural features, as in Dan *Lunderup* (lúndr), *Skovrup*, Swed *Skogstorp* (skǫgr), *Kvarntorp* (kvern); (iv) some 70–80% of *torp* names (unlike the older names in *bý*) have pers.ns. or personal designations as their first els., presumably those of the individuals who originally went out from the parent village to establish the new settlement. There is enough unambiguous evidence to show that the use of *þorp* in English p.ns. followed much the same basic pattern as in Denmark (cf. also K. Hald, *Fortid og Nutid* xi, 39ff).

(5) In assessing the use of ODan *þorp* in the Danelaw, we should bear in mind two things: one is that the material available for detailed study is from the counties of Cu, La, Nt, YE and YN, and a full account cannot be made until the surveys of YW, L, Lei and Nf in particular are completed. The second is the possibility of the Danes having substituted *þorp* as they did *bý* (cf. bý § 3, tūn § 10) for older English els.; Tholthorpe YN 21, for example, was *Þurulfestune* in 972 and *Turulfestorp* in DB, and similar substitutions may have affected other p.ns.

(6) The meaning 'a secondary settlement, an outlying farmstead or a small hamlet dependent on a larger place' would appear to be the right interpretation of *þorp* in the Danelaw as in Denmark, for the following reasons:

(i) It survives much more frequently as a secondary name than as a parish or township name and in many cases it still denotes only a small hamlet. Comparative figures for Nt, YE and YN are: 52 parish and township names (Nt 12, YE 28 including a heavy concentration of parish names in *thorpe* in Buckrose Wapentake, YN 12), 94 secondary names (Nt 27, YE 42, YN 25). In YW and L it appears to be even more common in secondary names. In many cases there are several such names in a single parish, as Northorpe and Southorpe in Hornsea par. YE or Easthorpe and Westhorpe in Southwell par. Nt; there is a large group of *thorps* round Wakefield YW and another near Sheffield YW. A good many *thorps* recorded in early sources have since disappeared—there are, for example, 7 such lost DB *thorps* in YN—and they could therefore be no more than very minor settlements. In L there are at least 22 lost *thorps* recorded (cf. *Lincoln Record Society* xix, pp. xlvii ff).

(ii) In a few cases there is evidence of the dependence of a *thorp* upon another place, as Ashwellthorpe Nf, where 8 acres of land were conveyed to Ashwell church (c. 1066 ASWills); Bishopthorpe YW was a residential manor of the Archbishops of York, and Littlethorpe YW was a *berewic* of Ripon YW at the time of the DB survey. Even after the Conquest, the idea persists, for Chapelthorpe YW was a chapel of ease of Sandal church, whilst Fyling Thorpe YN (olim *Prestethorpe*) and Priest Thorpe (near Bingley) YW belonged to the monks of Whitby and Drax respectively; Canonthorpe YW belonged to the canons of Nostell Priory, Kirkthorpe YW to the church of Warmfield and Monkthorpe L to the monks of Bardney.

(iii) As a simplex p.n. *þorp* is common, which suggests that settlements so named could have had only a limited and local importance and were not likely to have been large estates with independent rights. In YN 9 out of 36 *thorp* names are or were originally simplex. This kind of function has, of course, been obscured by feudal and manorial additions.

(iv) As in Scandinavia, *þorp* names are often combined with the names of the parent villages, as in Scotton Thorpe YW, Tattershall Thorpe L, Welwick Thorpe YE (all *Torp* in DB), and Thorpefield YN 187 was called *Petithorp juxta Thresk* 'Little Thorpe near Thirsk' in the 12th century (*v.* § 9 (*b*) v *infra*). Morningthorpe Nf (*Torp*, *Maringatorp* DB) and, if it is Scandinavian, Gestingthorpe Ess (*Gyrstlingaþorp* BCS 1306) may both be outliers of older settlements; the former in Ekwall's view is from an OE *Mæringas* 'the people of Meering or Mareham Nf' and the latter from a lost place named after the *Gyrstlingas*.

(v) The location of a *þorp* in relation to a larger place is often indicated by the addition of ēast, west, etc., as in Easthorpe YN, Northorpe, Southorpe YE, etc. (§ 9 (*b*) iv).

(vi) Pers.ns. form a high proportion of first els.; in a large sample some 65 % have pers.ns. as against 35 % with other els. or simplex. The proportion is not as high as in Scandinavia (cf. § 4 *supra*), but it is high enough to suggest that many of these new settlements were made by individuals from the parent villages.

(7) In most areas *þorp* was well established by the 11th century

and a surprisingly high number find record in DB; this is particularly true of YE, YN and the eastern and northern parts of YW, where about 85% of the *þorp* names are recorded in DB or earlier. In Nt the proportion is less at about 40% and in the rest of YW it is probably as low as 20%. The explanation of this is the continued use of *þorp* as a p.n. forming el. after the Conquest, esp. in a region like YW where there was still much land available for exploitation compared with east Yorkshire; names like Canonthorpe YW, Monkthorpe L and Priest Thorpe YW which recall post-Conquest monastic ownership (cf. § 6 (ii) *supra*) point in the same direction, whilst the affixing of pers.ns. of post-Conquest origin to simplex *þorp* names (as with Oakerthorpe Db probably named from *Ulkel*, whose son Robert was living there in 1224) shows that they could be the personal property of one man.

(8) As already noted, *þorp* in Danelaw p.ns. is of Danish rather than Norwegian origin: (i) The el. had barely reached Norway at the time of the Viking settlement in England (§ 3 *supra*). (ii) It sometimes embodies the name of the Danes, as in Danthorpe YE (**Danir**), never the names used of the Norwegians (**Norðman, Íri**). (iii) So far as pers.ns. can be distinguished as Danish or Norwegian, those of Danish origin are the only ones to be distinguished in *þorp* names, as in Authorpe L (ODan *Aghi*), Towthorpe YE (ODan *Tove*) etc. (cf. § 9 (*b*) ix *infra*); the only exceptions are Melkinthorpe We which may contain an OIr pers.n. and which is probably a later formation, and Tharlesthorpe YE 25, which was originally *Torueles-*, *Thoraldesthorp* and which sometimes has spellings with *T(h)arles-* due to the influence of Norw *Tharald* (cf. IPN 92); even in this p.n. it is a late 12th-century replacement of an older *Thorald* and not original. (iv) The distribution of *þorp* names shows that their greatest concentrations are in Y (esp. YE), L, Nt, Lei and Nf; they are found less frequently in adjacent counties We, Db, Hu, Sf, and occasional examples occur in Du, La, Bd, Hrt and Ess; this coincides very closely with the three main areas of Northumbria, the East Midlands and East Anglia which the Danes occupied and settled in the latter part of the 9th century.

(9) The following examples of *þorp* are a representative selection of the principal categories:

(*a*) As a first el. *þorp* is very rare, as in Thorpland Nf (**land**), except where other els. have been added in later times to a simplex

Thorpe, as in Thorpefield YN, Thorp Garth YE, as well as the more usual type of affix as in Thorpe Acre Lei (hafocere), Thorpe on the Hill YW, Thorpe Market Nf, Thorpe Thewles Du (þēawlēas), Thorpe Underwoods YW etc.

(*b*) As a simplex p.n. it is very common and was much more so in medieval times (cf. § 6 (iii) *supra* and (xii) *infra*), Thorp(e) *passim* in most Danelaw counties.

In compounds it is combined chiefly with ON and sometimes also with OE els.:

(i) An adj., as Littlethorpe YW (lytel), Newthorpe Nt, YW (nīwe).

(ii) A word describing vegetation, topography or some nearby feature, as Beasthorpe L, Besthorpe Nt (bēos), Burythorpe YE (berg), Gleadthorpe Nt (cf. glād), Grassthorpe Nt (gres), Howthorpe YN (hol), Layerthorpe YE (leirr), Moorthorpe YW (mōr), Staddlethorpe YE (staðol), Woodthorpe YW (wudu).

(iii) A word for a church or other building, as Chapelthorpe YW (chapel), Kirkthorpe L, YW (kirkja), Millthorpe L, Milnthorpe Nt, We, YW (myln).

(iv) A word denoting position relative to another place, as Aisthorpe L, Easthorpe Ess, Nt, YE (ēast), Everthorpe YE (yferra), Middlethorpe Nt, YW (middel), Northorpe L, YE (norð), Owsthorpe YE (austr), Southorpe L, Nth, YE (sūð), Westhorpe Nt, Sf (west).

(v) A p.n., often added later to an original simplex *Thorpe*, as Ashwellthorpe Nf, Ellington Thorpe Hu, Ewerby Thorpe L, Kilton Thorpe YN, *Scotton Thorpe* YW, Sneaton Thorpe YN, Tattershall Thorpe L, Welwick Thorpe YE.

(vi) A word denoting a person or a class of people, as Bishopthorpe YW (biscop), Canonthorpe YW (canoun), Coneysthorpe YN (kunung), Danthorpe YE (Danir), Ellenthorpe YN (æþeling), Kingthorpe L (cyne), *Laysingthorpe* L (leysingi), Priest Thorpe (prēost), Skinnerthorpe (skinnari) YW.

(vii) An ON pers.n. or by-name (the commonest type of compound), as Alethorpe Nf (*Áli*), Bilsthorpe Nt (*Bildr*), Bromskinthorpe Lei (*Brún-skinn* 'brown-skin'), Caythorpe YE (*Kári*), Flockthorpe Nf (*Floki*), Grimethorpe YW, Grimthorpe YE (*Grímr*), Hackthorpe We (*Haki*), Kettlethorpe YW (*Ketill*), Oakthorpe Lei (*Áki*), Scotterthorpe L (*Skalli*, also in the nearby

Scawby L and *Skalehau*, his burial-mound), Saxthorpe Nf (*Saxi*), Sibthorpe Nt (*Sibbi*), Streetthorpe YW (*Styr*), Swainsthorpe Nf, Swinethorpe L (*Sveinn*), Tholthorpe YN (*Þurulf*), Weaverthorpe YE (*Víðfari* 'far traveller'), Wilsthorpe Db, L, YE, Wilstrop YW (*Vífill*).

(viii) An ON woman's name, as Helperthorpe YE (*Hjalþ*), Ingerthorpe YW (*Ingiriðr*).

(ix) An ODan pers.n. as distinct from common Scandinavian (fairly common), as Authorpe L (*Aghi*), Bagthorpe Nf (*Bakki*), Boothorpe Lei, Bowthorpe Nf (*Bō*), Dowthorpe YE (*Duva*), Fleecethorpe Nt (*Flik*), Mowthorpe YE (*Múli*), Sunthorpe YE, Swinthorpe L (*Suni*), Tolethorpe R (*Toli*), Towthorpe YE, YN (*Tove*).

(x) An OE pers.n. (not common), as Addlethorpe L (*Eardwulf*), Edderthorpe YW (*Ēadrīc*), Edmundthorpe Lei (*Ēadmēr*), Ellenthorpe YW (*Æþelwine*), Yaddlethorpe L (*Ēadwulf*, adapted as ON *Jádúlf*).

(xi) An OIr pers.n. possibly in Melkinthorpe We (*Maelchan*).

(xii) A post-Conquest pers.n. or feudal el., usually added to a simplex name, as Countesthorpe ('countess'), Donisthorpe (OFr *Durand*) Lei, Herringthorpe YW (Jordanus *Heryng*), Oakerthorpe Db (*Ulkel*, cf. § 7 *supra*), Painthorpe YW (ME *Payn*), Perlethorpe Nt (*Peverel*), etc. There are also many feudal affixes with the simplex *Thorpe*, as Thorp Arch, Thorpe Audlin YW, Thorpe Bassett YE, Bochart Nt, Constantine St, Morieux Sf, Thorp Perrow YN, etc.

þræll ON, late OE, 'a thrall, a serf, a slave'. (*a*) Threlfall La (**fall**), Threlkeld Cu (**kelda**), Trailholme La (**holmr**).

þrēap OE, 'a dispute, a quarrel, contention', is recorded only in the sense 'band, troop', but its older meaning is retained in the derivative OE *þrēapung* 'reproof' and *þrēapian* 'to reprove, contend'. In p.ns. it is used, like **calenge**, **(ge)flit**, **strūt**, etc., of land over which there was a dispute (cf. NED s.v. *threap* sb. § 4). (*a*) Debateable Land Cu 38 (olim *Threpelands*), Threapcroft YW (**croft**), Threaphow La (**haugr**), Threapland Cu 271, YW (**land**), Threapthwaite Cu 337 (**þveit**), Threapwood Ch, Threepwood Nb (**wudu**).

***þremm, *þræmm** OE, 'a beam, a log', cognate with LG *traam* 'a balk, a beam' (which is probably the source of StdE *tram* 'framework', etc., cf. NED s.v.), MHG *drāme*, *dremel* 'a beam', Swe dial. *tromm* 'a log'. (*a*) Renville K 545 (feld), Tramhatch (hæcc), *Tremhuth* (hȳð) K 390, perhaps also Trimley Sf (lēah). [PrGerm **þramj-* in ablaut relation to OE *þrum* 'ligament'.]

þrēo (þrī masc., þrīm dat.) OE num. neut., fem., 'three', usually with words for 'mound', 'hill', 'tree' or 'measure of land', often in the dat. case. (*a*) Barrow Hills Sr 108 (olim *Threm burghen*), Rumbridge Sx 88, Three Barrows Hill D 286, Thrybergh YW (beorg), Ramacre Ess (æcer), Three Houses Hrt (hūs), Threo Wapentake L (haugr), *Tremelau* Hundred Wa (hlāw).

þrēpel OE (Angl), þrȳpel (WSax), 'an execution cross, a framework', is recorded in an OE gloss rendering Lat *eculeus* 'a wooden rack to which a body was fixed for execution' and is described as *genus tormenti* 'a kind of torture' (WW 116.13, 225.41); the compound *þrypel-uf* alternates with *wearg-rōd* 'felon cross' (ib. 180.13). The word survives as dial. *thripple* 'a framework attached to a cart to increase its load', being first recorded in that sense in the 15th century (NED s.v.). (*a*) Tripsdale YN 69 (dæl). [~ þrēap in the sense 'reproof', -el.]

*þresc, þersc OE, 'a thrashing, a beating', probably also 'threshing'. (*a*) Threshfield YW (feld). [~ OE *þerscan* 'to thresh'.]

*þresk ON, 'a fen, a lake', found as OSwed *thræsk*, Swed *träsk*. (*b*) Thirsk YN 188.

(ge)þring OE, 'a crowd, a throng'. (*a*) Dringwell D (wella). (*b*) Thriverton D 162 (olim *Thevethring*, from þēof).

þrittig OE num., 'thirty'. (*a*) Trenthide Do (hīd).

þriðjung ON, þriðing late OE, 'a third part', esp. 'the third part of a shire'; the term is used in a similar way in Norway and Iceland. Usually initial *þ-* (which became AN *t-*, cf. IPN 109) was absorbed by the final *t* or *ð* of the preceding word to give *Riding*. (*b*) East, North and West Ridings of Yorkshire, North, South and West Ridings of the Parts of Lindsey L.

þroc OE, 'a support, a post, a trestle', also 'a drain'.

(1) The word *þroc* is recorded chiefly in the OE spellings of p.ns., and also once independently to render Lat *mensa* 'a table' and once to gloss Lat *dentale* which is explained as 'the first part of the plough on which the share is fixed like a tooth' as an alternative to *sule-reost* lit. 'plough-rest'. It appears to be cognate with OHG *druh* 'a post, a shackle, a fetter'. It survives as dial. *throck*, *drock* which retained the technical meaning of 'the share-beam of a

plough'. The older meaning would seem to be 'prop, support' (as in OHG *druh*) and from this developed the more specialized meanings of 'table', 'plough-share beam' and probably something like 'beam, trestle' in such p.ns. as Drockbridge Ha (OE *þrocbriggæ* BCS 393, **brycg**, 'trestle or beam bridge'), Throckley Nb (**hlāw**) and the derivative **þroccen**.

(2) There was probably also another word *þroc* which survives in the dial. of Brk, W, So and Gl as *throck*, *drock* 'a covered drain, a flat stone covering a drain or ditch' which is also common in f.ns. in W 339. It is just possible that the significant idea here is 'the covering over a ditch to form a bridge' which would relate it more definitely with OE *þroc* 'a beam' (cf. § 1). But *þroc* in the sense 'drain' may equally well be connected with **þurruc** which also survives in the sense 'drain'; it could be an early contracted form of *þurruc*; at least the OE spellings of Rockmore W 339 (*þrocmere* BCS 508, *þroc-*, *þorc-*, *þorocmere* ib. 1080) indicate the possibility of some confusion between *þroc* and *þurruc*, whilst **þrūh** may also have added to the uncertainty. In some p.ns. the sense 'drain, dirty water' or the like, which *þurruc* has, would be more appropriate than 'beam, trestle', esp. when combined with **mere** 'pool'. The chief difficulty is in assuming that *þurruc* could be contracted to *þroc* so early. *v.* further **þurruc**. Drockmill Sx 446 (**myln**), Druckham Co (**cumb**), Rockamoor W 339 (**mere**), Throckmorton Wo 169 (**mere**, **tūn**), probably have the sense 'drain' or the like. Throcking Hrt 187 (ME *Throkyng*, *Thorkyng*, **-ing**[2]) is ambiguous.

***þroccen** OE adj., 'having or providing beams'. (*a*) Throckenholt C 278 (*þrokonholt* ASC 656E, '**holt** where beams were got'). [**þroc**[1], **-en**.]

***þrǫngr** ON adj., 'compressed, narrow'. (*a*) Throngham Cu (**holmr**). [~(**ge**)**þring**.]

þrop OE, 'a hamlet, an outlying farm'.

(1) This el. is found in OE only in the glosses where twice it is an alternative gloss to *tuun* (**tūn**) for Lat *competum* (OET 53.557, WW 365.24), once it glosses Lat *fundus* 'a piece of land, a farm, an estate' (WW 147.5), and once it is an alternative to *þing-stōw* 'assembly place' in another gloss to Lat *competum* (ib. 207.14), which in the same gloss is equated with Lat *villa* and which means, amongst other things, 'place of assembly' (*locus in quem conveniunt*, Du Cange). This gloss may reflect a vestige of a more original idea

of 'an assembly of people' which is also found in some of the cognates of *þrop* (cf. þorp § 4). In the other uses of OE *þrop*, however, there is nothing to recall such a meaning and the significant feature of the glosses is its equivalence to *tūn* 'enclosure, farmstead' and Lat *fundus* 'estate'; this may be confirmed by the only other occurrence of *þrop*, *þorp* in OE (which may however be ODan *þorp* and not OE *þorp*) in the twelfth-century record of the reputed grant by king Edgar to Peterborough of *ealle þa þorpes þe þærto lin, þæt is, Æstfeld and Dodesthorp and Ege and Pastun* 'all the *thorps* that pertain thereto, namely, Eastfield, Dogsthorpe, Eye and Paston' (ASC 963 E), all places in Nth round Peterborough, for which the meaning 'hamlets' or 'estates' is most probably correct. The entry is in fact translating *cum suis appendicis* of BCS 1258 and 1280 (the forgery the Peterborough writer was using), and since the entry itself is so late it may well be the ON and not the OE word that it should illustrate.

(2) The p.ns. containing this el. suggest, if anything, that as with ODan *þorp* it denoted a small secondary settlement, for (i) most places so named are insignificant and only a few have become parish names (for which reason many find no record in the earliest sources). (ii) It is frequently found as a simplex p.n. and therefore denotes a place of no more than local importance. (iii) Very often it is combined with words like hēah, sūð, upp, etc., which indicate its location relative to some larger or older settlement; Upthorpe Wo, for example, is so named because it is higher up than the much more important Alderminster a mile away. (iv) Some places would seem from their history and location to be dependent settlements; Neithrop O is in Banbury parish, Cokethorpe Park O is a hamlet in Hardwick parish, whilst Gestingthorpe Ess, if it is English (cf. * þorp § 6 ix), would seem to have originated as an outlier of the lost *Gyrstlingas*.

(3) The distribution of *þrop* is of interest. In the Danelaw it cannot be distinguished formally from ODan *þorp*, but it is possible that a few examples of the OE metathesized form *þrop* have persisted in Northumbria as in Throphill Nb, Thrope YW; p.ns. outside the Danelaw regularly have the metathesized *þrop*, and in the Danelaw metathesized forms of ODan *þorp* are unknown until the modern period; the existence of ME *þrop* spellings in the NCy may point therefore to OE *þrop*. It appears occasionally in some counties

bordering on the Danelaw, as in Nth and Wa, but here it is obviously difficult to be sure of an OE origin. In the rest of England, the el. is concentrated in W, Gl, Bk and Brk, O, and it is found occasionally also in the adjacent counties of Ess, Bd, Wa, St, Wo, So, Do, Ha and Sr; but it is not found in the SE (Kt, Sx) or the extreme SW (D, Co). Its provenance therefore suggests that whilst *þrop* was probably known to the Northumbrian Angles, it was typically WSax; it also suggests that on the Continent the Saxons were in a region which Germ *þorp* had reached before their migration to England and that the settlers in Kt had come from a more northerly part to which *þorp* had not spread at the time of their departure to England (cf. þorp § 1). The el. would also seem to be passing into disuse as a p.n. el. amongst the West Saxons at an early period, certainly before the progress of the settlement westward into D and Co. It is not possible to say whether the literary use of the word in ME is due to the persistence of OE *þrop* or to ODan *þorp*; the latter seems more likely.

(4) (*a*) Throphill (hyll), Thropton (tūn) Nb.

(*b*) As a simplex p.n., Thorpe Bk, Ess, Nth, Sr, Throop(e) Do, Ha, W, Thrope YW, Thrup Bd, Thrupp Brk, Gl, Nth, O, Stoneythorpe Wa (olim *Torp*); probably also Throapham YW (dat.pl.).

In compounds *þrop* is combined with:

(i) Words denoting position in relation to other places, as Astrop O, Easthorpe Ess, Eastrip So, Eastrop Ha, W (ēast), Dunthorp O (dūne in relation to Heythrop), Hatherop Gl, Heythrop O (hēah), Neithrop O (neoðera), Sedrup Bk, Southrop Gl, O (sūð), Upthorpe Wo (upp), Westhorpe Bk, Westrip Gl, Westrop W (west).

(ii) Words for nearby topographical or other features, as Burd(e)rop O, W (burh), Brookthorpe Gl (brōc), Eastrip W 94 (æsc), Eathorpe Wa, Eythrope Bk (ēa), Hilldrop W (hyll), Souldrop Bd (sulh).

(iii) Other significant words, as Tythrop O (twī).

(iv) Words denoting persons, as Cock-a-troop W (croccere), *Swanthorp* Ess, Swanthorpe Ha (swān).

(v) Pers.ns., as Adlestrop Gl, Bigstrup, Colestrope, Helsthorpe Bk, Huntingtrap Wo, Princethorpe Wa, Williamstrip Gl, possibly also Cokethorpe O, *Puttingthorp* So, Restrop W.

þrostle OE, 'a throstle, a thrush', as in *þrostlan well* BCS 1313. (*a*) Thrashnell W (halh). [Cf. þryscele.]

þrote OE, 'the throat', used in p.ns. in some undetermined sense, but presumably of 'something resembling a throat', such as 'a passage' or the like. (*b*) Young Stroat Sr 131, also in f.ns. *la Thrott*, etc. Sr 366.

þrūh (þrȳh gen.sg.) OE, 'a water-pipe, a conduit, a coffin', surviving as *through* (obs.) 'a coffin, a grave-stone'. (*a*) *Througham* Ha, Througham Gl (hām), Throwleigh D, Throwley St (lēah).

þrȳpel OE (WSax), 'a framework', *v.* þrēpel.

þryscele OE, 'a thrush', surviving as 15th century *thruschyl* and dial. *thrishel*, is a diminutive of OE *þrysce* 'a thrush' (*v.* -el). It alternates with þrostle in Threshelfords Ess. (*a*) Thrushelton D 210 (tūn), Thurlescombe D (cumb).

þrȳð OE, 'a troop, a host of warriors', also a prefix meaning 'strong, noble', found chiefly in OE poetry. (*a*) Thurlow Sf (hlāw, probably 'warriors' burial mould').

þūf OE, 'a tuft' not so far found in p.ns., but cf. the derivative and related els. þȳfel, þȳfelett, also OE *þūfig* 'leafy', *þuft* 'thicket'.

þunnr ON adj., 'thin, slender'. (*a*) Thonock L (eik). [~þynne.]

Þunor OE, the name of a heathen Saxon god, corresponding to ON *Þórr* (cf. Dickins 154–6); the distribution of p.ns. containing this el. suggests that the worship of this god was limited in England to the Saxons. (*a*) Thunderfield Sr (feld), Thunderley, Thundersley Ess 172, Thursley Sr 211 (lēah), Thundridge Hrt (hrycg), Thurstable Hundred Ess (stapol); cf. also the unidentified *þunorslege* BCS 208 Sx, *Þunreslea* ib. 393 Ha (lēah), *ðunres felda* ib. 469 W (feld).

Þunresdæg OE, 'Thursday'; for its use in p.ns. cf. Frigedæg. (*a*) Thursday Market Yk 299. [Þunor, OE *dæg* 'day'.]

þurruc OE, 'the bilge of a ship', is found in that or a similar sense in texts such as Chaucer's *Parson's Tale* (cf. NED s.v. *thurrock*); in OE it glosses *cumba*, *caupolus* (WW 181.35) 'the bilge of a ship'. It survives in dial. as *thurrock* and a contracted form *throck*, *drock* 'a ditch, a drain, a covered drain' as well as 'a heap of muck'. The word is probably a derivative of OE *þurh* 'through' and is related to þrūh 'a water-pipe, conduit'; probably its original sense was 'a passage, a channel for water', 'a drain' and then 'a place where filthy water collects' (as in a ship's bilge). *v.* also þroc § 2. (*b*) Thurrock Ess 129. [~OE *þurh* 'through', -uc, þrūh, þyrel.]

þurs ON, 'a giant'. (*a*) Thrushgill La (gil), *Thruslane* Yk (geil, lane), *Thursmare* YE 328 (marr). [~þyrs.]

þveit, þveiti ON, **thwēt** ODan, 'a clearing, a meadow, a paddock'.

(1) This el., which is ultimately related to OE *þwītan* 'to cut off, to whittle' (cf. (ge)þwit), has been taken to have had an original meaning of 'something cut off, a detached piece of land', but amongst the Scand appellative uses are ODan *thwēt* 'chip, splinter' (as well as 'grassy plot, meadow') and Swed dial. *tvet* 'a felled tree, splinter', whilst the related OE *(ge)þwit* also meant 'cuttings'. Knudsen (NK 109) was therefore probably right in thinking that the root meaning was 'something cut down' and the sense development from 'a felled tree' to 'a clearing' is a likely one; the meaning 'clearing, cleared ground' is found in Dan dials., in Norw and Swed p.ns., and in Norw dial. *tveit* 'a forest clearing, a plot of grassland in the forest or among cliffs' (Lindkvist 96ff). Knudsen (NK 107) notes that a very high proportion of the Dan p.ns. in *thwēt* are to be found in the old woodland areas of Vendsyssel and East Jutland. From this other meanings were evolved which include Swed *tvet* in p.ns. 'a detached piece of cultivated ground', ODan *thwēt* 'a grassy plot, a meadow', Norw *tvet* 'a meadow in the woods' and Icel *þveit* 'dry meadowland near bogland'.

(2) The word *þveit* was in productive use during and perhaps before the Viking Age in Scandinavia and is regarded as an older term than the later Norw *ruð* and Dan *rød* 'a clearing', for unlike the latter it was not used with pers.ns. which were introduced after the conversion to Christianity; it is found with pers.ns. of the Viking period and occasionally with the names of the heathen gods, but mostly with common descriptive adjs., as in Dan *Bredtved* (breiðr), *Langtved* (lang) or more often the names of natural features as in Engetved (eng), Næstved (nes), etc., a pattern which is constantly repeated in the Danelaw.

(3) In England this common el. is found only once in ME in a semi-appellative way in a passage cited by Lindkvist 97 from Dugdale vi, 1, *Langethweit et Stalethweit et alios thweiter qui pertinent ad Langethwest* (*sic*), 'Langthwaite (Cu 300) and Scawthwaite (*loc. cit.*) and other *thwaites* that belong to Langthwaite', where *thweiter* is the ON pl. **þveitar*. It does not recur in independent use until 1628 when a *twaite* is defined as 'a wood grubbed up and turned to arable' (NED s.v. *thwaite*); it survives in NCy dial. with the meanings 'a forest clearing, a piece of ground recovered from forest or waste, a low meadow', as well as 'the shelving part of a mountain

side' and 'a single house, a small hamlet'; these latter meanings are probably not genuine appellative uses but definitions recovered from the topography observed for places called *Thwaite*. In medieval documents places so called are frequently described as *campus*, *clausum*, *cultura* or *pastura*, all of which denote plots of ground of one kind or another. The very high proportion of ME examples of *þveit* which have disappeared suggests that it was rather a fugitive el. in current use for new clearings made in the ME period, many of which never became farmsteads. The most probable meaning of *þveit* in English p.ns. then is the original one of 'a clearing in woodland, probably used as meadowland, a meadow, a paddock or close'.

(4) The el. is found most frequently in the NW; there are, for instance, about 80 examples in Cu, at least 30 in We, about 40 in La and 30 in YN, and it is common in the western parts of YW. On the other hand it is rare in the remaining Danelaw counties; thus, YE has only 4 surviving examples and Nt 7 (though in both counties it is common in ME f.ns., cf. YE 328, Nt 291). This distribution is no doubt due to the NW counties having more forest and waste-land to exploit than the better developed eastern and midland counties. Lindkvist 100, however, thought that it reflected Norw influence, but the el. was used as much in Denmark as in Norway and since in fact so many of the p.ns. are ME formations the el. would appear to have been borrowed as an appellative in English and most p.ns. are to be derived from the ME word rather than directly from ONorw or ODan.

(5) (*a*) The el. is not used as a first el.

(*b*) As a simplex p.n., Thwaite(s) Cu, Nf, Sf, YE, YN, YW.

In compounds, it is found chiefly with:

(i) Adjs. referring to shape, size, location, etc., as Braffords YE, Braithwaite Cu, Y (**breiðr**), Easthwaite Cu (**austr**), -wood Nt (**ēast**), Langthwaite Cu, La, YN (**lang**), Micklethwaite Cu, YW (**mikill**), Short Wait YN (**sceort**), Smaithwaite Cu (**smár**).

(ii) Descriptive adjs., as Blaithwaite Cu (**bleikr**), Fairthwaite La (**fæger**), Greenthwaite YN (**grēne**), Ruthwaite Cu (**rūh**), Honeythwaite La (**unnýt**), Whyett YN (**hvítr**).

(iii) Nouns describing the ground or some nearby natural feature (common), as Cringlethwaite Cu (**kringla**), Falthwaite YW (**falh**), Froswick We (**fors**), Garfit Nt (**gor**), Hawthwaite La (**haugr**),

Hewthwaite Cu, Huthwaite Nt, YN (hōh), Holthwaite La (hol), Moorthwaite Cu (mōr), Raisthwaite (hreysi), Scrithwaite (skriða), Seathwaite (sǣ) La, Southwaite Cu (þōh), We (saurr), Stainfield L, Stonethwaite Cu (steinn), Swinithwaite YN, *Swithenthate* Cu (sviðinn, sviðnungr), Wallerthwaite YW, Walthwaite La (vǫllr).

(iv) Words for buildings, shielings, etc., as Bouthwaite YW (búr), Burthwaite Cu (búð, gen.sg.), Curthwaite, Kirkthwaite La (kirkja), Healthwaite YW (hǽli), Husthwaite YN (hūs), Laithwaite La (hlaða), Satterthwaite La (sætr), Scale Foot YN (skáling), Scalthwaiterigg We (skáli), Waberthwaite Cu (veiði, búð); Shoulthwaite Cu 314 may refer to a mill-wheel (hjól) and Crossthwaite Cu, We, YN, Crostwick, Crostwight Nf (cros) to stone crosses or sometimes to a meadow lying athwart something.

(v) Older p.ns., as Guestwick Nf (Guest), Legburthwaite Cu ('Legg's berg'), Subberthwaite (sol, berg), Tilberthwaite ('Till's burh') La, *Wakefeldthwayt* YW (Wakefield).

(vi) Tree-names, as Applethwaite Cu, We (æppel), Birthwaite YW (birki), Hawthornthwaite La (hagu-þorn), Roundthwaite We (raun), Slaithwaite YW (slāh), Thornthwaite Cu, We, YW (þorn), Wythwaite Cu (wīðig).

(vii) Words for wild vegetation (common), as Binthwaite Cu (binde), Brackenthwaite Cu, YW (brakni), Branthwaite (brōm), Bruthwaite (brēr) Cu, Kexwith YN (kex), Reathwaite (hrēod), Seathwaite (sef) Cu, Storwoods YE (storð), Thackthwaite Cu, YN (þak), Thistlewood (þistel), Wanthwaite (hvǫnn) Cu.

(viii) Words for crops, etc., as Beanthwaite (bēan), Big Forth (bygg) La, Haithwaite Cu, Haythwaite YN, Heathwaite La (hēg), Haverthwaite La (hafri), Linethwaite Cu (līn).

(ix) Words for animals, mostly domestic, as Calthwaite Cu (calf), Gristhwaite YN (gríss), Ornthwaite YW (orne), Rosthwaite La (3) (hross), Storthwaite YN (stirc); Ickenthwaite La (ikorni).

(x) Pers.ns. (which form less than 10 % of first els.), mostly ON, as Austhwaite Cu (*Áfastr*), Finsthwaite (*Finnr*), Gunnerthwaite (*Gunnarr*) La, Gunthwaite YW (*Gunnhildr* fem.), Hampsthwaite YW (*Hamr*), Mouthwaite YN (*Músi*), Outhwaite La (*Úlfr*), Wickerthwaite Cu (*Vígarr*); OIr, as Douthwaite YN (*Dubhan*), Yockenthwaite YW (*Eoghan*); post-Conquest, as Bassenthwaite Cu 263 (*Bastun*), Collingthwaite Nt 84 (*Colling*, tenant c. 1180), Godderthwaite Cu (*Godard*); cf. also Thethwaite Cu (þēof).

þvengr ON, **þweng** OE (ONb), 'a thong', with an extension of meaning to 'a narrow strip of land' in p.ns., as with Dan *tving* 'a narrow piece of land, perhaps fenced in'; cf. **þwang**. (*b*) Thwing YE 113.

þverr (**þvert** neut.) ON adj., 'athwart, lying across'. (*a*) *Thweregile* Cu 287 (**gil**), The Sikes YE (olim *Ouerwhart Sykes*, **sīc**).

þwang, þweng (**þwænga** pl.) OE, 'a thong', related to an OE derivative *geþwinglod* 'tied up, fastened up' (of the hair of the head), occurs several times in p.ns., and like the related ON **þvengr** probably denoted 'a narrow strip of land'; a similar sense development is noted for G *riemen* 'strap, thong' used as a f.n. with the meaning 'a long narrow piece of a field', and a development of this kind is also implied in the use of OE *strop* 'strap, band' as a ME f.n. *Strop* (YE 107). MLG *dwanc, dwenge* means 'a narrow place, a passage, a trap' and similar extensions of meaning are possible with *þwang*, as well as some such meaning as 'place where animals can be tied up, tethering place'. The occurrence of this word in p.ns. may recall legends, like those recorded in *Ynglingasaga* or Laȝamon, of a hide being cut into a long thong and used to delimit a tract of land. The form *þweng* (nom.pl. *þwænga, ðuuencgu*) is found in ONb (*Lindisf.Gosp.* Matt. xxiii. 5) and is, like ON *þvengr* (from which it cannot be distinguished), an *i*-mutated form of *þwang*. In ME this el. is sometimes difficult to distinguish from **twang** (*v.* **tang**). (*a*) Caistor L (olim *Þwongchastre*, **ceaster**), Fawn Wood Hrt (OE *æt þwang-tune*), Thongsleigh D (**lēah**). (*b*) Thong K, Nether-, Upperthong YW (at each end of a long ridge), Long Thong Nth; it occurs several times in ME f.ns. (W 448, Wa 333).

þweng OE (ONb), 'a thong, a strip', *v.* **þvengr, þwang**.

(ge)þwit OE, 'cuttings, chips', ***þwīt** OE, 'a clearing, a meadow', related (by ablaut) to **þveit**. An OE *þwīt* has been suggested by Ekwall (La 19) to explain certain NCy p.ns., Inglewhite La (*-white* 1662), Lillywhite Du (*-white* 1365) and Trewhitt Nb (*-wit* 12, *-wyt, -wyth* 13, *-wyth* 1346, *-whit(e), -whitte* 14–15), but none of these has any spellings such as *thwit* or *twit*, and they are therefore better derived from **wiht**. The only p.n. which does have appropriate spellings is Twitham K 539 (ME *Tuit-, Twit-, Thwit-, Thuitham*) and this may be from the suggested *þwīt*, but it is just as likely to be from the recorded OE *(ge)þwit* 'shavings, chippings of wood' which occurs as a variant reading for *sceafða* 'a cutting' in the OEBede iii, 17. Twetton K 62, which Wallenberg interprets as from *þwīt*, or rather another variant **þwǣte*, appears only as ME *Twetton* and is doubtful.

þȳfel OE, 'a bush, a thicket', evidenced chiefly in glosses (cf. WW 244.22) and in OE charters as in *to þam risc þyfele* BCS 687, *wiðig þeuel*, *þorn þiuel* ib. 781, and *on þone hundes þyfel* ib. 820, survives as ME *þuuele* (*Owl and Nightingale* 278) and possibly as NCy dial. *thivel* 'a pot-stick' (cf. NED s.v. *thivel*, where the difficulty of the sense-development is noted); the vowel length of *þȳfel* is uncertain but it might be directly from OE *þūf* 'a tuft'. There appears to have been some confusion between *þyfel* 'a bush' and **þefa**, **þefel** 'a thornbush' for *þyfel* occurs as *þeuel* in BCS 781 whilst in the compound *þefan-þorn þefa* is spelled *þyfe* and *þife* (cf. NED s.v. *theve-thorn*). (*b*) Thule D 439, Rixdale D 488 (**risc**). [~OE **þūf** 'a tuft', **-el**.]

***þȳfelett** OE (WSax), ***þēfelett** (Kt), 'a thicket'. (*b*) *Thevelette* Sr. [**þȳfel**, **-et**.]

þynne OE adj., 'thin, not dense, poor'. (*a*) Thinwood Co (**wudu**), Thynacombe D (**cumb**).

þyrel OE (Angl, WSax), ***þerel** (Kt), 'a hole, an opening (as in a wall)', adj., 'pierced, having a hole' and in some p.ns. possibly 'hollow'. (*a*) Durlett W (**geat**), Thirlmere Cu 35 (**mere**), Thirlstone, Thurlestone D (**stān**, the latter a rock with a natural hole), Thirlwall Nb (**wall**, a gap in the Roman Wall), Thurlbear So (**beorg**, perhaps a hill with a gap in it), Thurlibeer Co (**bearu**), Thurlow C (**hlāw**). (*b*) Threal's Fm Sx; Stanthorne Ch (**stān**). [PrOE **þyrhel*, ~OE *þurh* 'through', **-el**.]

þyrelung OE, 'piercing', used concretely in p.ns. of 'a hole, a gap, a hollow'. (*b*) Thurland's Drove C, Turleigh W 125. [**þyrel**, **-ing**[1].]

þyrne OE, **þyrnir** ON, 'a thorn-bush', is found chiefly in the Danelaw and many p.ns. are doubtless from the ON, but it is found in OE charter material (cf. Mdf 141); it is sometimes confused later with **þorn**, and is difficult to distinguish from the OEScand *Thyrni*. (*a*) Thrimby We (**bý**), Thrintoft YN (**topt**), Thrunscoe L, Thurnscoe YW (**skógr**). (*b*) Thirn YN, Thurne Nf; Farnham Nb, Thornholme YE, Thurnham La (dat.pl.); Caistron Nb (**kers**), Chawston Bd (**calf**), Henthorn La (**henn**), Lighthorne Wa (**leoht**), Stathern Lei (**staca**). [~**þorn**, **-e**.]

*þyrnett OE, 'a thorn copse'. (*b*) *Thernet* Ess, Thornets Sr. [~ þorn, -et, ~ þornett.]

*þyrning OE, 'a place growing with thorns', is possible in (*b*) Thurning Hu, Nf. [~ þorn, -ing[1].]

þyrnir ON, 'a thornbush', *v.* þyrne.

þyrre OE, thyr ODan, adj., 'dry, withered'. (*a*) Therfield Hrt (feld), Thirbeck Db (bekkr), Turville Bk (feld), Turtley D (clif).

þyrs OE, 'a giant, a demon'. (*a*) Thirlspott Cu (pott), Thursden La (denu), Trusey YE (haugr), Tusmore O (mere); cf. also *Thirsqueche* Nth 268 (queche). [~ þurs, and cf. Dickins 158.]

U

-uc, -oc, -c OE noun suffix, from PrGerm *-(u)k* (Kluge § 61), usually forming diminutives, as in (i) plant-names, such as **bēosuc, cammuc, galluc, hassuc, hleomuc, riscuc** (some of which are of obscure origin); (ii) animal- and bird-names, such as **bulloc, cādac, cranuc, dunnoc, hafoc, padduc, puttoc**, cf. also OE *ruddoc* 'a robin', *weoloc* 'a whelk'; (iii) topographical and other terms, such as **hylloc, lacuc, pearroc, pennuc, rimuc, sēoluc, þurruc**. In a few cases there may have been syncope of the vowel of the suffix, as in **halc** (from **halh**), **hulc** (from **hulu**). In some p.ns. this suffix may have been substituted for PrWelsh *-ǫg* (from **-āco-**), as in Craddock D, Ennickford Wo, Tarnock So. [Cf. RN lxxviii.]

ūf OE, 'an owl'. (*a*) Ousden Sf (**denu**).

ufan, ofan OE adv., 'over, above', in p.ns. of an elliptical type '(land) above'. (*a*) Oveney K (**ēg**).

***ufer** OE, 'a slope, a hill', *v.* **ofer**[2].

uferra OE adj., 'higher, upper', difficult to distinguish from **ofer** and **ufer**. (*a*) Overbury Wo (**burh**), Overton Ha, W (**tūn**), Ureby Cu, Yearby YN (**bý**). (*c*) Overpool Ch, Upper Helmsley YN (olim *Over-*), etc. [~ **ofer**[2], **ofer**[3].]

-ul OE noun and adj. suffix, *v.* **-ol**.

ūle (**ūlan** gen.sg., **ulena** gen.pl.) OE 'an owl', used in p.ns. of places like hills, old buildings, fortifications, etc., haunted by owls. The modern forms vary considerably. (*a*) Oldberrow Wo, *Oldborough* K (**beorg**), Oldcoates Nt, Ulcat Row, Ullcoats Cu (**cot**), Oubrough YE (**burh**), Outchester Nb (**ceaster**), Owley K (**halh**), Owlacombe D, Ulcombe K (**cumb**), Owl Head YW (**hēafod**), Ulley K (**lēah**).

úlfr (**úlfa** gen.pl.) ON, 'a wolf'. (*a*) Owlands YN (**lúndr**), Ullock Cu (2) (**leikr**), Ulpha Cu (**haugr**). [~ **wulf**.]

ulm OE, 'an elm-tree' (as in OE *ulm-trēow* WW 138.12). (*a*) Holmstead C, Ess (**stede**). (*b*) Nelmes Ess (**atten**). [Lat *ulmus* 'elm' as in G *ulme*; ~ **ylme, almr, elm**.]

-um OE, ON, dat.pl. ending.

(1) This is normal with a locative function in the OE spellings of p.ns. which have the final el. in the pl. (cf. also **-e**[2]), as in OE *æt Baðum* (ASC 906) now Bath So, *ad Hlidum* (BCS 214) now Lydd K, *æt norð healum* (ib. 1063) now Northolt Mx, as well as with

original folk-names or tribal names (esp. those in -ingas), as OE *In Gyruum* (Bede) now Jarrow Du or *æt Mallingum* (OET 434) now Malling K; cf. also æt, atten.

* (2) In the modern forms of p.ns. *-um* has usually been replaced by such forms as *-ham*, *-holme*, as in Newsham L, YN or Newsholme YE, YW, both from (*æt þæm*) *nīwum hūsum* '(at the) new houses' with the stress shifted to the final ending, as also in names like Windersome YE (*wind-hūsum*), Wothersome YW (*wudu-hūsum*). In Y there are a few examples of variation between the dat.sg. or nom.pl. and the dat.pl.; Blubberhouses and Woodhouse (near Leeds) YW, for instance, appear with ME *-huse*, *-house* and *-husum*, Coates L as *Cotes* and occasionally *Kotum*, *Cotun*; cf. also Downholme YN 270 (*Dune*, *Dunum*), Howe Bridge YN 44 (*Hou*, *Houm*).

(3) As Mawer (Problems 12ff) has pointed out, the dat.pl. type seems to belong to Anglian territory and it is much more frequent in the NCy than the Midl; that it is not due to ON influence is proved by its high incidence in Du and Nb and the fact that it is found more often with OE than with ON els. More precisely, the region east of the Pennines from Nb to Y, provides most examples with the greatest concentration in YE with over 30 such p.ns. But they appear sporadically everywhere in Anglian territory, as far south as Hitchin Hrt and as far west as Lindon Wo, Lidham St and Oaken Sa; but they are not very common in Cu, La and other counties to the west.

(4) Some instances occur in the south in OE times when the syntax demands the use of a dat., but they rarely survive; Carhampton So (OE *æt Carrum* ASC 833) is an example. They are, however, found somewhat more often after ME *atte* in surnames associated with p.ns., as in Cotton K 48 (cot), which in ME is occasionally *Cote*, *Cotes* but usually *atte Coten*, *atte Cotton* in the surnames of men who lived there. In the SCy OE *-um* was already appearing in an unstressed form *-an*, *-on* in late OE, as in *æt Sendan* BCS 1063 for Send Sr and it was therefore easily confused with the OE wk. noun pl. ending in *-an*. There are many instances in p.ns. of the extension of this southern weak pl. ending *-an* (ME *-en*) to strong nouns which should have had a pl. in *-es* (cf. -an § 4, -ena, and D xxxvi) and many SCy p.ns. which have ME *-en* alternating with *-es* arise from this new weak declension and are not survivals

of the dat.pl. *Hayne* D 369, for example, is ME *La Heghe*, *Heghen*, *Heghes* (gehæg) and Welwyn Hrt 144, which in OE is in the dat.pl. *Welingum*, *Welungum* (wilig), appears in ME as *Welewe*, *Welewes*, and the form *Welewen*(*e*) does not occur until 1220 and after; the same explanation is true of Wicken Ess 544, Nth 107 (wīc § 6*b*), and Willen Bk 26 (wilig), which is *Wily* in early ME and *Wylien*(*e*) from 1235 with *Wilies* sporadically.

(5) It is unnecessary to give examples in detail, as a typical sample is listed in YE 311. It is found mostly with simplex els., but compound p.ns., esp. with hūs and lēah also occur. The chief categories include:

(i) Topographical terms (common), as Bewholme YE (bjúgr), Burnham L (burna), Carham Nb, Carhampton So (carr), Chesham La (cis), Clotherholme YW (clūder), Crookham Nb (krókr), Croome YE (crōh), Deanham Nb, Denholme YW (denu), Downholme YN (dūn), Eyam Db (ēg), Fenham Nb (fenn), Hallam YW (hallr), Hallam Db, Hawne Wo (halh), Hillam YW (hyll), Holme on the Wold YE (haugr), Kelham Nt (kjǫl), Poolham L (pōl), Welham Nt, YE (wella), Yarm YN (gear).

(ii) Words for trees and wild vegetation, as Acomb Nb, YN, YW, Oaken St (āc), Askham We (askr), Farnham Nb, Thornholme YE (þyrne), Haslam La (hæsel), Hipperholme YW (hyper), Lindon Wo (lind), Riseholme L, Rysome YE (hrīs), Rusholme La (risc), Salome Wood Hu (salh), Stockham Ch, St (stocc).

(iii) Words for enclosures, clearings, etc., as Escombe Du (edisc), Leam, Lyham (lēah), Roddam (rod) Nb; also in compounds, Acklam YE, YN (āc, lēah), Cleatlam Du (clǣte, lēah).

(iv) Words for buildings and other structures as Bootham Yk (búð), Byram YW (bȳre), Coatham Du, YN, Nun Coton L, Cottam Nt, YE (cot), Howsham L, YE (hūs), Kilham (cyln), Laytham (hlaða) YE, Millom Cu (myln), Statham Ch (stæð), Wyham L (wīg); also in compounds with hūs (dat.pl. *hūsum*), as Loftsome YE (lopt-hús), Moorsholme YN (mōr), Newsham Du, L, YN, Newsholme YE, YW (nīwe), Wesham La (west), Windersome YE (wind), Wothersome YW (wudu).

(v) Words for farm or small settlement, as Airyholme, Eryholme YN, Arram YE (erg), Stokeham Nt (stoc), Throapham YW (þrop), Wigan Hu, Wykeham YN 45 (wīc).

(vi) Old tribal names, as Hitchin Hrt (*Hicce*), Ripon YW (Hrype).

under OE adv., prep., 'under, beneath, below', in p.ns. of an elliptical type denoting '(the place) under something (usually a hill)' and also with wood-names sometimes in the sense 'under the shelter of, under the jurisdiction of, near', esp. in affixes. (*a*) Underbarrow We (**beorg**), Underhill K (**helde**), Underley We (**lēah**), Underly He (**hlið**), Underriver K (**yfer**), Underwood Db (**wudu**). (*c*) As an affix, sometimes rendered by Lat *sub*, as Shipton under Wychwood O, Thorpe Underwood(s) Nth, YW, Weston Subedge, Wotton under Edge Gl.

-ung, -lung OE noun suffix, with the same function as **-ing**[1]; it does not cause *i*-mutation and is always replaced in ME by *-ing*.

unnyt OE, **únytr** ON adj., 'useless'. (*a*) Honeythwaite La 196 (**þveit**).

unþanc OE, 'thanklessness, displeasure', is used in p.ns. and f.ns. to describe land occupied by squatters against the owner's wish. (*b*) Unthank Cu 193, Nb. (*c*) Newton Unthank Lei.

únytr ON adj., 'useless', *v.* **unnyt**.

upp, ūp, uppe OE adv., **uppan** OE prep., **upp, uppi** ON, **up, uppe** ME adv., prep., 'up, higher up, upon', are no doubt to a large extent used in elliptical formations to denote '(land) higher up than something else' (esp. with topographical els.); this is certainly true of the type *upp-in-tūne* '(land) higher up in the village', as in Upton Ess, and when it forms a prefix to river-names in the type Upavon. In other cases it denotes 'the higher one' of two villages (as in Upleatham as distinct from Kirkleatham YN) and 'a place with a lofty situation' (esp. in the names of buildings, farms, etc.). (*a*) It is usually found with (i) topographical els., as Offord Hu (**ford**), Uplands K (**land**), Upleatham YN (**hlið**), Upnore K (**ōra**), Upwood Hu (**wudu**); (ii) r.ns. and words for 'water' (sometimes as an affix), as Upavon W (R. Avon), Up Cerne Do (Cerne), Upleadon Gl (R. Leadon), Upottery D (Ottery), Uphill So (**pyll**), Upwell C (**wella**); (iii) words for buildings, farms, etc., as Upchurch K (**cirice**), Upham Ha, W (**hām**), Uppington W (**hām-tūn**), Upsall YN (2), Upsland YN (**salr, lúndr**), Upthorpe Wo (**þrop**), Upton Bk, Brk, Ch *et freq* (**tūn**). (*b*) Westup Sx 266 (**west**). (*c*) Uplitherland La, Kingston upon Hull YE, etc. (cf. **on, super**).

uppan OE prep., 'upon', *v.* **upp**.

ūr OE, 'a bison', recorded only as the name of the rune for U. (*a*) Urpeth Du (**pæð**), Urswick La (**sǣ, wīc**). [~ON *úrr* 'a kind of ox'.]

ūt, ūte OE, **út, úti** ON adv., 'outside, on the outskirts', used elliptically to describe '(a place) lying on the outskirts or further away from something' (cf. also **būtan**), but mostly as an affix with an adj. function 'outer, more distant'. (*a*) Outgate L (**gata**, road leading out of the town), Outwell C (**wella**) and the common f.n. *Outfield* (e.g. *lez Owtfeld* Cu 325, etc.). (*b*) Westout Sx 320 (land outside the west gate of Lewes). (*c*) Out Newton, Owthorne, Rysome Garth (olim *Utrisum*) YE. [~**ūterra.**]

ūterra, ūtera OE adj., 'outer, lying on the outside, more remote'. (*a*) Outerness Hu (**næss**), Utterby L (**bý**). (*c*) Dearsden YE 170 (olim *Vtter-* as distinct from *Haym-deresdun* 'home Dearsden' cf. **heim**). [~**ūt, ytri.**]

ūt-gang OE, **út-ganga** ON, 'an exit, a way out'. (*b*) (The) Outgang Cu 301, Nt, YE 137, and in f.ns. (as Cu 496, Nt 292); cf. also *Utganger* (a street in Selby) YW (ON pl. *útgangar* 'exits from the town'). [**ūt, gang.**]

-uð OE noun suffix, *v.* **-oð.**

V

v had the value of [w] in ON and also in the Celtic and British forms cited in this work (practice varies and the British sound is represented by some scholars as *u̯* or *w*). OFr *v*, ME *v* both had the value of [v].

vacherie OFr, ME, 'a vaccary, a dairy farm'. (*b*) Vachery Sr (from 1242), Chalwood Vetchery Sx.

***vǽtt-vangr** ON, 'a field for the trial of a legal action', cannot formally be distinguished from OE *se weta wang* 'wet meadow' (*v.* **wēt**), but the topography is decisive in (*b*) Wetwang YE 128. [ON *vǽtti* 'witness, evidence', **vangr**, cf. *Sagabook* iv, 102, 106.]

val, vals OFr, **vale** ME, 'a vale, a wide valley', esp. in p.ns. of Fr origin. (*a*) Vale Royal Ch (Fr *roial* 'royal'), Vaudey L (Fr *dieu* 'God'). (*b*) Vale Fm Sx 343; Beauvale Nt (**bel**), Jervaulx (R. Ure), Rievaulx (R. Rye) YN, Merevale Wa, Merryvale He (**myrig**), Perivale Mx (**pirige**), Pickering Vale YN, the Vale of Evesham Wo, etc. (*c*) Staunton in the Vale Nt. [~ Lat *vallis*.]

valee OFr, **valeie** ME, 'a valley'. (*b*) Vallis So (from 1296); cf. also C 348, Hrt 260. [~ **val**.]

vangr ON, 'a garden, an in-field'. (*b*) Whangs Cu and in ME f.ns. (as C 348, Ess 592, Hu 296, L, Nt 292, Nth 270, etc.). [~ **wang**.]

vápnatak ON, **wæpengetæc** late OE, **wapentac** ME, 'a wapentake, a sub-division of a county', corresponding to OE **hundred**; it was used in the Danelaw counties of Y, L, Nt, Lei, Nth. [*v.* NED s.v. and Anderson xxi–xxiv.]

vargr ON, 'a wolf', also 'an outlaw who has violated a holy place'. (*a*) Wragholme L (**holmr**), Wragmire Cu (**mýrr**). [~ **wearg**.]

varp, varpa, verp ON, lit. 'a casting (up)', used in two distinct senses in Norw p.ns., (i) 'a place where fishing nets are cast' and (ii) 'a heap of stones, a cairn' (NGIndl 84). Formally this may be found in (*b*) Ruswarp YN 125 (**hrīs**), but cf. the cognate **wearp**.

varða, varði ON, 'a cairn, a heap of stones', esp. one on the top of a hill (probably as a look-out place). (*a*) Ward Hall Cu (**hóll**) Warbreck La (**brekka**), Warcopp We (**copp**), *Watchcommon* Cu 103 (OIr *Colman* pers.n.), Wath Cote YN (**cot**). [~ **weard**.]

vatn (**vatns, vats** gen.sg.) ON, 'water, fresh water, a lake'. (*a*) Wasdale We (gen.sg., **dalr**), Watendlath Cu (**endi**). (*c*) Thornton Watlass YN (**lauss**). [~ **wæter**.]

vátr ON adj., 'wet'. (*a*) Waitby We (**bý**), Waithwith YN (**viðr**); it replaces **wēt** in Watton YE 158 (*Uetadun* Bede, **dūn**).

vað ON, 'a ford', used in much the same way as **ford**. (*a*) Wassand YE (**sand**). (*b*) Wath Cu, YN, YW; Waithe L (from *vaði* dat.sg.); probably Wass YN (pl.). In compounds, it is found with (i) adjs. relating to size, etc., as Braworth YN (**breiðr**), Broadwath Cu (**brād**), Langwith Nt, Langworth L (**lang**), *Scamwath* La (**skammr**); (ii) words descriptive of the bed of the ford, as Helwath YN (**hella**), Lairthwaite Cu (**leirr**), Sandwath Cu, Sandwith Cu, YW (**sand**), Slapewath YN (**sleipr**), Stenwith L (**steinn**); (iii) topographical or other descriptive words, as Crookwath (**krókr**), Dubwath (**dubb**) Cu, Flawith YN (**flaða**), Howath La (**haugr**), Rainworth Nt (**reinn**), Solway Firth Cu (**súl**); (iv) animal names, as Lambwath YE (**lamb**), *Noutwath* Cu (**naut**); (v) pers.ns. or other pers. designations, as Conjure Alders Nt (**kunung**), Calceworth L, Kersey Bridge Cu, Mulwith YW, Ravensworth, Snilesworth YN, Winderwath We. [~**wæd**.]

veggr ON, 'a wall', in ODan also 'a boulder' and in Norw p.ns. 'a mountainous wall, a steep cliff'. (*b*) Stanwick YN 296 (ancient rock entrenchments), Stanwix Cu 108 (Hadrian's Wall) (**steinn**).

veiðr ON, 'hunting, fishing, a place for hunting or fishing'. (*a*) Waitham La, Wedholme Cu (**holmr**), Waberthwaite Cu (**búð**, **þveit**). (*b*) Ingoe La (pers.n.).

vél ON, 'a trick, a snare', *v.* **wīl**.

venelle OFr, **vennel** ME, 'a narrow lane in a town'. (*b*) The Vennel (Wilton) W, *Blind-Venell*, etc., Cu 496. [MedLat *venella*.]

vengi ON, 'a field', recorded only in a general sense. (*b*) Wing R. [~**vangr**.]

vennel ME, 'a narrow lane', *v.* **venelle**.

ventā Brit, of unknown meaning; this el., however, occurs as a simplex British town-name in classical sources (*Venta Belgarum*, *Venta Icenorum*, etc.). On the forms. *v.* Jackson 278, 282, etc. (*a*) Winchester Ha (**ceaster**).

verk ON, 'work, a work', no doubt having in the Danelaw the sense of OE **weorc** 'a military or defensive work, a fortification', though this does not appear to be found in Scandinavia. (*b*) Foremark Db (**forn**).

***verno-** Brit, gwern Welsh, 'alders'; it is recorded in Gaul *Vernetum* (DEPN). (*a*) Warren Burn Nb, Werneth Ch, La (with a suffix *-eto-*, as in the Gaul name cited).

verp ON, 'a casting up, a cairn, etc.', *v.* **varp**.

vestr (**vestri** dat.sg.) ON sb., used also as adj., **vest-** ON pref., 'west, westerly', **vestri**, **vestari** ON comp., 'more westerly', indistinguishable from **wester** and **westerra**. (*a*) Westby L, La, YW, Westerby Lei (**bý**), Westerdale YN (**dalr**). [~**wester.**]

veðr ON, 'a wether-sheep'. (*a*) Wetherby YW (**bý**). [~**weðer.**]

vík ON, 'a small creek, an inlet, a bay', also seems to have been used in Norw p.ns. of 'a nook, a hollow' (NGIndl 85) and both senses are found in NCy dial. *wyke* 'a small bay in an inland lake', esp. in Lakes Windermere, Esthwaite and Coniston Water (EPN 62), and *wick* 'a corner, an angle, a hollow'. It is rare as a p.n. el. and examples are found mostly on the coast. (*a*) Wigtoft L (**topt**). (*b*) Blea Wyke YN, Blowick La (**blár**), Lowick La (**lauf**), Catwick, Ravenswyke, Runswick Bay YN (pers.ns.).

víkingr ON, 'a roving pirate, a viking', was already known in OE as *wicing*, but it is usually difficult to distinguish from the ON pers.n. *Víkingr* (cf. Feilitzen 405). (*a*) Wickenby L (**bý**), Wiganthorpe YN (**þorp**), Wigginton YN, Wigston Lei (**tūn**). [~**wīcing.**]

vin ONorw 'a meadow, a pasture', which is a typical p.n. el. in Norway and some adjacent parts of Sweden, is thought to have been at least obsolescent by the period of the Norw settlement in England in the 10th century. It is found in the Orkneys and Shetlands, where the Norse settlement was much earlier, but it is not found in Iceland and it is doubtful whether it is found in England though examples of its use have been suggested. The whole history of this el. has been very satisfactorily dealt with by Valter Jansson, *Nordiska Vin-namn* (Uppsala 1951). The two suggested English examples are Rosewain Cu 334 (ME *Rossiwin*, *Rossewyn*, *Rosewin*, from **hross** 'a horse') and Tossan Nb 199 (ME *Thos(s)an*, *Tossan*, *Tossen*, thought by Mawer to be parallel to Swed *Tossene* or *Tos-vin* 'flax field'). In view of the improbability of *vin* persisting long enough in Norway to be a living el. in the 10th century, it is on the face of it unlikely to enter into either of these p.ns. Rosewain is undoubtedly a compound of **hross** and OE **gewinn** 'fight' (the spelling *Rossiwin* points to this) and the name is a close parallel to compounds with **gefeoht** which also recall the early sport of horse-fighting. The spellings of Tossan do not in any way support *vin* as the final el. and the name may well be of non-Germanic origin.

vindr ON, 'wind', *v.* **wind**[1].

vine OFr, ME, 'a vine'. (*b*) Vine Street (Lincoln) L (*Vinea* Hy 2), *et freq*; it alternates with OE *wīn* in **wīn-geard**.

vinȝerd ME, 'a vineyard', with OFr **vine** 'vine' for OE *wīn*, usually replaces **wīn-geard**.

viniterie ME, 'a small vineyard', is found in f.ns., *le Vyntre*, etc., C 348, The Vintry Ln.

vinstri ON, 'the left one' in r.ns. as in Norw *Vinstra*. (*b*) R. Winster La, We. [*v.* RN 463.]

vinter OEScand, 'winter', *v.* **winter**.

vinye ME, 'a vine', a variant of **vine**. (*b*) Phoenice Fm Sr 100. [~OFr *vigne*.]

við ON adv., prep., 'beside', *v.* **wið**.

víðir ON, with ODan, 'a willow, a withy'. (*a*) Withgill YW (**kjǫlr**), Wythburn Cu 315 (**burna**), Wythwaite Cu (**þveit**). [~**wīðig**.]

* **viðr** (**viðar** gen.sg., **viðir** nom.pl.) ON, 'a wood', also (but less often) 'a tree, a tree-trunk'. It occasionally replaces OE **wīc** as in Bubwith, Cottingwith (pers.ns.), Skipwith (**scēap**) YE and perhaps Skirwith Cu (**skírr**), and **wudu** in Beckwith (**bēc**), Tockwith (pers.n.) YW. It is not as common as **skógr** or **lúndr**. (*a*) Witherslack We (gen.sg., **slakki**). (*b*) Askwith YW (**askr**), Blawith La (**blár**), Hartwith (**hjǫrt**), Menwith (**gemǣne**) YW, Nutwith (**hnutu**), Rookwith (**hrōc**) YN, Swinn Wood L (pers.n.), Yanwath We (**jafn**). [~**wudu**.]

vǫgn ON, 'a grampus', suggested by Ekwall for (*a*) Walney La 205 (**ey**), but *v.* **wagen**.

vǫllr (**vallar** gen.sg., **velli** dat.sg.) ON, 'a meadow, a pasture, a paddock'. (*a*) Wallerthwaite YW (gen.sg.), Walthwaite La (**þveit**), *v.* also **þing-vǫllr**. [~**wald** § 2.]

vǫr (**varar** gen.sg.) ON, 'a fenced-in landing place'. (*a*) Wartop Lei (**topt**). [~**wer**.]

* **vrá**, **rá** ON, 'a nook, a corner of land', is used in Scand p.ns. of 'a secluded or outlying place, a patch of cultivated ground jutting out from the main grounds of an estate'; cf. Lindkvist 198. This el. remains in dial. use as *wro* 'a nook, a secluded spot, a cattle shelter'. Initial *w*-, which was lost at an early date in Iceland and parts of Norway, is always retained in ME in the Danelaw. The el. is fairly frequent in ME f.ns. (C 348, L, Nt 292, Nth 271, YE 328, YN 331, Lindkvist 198ff). (*a*) Wrayton La (**tūn**). (*b*) Wray YW, Wrea La, Wreay Cu. In compounds, it nearly always occurs with significant

words, often denoting vegetation, as Benwray (bēan), Bramery (brōm) Cu, Capernwray La (kaupmaðr), Dockray Cu (docce), Haverah YW (hēg), Lacra Cu (lauk), Murrah Cu (mōr), Rowrah Cu (rūh), Thackray YW (þak), Whiteray La (hwīt).

vrangr ON adj., 'crooked', *v.* **wrang.**

vreini, reini ON, 'a stallion'. (*a*) Wrynose Cu, La, We (hals). [~**wrǣna.**]

***vrengill** ON, 'something twisted', *v.* **wrengel.**

W

wacen OE, 'watch, vigil', also in p.ns. 'a watching place'. (*b*) Ewekene's Fm Sr 265 (**ēa**). [**wacu**, **-en**.]

wacol OE adj., 'watchful, vigilant, watching'. (*a*) Wechylstone K (**stān**). [**wacu**, **-ol**.]

***wācor** OE, 'an osier, a willow twig, wicker', related by ablaut to OSwed *vīker* 'willow', ModE *wicker*, OE *gewīcan* 'to give way, yield', and *wāc* 'weak' (cf. DEPN 467); it would be difficult to distinguish from OE *wacor* adj. 'watchful, watching' which has been suggested for Wakerley Nth 172 (used substantivally, *wacralēah* 'the watchers' wood'). (*a*) Wackerfield Du (**feld**). (*b*) Wacker Co.

wacu OE, 'a watch, a wake', evidenced in OE only in the compound *niht-waco* 'night-watch'; in p.ns. it may refer to an annual festival or wake, a meaning first evidenced c. 1225; there was, for example, a great annual fair at Wakefield YW at which the well-known cycle of plays was no doubt presented in late medieval times (cf. Ekwall, Studies[2] 189). (*a*) Wakebridge Db (**brycg**), Wakefield Nth, YW (**feld**). [~OE *wacian* 'to be awake, to watch'.]

wād OE, 'woad', used as a dye and apparently cultivated in England in OE times and later; it is indigenous near Tewkesbury Gl (cf. Wo 221 and note). It is found in several OE charter names, *wadbeorh* BCS 1299, *wadbeorgas* ib. 183, *wadleah* ib. 1222, *wadlond* ib. 356, and later f.ns. (Nt 286, Nth 273, W 271). (*a*) Odell Bd, Woodhill W (**hyll**), Wadborough Wo 221 (**beorg**), Waddon Do, Sr (**dūn**), Wadley Nb (**lēah**), Watton Hrt (**tūn**).

***wāden** OE adj., 'growing with woad', difficult to distinguish from an OE pers.n. *Wada*, is possible in (*a*) Wadden Hall K (**halh**). [**wād**, **-en**, cf. OE *wǣden*.]

(ge)wæd OE, 'a ford'. (*b*) Wade Sf, *Wathe* Wt, Wadebridge Co; Biggleswade Bd (pers.n.), Broxwater Co (**frosc**), Cattawade Sf (**catt**), Iwade K (**īw**), Landwade C (**lang**). (*c*) St Nicholas at Wade K. [~**vað**, OE *wadan* 'to go, move', the sense 'wade' occurring only in *oferwadan*; cf. NED s.v. *wade*.]

***wæferce** OE, 'a spider', a derivative (a parallel formation to **lāwerce**) of OE (*gongel*)-*wæfre*, *wæfer*-(*gonge*) 'spider', is possible in (*a*) Warkleigh D 349 (**lēah**), Warkworth Nth 63 (**worð**). [~OE *wefan* 'to weave'.]

*wǣfer(e) OE (WSax), 'a winding stream', *v.* wēfer(e).

wæfre OE adj., 'unstable, restless, wandering', *wæfer OE, 'that which wanders', probably enter into some p.ns. and r.ns. in *Waver-*, but there is some doubt about their interpretation. The following points should be taken into account:

(1) These words are ultimately from a PrGerm root *web-*, *wab-*, *wǣb*, 'move back and forth', which produced OE *wefan* 'to weave', wæferce 'spider', *wafian* 'to move the hands back and forth' (late ME *waven* 'to wave', also ON *vafa* 'to vacillate') and ME *waveren* 'to wander'. The length of the vowel in OE *wæfre* is uncertain, but p.n. spellings and its later history suggest that it was short; the lengthened grade *wǣf-* appears in wēfer(e).

(2) In the name of a river such as the Waver Cu (with Wavermouth and Waverton, *v.* mūða, tūn), which follows a very devious course, we may have, as Ekwall (RN 440) notes, OE *wæfre* itself, signifying 'the wandering one'; cf. also wēfer(e). In Brownsover and Churchover Wa 100, the el. seems also to be an old name for the R. Swift (not recorded as *Swift* before 1577), since some local r.n. of this form is referred to in *aquam voc. Wovere Watir* in an undated document cited by Dugdale; the R. Swift is characterized by countless bends and twists in its course to the Avon.

(3) In other p.ns., however, such a sense is obviously improbable for the constant recurrence of an undocumented r.n. forming an el. in so many p.ns. would be remarkable; Woore Sa, at any rate, is on the top of a hill and a r.n. is there impossible, and although Waverley Sr is in a loop of the R. Wey there can hardly be any question of *wæfre* being an old name for the Wey which is said to have been so called from as early as 675; the documents adduced as evidence for this, such as the Latin bounds to BCS 34, or BCS 955 (dated 956), are not contemporary but may reflect genuine material (BCS 39 and 563 are spurious). The combination of *wæfre* with lēah and trēow as well as dial. *waver* 'a young tree left standing by itself in a felled wood' indicates some connexion with 'tree'. Ekwall (DEPN 478) notes the occurrence of *waver* in Continental Germ p.ns. like Du *Waverlo*, *Waverwald* (from *lo* 'wood', *wald* 'forest') and Fr *Woevre* (olim *Wabra silva*), which provide similar contexts, whilst the latter is further evidence of a sb. which is certainly found in such English p.ns. as Woore Sa. In such names *wæf(e)re* may well be an old *nomen agentis* 'that which

sways or shakes', hence 'a swaying or shaking tree'; Duignan even adds (Sa 261) 'aspen tree', which is at least feasible. There is, however, much to be said for taking *wæfre* to mean no more than 'a swaying tree', bearing in mind the dial. use of *waver* of 'an isolated young tree', no doubt one which sways dangerously in the wind.

(4) Other possibilities in p.ns. include the meaning 'swampy ground', which is found in the cognate LGerm *waver* 'quaking bog' (with a sense development paralleled by **cwafen** and **wagen**) and this may occur as dial. *waver* in the sense 'a common pool'; such a meaning at least would suit the topography of Waverley Sr.

(5) In some of the p.ns. we may have to postulate a form *wafre* or *wafor*, for in the WMidl at any rate *wæfre* should have become *wefre* and there are no traces of spellings like *wevre* in ME. On the other hand in Brownsover, Churchover Wa and Woore Sa, a ME form *Wovre* appears sporadically from the end of the 13th century and more frequently in the 15th; these may be rounded forms due to the influence of *w*- but are more likely to be due to confusion of *wavre* with the common el. **ōfer** in p.ns.

(6) (*a*) Warton St, Wa 23, Wharton He, La 43 (**tūn**), Waverley Sr 174 (**lēah**), Wavertree La 112 (**trēow**).

(*b*) Brownsover, Churchover, Cesters Over Wa, R. Waver Cu, Woore Sa.

wægn, wægen, wǣn OE, 'a wagon, a cart', usually in p.ns. to denote the fitness of a ford, road, etc. for the passage of a wagon. The OE contracted form *wǣn* sometimes appears in ME spellings as *Wen-*. (*a*) Wainfleet L (**flēot**), Wainforth YW, Wangford Sf (**ford**), Wainscarre Nt 69 (described as *venella* 'lane'), Wainscarth Cu 343 (**skarð** 'a gap'), Windgate YN (**gata**), Winnowsty L (**wella, stig**).

***wæl**[1] (Angl, WSax), ***wel** (Kt, Merc), 'a corpse', is usually found in a collective sense 'the slain', but it refers to a single corpse in *blodig wæl* (*Beowulf* 448) and to single corpses in *walu feollon* (ib. 1042) and *crungon walo* (*Ruin* 26). It is possible in (*a*) Wellesbourne Wa (**burna**) with Merc *wel* alternating with *wæl* in the medieval spellings which are otherwise difficult to explain; for similar compounds cf. **dēad, līc, wearg.**

wǣl[2] OE (WSax), 'a deep pool', *v.* **wēl**[2].

wælla, wælle OE (Merc) 'a well, a spring', *v.* **wella.**

***wællere** OE (Merc), 'a salt-boiler', *v.* **wellere.**

wælm OE (Merc), 'a spring', *v.* **welm**.

wær[1] OE, 'a weir', *v.* **wer**.

wǣr[2] OE (WSax), 'an agreement, a compact, a treaty', difficult to distinguish from **wer** except on topographical grounds. (*a*) Warley Ess 133 (**lēah**).

wǣrloga OE, 'a traitor', *v.* **wērloga**.

wærna[1] OE, 'a wren', *v.* **wrenna**.

***wǣrna**[2] OE, 'a stallion', *v.* **wrǣna**.

wærnægel OE, 'a hard tumour', used as a nickname for a hill. (*b*) Warnell Cu 152.

(ge)wæsc OE, 'washing, a flood', recorded only in a gloss to *aquarum alluuio* 'inundation of waters' (WW 179.35), occurs in late ME with the sense 'a sandbank or part of the shore which the sea floods at high-tide' and 'a low-water ford across a tidal estuary'. Apart from topography, this el. cannot be kept separate from **wæsce** and very often from **wæsse**, for *-sh* often had the AN spelling *-s* in p.ns. (IPN 113–17). (*a*) Washford D, Trewashford Co (**ford**). (*b*) The Wash L-Nf, Horish K (**horu**), Strangeways La 33 (**strang**), probably *Arnewas* Hu (pers.n.).

wæsce OE, 'a place for washing', is recorded in OE only in the charter references to **scēap-wæsce**. It is difficult to keep apart from **(ge)wæsc** and **wæsse**. (*a*) Washbourne D (**burna**), Washbrook Sf (**brōc**), Washway L (**weg**). (*b*) Probably Allerwash Nb (**alor**).

***wæscel(s)** OE, **waschel** ME, 'a bath, a washing vessel', perhaps also 'a washing place', found as a ME f.n. el. (Ess 592) and in (*a*) Washall Green Hrt 185 (**halh**). [**wæsce, -el, -els.**]

***wæsse** (**wassan** wk.obl.) OE (Angl, WSax), ***wesse** (Merc), 'a wet place, a swamp, a marsh', is not on independent record, but is found often enough in the OE spellings of p.ns. to be a certain el. (cf. RN 437); it is from PrGerm **wat-so*, cognate with Norw *vassa* 'to wade', OSwed *vass* 'reeds', and related in a different grade to **wēt**. It is sometimes difficult to distinguish from **gewæsc** and **wæsce**, but is of much more common occurrence than either. Apart from Allerwash Nb, which has ME spellings in *-was* and in *-wasch* from 1323 and which is not on marshy ground (although it stands on the north bank of the Tyne), the el. has a typically WMidl provenance; Allerwash and perhaps some other suggested examples are to be derived from *wæsc(e)* with AN *-s* for *-sh*. The Merc form *wesse* (obl. *wassan*) is well-evidenced in the spellings of the p.ns. (*a*)

Washbourne Gl (**burna**). (*b*) Possibly R. Wash L-Lei; Alrewas St (**alor**), Bolas Sa (pers.n.), Broadwas Wo (**brād**), Buildwas Sa (**gebyldu**), Hopwas St (**hop**[1]), Rotherwas (**hrīðer**), Sugwas (**sugga**) He.

wǣt OE (WSax) adj., 'wet', *v.* **wēt**.

wæter OE, 'water, an expanse of water', usually denotes in p.ns. and r.ns. either 'a lake, a pool' (esp. in the NW) or 'a stream, a river', both meanings being first independently recorded in ME (NED s.v. *water* sb. § 12); as a first el. it often has an adj. function 'wet'. (*a*) Wardington Hrt, Waterden Nf (**denu**), Watercombe Do (**cumb**), Waterham K (**hamm**), Waterholmes YN (**holmr**), Watershute D (**scīete**), Waterton L (**tūn**). (*b*) Water Fm Sr, Sx, etc. When used of lakes it often incorporates a p.n. or r.n. as its first el. as in Crummock Water Cu, Hawes Water We, Derwent Water, Loweswater (**lauf**, **sǣ**), Cu, Malham Tarn YW (olim *Malgewater*), Semerwater YN (**sǣ**, **mere**), but occasionally a pers.n. as in Bassenthwaite (olim *Bastunwater*), Ullswater Cu. When it means 'stream, river', it is usually combined with (i) descriptive adjs., as Blackwater Ess, La, Sr (**blæc**), Broadwater Ess, Sx 192 (**brād**, cf. OE *bradan wætere* BCS 819), Freshwater Wt (**fersc**), Loudwater Bk (**hlūd**), Shallow Water Co (**cald**), Southwater Sx (**sūð**). (*c*) As an affix, often rendered by Lat *juxta aquam*, *Water* is prefixed to Eaton O, W, Fryston YW, Fulford YE, Orton Wa, Stratford Bk; Waterstock O; Allerton Bywater YW, Bourton on the Water Gl; Thorpe by Water R; Westley Waterless C (**lēas**, cf. **vatn**).

wæter-gefall OE, 'a waterfall, a cascade' and later 'a rapid', probably also 'a place where a stream disappears into the ground' as in Waterfall St. (*b*) Waterfall YN, Watervale D 214; cf. also Nt 292, Wa 333. [**wæter**, **(ge)fall**.]

wæter-scipe OE, 'an expanse of water', also 'a conduit, a water channel'. (*b*) Water Sheep, *Watership(pe)* Ess 592, Hrt 127, *Watership Lane* W. [**wæter**, **-scipe**.]

***wǣðe** OE, 'hunting', found in OE *wæðeburn* BCS 1282; it is a derivative of **wāð**. (*a*) Waverley Wa (**lēah**), possibly Wedmore So (*Weþmor* ASC 878 A with loss of *-e* in the compound). [~ **veiðr**, OE *wǣðan* 'to hunt'.]

***wǣðe-mann** OE, 'a hunter'. (*a*) Wembdon So (**dūn**). [**wǣðe**, **mann**.]

wāg OE, 'a wall', is possible in (*a*) Wooburn Bk 196 (*burna*, late OE

Wa-, ME *Wau-*, *Wou-*, also *Wogh-* etc.) in some such sense as 'stream with its banks walled up', since this offers the best explanation of the medieval spellings. The interpretation is, however, difficult and Ekwall (DEPN s.n.) may therefore be right in ignoring the earliest spellings in *Wau-* and referring the first el. to wōh 'crooked', as this offers an easier explanation of the modern form [u:bən] and is not an inappropriate description of the winding stream. [~ veggr.]

*wagen OE, 'a quagmire, quaking sands' and the like, related to OE *wagian* 'to move' and ME *waze*, *wawe* 'a wave' (cf. NED s.v. *waw*), has been proposed by Ekwall, RN 440. For a similar sense development cf. cwafen, wæfre § 4. (*a*) Warne D 201 (fenn), R. Waveney Nf-Sf (ēa), probably also Walney La (ēg). (*b*) Wawne YE 44. [OE **wagu* 'wave', -en.]

waite ONFr, ME, 'a watch, a look-out, a look-out place'. (*a*) Waite Hill W, Waytail Gate YN (hyll). (*b*) Waits House YN, White D.

wala OE, gen.pl. of walh 'a Welshman, a serf'.

*walc OE, 'fulling, the dressing of cloth', not independently recorded (but cf. walcere). (*a*) *Walkemulne* YE (myln, from 1241), Walkern Hrt (ærn, from DB).

walcere OE, 'a cloth-dresser, a fuller', once recorded in OE as a gloss to Lat *fullo* (WW 407.29) and in ME as a surname *Walker*. (*a*) *Walkergate* (Lincoln) L (gata), possibly Walkerith L (rið). [walc, -ere.]

wald OE (Angl), weald (Kt, WSax), 'woodland, a large tract of woodland, high forest-land'.

(1) That *wald* denoted 'woodland' is clear from such references in the OE charters as those to *silba quæ appellatus est Cæstruuarouualth* (BCS 175) 'the wood which is called the *wald* of the chester-dwellers' (that is, of the men of Rochester K) and to *in commune saltu id est on Cæstersæta walda* (ib. 303) 'in the common wood, that is in the *wald* of the chester-dwellers' (also Rochester). There is little in OE literary sources to indicate the precise meaning; *on wuduwaldum* glosses Lat *in saltibus* (WW 426.35) and in the OE *Orosius* (i, 1, iii, 3) *weald* also translates Lat *saltus* 'a forest glade, a passage through a forest'. In *Genesis* 839 it is in apposition to holt 'wood' in *uton gan on ðysne weald*, *innan ðisses holtes hleo* 'let us go into this *weald*, into the protection of this wood', and in ASC 893 A the Weald of Kent is described as a forest, *ðæs miclan wudu*

eastende ðe we Andred hataþ . . . seo ea lið ut of ðæm walda 'the east end of that great wood that we call Andred . . . the river flows from that *weald*'. These contexts, along with others less definitive such as *wulf in walde* 'the wolf in the *wald*' (*Judith* 206) or ME *te wilde* * *deor þet on þeos wilde waldes wunieð* (*St Marherete* 23), all point to *wald* meaning 'woodland', whilst OE *Andredesweald*, the Weald of Kent, points to its application to a tract of woodland of considerable extent, as do other names first evidenced in ME such as the Cotswolds Gl, the Yorkshire Wolds YE, etc.

(2) This meaning of 'woodland' is also general in the cognates in the other Germ languages, as OHG, MHG *wald* 'forest, waste-land', MHG *walt* 'timber', OFris, OSax *wald* 'forest'; ON *vǫllr* appears to have lost its connexion with woodland and to be used only of 'a meadow, a pasture', probably evolved from the idea of 'a forest glade' implied in the Lat *saltus* which OE *wald* glosses.

(3) With the clearing of the large forest-tracts, some of which like the Weald of Kent were on high ground, the term *wald* came to lose its association with woodland and now described the newly developing type of landscape; in ME there are few allusions to *wald* meaning 'woodland', but there is an increasing number of contexts which suggest the sense 'hill, down' (as in *Y*^{e} *Walde, alpina* in *Catholicon Anglic.* 406.2) and 'a piece of open country, an elevated stretch of open country or moorland' (as in Laȝamon's *Brut* 10001, *Stod þe wundliche wude amidden ane wælde* 'the wicked wood amidst a *wælde*'; for *wald* in l. 16461 the later manuscript of the *Brut* reads *felde* (*v.* feld 'open country'); cf. NED s.v. *weald*, *wold*. This kind of distinction between open country and woodland is revealed in the p.ns. Old Hurst (olim *Waldhirst*) and Woodhurst Hu 211, 229; the district must once have been called *hyrst* from its being a well-wooded area but clearly only Woodhurst retained that character. Similarly in the later form *Wild* [waild] found in K, Hrt and C, *weald* has been assimilated to the common noun *wild* which was probably more accurately descriptive of the terrain when the change took place.

(4) Although this new appellative use of *wald* arose in ME and adequately describes the contemporary state of large areas whose names incorporate the el., like the Cotswolds or the Yorkshire Wolds or the large areas of high clayland called *Wold* and Croydon Wilds, etc. in C, there is little evidence that such a meaning was

ever used in p.ns. which had for the most part originated when *wald* still retained its old meaning of 'woodland'. It may, however, be found in some minor ME names (C 348, Ess 592, Nt 293, Nth 271, Wa 333) and in the common MedLat *waldum* in expressions like *in Waldis de Brunne* C, etc.

* (5) The two OE dialectal forms, Angl *wald* and Kt, WSax *weald* produced (i) ME *wāld*, later ME *wōld* (StdE *wold*), in the NCy *wald*, and (ii) ME *wēld* (StdE *weald*) respectively. OE *wald* as a first el. kept its original short vowel in compounds and therefore appears as *Wal(d)*-. ME *wēld* (from *weald*) develops a form *wild* as in Wild Fm Hrt 62 or Croydon Wilds C; when ME *ē* was raised to [i:] in ModE it was sometimes spelt *weild* and *wild* and the latter then had a new spelling pronunciation [waild] (cf. also § 3 *supra* and a similar spelling pronunciation of cinu). StdE *wold* often replaces *weald* in SCy p.ns. and *wald* in the NCy.

(6) The provenance of Angl *wald* and Kt, WSax *weald* in p.ns. has some importance for the linguistic boundaries of OE, which Ekwall has demonstrated (OEDials. 5 ff); evidence since collected confirms Ekwall's conclusions; briefly, *weald* forms are found as far north as the Hu border of C, in Ess, Hrt and to some extent Bd, Hu, O, Gl. But in these border counties, ME *wold* (later dial. *old*) has often penetrated from the Midl. In Kt, Sx and the rest of Wessex *weald* is normal but is occasionally replaced by StdE *wold*.

(7) (*a*) Old Hurst Hu (hyrst), Oldridge D, Waldridge Bk (hrycg), Waldershare (ware, scearu), Walderslade (slæd) K, Waldron Sx (ærn), Walgrave Nth (grāfa), Waller Fen C (hlāw, fenn), Waltham Brk, Ess, Ha, K, Lei, L, Sx (hām); Wauldby YE (bȳ), Woolden C (dūn); *wald* may also be found in some of the Waltons, but *Wald-tun* never occurs in OE spellings (cf. also walh, wall).

(*b*) As an original simplex name, from *weald*, The Weald K-Sx, Weald Bk, Hu, O, North and South Weald Ess, Wield Ha, Wild Fm Hrt, Croydon Wilds C, Westbury Wild Bk; from *wald*, Old Nth, The Wolds L, Nt, YE. In compounds, Hammill K (hamel), Harrold Bd (hār), Hawold YE (haugr), Hockwald (hocc), Methwold (meðal), Northwold (norð) Nf, Prestwold Lei (prēost), Southwold Sf (sūð), Studdal K (stōd); with pers.ns., The Cotswolds Gl, Wo, Coxwould YN, Cuxwold L, Sibertswold K, Stixwold L; with folk-names in -ingas, Easingwold YN, Horninghold Lei, Ringwould K.

(*c*) As an affix, Old Weston Hu, Wold Newton YE, Newton le Wold L, Dry Drayton C (olim *Walddraitton*).

walh (**wales** gen.sg., **walas** nom.pl., **wala** gen.pl.), OE (Angl), **wealh** (Kt, WSax), 'a foreigner, a Welshman, a serf'.

(1) This el. has been thought to have originated in the name of the Gaulish tribe, the *Volcae* mentioned by Caesar, and to have been borrowed as PrGerm **walχaz* (sg.) to denote a foreigner, particularly a Gaul or Celt. The sense 'foreigner' is often retained but usually with more specific reference to particular foreigners with whom the Germanic peoples came in contact, as in OHG *Wal*(*a*)*h* 'a Celt' or 'a Roman', ON *Valir* 'the Gaulish people, Frenchmen', Dan *vælsk*, Swed *välsk* 'French, Italian, Welsh'; it is also retained in compounds like OE *walh-hnutu* 'walnut' and *walh-more* 'parsnip, carrot' (lit. 'foreign root'), *wealh-stod* 'interpreter'.

(2) In England the meaning 'foreign' occurs once (from the context) in *Riddle* 71.10, *ic . . . mearcpaþas wala træd, moras pæðđe* 'I trod the roads of the foreigners, I traversed the moors', once in the gloss *barbarus, walch siue ungerad* 'foreign, *walch* or ignorant' (WW 361.29) and once, meaning 'Roman', in the gloss *jus quiritum, weala sunderriht* 'Roman citizenship', which another gloss renders *Romwara sundorriht* (ib. 429.4). Its chief use, however, was to describe the native Britons, both those who remained in England and those who had moved into Cornwall and Wales (whose names are of course derived from the OE pl. *Walas*); cf. BT s.v. In addition, *walh* was commonly used of 'a serf, a slave'; for instance in the Gospel Matt. xxiv. 50, Lat *servi* 'of a servant' is translated by *ðæs weales*, which corresponds to *ðræles* 'thrall's' in *Lindisf. Gosp.* and *esnes* 'servant's' in *Rushw. Gosp.* In other literary and legal contexts the meaning 'serf' is also apparent.

(3) In p.ns. the choice of meaning lies between 'Briton, Welshman' and 'serf' (cf. IPN 18), and in many cases it is an impossible one; indeed with many of the Waltons (which have no ME *Waletun* spellings) it is a problem whether we have *walh* at all or **wald**, **wall** or **walu**. In some names like Cornwall and Wales, Wallasey Ch, Wales YW, *walh* may well have the meaning 'Welshman', but in the majority of names 'serf, slave' is much more likely. Few names in *Wal-* bear the mark of any great antiquity and historically they should do so, for the presence of Britons or Welshman in a place

could only find record in a p.n. whilst they kept their separate identity as foreigners to the English; there are, for example, no certain compounds with an old el. like hām. It is also remarkable how little evidence there is for these *Wal-* names in OE; only two, Walden Hrt (*on Wealadene* KCD 1354) and Walworth Sr (*Wealawyrð*, *-wurð* KCD 715, 896), have a recognizable OE form and the other two, Walcote L (*Walecote* KCD 806) and Walton on Trent Db (*Waletun* BCD 772), are obviously from late copies; the uninflected *walh* occurs in Walter Ess 239 (*walhfare* KCD 813) and in an unidentified *wealhgeat* BCS 1282. The word cot which is frequently combined with *walh* generally denotes 'a humble dwelling' and would be very appropriate if *walh* had the sense 'serf' (cf. cot § 3); it would be parallel to the use of gebūr, ceorl, cild, swān, etc., in similar contexts.

(4) The forms of this el. vary somewhat. The Angl. nom.sg. *walh* (which is rare) survives as *Wal-*; the gen.sg. *Wales* which sometimes appears as *Wals-*, in Walsall St (hall), Walshford YW (ford), Walsworth Gl (worð) is as likely to be the OE pers.n. *Walh*; the nom.pl. *walas* is found as Wales and the gen.pl. *wala* as ME *Wale-*, later *Wal-*. The WSax broken form *wealh*, with gen.sg. *weales*, and nom. and gen.pl. *wealas*, *weala* does not survive, except rarely as in Wella Brook D; Wellesbourne Wa (OE *Weles-*, ME *Weles-*, *Wales-* later *Welles-*) and Wellesley So (lēah) have been derived from the WSax gen.sg. *weales*, but though this might be right for Wellesley, it is improbable in a Wa p.n. (cf. wæl[1]). Most OE grammars assume, presumably from the metre of certain OE poetic half-lines which contain *feores*, gen.sg. of *feorh* 'life' and which would in this lift usually have a long syllable, that with loss of *h* in the oblique cases there was compensatory lengthening of the short vowel; *wales*, *walas*, *wala* are assumed to be *wāles*, *wālas*, *wāla* and so too *wēales*, *wēalas*, *wēala*; Bülbring § 529 suggests that there had been lengthening but the short vowel was restored from the nom.sg. It is remarkable that this restoration of short vowels was everywhere so complete that nowhere in ME or ModE is there a single trace of this supposed lengthening; *walas* itself is always *Wales*, never *Woles*, and with words like *halh*, the dat.sg. invariably produces *Hale*, not *Hole*, which it would have done if the vowel had been lengthened in OE; the metrical evidence upon which the theory of lengthening was based is of doubtful value, for the

rhythmical patterns of OE verse, like the word patterns, had become traditional.

(5) (*a*) From *walh* nom.sg., Walford (Ross) He (**ford**), Walter Ess 239 (**fær**); from *wala* gen.pl., Walbrook Mx, Walla Brook, Wella Brook D (**brōc**), Walburn YN (**burna**), Walcot(e), -cott Brk, L (3), Lei, Nf, Nth (2), O, Sa (2), W, Wa (2), Wo (**cot**), Walden Ess, Hrt, YN (**denu**), Wallon Brook Wa (*walhǣme* 'the dwellers at Walcote', **brōc**), Wallasey Ch (**ēg**, with ME *ei* added again), Wallington Brk, Sr, Walton (ME *Waletun*) Ch, Db (2), Ess, K, La (4), Lei, Sf, Sr, St (3), Sx, YW (2), *Walton* YN (**tūn**), Walmer K (**mere**), Walpole Sf (**pōl**), Walworth Du, Sr (**worð**).

(*b*) Wales YW, Cornwall.

[~**welisc**; cf. also Jackson 227–8.]

wall OE (Angl), **weall** (Kt, WSax), 'a wall'.

(1) This el. is used in OE of 'the wall of a house or building', but chiefly of 'a rampart of stone, earth or other material for defence' (as in OE *andlang þære wealdic* BCS 969, cf. **dīc**), and of 'the defensive wall enclosing a town'. It also had in OE an extension of meaning to 'cliff', esp. in poetry (cf. BT s.v.) but it is doubtful if this use is found in p.ns. The commonest application in p.ns. is to defensive Roman works; the examples from Cu and Nb refer to Hadrian's Wall and those in Nf to a Roman bank. In some others it alludes to a town-wall. It is not improbable that a few of the Waltons contain *wall* (cf. Zachrisson, *Romans, Kelts and Saxons* 39ff), the compound *wall-tūn* denoting 'a farmstead protected by a surrounding rampart', but such a compound is not evidenced in OE. Angl *wall* forms have predominated everywhere.

(2) (*a*) Walby Cu (**bý**), Walker (**kjarr**), Wallbottle (**bōðl**), Wallsend (**ende**) Nb, Walton Cu 114 (**tūn**), Walwick Nb (**wīc**), all referring to Hadrian's Wall; Walcot So (**cot**, outside the walls of Bath); Walpen Wt (**penn**); Walpole (**pōl**), Walsoken (**sōcn**), West Walton (**tūn**) Nf, all three near the Roman embankment; Walton Cu 431 (suggested to be '**tūn** with a defensive wall'), Walton Grounds Nth 58 (**tūn**, near Roman remains), Warsergate Nt 21 (**geset**, near the town wall).

(*b*) Wall St (referring to the walls of Roman *Letocetum*, Lichfield), Wall Heath St (ancient earthworks); Bestwall Do (**bī**, **ēastan**), Bewell Street (Hereford) He (**bī**), East Wells (in Wells) So (**ēastan**), all referring to town walls; Blackwall Mx (**blæc**, a bank to restrain the R. Thames), Parkwalls Co (pūca, 'haunted ruins'), Thirlwall Nb (þyrel, 'gap in Hadrian's Wall'), Whitewalls Co (wīd, alluding to prehistoric stone buildings).

(*c*) Aston le Walls Nth 32 (near Walton Grounds (*a*) *supra*).

[A Continental Germ loan from Lat *vallum* 'rampart', found also in OSax *wal(l)*, OFris *wall*.]

*walt OE (Angl), *wealt (WSax) adj., 'unsteady', found only in OE *unwealt* 'steady, firm' (that is, 'not rolling') has been suggested by Ekwall for (*a*) Walford Do (ford), Welton Nb (denu), but there are phonological as well as semantic difficulties, esp. in the freq. ME *Welte(s)*-spellings for Welton. A pers.n. from this word would be preferable in most p.ns.

walu OE, 'a ridge of earth or stone' (also 'a weal'), is found in a topographical sense only in OE and then only in such charter references as *on ða ealdan wale*, *be wale* KCD 741, where the whole context 'on the old *wale*, then to the western cottages of *corfget* (a gap no doubt in the *wale*), south by the *wale* to the corner of the dike' suggests some kind of earthwork, and also *in stanwale*, *andlang ðære wale* ib. 778 and *on ða eastlangan dicwale* ib. 1174; the only evidence for meaning is in these three examples of its use which suggest by the contexts something like 'ditch' or embankment'; the normal meaning 'weal' suggests 'a raised strip of earth'. (*a*) Easole K (ēs), Holwell Do (hol).

wamb, womb OE, 'womb, belly', used in a topographical sense 'a hollow' (cf. NED s.v. § 3), as in *on ondoncilles wombe* (probably an error for *on ðon cilles wombe*) BCS 1240, or 'a lake', as in Swed *Vambsjön* (DEPN 502). (*a*) Wombridge Sa (brycg), Wombwell YW (wella).

wandale, -daile, -dole ME, 'a share of land', in NCy dial. 'a share of the common arable land of a township'. (*b*) Wan Dale YE, Wandales Cu, YE, YN 59, Wandhills YN, fairly common in ME f.ns. (as Cu 497, Nt 292, Nth 274, YE 328, YN 331). [ON *vǫndr* 'a wand, a shoot, a measure', dāl, deill.]

wang OE, 'a piece of meadowland, an open field', is rare, and in the Danelaw cannot be distinguished from vangr. (*a*) Wangfield Ha (feld), Wangford (Southwold) Sf (ford).

wann OE adj., 'dark'. (*a*) R. Wenning YW (-ing²), Wampford D (ford).

wante ME, 'a path', *v.* wente.

wapentac ME, 'a wapentake', *v.* **vápnatak.**

wapol OE, probably 'a pool, a marsh', is recorded only in a gloss in the sense 'bubble, froth' (Lat *famfaluca*, WW 21.18, 402.10), but there is a derivative verb *wapolian* 'to bubble, pour forth' and cognate with it is OFris *wapul* 'pool, mire'. It is possible in (*a*) Waplington YE (-**ing**[4], **tūn**); it is improbable on phonological and topographical grounds in Wapley Gl, YN, Wapping Mx.

-ware (**-wara** gen.pl.) OE pl., 'dwellers', is used only in combination with prefixed words as in *burh-ware* 'burgesses', *eorð-ware* ('earth dwellers', or p.ns. as in *Cantware* 'men of Kent', *Lynware* 'men of Lynn (Nf)'. It is fairly common in p.ns. to denote 'the dwellers in a place' and has much the same function as **sǣte**, as in *Cæstruuaro-uualth* BCS 175 beside *Cæstersætawalda* ib. 303, both referring to 'the chester-dwellers', that is, the men of Rochester K. As a rule in p.ns. such folk-names are first els., but occasionally they become p.ns. themselves, as in *regione quæ dicitur Merscuuare* (BCS 214) 'the district which is called "the marsh dwellers"' (that is, Romney Marsh K). It is common in K. (*a*) It is the medial el. in Burnarsh (**burh** of Canterbury, **mersc**), Felderland (**feld**, **land**), Tenterden (Thanet, **denn**), Waldershare (**wald**, **scearu**), Worthgate (Wye, **geat**) K; *v.* also **Cantware.** (*b*) Clewer Brk, So (**clif**), Ridware St (**rhyd**). [~OE *warian* 'to guard, inhabit'.]

wareine ME, 'a game preserve' and somewhat later 'a piece of ground for the breeding of rabbits, a warren' (cf. NED s.v., first recorded in *Piers Plowman* Prol 163). It is frequent in later minor names. (*b*) Aldbourne Warren W (from 1307), Dawlish Warren D (from c. 1280). [ONFr *warenne.*]

warener, warnere ME, 'a game-keeper, one in charge of a rabbit warren'. (*a*) Warner's Copse W. [~**wareine.**]

waroð, wareð, warð OE, **warth** ME, 'a shore, a beach', in dial. 'a flat piece of land or meadow along a stream or the shore'; in some p.ns it seems to mean 'marshy ground near a stream'; cf. OHG *warid* 'a piece of dry ground amidst marshes'. (*a*) Warleigh D (**lēah**), Warwick Cu (**wīc**). (*b*) Ward D (3), Warth Gl, Warth's Old Halves C. [~**wereð.**]

warð OE, **warth** ME 'a shore', *v.* **waroð.**

waru[1] OE, 'a shelter, defence, guard', is probable in (*a*) Warden Nb, Nth (**dūn**). [~**ware.**]

waru[2] OE, 'a weir', *v.* **wer.**

waschel ME, 'a washing place', *v.* wæscels.

wāse (wāsan obl.) OE, wōse ME, 'mud', is recorded in OE as a gloss to Lat *cenum* and *lutum* 'mud, mire' and is once an alternative to *fæn* (fenn) (WW 11.15, 203.45, etc.); it is cognate with ON *veisa* 'a stagnant pool' and related to wisc, wisse (cf. Zachrisson, *PN in *vis, *vask*, RN 437). It occurs several times in OE charters for Brk, as *Wase* BCS 1222, *Wasan* ib. 777, 1047 (Appleton) and 977, 1221 (Fyfield), but these have not yet been identified clearly enough with any special feature in local topography to suggest a meaning less general than 'ooze, mud, muddy place, marsh'. (*a*) Western D (þorn). (*b*) Oozedam Ess, Ooze Ditch (Buckland) Brk, R. Ouse Sx 6, Ouse Brook Wa 4, Chalkwell Oaze Ess. (*c*) Wapping Mx (olim *atte Wose*).

waste ME, 'wasteland', *v.* wēste.

wāð OE, 'chase, hunting'. (*a*) Watford Hrt, Nth (ford). [~wǣðe, OE *wāðan* 'to wander, flee'.]

weala OE gen.pl. of walh, 'a Welshman, a serf'.

weald OE (Kt, WSax) 'woodland', *v.* wald.

wealh OE (Kt, WSax), 'a Welshman, a serf', *v.* walh.

weall OE (Kt, WSax), 'a wall', *v.* wall.

*wealt OE (WSax) adj., 'unsteady', *v.* walt.

weard OE, 'watch, ward, protection'; the sense 'watch' is usual in p.ns., esp. with words for 'hill' (cf. also tōt); it also came to be used of 'a district', as in the Wards of Cu, Du, Nb, We (cf. Anderson xxivff). Its form has sometimes been influenced by that of the cognate ON *varði*, as in Warboys Hu. (*a*) Wadloo C, Wardlow Db (hlāw), Warby Nt (beorg), Warden Bd, Du, K, Nb (dūn), Wardhedges Bd (hecg, 'a protecting hedge'), Wardle Ch, La, Warthill YN (hyll), Wardour W (ōra), Ward's Hurst Bk (hyrst), Warton La, Nb, Wharton L (tūn); *v.* weard-setl. (*b*) Wolford Wa 302 (wulf, 'a defence against wolves'), Naworth Castle Cu 67, Westward Cu (a division).

weard-setl, weard-seld OE, 'a guard-house, a watch house', often in lofty situations; OE *weard-setl* (Crawf 72), *weardsetl* BCS 179, for example, have been identified with Beacon Hill Ha, D. (*b*) Warshill Top, Wassell, Wasthills Wo 253. [weard, setl.]

wearg OE, werg (Angl), 'a felon, a criminal, an outlaw'. (*a*) Horrell Co, Wreighill Nb (hyll), Warnborough Ha, Wreighburn Nb (burna); *v.* also wearg-rōd, wearg-trēow. [~vargr.]

wearg-rōd OE, 'gallows, a scaffold'. (*b*) Worgret Do. [**wearg, rōd.**]

wearg-trēow OE, 'a gallows, a tree where felons were hanged', recorded only in an OE charter, surviving as ME *waritreo*. (*b*) Warter YE. [**wearg, trēow.**]

wearm (**wearman** wk.obl.) OE adj., 'warm'. (*a*) Warmden La (**denu**), Warmley Wa (**lēah**), Warmhill D (**hyll**), Warmmacombe D (**cumb**), Warmwell Do (**wella**).

wearp, wearpe OE, 'warp', also denoted (i) 'an osier or twig' such as is used in basket-making (cf. *wearp-fæt* 'wicker-basket') and in the sense 'osier or twig' it may be found in Ruswarp YN 125 (**hrīs** 'brush-wood'); (ii) 'silted land' or the like which is evidenced in dial. *warp* 'sediment deposited by a river' and *warp-land* 'land formed by the silt of a river', probable in Salwarpe Wo 306 (**salu**), where it may refer to the flooding and silting up of salt-pits near the river (this could also be the sense in Ruswarp which is situated on the bank of the R. Esk). The root meaning 'what is thrown up' occurs in the related OE *geweorp* (which has influenced some of the early spellings of Salwarpe) as well as ON **varp** 'cairn' and LG *werp* 'a dam, a dike' in *Antwerp*, *Neuwarp*. [~OE *weorpan*, ON *verpa* 'to throw'.]

weax OE, 'wax', in p.ns. probably in allusion to places where bees' wax was produced or found. (*a*) Waxholme YE, Wexham Bk (**hām**), Wexcombe W (**cumb**).

webba OE, 'a weaver'. (*a*) Webland D (**land**).

***wedering** OE, 'a place for giving shelter from the weather', has been suggested for (*b*) Withering Sx 95 (on the coast). [OE *weder* 'weather', **-ing**[1].]

***wēfer(e)** OE (Angl), ***wǣfer(e)** (WSax), 'a winding stream', related to **wæfre** by ablaut (the latter being from PrGerm **wab-*, and the former from the lengthened grade **wāb-*, PrGerm **wǣb-*). This el. is probable in the r.ns. Weaver Ch (with Weavercote and Weaverham) and *Weaver* W (surviving in Weavern Fm). Both have very winding courses.

weg OE, 'a way, a path, a road', but not usually an urban road; it denotes a great variety of tracks, from one used by animals (as in Hartington Nb) to a great Roman road like the Fosse Way or the ancient British track of Icknield Way. It is a very common el. in D and fairly common in W and So; it also occurs in ME minor names (as Bk 259, C 348, Ess 593, Hrt 260, *et passim*). In the NCy its place has been largely taken by gata.

(*a*) Wayford So, Wifford D (ford), Wayton Co (tūn), Weybread Sf (brǣdu), Whaley Ch (lēah).

(*b*) Way(e) D (17). In compounds it is usually found with:

(i) Words describing the track, as Broadway Hu, So, Sr, W, Wo (brād), Cheeseway D (cis), Fulloway W (fūl), Holwey So, Holloway D, Mx, W (hol), Sharpway Wo (scearp), Stanway Ess, Gl, He, Sa, Stowey So (stān, 'paved'), Stantway Gl (stāniht), Stony Way O (stǣniht), Yelloways D (ald); cf. also Flotterton Nb (flot, tūn).

(ii) Colour adjs., as Greenaway D (grēne), Whiteway D, Do (hwīt), perhaps some of the Radways D, etc. (rēad).

(iii) Animal names, as Hartington Nb (heorot, tūn), Shipway K (scēap); cf. also OE *horsweg* BCS 299, *swinweg* ib. 801.

(iv) Words denoting goods habitually transported, as Barlichway Wa (bærlic), Hayway O, Wo (hēg), Salt Way O, Wo, etc. (salt).

(v) Words indicating fitness for a particular use, as Cartway W (cræt), Radway Wa, Roadway D, Rodway So (rād).

(vi) Words for vegetation, as Barkway Hrt (beorc), Broomway Ess (brōm), Spurway D (sprǣg), Trow Lane W (trēow).

(vii) Topographical terms, as Halsway So (hals), Hillway Wt (helde), The Mareway C 27 (gemǣre), Ridgeway O, K, Wo *et freq*, Rudgeway Gl, St (hrycg).

(viii) Words indicating direction or the object or place to which the road leads, as Northway, etc. (*passim*), Port Way O, Wo *et freq* (port), Wickey Bd (wīc), Workway W (geweorc).

(ix) Words denoting people, as Kingsway *freq* (cyning), *Meaning Way* O (gemǣne); pers.ns., as Garmondsway Du, Thoresway L, Tidgeon Way O 4 (cf. also Wo 4); folk-names, as Buckingway C 173 (*Buccingas* 'the men of Boxworth'), *Fielden Way* C 23, O 1, Wa 8–9 (filde).

[~wægn, ultimately related to Lat *vehere* 'to carry'.]

*wel[1] OE (Kt, Merc), 'a corpse', *v.* wæl[1].

wēl[2] OE (Angl, Kt), wǣl (WSax), 'a deep pool, a deep place in a river, a whirlpool'. (*b*) Weel, Wheel Hall YE; Sale Wheel La (salh), Thelwall Ch (þel).

welig OE (WSax), 'a willow', *v.* wilig.

Welisc OE (Angl, Kt), Wielisc, Wilisc (WSax), adj., 'Welsh'. (*c*) Welsh Bicknor He. [~walh, -isc.]

wella, well(e) OE (Angl, Kt), **wiella, wielle, will(a), wyll(a), wylle** (WSax), **wælla, wælle** (Merc), 'a well, a spring, a stream'.

(1) This very common el., which occurs as a strong and weak masc. and a weak fem. noun in OE (gen.sg. *welles*, *wellan*, gen.pl. *wella*, *wellena* etc.), denotes chiefly 'a spring of water', from the root meaning of 'that which bubbles up' (cf. OE *weallan* 'to boil or bubble up', ON *vella* 'to well up, boil'), and frequently translates or glosses Lat *fons*, *fontana*. In a great many p.ns. it means no more than 'spring'. It does, however, appear to have had also the meaning 'stream, river' in the OEBede where it renders Lat *fluvius* (i, 7), and in the *Orosius* Lat *flumen* (iv, 7). The sense 'stream, esp. a stream fed by a spring' is well-evidenced in p.ns. and r.ns. like R. Cherwell O, R. Irwell La.

(2) The el. is found with great frequency in most parts, but in the NCy its place was largely taken by **kelda**, and in the SCy to some extent by **ǣwell, ǣwelm, funta**, etc. The reasons for its common occurrence in early p.ns. were of course the importance of a local water-supply in early rural economy and the customs and religious beliefs associated with springs.

(3) The three main OE dialectal types which arose from the different effects of breaking and *i*-mutation, were:

(i) Angl, Kt *wella*, *welle*, which remains in StdE and which from late OE times has gradually extended its provenance outside the Anglian and Kentish dial. areas; in ME, for example, it is the only form found in K, Sx, Sr, Bk, Nth, most of Wa and all counties to the east and north, and it had become almost the only form current in other counties like O, W, Gl; in modern times StdE *well* has become general everywhere.

(ii) WSax *wiella*, *will(a)*, *wille*, generally represented in ME by *will(e)* in the SW counties of Co, D and So, and often surviving there as *will* (Will, Halwill D, etc.), whilst late WSax *wyll(a)*, *wylle* is found in ME as *wulle* in Do and Ha and occasionally in W (as in the spellings of Godswell W 148, Groundswell 31, Ludwell 189); this sometimes persists, as in Wool, Woolcombe Do.

(iii) Merc *wælla*, *wælle* (which is found in OE mainly in texts like the Merc *Rushw. Gosp.* or *Vesp. Psalt.*) became ME *walle* and is then difficult formally to distinguish from **wall** 'a wall'. The counties in which *wælla* occurs with the greatest frequency are Wo, He, Sa, St, Db, Ch; it is fairly well represented in south La and the adjacent parts of south-west YW (as in Wormald), and occasional ME *walle* spellings are found in Wa (xxvi), O (xxxi) and Gl. In the WMidl it often remains, as in Wall Sa, Colwall He, Crabwall Ch, Crosswall He, etc.; there are one or two *Wal-* forms in Bd (as in Wallpool 202), but these are 18th-century and are not significant. Although these variant forms have long been in the process of replacement by StdE *well*, their older provenance has great importance in the geography of OE dialects; cf. Ekwall, OEDials. 4 ff.

(4) (*a*) From Angl, Kt *wella*, Welborn, -bourn, -burn L, Nf, YN (**burna**), Wellbrook K (**rāw**), Welbury YN (**burh**, the spring is now called Hali Well), Welby L (**bý**), Welford Gl (gen.pl., **ford**), Wellow Nt (**haga**), Welton Cu, L (3), Nth, YE (**tūn**), Welwick YE (**wīc**). From Merc *wælla*, Walford He, Sa (**ford**). From WSax *wi(e)lla*, Wilcot W (**cot**), Willesden Mx (**dūn**), Wilton So, W (**tūn**). From late WSax *wylla*, Woolcombe Do (**cumb**).

(*b*) Wall Sa (3), Well K, L, YN, Wells Nf, So, Wool Do; Welham Nt, YE (dat.pl.).

In compounds, *wella*, etc., is combined chiefly with the following categories of words:

(i) Words for size, shape, etc., as Bradwall Ch, Bradwell Bk, Ess, Sf, Broadwell Gl, Sx (**brād**), Cranwell Bk (**crymbed**), Cromwell Nt, YW (**crumb**), R. Irwell La (**irre**), probably all denoting streams; Holwell Hrt (**hol**), Littals Wo (**lytel**), Trendwell D (**trendel**), Tuelldown D, Twywell Nth (**twī**).

(ii) Adjs., etc., describing the water, as Brightwell(s) Brk, Hrt, Britwell Bk (**beorht**), Caldwall Wo, Caldwell YN, Cauldwell Bd, Chadwell Ess, W, Chardwell Ess, Cholwell Co, D, So (**cald**, **ceald**), Colwall He, Colwell Wt (**cōl**), Framwellgate Du (**fram**), Gorrell, Gorwell D (**gor**), Harwell Nt (**hēore**), Loudwell Sx, Ludhill YE, Ludwell So, W (**hlūd**), Prittlewell Ess (**pritol**), Shadwell Mx (**sceald**), Sharnal K (**scearn**), Sherwill D (**scīr**), Wallingwells Nt ('bubbling', cf. **-ande**), Warmwell Do (**wearm**), Whistlewell D (**hwistel**).

(iii) Words for stone, etc., as Cawkwell L, Chalkwell Ess, K (**calc**, **cealc**), Greetwell L (**grēot**), Sandwell D, St (**sand**), Stanwell Mx, Stowell Gl, So, W (**stān**), Stoneywell St (**stānig**).

(iv) Colour adjs., as Blackwell Bk, Wo (**blæc**), Greenwell D (**grēne**), Radwell Bd, Hrt, Redhall Wo (**rēad**), Velwell D (**fealu**), Whitwell Hrt, Sr (**hwīt**).

(v) Names of living creatures haunting the well; large animals, as Hartwell Bk, D, St (**heorot**), Oxhall Wo (**oxa**); birds, as Crawl YN, Crowell Sx (**crāwe**), Culverswell D (**culfre**), Goswell (**gōs**), Hanwell (**hana**) Mx, Hauxwell YN, Hoxall Wt (**hafuc**), Wrenwell D (**wrenna**); frogs, snails, etc., as Crabwall Ch (**crabba**), Freshwell Ess (**forsc**), Frogwell D (**frogga**), Snail(s)well C, Hrt (**snægl**), Tathwell L (**tāde**).

(vi) Names of plants, esp. aquatic plants, as Barnwell Sr (**bere**), Bunwell Nf (**bune**), Carswalls Gl, Carswell D, Caswell Do, So, Cresswell Nb, St, etc. (**cærse**), Miswell Hrt (**mysse**), Muswell Bk, Mx (**mēos**), Pirzwell D (**pise**), Raywell YE (**ragu**), Sparkwell (**spearca**), Spirewell (**spīr**) D.

(vii) Tree-names, etc., as Adder Wells Sx (**æppel-trēow**), Ashwell Ess, W (**æsc**), Aspinwall La (**æspen**), Heswall Ch, Hors(e)well, Horswill D (**hæsel**), Salford Wo (**salh**), Stockalls Hrt, Stockwell He, Gl, Sr (**stocc**), Stumpwell Bk (**stump**), Trowell Nt (**trēow**), Widewell D (**wīðig**).

(viii) Topographical and other terms indicating location, as Amwell Hrt (**hamm**), Backwell So (**bæc**), Blindwell D (**blind**), Colwell D (R. Coly), Churchill D 307 (**crūc**), Hipswell YN (**hyppels**), Howell Sr (**hōh**), Lipwell K (**hlēpe**), Quobwell W (**cwabba**), Shadwell Nf, O, YW (**scēad**), Shadwell Lei (**scēað**), Wiswell La (**wise**), Yarwell Nth (**gear**).

(ix) Words for a vessel or receptacle for water or some structure over a well, as Beardwell W, Bedwell Hrt, Mx, Bidwell Bd, etc. (**byden**), Canwell St (**canne**), Wherwell Ha (**hwer**); cf. also **cetel**, *Stoppewelle* O 16 (**stoppa**); Brindiwell D (**breden**, probably in allusion to a wooden covering), Thatto La (**þēote**).

(x) Words indicating ancient customs, esp. for wishing wells, healing springs, etc., as Botwell Mx (**bōt**), Elwell Do, Holywell L (**hǣl** 'omen'), Fritwell O (**freht** 'augury'), Orwell Bury Hrt 159 (**hord**, from the dropping in of treasure for luck), Rumwell So, Runwell Ess (**rūn**, 'secret').

(xi) Words for persons, as Bridals Co, Bridewell W, Bridwell D (**brȳd** 'bride', probably a fertility spring), Bannall's Fm Wo, Banwell So (**bana**), Childwall La (**cild**), Churwell YW (**ceorl**), Dringwell D (**þring** 'a crowd'), Maidwell Nth (**mægden**).

(xii) Words with a religious association, as Godswell W (**god**), Haliwell Mx, Halliwell La, Hallwell Co, Halwell, -will D, Holy

Well, Holywell Bk, Hu, K, Mx, Nb, O, Wo, YW *et passim* (hālig), Eccleswall He (eclēsia); the names of saints and other holy persons, as Austle Co (St Augustine), Baywell Wo 121 (*Bægia* to whom the land was granted for a monastery, BCS 139), Dewsall He (St David), Hinderwell YN 138 (St Hild of Whitby), Kimberwell Bd 117 (St Cyneburg), St Helen's Well YE (St Elene).

(xiii) Pers.ns. (fairly common), as Brownswell D, Caversall St, Chatwall, -well Sa, St, Dudswell Hrt, Hemswell L, Rimswell YE, Treswell Nt, Wirswall Ch, etc.

*wellere OE (Angl), wyllere (WSax), *wællere (Merc), 'a salt boiler', found only in OE *wylleres seaðan* KCD 691 and first independently evidenced in late ME (NED s.v. *weller*); it might be confused with the OE pers.n. *Wilhere* (as in Willersey Gl) in the WSax area. The Merc form is found in (*a*) Wallerscote Ch (cot). [~OE *w(e)allan* 'to boil, seethe', -ere; ~wella.]

welm OE (Angl, Kt), wielm, wylm (WSax), wælm (Merc), 'a surging or welling up of water, a spring', is infrequent in this sense in literary documents; it is there usually associated with fire or the surging of the waves and, figuratively, with rage. In p.ns. it denotes 'a spring, the source of a stream'; cf. ǣ-welm. All three OE dial. forms are recorded, but the only one that survived was Merc *wælm*, ME *walm* (cf. NED s.v.); this Merc form had a wide currency in OE; it is noteworthy that this also occurs in a Nth p.n. (*a*) Wansford Nth 245 (ford, cf. also Hu 198, OE *wylmes-*, ME *Welmes-*, *Walmes-*). (*b*) Walmspout Wo 67 (ME *Welme*). [~ON *ólmr* 'rage', MHG *walm* 'passion, heat', PrGerm **walmiz*; ~wella.]

wemm OE, 'a spot, a blemish, filth', probably used in p.ns. of 'a filthy place'; the unmutated *wamm* is best evidenced in the figurative sense 'disgrace, impurity'. OE *wemm* and *wæmm* are both on record and survive as *wem* (NED s.v.). There is no evidence for the meaning 'marshy place' sometimes proposed. (*a*) Whempstead Hrt 143 (stede). (*b*) Wem Sa.

*wende OE, 'something which bends', possibly used in p.ns. in a topographical sense and therefore of similar meaning to (ge)wind 'a bend'; cf. ME minor names C 349 where it refers to bends in both streams and roads. (*a*) Wenden Ess (denu), Wendy C 67 (ēg). [An *i*-mutated form of OE *wand*, the pa.t. grade of *windan* 'to wind', found also in ON *vǫndr*, ME *wand* 'a shoot, a willow shoot' and in OE *wandrian* 'to wander'; cf. also *wendan* 'to wend'.]

wending ME, 'a turning, a bend in a road', is found in ME minor names like *le Wending* YE 328. [**wende**, **-ing**[1].]

***wendsum** (earlier ***wændsum**) OE adj., 'winding' (cf. Bradley E & S i, 34). (*b*) R. Wantsum K, R. Wensum Nf. [~**wende**, *-sum* adj. suffix.]

wenn, wænn OE, 'a wen, a tumour', used of a barrow or mound which might be thought to resemble such an excrescence. (*a*) Wamborough So, Wanbarrow Sx 275, Wanborough Sr 151, W 283 (**beorg**), possibly also in Wanstead Ess 109, Ha (**stede**).

wente ME, 'a path, a way', found in later use with numerals (cf. NED s.v. *went*), and also in f.ns. as *went*, *want* (Cu 497, Ess 593, Hrt 260, Nt 287, etc.). It belongs chiefly to EAngl, the EMidl and the NCy. (*a*) Wentford Sf, Winsford D (**ford**). (*b*) Four Wantz, Four Wents Ess, Four Want Ways Hrt (**fēower**). [~OE *wendan* 'to go', **wende**.]

wēod OE, 'a weed', also 'a herb, grass'. (*a*) Weddicar Cu (**æcer**), Wedhampton W (**hām-tūn**).

wēofod, wīobud OE, 'an altar' (heathen or Christian), remained in use till the 15th century (NED s.v. *weved*). (*a*) Wilson D (**stān**). [~**wēoh**[2], OE *bēod* 'table'.]

wēoh[1] OE, 'an idol, a shrine', *v.* **wīg**.

wēoh**[2] (wēon** wk.obl.) OE adj., 'holy', as in OE *æt Weonfelda* BCS 888, *Weondune*, Symeon of Durham's name for the place of the Battle of *Brunanburh*, and the compound **wēofod**, suggested by Ekwall (DEPN) for (*a*) Wembury D (**burh**). [~Goth *weihs*, OHG *wih* 'holy', ~**wīg**.]

(ge)weorc OE, 'a work, a building structure', esp. in p.ns. 'a fortification', as in Newark Nt 199 (as distinct from *Oldwark* Nt 222, the old fortification of Roman *Margidunum*) or War Coppice Sr 310 (near an old earthwork). It was also used of 'a building'; Newark Priory Sr 148 was originally *Aldebury* 'old manor' (**ald**, **burh**), but with the foundation of the Priory it became Newark (also Lat *Novus Locus* 'new place'). (*a*) Walkwood Wo (**wudu**), Workway W 318 (**weg**, near the ancient camp on Knap Hill). (*b*) Wark Nb (2), War Coppice Sr; Aldwark Db, YN, YW, *Oldwark* Nt (**ald**), Butterwork (Lincoln) L (**būtan**, 'outside the city wall'), Hill Barn W 320 (olim *Hulwerk*, **hyll** near an earthwork), Inswork Co (**inis**), Newark Nt, Nth, Sr (**nīwe**), Southwark Sr ('Surrey men'). [~**verk**.]

weorf OE, 'draught cattle, a beast of burden, a colt' (cf. Crawf 130 and

Ekwall, Studies² 63–4). (*a*) Warley Sa, Wo, Worsley Wo (**lēah**), Warracott D 200 (**geat**).

weorod, werod OE, 'a host, an army, a throng'. (*a*) Wuerdle La 57 (**hyll**).

weorð, weorðig OE, 'an enclosure', *v.* **worð, worðig**.

wer, wær OE, 'a weir, a river-dam, a fishing-enclosure in a river'; on the form *wær* cf. **bere**; there was also a form *waru* in the compound *on ða mylen-ware* 'a mill dam' (KCD 479). (*a*) Wareham Do, Warham He, Nf (**hām**), Warehorn K (gen.pl., **horn**), Warford Ch (**ford**), Wargrave Brk (**grāf**), Warleigh So (**lēah**), Werrar Wt (**ōra**). (*b*) Ware Hrt (pl.), Weare D, So; Brockweir Gl (**brōc**), Dunwear So, Edgware Mx (pers.ns.).

wer-cok ME, a small bird, first recorded in 1420 (NED). (*a*) Warcockhill La 44 (**hyll**, c. 1280). [Ekwall relates *wer-* to **wōr**.]

***wereð, *weroð, *werð** OE, 'a marsh' or the like, an *i*-mutated form of **waroð** and corresponding to OHG *werid* 'an island in a river'. The exact meaning is not clear, but *werth* is a common p.n. term for 'a marsh' along the Thames (Ess 569, 595); cf. also Hrt 260. It is found chiefly in Ess in Dengie Hundred and is first recorded there c. 1170. (*b*) Broadward (**brād**), Burwood (**burh**), Coleward (**cule**), Labworth (**lobb**), Ringwood (**hring**), Rugwood (**rogga**), Tilletsmarsh (**til**), Twizzlefoot (**twisla**) Ess.

***wering, *wæring** OE, 'a river-dam', is possible in (*a*) Warrington La (**tūn**), Warwick Wa 260 (**wīc**). [**wer, -ing¹**.]

wērloga, wǣrloga OE, 'a troth-breaker, a traitor, a warlock'. (*a*) Warlaby YN (**bý**).

***werpels** OE (Angl, Kt), ***wierpels, *wyrpels** (WSax), 'a path', surviving in Sx dial. *warple, wapple* 'a bridle-path, a cart-track, a track in the common field', evidenced in modern usage from 1565 (NED s.v. *warple*, cf. also f.ns. in Mx 204). It is a derivative of **wearp**, the primary meaning of which is 'something thrown up' and no doubt the idea behind *werpels* is that the earth was thrown up to the sides, as in ditching, when the track was levelled or much used (cf. a similar use of LG *werp*). Most p.ns. properly have ME spellings *Werples-* from the Angl and Kt *werpels*; there is some difficulty in the phonology of Wirples Moss La 123 (ME *Wirples-*) which can hardly be from the WSax form *wierpels*; it might, however, represent a different ablaut grade *wurp* (as in OE *gewyrp* 'a heap' (Mdf 59) or *wyrpel* 'a falconer's jess'). (*a*) Wapsbourne Sx

298 (burna), Warple Road Sr 39 (weg), Warpsgrove O 123 (grāf), Wirples Moss La (mos), Worplesdon Sr 161 (dūn). [~wearp, -els.]

*werð OE, 'a marsh', *v.* wereð.

*wesse OE (Merc), 'a swamp', *v.* wæsse.

west OE, adj., adv., 'western, west'; the adj. and adv. uses are difficult to separate in many p.ns.

(1) The adj. use is common in many names which denote places lying to the west of another older place or facing the west, or lying west in relation to another similar place, as in (*a*) Wesham La (hūs, dat.pl.), Westbury Bk, Gl, Ha, Sa, Wo, W (burh), Westhide He (hīd), Westley C, Sf (lēah), Westminster Mx (mynster), Weston *passim* (tūn), Westwick C, Du, Nf, YW (wīc). (*c*) As an affix it is very common as *West* prefixed to Ashford D, Ashton W, Burton Sx, Hardwick YW, etc.; in West Horndon Ess (olim *Thorndun*) and West Riding YW (olim *West Thrithing*) the initial consonant of the p.n. has been absorbed by the affix.

(2) As with ēast, etc., the adv. use of *west* is less frequent since westan is the usual OE word in elliptical p.n. formations; it may appear in Westington Gl, which is no doubt the type *west in tūne* '(land) west in the village'.

westan OE adv., 'west, west of', used in p.ns. elliptically, for '(place) west of something', as in OE *uuestan ae* '(place) west of the river' BCS 45. (*a*) Westbourne Mx (burna), Westbrook Brk (brōc), Westwood K (OE *beuuestanuudan* BCS 323, wudu).

wēste, wēsten OE, waste ME, 'waste-land'. (*b*) *Holewest* K 483 (hol); it occurs in f.ns. in Wa 333.

*wester, -ar (westra(n) wk.) OE adj., 'west, western', as in *se westra crochyrst* BCS 1125 and *se westra east healh* ib. 1208; it is cognate with ON vestr, OFris *wester*, OLG *westar* and survives as dial. *wester* (NED s.v.); it is found in p.ns. like Wester K 139 (gē), Westerham K (OE *Westarham* BCS 558, hām), Westerfield Sf (feld), Westerleigh Gl (lēah), Westerton Sx (tūn), but it is difficult to distinguish from vestr and westerra.

westerne (westerra comp., westmest superl.) OE adj., 'west, western, westerly'; the comparative may occur in some p.ns. in *Wester-* like Westergate Sx (olim *West-*, *Westregate*, geat), or Bowood D 84 (*westeraboue wode*, lit. 'more westerly above the wood') but it is difficult to distinguish from wester. The superl. is found in Westmeston Sx (tūn).

westerra OE comp.adj., 'more westerly', *v.* **westerne.**

westmest OE superl.adj., 'most westerly', *v.* **westerne.**

wēt (**wētan** wk.obl.) OE (Angl, Kt), **wǣt** (WSax), adj., 'wet, damp'. It is used as a sb. in OE *hrunig fealles wæt* BCS 1307 (Runfold Sr). (*a*) Watton YE, Wetton St (**dūn**, cf. **vátr**), Weeting Nf (**-ing**[2]), Weetwood Nb, YW, Wetwood St (**wudu**), Wettenhall Ch (**halh**), Wheatshaw La (**sceaga**), Whetty Wo (**gehæg**). [~ **vátr**; **wæter**, by ablaut.]

weðer OE, 'a castrated ram, a wether'. (*a*) Waresley Hu, Wetherley C (**lēah**), Weatheroak Wo (**āc**), Wetheral Cu (**halh**), Wetherden Sf (**denu**). (*c*) Watermillock Cu. [~ **veðr**, ***wiðer.**]

weyour ME, 'a pond', rendered *piscina* in *Promptorium Parvul.*, is found only in ME and later f.ns. such as a fishpond called *Wayer* (1229), *le Wayer* (1326), C 350, Hrt 260, Ware Field Ess 594, etc. [~ OFr *gayoir* 'to bathe (a horse)', AN *wayour.*]

whin ME, 'gorse', *v.* **hvin.**

whinny ME adj., 'covered with gorse', *v.* **hvin.**

whippel-tre ME, a tree of some kind, as in Chaucer's list of trees in the *Knight's Tale* 2065; it is possible in a much contracted form in (*a*) *Whyperley* Bd 159 (**lēah**). [Possibly related to **hwippe, -el, trēow.**]

wīc (**wīc** nom.pl., **wīcum** dat.pl.) OE, 'a dwelling, a building or collection of buildings for special purposes, a farm, a dairy farm' and in the pl. 'a hamlet, a village'.

(1) OE *wīc* was a Germ loan from Lat *vicus* 'a row of houses, a street, a city district', the root idea being 'a collection of dwellings' which remained in some Germ languages, as in Goth *weihs* 'village', MLG *wīk*, OHG *wīch* 'town'; in others it denoted 'a single dwelling', as in OSax *wīc*, OFris *wīk* and also OHG *wīch* 'a house, a dwelling place'. In OE it was often associated with Lat *vīcus* in the sense 'quarter of a town, a town' (which is retained in OE *wīc-gerēfa* 'bailiff, tax-gatherer') and it possibly refers occasionally to the remains of a Roman *vicus* (*v.* **wīc-tūn**). In OE literary documents it had a variety of uses, of which the commonest was 'a dwelling' (translating Lat *mansio*, as, for instance in the OEBede). In this sense it enters into some compounds like **wīc-stede** and **wīc-stōw**, and the original notion of 'a collection of buildings' is effected by the frequent use of the pl., often denoting 'the dwellings (of men)'; this pl. usage led to the sense 'hamlet, village' which

survived at least till ME (NED s.v. *wick* sb. 2). No doubt in a good many p.ns. with *wīc* in the sg. it denotes 'a dwelling' and in a few instances it seems also to have denoted 'military quarters, a camp', as in here-wīc; in the *Psalms* lxxvii, 28, *on middan ða wic* renders Lat *in medio castrorum* (the *Vesp. Psalt.* has *in midla ferd-wica*, with ferd). Similarly in p.ns., the idea of 'a hamlet or village', that is a collection of buildings, is expressed by the pl. as in a good many names like Wix, Wyken, Wycombe.

(2) There is in fact no unambiguous evidence that *wīc* itself denoted 'a hamlet' in OE (though NED cites ME examples). Although its paradigm is not completely recorded, it appears to have been originally a neut. noun with an unchanged pl. *wīc*; through the frequent use of the neut. acc.pl. (*on*) *þa wīc* it came to be regarded as a fem. acc.sg. (despite the absence of the fem. case ending *-e* in *wīc*) and the word was then sometimes wrongly treated as a fem. noun but always without case ending in expressions like *to anre wic*. The several examples cited to establish the meaning 'village' always have this ambiguous form (*þa*) *wic*, which is as likely to be pl. as sg. as in the OEGosp. Matt. xxi. 2 *Gaþ on ða wic* 'Go into the village' (for Lat *castellum* 'a fortified house', etc., *v.* castel), Mark viii. 23 *He lædde hine butan ða wic* 'he led him (the blind man) out of the town' (Lat *extra vicum*), and the gloss *castellum, wic uel lytel port* (WW 140.40, *v.* castel, port[2]), in all of which *wic* could be pl. The only probable sg. example is in Acts xii. 10 *Hi comon to anre wic* where *wic* sg. renders Lat *vicus* in the sense 'quarter of a town, street'). It is in fact the use of the pl. that effectively gives OE *wīc* the meaning 'hamlet, village', which was in late OE and ME acquired by *wīc* sg. because of the identity of the sg. and pl. forms.

(3) Place-names provide some evidence that a *wīc*, like a cot, came to be associated with buildings used for particular occupations and manufactures. Some of the compounds connected with trades and farming mentioned *infra* (cf. also 6 (*b*) viii *infra*) may have denoted places where the various commodities were produced or prepared, but perhaps also store-houses where the products could be bought, for *wīc* is found in combination with cēap, and a *saltwich* is described as *unam portionem mansionis in wico emptorio salis* 'a portion of a house in a *wic* for the sale of salt' (BCS 138, cf. § (iii) *infra*). It is not possible to say if this is a reflexion of some older

application of Lat *vicus* 'street, quarter' to 'a street or quarter where particular trades concentrated', as they did in later medieval times; the compound wīc-stōw implies 'a place where people gathered' and it may have been a place where they gathered for trade; cf. also wīc-tūn. The principal uses are distinguished as follows:

(i) OE *wīc* denoted dwellings and buildings with a variety of interests other than agricultural, as may be gathered from its combination with words like bærs, fisc, fiscere in allusion to fishing and words like col, hamor, myln, salt, smið (cf. § 6 (*b*) viii, ix, xi *infra*) in allusion to crafts. It is doubtful whether *wīc* had any special religious connotation (like stoc or stōw), for most p.ns. which incorporate the names of ecclesiastics (ancra, hālig, munuc, nunne, prēost) do not indicate religious houses and foundations but merely property owned or enjoyed by them.

(ii) As a particular development of the idea of 'a building for a particular occupation', its principal meaning was 'farm', esp. 'a dairy farm', judging by the frequency with which it was combined with words denoting farm-stock and farm produce, as also by the compounds bere-wīc and heorde-wīc. It is, however, noteworthy that apart from *bere-wīc* the el. is rarely combined with words indicating arable farming but frequently with words denoting dairy produce; butere and cēse and words for dairy cattle are common, and those with bēo, hunig, gōs, henn, etc., indicate an association with other kinds of food production, but els. like scēap, wull and gearn show that a *wīc* could be concerned with sheep-farming (*v.* esp. § 6 (*b*) ix, x *infra*). The course of its semantic development is difficult to follow; doubtless it began by denoting 'a dwelling' and then 'a dwelling or building associated with some kind of productive farming', for Lydwicke Sx 160, Strudgwick Sx 107, etc., were described as pastures belonging to Annington in BCS 961 and Gotwick Sx as one belonging to Washington ib. 834; the prefixing of noun-qualifiers like bere, butere, heorde, oxa, scēap, etc., implies that *wīc* by itself meant no more than 'farm', clearly 'a local outlying or dependent farm' if we take into account the relation of Lydwicke and other Sx *wīcs* to their parent villages as well as the very large number of simplex p.ns. containing this el.—they are esp. common in West Sussex, W and D—and those like Hampton Wick Mx which embody older p.ns. Besides this certain places are known to be dependent farms: Eastwick and Westwick YW were outliers of Ripon YW, Monkwith YE was a *berewic* of St John's Beverley; Cannock Ess 378 belonged to St John's Abbey, Monkswick Ess 150 to Westminster Abbey, and Bathwick So to the Abbess of Wherwell. The limitation of *wīc* to 'dairy farm' is first found in DB, esp. in Ess where it long survived as an appellative with this meaning; as late as 1729 there is a reference to 'a wick or dairy of 20 cows in St Osyth' (Ess 594).

(iii) A word *wich* has been isolated with the meaning 'salt works, brine spring' (*v.* NED s.v.), partly on the basis of OE names in *wīc* denoting places which also happened to have brine workings and from the passage already mentioned in a spurious OE charter (BCS 138, a 14th-century manuscript) which refers to *unam portionem mansionis in wico emptorio salis quem nos Saltwich vocamus.* Here, of course, *wīc* means no more than 'dwelling, dwelling or building associated with a trade', which has already been noted as a general meaning of *wīc* (*v.* § 3 (i) *supra*). But the coincidence of several well-known places in Wo and Ch being called *wic* (like Droitwich Wo, Nantwich, Northwich Ch) and being famous for their salt-workings led antiquarians like Camden (*Britannia*, i, 607) who talks of 'famous salt-wiches [the original Latin has *salinæ*] where brine or salt water is drawne out of pittes' to conclude that *wīc* meant 'salt working'.

(4) The el. *wīc* is found everywhere, but it is particularly common in the SCy, esp. in Ess, Sx, W, D. From the distribution it would not appear to have been a very active element in the oldest period of OE, for it is rarely found with archaic els. such as folk-names in *-ingas*. A high proportion of *wīc*-names find no mention in DB; they were therefore largely minor settlements and many of them must belong to the period when *wīc* meant no more than 'farm' or 'dairy farm', esp. in counties like Ess, Sr, West Sx, W and D. Some are certainly post-Conquest; Holywick Bk 179 belonged to Medmenham Abbey which was founded in 1204 and though Holywick might conceivably be an older name the evidence suggests that it was called 'holy *wic*' because of its conveyance to the Abbey in the first years of the 13th century. Over a third of the p.ns. in *wīc* are simplex names, suggesting that they were minor settlements of no more than local importance; a good many unidentified examples occur in some counties (as Bd 297, Ess 594, Hrt 260, Mx 204, etc.),

which also indicates the minor character of many such places. Not more than a quarter have pers.ns. as their first el., but a good many have other words denoting people, like fiscere, hunta, nunne, prēost, etc. (*v.* § 6 (*b*) xi *infra*). It is rarely found with an ON el.

(5) The chief current forms of *wīc* in simplex p.ns. are Wike, Wick, Week; *Wike* is normal from the nom.sg. *wīc*, *Wick* has undergone early shortening or is a spelling pronunciation and *Week* may be from an early ME shortened *wice* dat.sg. with lengthening in the open syllable, but it seems mostly to be a local SW form and spellings like *Weke* first appear in the 15th century. The alternative forms *-wich* and *-wick* as a final el. are parallel to those of dīc (*ditch* and *dike*); *-wich* is regularly developed from the nom.sg. and *-wick* from the obl. cases like dat.pl. *wicum.* In Y the el. was sometimes replaced by *-with* (as in Bramwith YW, Monkwith, Skipwith YE), probably through the influence of p.ns. in ON viðr, and partly through ME scribal confusion of *c* and *t* (*wic* and *wit*) which was later reflected in pronunciation when the p.n. spelling in *-wit* (AN for *with*) was stabilized. It is sometimes difficult to distinguish from wice.

(6) (*a*) As a first el. *wīc* is rare except in the compounds wīc-hām, wīc-stōw and wīc-tūn; Weekaborough D (beorg), Wickhampton Nf (hām-tūn), Wickey Bd (weg), Wickham C (hamm), Wickmere Nf (mere), Wighill YW (halh), Wigford L (ford), Wigton YW (dūn near Wike YW), Witchampton Do (hǣma-tūn), Wychbold Wo (bōðl).

(*b*) As a simplex p.n. it is very common (cf. § 4 *supra*), often in the plural (cf. § 2 *supra*), Week(e) Co, Ha, So, Wt, Wick Brk, Gl, So, Wo, Wickwar Gl (*-war* is a feudal affix), Wike YW (all from the dat.sg. *wice*); Wix Ess (from a new ME pl. *wikes*); Ashwicken Nf, Wicken C, Ess, Nth, Wyken Wa, Wykin Lei, Wigan Hu (some of which have ME *Wikes* alternating with *Wiken*, mostly a new wk. ME nom.pl., cf. -um § 4, occasionally an OE dat.pl.); Wycombe Lei, Wykeham YN 45 (dat.pl. *wīcum*).

In compounds, it is chiefly found with significant els. in the following categories:

(i) Adjs. of direction and location, as Astwick Bd, Eastwick YW (ēast), Middlewich Ch (middel), Netherwich Wo (neoðera), Norwich Nf, Northwich Ch (norð), Owstwick YE (austr), Southwick Du, Gl, Ha, Nth, Sx, W (sūð), Westweek D, Westwick YW (west).

(ii) Descriptive words, as Droitwich Wo (drit), Longwick Bk

(lang), Nantwich Ch (ME *named* 'well-known'), Shernick Co (scearn), Terwick Sx (tord).

(iii) Topographical words, as Brookwick Sr (brōc), Combwich So (cumb), Dorweeke D (dor), Fenwick Nb, YW (fenn), Fordwich K (ford), Landwich Ess (2) (land), Lydwicke Sx (hlið), Markwich Sr (mearc), Neswick YE (nes), Pickwick W (pīc), Rudgwick Sx (hrycg), Sandwich K (sand), Standerwick So (stǣner), Strudgwick Sx (strōd), Warwick Cu (waroð), Wa (wering), Woodix So (wudu).

(iv) Older p.ns., some lost, others later additions, as Bathwick So (Bath), Buddleswick D 396, Clapton Wick So, Eton Wick Bk, Hampton Wick Mx, Kimble Wick Bk, Lenchwick Wo (Lench), Sunderlandwick (sundor-land), Withernwick (a lost *Withthorn*) YE.

(v) River-names, as Alnwick Nb (R. Alne), Exwick D (R. Exe), Lowick Nb (R. Low).

(vi) Names of wild plants, as Blatherwycke Nth (blæddre), Bromwich St, Wa, Wo (brōm), Dilwick Bd (dile), Redwick Gl (hrēod), Rushwick Wo (risc).

(vii) Tree-names, as Aldridge St (alor), Ashwick So (æsc), Hazelwick Sx (hæsel), Slaughterwicks Sr (slāh-trēow).

(viii) Significant words connected with use, occupation, buildings, etc., as Flitwick W (geflit 'dispute'), Hammerwich St (hamor, perhaps in the sense 'smithy'), Harrowick Bd (hearg), Holywick Bk (hālig), Keepwick Nb, Kepwick YN (cēap with ON *k*-), Milwich St (myln), Sheldwick K, Shelwick He (sceld).

(ix) Words for products, esp. dairy produce, as Bastwick YE (bæst), Benwick C (bēan), Butterwick Do, Du, L, We, YE, YN (butere), Cheswick Nb, Wa, Chiswick C, Ess, Mx (cēse), Keswick Cu, Nf, YW (cēse with ON *k*-), Colwich St, Colwick Nt, Wo (col 'charcoal'), Honeywick Sx (hunig), Saltwick Nb (salt), Spitchwick D (spic), Woolwich K (wull), Yarnwick YN (gearn).

(x) Names of domestic animals, birds, etc., esp. those producing food, etc., as Bewick Nb, YE (bēo), Bulwick Nth (bula), Chelvey So (calf), Conrish W (cūna gen.pl. of cū), Cowick D, YW, Cowix Sr (cū), Fuge, Fuidge D (feoh), Fulwich K (fugol), Gatwick Sr, Gotwick Sx (gāt), Goswick Nb (gōs), Hinwick Bd (henn), Oxwick Nf (oxa), Roderwick L, Rotherwick Ha (hrīðer), Shapwick Do, So, Shopwyke Sx (scēap), Skipwith YE (scēap with ON *sk*- and *wīc* replaced by viðr), heorde-wīc; cf. also Baswick YE 72 (bærs 'perch'), Fishwick La (fisc).

(xi) Words denoting people, esp. groups of people, tradesmen, craftsmen, ecclesiastics, etc., as Ankerwyke Bk (**ancra**), Cannock Ess (**canoun**), Fisherwick St (**fiscere**), Huntwick (**hunta**), Kildwick (**cild**, with ON *k-*) YW, Knightwick Wo (**cniht**), Monkswick Ess, Monkwith YE (**munuc**), Nunwick Nb, YW (**nunne**), Prestwich La, Prestwick Bk, Nb (**prēost**), Smethwick Ch, St, *Smithwick* Sx (**smið**), Swanage Do, Swanwick Ha (**swān**).

(xii) Folk-names, probably already stabilized p.ns. when *wīc* was added, as Cottingwith YE (**-ingas**), Spaldwick Hu (**spalde**).

(xiii) Pers.ns., not common, as Ardwick La, Chadwick Wa, Wo, Chelmick Sa, Gotherswick La, Heckmondwike YW, Hunwick Du, Orgarswick K, Osbaldwick YN, Tadwick So, Wistanswick Sa.

wice (**wican** gen.sg., **wicena** gen.pl.) OE, 'a wych-elm' or other tree with pliant branches. (*a*) Wichenford Wo, Wishford W, Witchford C (**ford**), Wicheves La (**efes**), Witcham C (**hamm**). (*b*) Horwich La (**hār**).

***wīc-hām** OE, 'homestead near a *wīc*, homestead with a dairy farm', is not recorded in OE (except in p.n. spellings), but it occurs often enough to be regarded as an appellative compound. Its exact meaning is obscure. (*b*) Wicham K, Wickham Brk, Ess, Ha, Hrt, K, Wykeham L (3), YN 99, Wykham O. [**wīc**, **hām**.]

wīcing OE, 'a pirate', was already in use in OE before the Viking invasions and NED points out the existence of another WGerm cognate in OFris *witsing* as well as OE *wicing-sceaða* for Lat *piraticam* in an 8th-century gloss (OET 87); an Anglo-Frisian origin is therefore probable. The cognate ON **vikingr** was introduced in the Danelaw later, certainly as a pers.n., and the OE and ON words cannot be kept apart. (*a*) Whissendine R (**denu**), Whissonsett (**geset**), Witchingham (**hām**) Nf. [**wīc**, **-ing**[1].]

wīc-stōw OE, 'a dwelling place, a camp', is recorded in these senses in OE; the meaning 'dwelling place' is more likely in p.ns.; the significance of *stōw* is that of a place where people gathered together for a purpose. (*b*) Wistow Hu 228 (described as a *Kingestune* in 974), YW. [**wīc**, **stōw**.]

wīc-tūn OE, 'an enclosure with a dwelling or a *wīc*', is recorded in OE in the *Paris Psalter* with the sense 'porch, vestibule' and in ME *wicke-tunes* in the *Owl and Nightingale* 730, where it is said to denote something like 'religious establishments'. In p.ns., however, the more literal sense '*tūn* with a *wīc*' is likely. In one or two instances, the *wīc* may be a Roman *vicus* (Market Weighton YE 230 lies on a Roman road). In others some other meaning of *wīc* is to be sought; Witton Wo 289, like Wychbold Wo, is near the *wīc* of Droitwich and Witton Ch is near Northwich. It has been suggested (Wo 289) that in these cases the *wīc* itself was the industrial centre (cf. also wīc § 3) and the *wīc-tūn* the dwelling place. This meaning 'dwelling places' (without further limitation) would also suit the *Owl and Nightingale* passage. (*b*) Market Weighton YE, Wighton Nf, Witton Ch, Wa, Wo, Wyton Hu. [wīc, tūn.]

wīd (wīdan wk.obl.) OE adj., 'wide, spacious'. (*a*) Whitcombe Do, W, Widcombe So, Witcombe Gl, Wydcombe Wt (cumb), Widemarsh He (mersc), Widnes La (næss), Widnell Bk (halh), Willock C (lacu), Woodbatch Sa (bece).

widu early OE, 'a wood', *v.* wudu.

wielle, wiella OE (WSax), 'a well, a spring, a stream', *v.* wella.

***wierpels** OE (WSax), 'a path', *v.* werpels.

wīf (wīfes gen.sg., wīfa gen.pl.) OE, 'a woman'; the meaning 'wife, married woman' was already current in OE (as in *Rushw. Gosp.* Matt. i. 24, where it renders Lat *conjugem*). (*a*) Westoe Du, Westow (stōw), Winestead (stede), Wyton (tūn) YE.

wifel OE, 'a weevil, a beetle', is difficult to distinguish from the pers.ns., OE *Wifel* and ON *Vífill*, in p.ns. like Wilsford L, W (ford), Wilsill (OE *Wifeleshealh*), Wilstrop (þorp) YW, etc. (*a*) *Wivelridge* Sx (hrycg).

wīg, wēoh OE, 'an idol'; although not recorded, the meaning 'holy place, shrine' is suggested by the use of *wīg* as a final el. (as in OE *cusanweoh* BCS 72 Sr) and in simplex p.ns.; it meant 'holy place, temple' in OSax *wih*, ODan *wī*, OSwed *vī*, *vǣ* (as in Dan *Odense*, Swed *Odensvi*, *Torsvi* containing the names of the heathen gods Othin and Thor, NK 79, 166). In the few literary references in OE, *wīg* has a heathen association and p.ns. containing it are probably of great antiquity. Cf. Dickins 152. The OE forms *wīg* and *wēoh* which later became *wy*(*e*)- and *wee-* respectively arose in this way; *wīh* was broken to *wīoh* and this gave (i) Kt *wīoh*, later WSax *wēoh* and and (ii) Angl *wīh* with smoothing before *h*; *wīg-* is normal in the inflected cases (cf. Bülbring § 489) and is a later alternative spelling for *-h* (Brunner § 214); cf. the forms of burh, byrig, lēah, lēage, etc. (*a*) Waden W, Weedon Bk 85, Nth 30, 45 (dūn), Weeford St (ford), Weeley Ess, Weoley Wo 350, Wheely Fm Ha (*on weoleage* KCD

780), Whiligh, Whyly Sx 401, 454, Willey Sr 175 (lēah), Wyeville L (wella), Wyfold O lii, 46, *Wyfold* Hundred Brk (fald). (*b*) Weyhill Ha, Wye K (OE *Uuiæ*); Wyham L (dat.pl.); Patchway Sx 309 (pers.n.). [~wēoh².]

wigga OE, 'a beetle' (surviving in *earwig*), may be found in some p.ns. Ekwall (DEPN) has suggested that in Stanwick Nth 196 (OE *Stanwigga*) and Wigston Parva Lei (OE *Wicgestan*), both combined with stān, we have the same word in a more original sense, such as 'that which moves', which is retained in ModE *wiggle* and MLG *wiggen* 'to move'; that both p.ns. would therefore denote 'a logan stone'. As a first el. it cannot be distinguished from the OE pers.n. *Wicga* as in (*a*) Wigley Db, Ha (lēah), Wigwell Db (wella).

*wiht OE, 'a bend', found in OE only in p.n. spellings, has some topographical application such as 'a curving recess, a bend in a river or valley' (cf. Mawer, Problems 46); it occurs in ME in *Binnewiht*, an alternative name for Bingley's Island K (OE *binnan ea* 'within the river', cf. KPN 132 and binnan). It is common in ME f.ns. in C 351, where it appears to have denoted 'land included in the bend of a stream' and probably also 'a close surrounded by winding ditches'. (*a*) Utton's C 173 (tūn), Wetmoor St (mōr, a bend in the R. Trent), Whitehill O 286 (hyll, a curved hollow), Wightfield Gl (feld, a bend in the R. Severn), Witley Wo 183 (lēah, the sinuous course of Shrawley Brook), Wytham Brk (hām, a bend in the R. Thames). (*b*) Great Whyte Hu xli, 217 (the bend of a stream); probably also in Inglewhite La (on a hill in the fork of two streams), Littlewhite Du (a side-valley), Trewhitt Nb (bends in Wreigh Burn), which have been derived from þwit, but no *thwit* spellings occur; cf. also ME f.ns. in C 351. [~OE *wican* 'to yield', that is, 'to give way, to bend'.]

wīl late OE, 'a wile, a trick', probably used of some kind of contrivance 'a gin, a trap, a snare'; the cognate ON *vél* was, for example, used of 'a device for catching fish'; NED (s.v. *wile*) has suggested that *wīl* may be a loan from ON *vél* (earlier **vihl-*), since it is not recorded in English before the 12th century (ASC 1128 E) and usually has a Danelaw provenance; the SCy p.ns. are rather late, but a native OE *wīl* would not be out of the question (cf. Ekwall, Studies² 156–7). (*b*) Wild Brk, Monkton Wyld Do; Wylam Nb (dat.pl.).

wilde (wildan wk. obl.) OE adj., 'wild, uncultivated, desolate', is not common in p.ns. (*a*) Weald Moors Sa, Wildmore L (mōr, cf. *wilde moras* in *Orosius* i, 1), Wildhill Hrt (hyll), Wildwood Sr (wudu), Willand (land), Willyards (geard) D; it has been suggested for Wilton He, YE, YN (tūn), but cf. wilig, which is preferable since *wilde* is found only with topographical words.

wilder, wild-dēor OE, 'a wild beast, a deer', was found already in OE in a contracted form, with gen.sg. *wildres* and gen.pl. *wildra* (cf. BT s.v. *wilder*). (*a*) Longdon Marsh Wo 209 (olim *Wildres Mareys*, mareis), Wilders Moor La (hyrst); *Wilderehey* Ess 374 (gehæg). [An old *-os-* stem, PrOE **wildor*, pl. *wildru* (~wilde), remodelled as a compound of *wilde* and dēor.]

***wilig** OE (Angl), **welig** (WSax), 'a willow'.

(1) The two forms *wilig* and *welig* certainly existed in OE; *welig* is the common one found on independent record, as in *on welgum* (Blickling Glosses, OET 123), *weliges leaf* (Leechdoms ii, 156), in the OE spellings of p.ns. like Welford Brk (*æt Weligforda* BCS 877, 963) and Wellow Wt (*æt welig* ib. 553), and in a few unidentified charter names like *on welewe* ib. 391, *to ðam greatan welige* ib. 924 *ða welegas* ib. 792. On the other hand, *wilig* is not found independently in OE and in p.ns. only twice in the OE spellings of Wilbury Hrt (*fram wiligbyrig* Crawf 25) and Willoughby Wa (*wyliabyg* BCS 978); OE *be wilig* BCS 500, etc., refers to the R. Wylye W 11 (a Brit r.n.) and is not relevant. After the Conquest spellings in *Welge-*, *Weli-*, *Wel-* survive in Brk and Wt; they occur also in Hrt and Bd but there they are invariably replaced at an early date by *Wil-*. In EAngl, the Midl and WMidl as far north as YE, *wilge-* and *wilwe-* regularly appear from the time of DB. It would seem therefore from the material so far available that *welig* was the WSax form and *wilig* the Anglian; as far as ME literary usage is in evidence—and there is a curious lack of it before the 14th century—it would tend to confirm this distinction (cf. NED s.v. *willow*).

(2) The relationship of *welig* and *wilig* is obscure. The better recorded OE form *welig* is thought to be from a PrGerm root **walg-*, **welg* (NED s.v. willow) but it survives only in WSax as already noted (§ 2 *supra*); *wilig*, which has a wide currency in Midl p.ns. but is rare in OE spellings, may be very old, and is paralleled by MHG *wilge*, OLG *wilgia* (as also by OE *wilige* 'a basket' and the adj. *wiliht* 'growing with willows' which occurs only in the OE f.n. *on wylihte mædwan* KCD 662). If the root is *welg-*, the OE *-i-* in the suffix is svarabhaktic (Wright, OEGr § 220).

(3) Some later spellings vary between *Willi-* (as in Willitoft) and *Willough-* (ModE *willow* in late minor names); the former is from the OE nom.sg. *wilig* and the latter from oblique cases, dat.sg. *wilge*, gen.pl. *wilga*. An OE form *wiluh*, postulated (C 305) to explain ME *wilugh-*, is improbable; *wilugh-* is a typical ME development of *wilg-*.

(4) The early provenance of *welig* and *wilig* is limited; as already noted (§ 1), *welig*, which is not common in p.ns. is found only in Hrt, Brk and Wt, and *wilig* is for the most part restricted to the Midl, not being found in NCy p.ns. This limitation of use was probably because other words for 'willow' such as wīðig were available. In modern minor names and f.ns. StdE *willow* is common in most parts.

(5) (*a*) From *welig*, Welford Brk (ford); from *wilig*, Wilbury Hrt (burh), Wilby Nf, Nth, Sf, Willoughby L (4), Lei, Nt, Wa (bý), Willey Ch, He (lēah), Willitoft YE (topt), Willoughton L (tūn).

(*b*) From *welig*, Wellow Wt (dat.sg.), Welwyn Hrt (dat.pl., also DB *Welge*, *Wilge*, *Wilie*); from *wilig*, Willen Bk, Willian Hrt (pl.); Prickwillow C (pricca).

*wiligen OE adj., 'growing with willows', may be found in some p.ns., but it would be indistinguishable in ME from wilign (cf. also wīðign). (*a*) Willenhall Wa, Winnall He (halh). [wilig, -en.]

*wilign OE, 'a willow' or 'a willow copse' (cf. Wa 190), (*a*) Willington Bd, Db (tūn). (*b*) Wilne Db. [~wilig, -en or -ign.]

wince (wincan gen.sg.) OE, 'a winch', is recorded in OE only in the sense 'winch, pulley' (WW 416.6) and in the compound *hleape-wince* 'lapwing' (so called from its leaping twisting flight); it developed from 'winch' the meaning 'a well wheel' and then 'a well' by 1400 (NED s.v. *winch*); these have not so far been found in p.ns. It is related to a series of words which go back to PrGerm **wink-*, **wank-* 'to move sideways', such as OE *wancol* 'unsteady', OHG *wanc* 'turning', OSax *wankon* 'to waver', OE *wincian* 'to wink', etc. (NED s.v. *wink* vb. 1), and it has a derivative wincel 'nook, angle, corner'. It has been suggested therefore that in p.ns. *wince* has a similar sense, 'that which turns to one side', that is, 'a sharp bend in a river or valley, a corner', which is topographically suitable. (*a*) Wincham K (hām). (*b*) Winchbottom Bk 203, Winches Hrt 99 (there is a *Winchfield* from wincel in the same par.), Winch-hill Hrt; it is also possible in Lower Winchendon Bk 111 (dūn).

***wincel** OE, 'a nook, a corner', found only in the OE spellings of p.ns. (Mdf 151); its meaning 'corner' is deduced from its cognate OHG *winkil* 'corner' (cf. also fenkel²) and from the topography of the places so named; it may denote 'a sharp bend in a river or valley', 'a corner of land in the hills' and the like. (*a*) Wichling K (mere), Winchcomb Gl, K 383 (cumb), Winchelsea Sx (ēg), Winchfield Ha, *Winchfield* Hrt (near Winches, *v.* wince) (feld). (*b*) Aldwinkle Nth (pers.n.). [wince, -el.]

wind¹ OE, vindr ON, 'wind', used in p.ns. to denote places and esp. houses with windy exposed situations; cf. also wind-geat. (*a*) Winder La, We (erg), Windersome YE (hūs, dat.pl.), Windhill K YW, Windle La, Winthill Wo (hyll), Winscales Cu (skáli), Winsetts YE (geset).

(ge)wind² OE, 'something winding, a winding path, a winding ascent', glossing Lat *circuitus*, *ascensus* (WW 145.17). It was probably used also to denote 'a winding stream'. (*b*) Chetwynd Sa (pers.n., here 'an ascent'), R. Ouse Sx 6 (olim *aqua de Midewinde*, midd). [~OE *windan* 'to wind'.]

-winde OE, 'a climbing plant', occurs as a suffix in plant-names such as OE bed-winde, *nǣdre-winde* 'adderwort', *wudu-winde* 'woodbine'. [~OE *windan* 'to wind, entwine'.]

***windels** OE, 'a winding gear, a winch, a windlass', which is found in OE only in p.n. spellings, has been suggested by Ekwall (DEPN 498) to enter into certain p.ns., Windsor Brk, Winsor D, Ha, Broadwindsor Do; it is always combined with ōra 'a bank, a shore' and it would be an unusual coincidence for such a combination so often repeated to embody either a pers.n. *Windel* (which is not on record in OE) or the recorded OE *windel* 'a basket' (which is also found in a different sense in the compounds *windel-strēaw* 'a long withered grass' and *windel-trēow* 'a willow'). As a technical term *windels-ōra* 'a shore or bank with a winch for pulling up boats' might well repeat itself in this way. The word *windlass* itself is not recorded before 1400 and is of obscure origin, but it may well be from this OE *windels*. [~OE *windan* 'to wind', -els.]

***wind-geat** OE, 'a wind-swept gap or pass', is not independently recorded, but is found in the OE p.n. *to winde geate* BCS 1066 Ha and in p.ns. (*b*) Windgate Wt, Wingate D, Du, Nb, Sr, YW, Winnats Pass Db. In one or two names, where the topographical conditions are dubious, the meaning 'swing gate' has been suggested, as for Wingate(s) K 446, La 44. [wind[1] or OE *windan* 'to wind', geat.]

wīn-geard OE, 'a vineyard', is found in ME p.ns. and minor names (C 352, Ess 595, Hrt 260, Sr 366), sometimes rendered by Lat *vinea* and usually replaced by ME vinȝerd. (*a*) The Vineyard(s) C 130, He *et freq*, Winyard W. [OE *wīn* 'vine' from Lat *vīnum*, geard.]

***winn[1], *wynne** OE, 'a pasture', is not recorded in English but a word of this form appears in a number of p.ns. found in OE; as a final el. it occurs but once. The cognates of *winn* include ON vin, Goth *winja*, OHG *winne* (from PrGerm **winjaz*) and for *wynne* there is OHG *wunnja* (from a different grade, PrGerm **wunja-*). These words mostly have the sense 'pasture, meadow'. This el. would be difficult to distinguish from (ge)winn 'strife, contention' which may be found in some of the following p.ns. (*a*) Umborne D, Wimborne Do (*æt Winburnan* ASC 718, etc., *Winburna* BCS 114), Wombaford D (burna), Winch Nf (wīc), Windley Db (lēah), Windridge Hrt (hrycg), Winford Wt, Wonford D (*Wynford* BCS 721, ford), Wingfield Db (*Wynnefeld* ASWills), Winnersh Brk (ersc), Winton We (tūn). (*b*) Heddon Nb (pers.n.).

(ge)winn[2] OE, 'a fight, a conflict, dispute', may be found in some p.ns. thought to be from winn[1], probably to denote places in dispute (cf. þrēap) or the scene of a fight. It is much more probable in Rosewain Cu 334 (hross) than ON vin; for a similar allusion to horse-fighting, *v.* (ge)feoht. [~OE *winnan* 'to fight'.]

***winn[3]** PrWelsh, gwyn Welsh adj., 'white, fair, holy'. The older form is found in names like (*a*) Wendover Bk (dubro-), Wenlock Sa (*loc* 'monastery'), Winford So, Wynford Do (Welsh *ffrwd* 'stream', cf. also *Wenferð* BCS 513–4, the stream-name which is found in Wanerton Wo), and the later Welsh form in Drefwen (tref), the Welsh name of Whittington Sa (hwīt).

winter[1] OE, vinter OEScand, 'winter', in p.ns. referring to streams that run or places that are used in winter. (*a*) Winkelbury W (burh), Winter Beck Nt (bekkr), Winterfold Wo (fald), Wintersett YW (geset), Winterton Nf (tūn), Wintry Park Ess (gehæg); *v.* also winter-burna.

***winter[2]** OE, 'a vineyard', has been proposed as a loan from Lat *vinitorium* for (*a*) Midwinter D 435, Radwinter Ess 512, though alternative explanations, such as 'Rædwynn's tree' are possible (DEPN).

winter-burna OE, 'a winter stream', that is, one which flows or becomes a torrent only in winter; it is an alternative gloss to **burna** for Lat *torrens* in *Lindisf. Gosp.* John xviii. 1. It is found in OE charter names (as in BCS 226, 467, 667). (*b*) R. Winterborne Do, Winterbourne Bk, Gl, Sx, W, Winterburn YW. [**winter, burna.**]

wīr, wȳr OE, 'myrtle, bog myrtle', as in OE *wirdene* BCS 246, *wirhangra* ib. 801 (cf. Mdf 151), glosses Lat *myrtus* 'myrtle' (OET 76, WW 269.25). (*a*) Wirral Ch, Worrall YW (**halh**), Wyrley St (**lēah**).

wisce, wixe OE, 'a marshy meadow', is found in OE charter names such as *to stucan wisc* BCS 707, *on ceab wisce* ib. 782; BCS 576 *an miclan wisce vi æceres mæde* suggests the word denoted 'meadowland' (cf. **mǣd**). It is found in ME f.ns. (Nt 293, Sx 562, W 450) and it survives as Sx dial. *wish* 'a piece of marshy meadowland, a piece of land in the bend of a river liable to floods'. Ekwall (RN 465) notes a possible cognate in the Swed r.n. *Viskan*; cf. also LG *wisch(e)* 'meadow' and the related words *wase, wisse*, and Zachrisson, *PN in *vis, *vask* 21 ff. In p.ns. it frequently takes the form *wis* through AN influence (cf. **wæsc**). (*a*) *Westbeach* K (**bece**), Whistley Brk (**lēah**), Wishworthy Co (**ford**). (*b*) Weaks, Wish Sx, The Wish K, R. Wiske YN (with ON *-sk*); Buckwish Sx (**bōc**), Cranwich Nf (**cran**), Dulwich Sr (**dile**), R. Erewash Nt (**irre**).

***wise** OE, probably 'a river, a swamp', found in OE only in p.n. spellings, is related to **wāse** and **wisse** and G *wiese* 'meadow'; these suggest a sense 'marsh, swamp'. (*a*) R. Wissey Nf (**ēa**), Wiswell La (**wella**). [*v.* RN 466–7.]

***wisp, *wips** OE, 'a wisp', possibly in some sense like 'thicket, brushwood' (cf. WFris *wisp* 'a twig, a wisp of straw'), probably found in ME as The Whisp R, and suggested (DEPN) for (*a*) Wispington L (**tūn**).

***wisse** OE, 'a meadow, a marsh' or the like, related to **wisce**, has been suggested by Ekwall for (*b*) Hautbois Nf; it is, however, difficult to distinguish from **wisce**, which often had medieval AN spellings in *wisse*.

wist OE, 'being, existence', probably in some such sense as 'resting place, lair, dwelling' (cf. OE *hūs-wist* 'house', *nēahwist* 'neighbourhood' and OHG *wist*, ON *vist* 'a stay'), also used in Sx for a land-measure; cf. also Sx 562. (*b*) Downash Sx 452 (**dūn**), Foxwist Ch (**fox**).

wita (**witan** gen.sg., **witena** gen.pl.) OE, 'a councillor', is possible in (*a*) Witham Ess (hām), and in the gen.pl. in Whitstable (a hundred) K (stapol).

with ODan, 'a willow', *v.* viðir.

wið OE, við ON adv., prep., 'against', used in p.ns. in the sense 'near, beside' (as opposed to ūt), is probable in (*a*) Withernsea YE 26 (þorn, cf. the nearby Owthorne from ūt), Wythemail Nth 129.

*wiðer[1] OE, 'a ram, a wether', a secondary form of weðer (cf. OHG *widar*, Goth *wiþrus* 'a lamb'), suggested (DEPN) for (*a*) Withersdale (dæl), Withersfield (feld) Sf.

wiðer[2] OE adv., prep., 'against, opposite', cannot easily be distinguished from wiðer[1], but has been suggested for (*a*) Worsted's Fm Sx 334 (stede).

wīðig OE, 'a withy, a willow', found in OE chiefly in glosses and p.ns. (cf. Mdf 152), is fairly common in p.ns., but is difficult to distinguish sometimes in ME from wīd and wiððe, except when it continues to be spelt *withi-* (which is often only a sporadic form); in view of the fact that such p.ns. retain *withi* only occasionally and usually have *withe-*, other p.ns. which exhibit only the latter spelling, like Widmere Bk (mere) or Wythop Cu (hop), may well be from *wīðig* rather than *wiððe* 'a thong'. (*a*) Weethley Wa (lēah), Weeton La, YW, Widdecombe, Widdicombe D, Witcombe So, Withycombe D, So (cumb), Widford Ess, Hrt, O, Wytheford Sa (ford), Withiel So (lēah), Withybrook Wa (brōc), Withyhook Do (hōc), Withypool So (pōl), Wyddial Hrt (halh). (*b*) The Wergs St (pl.), Hoarwithy He (hār). [~víðir, wiððe, -ig.]

*wīðigen OE adj., 'growing with willows, made of withies', cannot be distinguished in p.ns. from wīðign; it is possible in some p.ns. cited s.v. wīðign. (*a*) Withnell La (hyll). [wīðig, -en.]

*wīðigett OE, 'a willow copse'. (*b*) *Wythiette* Sr. [wīðig, -et.]

*wīðign OE, 'a willow, a willow copse', surviving as dial. *withen* 'a willow holt', may be found in some p.ns. but it is impossible to distinguish it as a first el. from wīðigen adj., but since tūn is not often combined with adjs. of this kind, it may well be found in (*a*) Widdington Ess, YW, Winton La, Witherington W, Withington Ch, He, La, Sa (tūn); Widdington W (denu). (*b*) Withens, Withins YW (*freq*). [wīðig, -en, -ign.]

wið-innan OE adv., 'within, inside (the city walls)'. (*c*) Bridge Ward Within, Cripplegate Within, Farringdon Within Ln, Faversham Within K; cf. extra, wið-ūtan.

wiððe OE, 'a withe, a tie, a thong, an osier or twig used as a band', may be found in some p.ns. to describe places where such withes were got; it may also have meant 'willow' (as it did in ME), but in that sense ME *withe* is more likely to have been a reduced form of **wīðig**. It is possible in (*a*) Withcote Lei (**cot**, made of plaited osiers or the like or where they were worked). [~OFris *withthe*, MLG *wedde*, ON *við*; ~**wīðig** by ablaut.]

wið-ūtan OE adv., 'outside (the city walls)'. (*c*) Newton Without W, and ward names in the City of London like Cripplegate Without, Farringdon Without, Faversham Without K. Cf. **extra**.

Wixan (**Wixena** gen.pl.) OE, a tribe known from the Tribal Hidage (BCS 297), probably settled in the L district (cf. Wo 16). (*a*) Uxbridge (**brycg**), Uxendon (**dūn**), Waxlow (**lēah**) Mx, Whitsun Brook Wo (**brōc**). [Cf. Ekwall, NoB xli, 149.]

wōcig OE, 'a noose, a snare', found only in glosses (Napier 962). (*b*) Wookey So. [~**wōh**, **-ig**.]

Wōden OE, a heathen Germanic god, corresponding to **Óðinn** and nicknamed **Grīm**. Cf. Dickins 154–5. The variation between *Wōden-* and *Wēden-*, which is very old (it is found also in OFris), has not been satisfactorily explained, but *Wēden-* is no doubt an *i*-mutated form. (*a*) Wansdyke Ha, W, So (**dīc**, the great British defensive work, cf. also **Grīm**), Wednesbury (**burh**), Wednesfield (**feld**) St, Wensley Db (**lēah**), Wenslow Bd (**hlāw**), Woodnesborough (**beorg**), Wormshill (**hyll**) K.

Wōdnes-dæg OE, 'Wednesday' (cf. Sr 410). (*a*) Wednesday Market (Beverley) YE. [~**Wōden**, OE *dæg*.]

wōh (**wōgan**, **wōn** wk. obl.) OE adj., 'twisted, crooked', applied esp. in stream-names. (*a*) Oborne Do, Woburn Bd, Wombourne St (with *Wōmburnan* shortened to *womburne* and so spelled *Wom-*, *Wam-* in ME, cf. a similar change in **brōm**) (**burna**), Wambrook So (**brōc**), Warridge Wo (**hrycg**), Wonersh Sr (**ersc**), Worhope K (**hop**).

***wōr** OE, a bird (as in OE *wōr-hana*, *wōr-henn*, Du *woerhaan* 'wood-grouse', probably so named from its wandering flight, cf. **wōrig**), has been suggested for some p.ns. (cf. Ekwall, Studies[2] 95). (*a*) Woodspring (**spring** 'copse'), Worle (**lēah**) So.

***wōrig** OE adj., 'wandering, winding', related to OE *wōrian* 'to wander', *wērig* 'weary, troubled' (cf. also **wōr**), was probably used as a r.n. (*b*) R. Worf Sa, and possibly R. Were W (cf. also Warminster W, OE *Worgemynster* BCS 591).

worð, weorð, wurð, wyrð OE, 'an enclosure'.

(1) This el. is cognate with OSax **wurð**, 'soil' and MLG *wurt*, *wort* 'a homestead', and has derivatives **worðig** and **worðign**. In one or another of its forms it is of frequent occurrence in names in the OE charters and in biblical glosses. In the charter material the meaning is not altogether certain for there it is used of places which vary in size from an *aliquantulum terrae* (actually 4 hides) at Chelworth W (BCS 585) or 5 hides at Brinkworth W (KCD 817) to 120 hides at Worth Brk (ASWills); in several cases it seems to refer to small places which could be described as Lat *villa*, *villula* or *viculus* (cf. BT s.v.). It is associated with **hege** 'a hedge, a fence' in *on weorðe hege forð be ðan hege on weorð apeldre* 'to the *weorð* hedge, along the hedge to the *weorð* appletree' in BCS 955 (cf. Sr 132 n.), which suggests that a *worð* was an enclosure of some kind, a sense confirmed by the derivative **worðig** and by some p.n. combinations such as Hurworth Du ('hurdle') or Shuttleworth Db, etc. (cf. **scytels**); cf. OE *tuneweorð* BCS 994 and *tunles weorð* ib. 820, which appear to denote enclosures with and without fences (*v.* **tūn** § 2), and § 6 (*b*) iv *infra*.

(2) In the glosses *worð* is an alternative to *plægiworð* 'playground' and *plæce* 'open space' for Lat *platea* 'open place, street' (*Durham Ritual* 36, *Lindisf. Gosp*. Matt. vi. 5), and it also renders Lat *atrium* 'forecourt, temple'. It is not possible with the available evidence to suggest that the word meant more than 'an enclosed space, an enclosure'. In p.ns. there are surprisingly few *worðs* which are associated with crops or animals or, like Butterworth La, YW (**butere**), with other agricultural activities (cf. § 6 (*b*) v *infra*); those with tree-names and wild plant names are fairly common and those with pers.ns. extremely so. It would not therefore seem necessarily to denote an enclosure for agricultural purposes, but it may have been one enclosing a dwelling.

(3) The el. is clearly in early use in the OE period, for it is found in documents as early as the 7th century and there are a few compounds with folk-names in **-ingas** and with **hām**; the almost complete absence of so common a p.n. el. from the literary records of OE would suggest that it was obsolescent or obsolete in the literary period; many *worths* have become parish names and are recorded in DB. But the very high proportion of pers.ns. as first els. (about 75 %) suggests that it continued in living use as a p.n. el. for some

time or that these enclosures were individual and personal possessions and it may well be that the *worð* was something like a topt, the small enclosure in which a single dwelling stood in the settlement. The el. is very rare with ON els. and it does not appear to be combined with post-Conquest pers.ns. as the derivative worðig is. In many cases a *worð* developed into a homestead and then a village or manor, but often, esp. in La and YW, it denotes places which are still small single homesteads often in remote situations, and there are a good many ME examples which have not survived (Bk 259, C 352, Ess 595, Hrt 260, Mx 205, Sr 366, Sx 562, W 450, Wa 334). The use of the word in *Lindisf. Gosp.* (cf. § 2) suggests that it continued in living use longer in the far north than elsewhere.

(4) The el. is common in Sr, Sx and fairly so in Nb. It is fairly well represented in the Midl counties from south La and south-west YW to W, but it is rare in Ess, Bk and O, as well as in Wo and some other WMidl counties where its place was taken by worðign; in YE, YW north of the R. Wharfe, YN and Cu it is practically unknown. In the SW counties it interchanges a good deal with worðig and on the fringes of the WMidl with worðign.

(5) Most ME and modern spellings go back to OE *worð* but in OE (WSax) documents *weorð* and *wyrð* are common. These forms can be explained in various ways as arising in OE itself, but in all probability *worð* and the *i*-mutated *wyrð* represent a different ablaut grade from *weorð*.

(6) (*a*) As a first el. *worð* is rare, Worstead Nf (stede), Wortham Sf (hām).

(*b*) As a simplex p.n., Worth Ch, Do, K, Sx, Wortha Co, Highworth W, Littleworth Brk.

In compounds it is found with:

(i) Adjs., usually descriptive, as Aldworth Nb (ald), Heworth Du, YN (hēah), Longworth (lang), Rumworth (rūm) La.

(ii) Topographical words, as Clayworth Nt (clawu), Edgeworth La, Gl (ecg), Ewart Nb (ēa), Eyworth Bd (ēg), Greatworth Nth (grēot), Ranworth Nf (rand), Saddleworth YW (sadol).

(iii) Old p.ns. and r.ns., etc. (rare), as Hamptworth W (hām-tūn), Minsterworth Gl (mynster, St Peter's Gloucester), Tamworth St (R. Tame, cf. also worðig), Wardleworth La (Wuerdle).

(iv) Words connected with 'hedge' or 'enclosure', as Cotchford Sx (queche), Faldingworth La, Fallingworth YW (falding), Hay-wards Heath Sx (hege), Hurworth Du (hurð), Letchworth Hrt (lycce), Shuttleworth Db, La, YW (scytels), Twigworth Gl (twigge).

(v) Animal names, rare but possible in Chafford Ess (calf), Hinxworth Hrt (hengest); cf. also Beauworth Ha (bēo), Duckworth La (dūce).

(vi) Tree-names, as Ashworth (æsc), Hollingworth (holegn) La, Lindworth Wo (lind), Oakworth YW (āc), Plumford K (plūme), Turnworth Do (þorn), Wythwood Wo (wīðig).

(vii) Names of wild plants, as Clarewood Nb (clǣfre), Farnworth La (fearn), Nettleworth Nt (netele), Rishworth YW (risc), Thistleworth Sx (þistel), *Wratworth* C (wrætt).

(viii) Folk-names, rarely, as Abinger Sr, Worlingworth Sf (-ingas), *Walworth* C, Walworth Sr, W (walh, probably in the sense 'serf').

(ix) OE pers.ns. extremely common, as Ashmansworth Ha (*Æscmēr*), Awsworth Nt (*Ald*), Badgeworth Gl (*Bæcga*), Bayworth Brk (*Bǣga*), Bengeworth Wo (*Beonna*, -ing[4]), Chaddleworth Brk (*Ceadela*), Chelwood So (*Ceola*), Hanworth Nf (*Hagena*), Hawksworth YW (*Hafuc*), Isleworth Mx (*Gīslhere*), Madginford K (*Mæghild* fem.), Padworth (*Peada*), Seacourt (*Seofeca*) Brk, Tedworth Ha (*Tuda*), Wandsworth Sr (*Wendel*), *et freq.*

(x) ON pers.ns. (rare), as Torworth Nt (*Þórðr*).

worðig, weorðig, wurðig, wyrðig OE, 'an enclosure'.

(1) This el. is used much more frequently in OE texts than **worð** from which it is derived (cf. BT s.v.), but in p.ns. has a more restricted provenance. It has much the same meaning as *worð*. Its primary sense of 'enclosure' is quite clear in the Laws of Ine where it is stated that 'a ceorl's *weorðig* or *wurðig* shall be fenced in (*betyned*) summer and winter', and in KCD 811 the *þreom worðigan* of the bounds (vi, 244) corresponds to Lat *agellorum* 'small plots of ground' in the charter (iv, 150). Otherwise, *worðig*, as an alternative to croft and tūn glosses Lat *predium* 'property' and *fundus* 'estate' (BT and Suppl s.v.), meanings which evolved as the original enclosures themselves developed into larger settlements. The p.ns. which contain *worðig* add little to this, for it is combined with other els. and esp. pers.ns. in much the same way and in much the same proportions as *worð*. The el. survived much longer in the SW than *worð* did elsewhere, for in ExonDB there are a good many

p.ns. in *worðig* which are compounded with the names of tenants who were living 1066–86.

(2) The form *worðig* appears from p.ns. to be a distinctively SW word, for it is extremely common in D and So and survives occasionally in the neighbouring counties of Co, Do, Ha, W and Gl. In OE it is more widespread, being found as far north as St and Db in such p.ns. as *Tome-*, *Tameworðig* (BCS 293, ASC 922 A, etc.) for Tamworth St and *Norðworðig* (c. 1000 Saints), the old name for Derby Db. It is difficult to say whether all these are genuine local forms or merely spellings due to WSax scribal practice; the latter would explain late instances at least, for in Tamworth *worthi* spellings are not found from the time of DB; in the isolated *Benigwrthia* BCS 125 (12th century) for Bengeworth Wo 95 (which otherwise has *-wyrð(e)*, etc.) *-wrthia* is merely a latinization. In ME *worthi* appears mostly in the later spellings of p.ns. that usually have *worth* earlier, and this replacement of *worth* by *worthi* is very common in D and So and extends to the neighbouring counties, as in south Gl in such p.ns. as Worthy, Ashworthy or Rangeworthy.

(3) (*b*) Worthy D, Gl, Ha, W. In compounds, it is found with:

(i) Adjs., esp. describing position or shape, etc., as Highworthy (**hēah**), Langworthy (**lang**), Smallworthy (**smæl**), Widworthy (**wīd**), Wrangworthy (**wrang**), Yalworthy (**ald**) D.

(ii) Topographical words, as Bowerthy D (**boga**), Canworthy Co (**carn**), Eworthy D (**ēa**).

(iii) Words for buildings and the like, as Curworthy (**cweorn**), Silworthy (**sele**) D, Wringford Co, Wringworthy D (**wringe**); cf. also Rangeworthy Gl (**hrynge**).

(iv) Animal names and other agricultural terms, as in Stitworthy D (**stott**), Honeyford D (**hunig**).

(v) Plant- and tree-names, as Clatworthy So (**clāte**), Fernworthy (**fearn**), Neopardy (**nēp**), Nettleford (**netele**) D, Selworthy So (**sele**), Thornery, Thornworthy D (**þorn**).

(vi) Folk-names, as Wallaford, Wallover D (**walh**).

(vii) Pers.ns., extremely common, as in Blatchworthy D (*Blæcci*), Chilsworthy Co (*Cēol*), Ebsworthy D (*Ecgbald*), Elworthy So (*Ælla*), Hamsworthy (*Heremōd*), Natsworthy (*Hnott*), Wilsworthy (*Wifel*), Woolfardisworthy (*Wulfheard*) D, *et freq*, as well as post-Conquest names, as Derworthy, Stroxworthy, etc., D.

[**worð**, **-ig**.]

worðign OE, 'an enclosure', is used in much the same way as **worð** and **worðig**. It is on record in OE in the *Psalter* and the OEBede (BT s.v. *worðig* and cf. Schlutter, Angl xliii, 99–100), and it survives as WMidl dial. *worthine* (NED s.v.). In p.ns. it is typically WMidl, being esp. common in He and Sa and being found in other WMidl counties, south La, Ch, St, Wo and north Gl and sporadically in other neighbouring counties, where it has usually been replaced by the more common *worð*. It is also found as an occasional spelling for *worð* and *worðig* in D, where it sometimes persists. There is one example from the NCy in the LVD spelling in *-wurthin* for Shoresworth Nb and Ekwall has suggested that Worthing Nf is also from this el.; there are also ME examples like *le Worthene* in Ess 595. Even so, it is most prolific in the WMidl. (*a*) Worden, Worthen D, Worthin Sa. In compounds it is found with (i) significant words, as Bradworthy D (**brād**), Cheswardine Sa (**cēse**), Chickward He (**cicen**), Faldworthings La (**fald**), Northenden Ch (**norð**), Virworthy D (**feor**); (ii) topographical words, as Bredwardine He (**brerd**), Brockworth Gl (**brōc**), Carden Ch (**carr**), Lapworth Wa (**læppa**), Ridgwardine Sa (**hrycg**), Ruardean Gl (**rhiw**), Shrawardine (**scræf**), Stanwardine (**stān**) Sa; (iii) old p.ns. and r.ns., as Leintwardine (R. Lent), Lugwardine (R. Lugg), Marden (Maund) He, Wrockwardine Sa (The Wrekin); (iv) pers.ns., as Badgworthy D, Bedwardine Wo, Ellardine, Ingardine Sa, Pedwardine He, Tollardine Wo. [**worðig**, **-en**, **-ign**; on the common later WMidl development to *-wardine* cf. Jordan § 35.1.]

wræcca OE, 'an outlaw', *v.* **wrecca**.

***wrǣna**, ***wǣrna** OE, 'a stallion', related to OE *wrǣne* adj. 'lustful' and ON *reini*, OLG *wrēnio* 'stallion', has been suggested by Ekwall, Studies[2] 67–8, for some p.ns. in *Warn-*; some of these could equally well be from **wrenna** or its metathesized form *wærna*. (*a*) Warmfield YW (**feld**), Warnham Sx (**hām**), Wrantage K (**etisc**), Wrinstead K (**stede**).

wrænna OE, 'a wren', *v.* **wrenna**.

***wrǣsel** OE, 'something twisted or knotted', such as 'a piece of rough ground' or 'a twisting river'. (*b*) Wressell YE 242. [~**wrāse**, **-el**.]

***wrǣst** OE, 'something twisted', such as 'broken or contorted ground', possibly also 'a thicket'. (*b*) Wrest Bd 162, Wrest Wood Sx 494. [~**wrāse**, **-t**, ~ON *vreist* 'a ring made of withies'.]

wrætt, wrætte OE, probably 'crosswort, hellebore', found chiefly in EAngl p.ns., (*a*) Wratton Hrt, Wretton Nf (**tūn**), Wratting C, Sf (**-ing²**), *Wratworth* C (**worð**), Wretham Nf (**hām**).

wrang OE adj., **(v)rangr** ON adj., 'crooked or twisted in shape'. The OE word is thought to be a loan from ON *vrangr* (cf. NED s.v. *wrong*), but it may be native as it is found in OE *on wrangan hylle* 944 BCS 801 Brk, which is rather early for a loan of this kind in Brk. It is used once as a noun in Wulfstan's *Homilies* xlii, 203 in late OE, and a WGerm cognate exists in MLG *wrangh* 'sour, bitter'; in p.ns. it is usually combined with OE els. It is not common, as the idea could be expressed by other els. such as OE **wōh**. (*a*) Wrampool La (**pōl**), Wrangbrook YW (**brōc**), Wrangling C (**land**), perhaps also Wrangaton, Wrangworthy D (**tūn, worðig**). [~**wringe**, by ablaut.]

***wrangel** OE, 'a twisted place or stream', *v.* **wrengel**.

wrāse OE, 'a knot, something twisted', as of 'broken contorted ground', 'a hill'. (*b*) Wrose YW (a steep hill), Wraysholme La 197 (dat.pl., alluding to a ridge and knolls). [The root idea of *wrāse* and its derivatives, **wrāsen, wrǣsel, wrǣst**, and OE *wrǣstan* 'to bend, to twist', as well as of **wride** and OE *wrīðan* 'to twist', is 'bend, twist, contort'.]

* **wrāsen** OE, 'a band, a tie', probably used in some topographical sense of 'something bent or twisted'; the p.ns. are associated with either ancient roads or earthworks and the meaning 'contorted, broken ground' would be appropriate, as in **wrāse**. (*b*) Wrens Nest Hill Wo 290, Grimsworth Hundred He, *Grimes Wrosen* Ess, Wa (**Grīm**). [**wrāse, -en.**]

wraðu OE, 'a prop, a support', possibly used of the piles or timbers on which a building might be erected. (*a*) Wrafton D 45 (**tūn**).

wrecca, wræcca (wreccena gen.pl.) OE, 'a wretch, a fugitive, an outlaw'. (*a*) Ratchwood Nb (**wudu**), Wrekendike Du (**dīc**), Wretchwick O (**wīc**).

***wrengel, *wrangel** OE, ***vrengill** ON, 'a crooked place or stream', with which Ekwall compares Norw dial. *vrengjill* 'a twisted tree' and the Norw r.n. *Rangla*. (*b*) Wrangle L. [~**wrang, -el.**]

wrenna, wrænna, wærna OE, 'a wren', is difficult to distinguish in p.ns. from **wrǣna**, but it may occur in such p.ns. as (*a*) Warnford Ha (**ford**), Wrenbury Ch (**burh**), Wrenwell D (**wella**), etc.

***wrēo, *wrīo** OE adj., 'twisting', related to OE *wrīgian* 'to turn, twist, bend', MLG *wrīch* 'perverse', ModE *wry*; used as a r.n. (*b*) R. Wring So (OE *Wring* BCS 606 'the twisting one', -ing², hence Wrington); cf. also OE *Wryoheme* BCS 606 (hǣme) in the same district.

*wrēode OE, 'a shelter, protection', related to OE *wrēon* 'to cover, clothe, protect, defend', is more likely on phonological grounds than wrid(e) for (*a*) Rednal Wo 356 (halh).

wrīd, wrīð OE, 'a shoot, a bush', gewrīd OE, 'a thicket', are both probably related to OE *wrīdan* 'to grow, to flourish' but *gewrīd* may be connected with OE *wrīðan* 'to twist' (cf. wrāse). The meaning 'thicket' is perhaps more likely in p.ns. (*a*) Rytham YE (holmr), Wothorpe Nth (þrop). (*b*) Easewrith Hundred Sx 146 (ēs).

*wride OE, 'a winding, a twist, a bend', suggested (DEPN) for (*a*) Wordwell Sf (wella, OE *æt wridewellan* BCS 1018). (*b*) Wryde Bridge, Wryde Croft C 282. [~OE *wrīðan* 'to twist', ~wrāse.]

*wrīdels OE, 'a thicket'. (*a*) Woodlesford YW (ford). [wrīd, -els.]

wringe OE, 'a press', 'a cheese- or a cider-press'. (*a*) Ring-, Wringford Co, Wringworthy D (worðig). [~OE *wringan* 'to twist, to wring, to press out', wrang.]

*writol OE adj., 'bubbling'. (*a*) Writtle Ess 277 (OE *writolaburna*). [~OE *writian* 'to chirp, to chatter', cf. pritol.]

wrīð OE, 'a bush', *v.* wrīd.

*wrocc, *wrōc OE, a bird of prey, 'a buzzard', related to Swed *vråk* 'a buzzard' (cf. Ekwall, Studies² 96ff). It is found esp. with halh and may sometimes be used as a pers.n. (*a*) Roxhill Bd (hyll), Wraxall Do, So, W, Wroxhall Wa, Wt (halh), Wroxham Nf (hām), Wroxton O (stān).

wroht OE, 'accusation, crime, quarrel', as in OE *wrohthangra* KCD 1283 (on a boundary), suggested to refer to land in dispute in (*a*) Wrautam Wa 189 (holmr, on the parish boundary), *Wroughthull* Hrt (hyll).

wrōt OE, 'a snout', used in some topographical sense such as 'a spur of land, a hill projecting forward like a snout'. (*b*) Wroot L.

wudig OE adj., 'wooded'. (*a*) Odiham Ha (hām), Woodyates Do (geat), Wootton Wt (tūn). [wudu, -ig.]

wudu, earlier widu, OE, 'a wood, a grove, woodland, a forest', also 'wood, timber'; the latter sense being sometimes found when *wudu* is a first el. with words for buildings, and other structures (ærn, cot, hall, hūs, brycg). For the most part, however, *wudu* means 'a wood, a tract of woodland'. The earlier form *widu* is kept in a few p.ns. and also appears sporadically in the OE and ME spellings of some others such as Woodford Ch, Woodhay Brk, Ha, Wootton Wawen Wa, but by the 8th century *widu* had usually become *wudu* by back-mutation (Bülbring §§ 235, 264).

(*a*) From *widu*, Withern L (ærn), Witton Nb, Nf, YN (2) (tūn). From *wudu*, Woodbarrow So, Woodborough W (beorg), Woodbrough Nt (burh), Woodbridge Sf (brycg), Woodchester Gl (ceaster), Woodchurch Ch, K (cirice), Woodcote, -cott Ch, Ha, O, Sa, Sr, Wa (cot), Woodford Ch, Co, Ess, Nth, W (ford), Woodhall L *et freq* (hall), Woodham Ess, Sr (hām), Woodhay Brk, Ha (gehæg), Woodhouse Lei, Sa, YW *et freq*, Wothersome (hūs, dat.pl.), Woodkirk (kirkja) YW, Woodstock O (stoc), Wootton Bd, Brk, Do *et passim*, Wotton Bk, Gl, Sr (tūn).

(*b*) Wood Sx; Woodham Du (dat.pl.). In compounds it is usually found with:

(i) Tree-names, as Ashwood Nth, St (æsc), Beckwith YW (bēc, wudu replaced by viðr), Birchen Wood Sx (bircen), Buckwood Hrt (bōc), Hazelwood Sx, YW (hæsel), Iwood So (īw), Linwood Ha, L (lind), Selwood So (salh).

(ii) Words for timber, posts, etc., as Borthwood Wt (bord), Col Wood K (col[1]), Spar Wood Sx (spearr), Timberwood K (timber), Yokewood Nth (geoc).

(iii) Plant-names, as Broomwood Nt (brōm), Marchwood Ha (merece).

(iv) Bird-names, as Cawood La, YW (cā), Coquet Nb (cocc[2]), Cornwood Wo (cran), Crow Wood Nt (crāwe), Earnwood Sa (earn), Hanwood Sa (hana), Henwood Co (henn), Snip Wood Bk ('snipe').

(v) Animal-names, as Harewood He, YW (hara), Oxenwood W, Oxwood Hrt (oxa).

(vi) Adjs. and advs. denoting position, etc., as Astwood Wo, Eastwood Nth (ēast), Bestwood Wo (bī, ēastan), Inwood W (in), Northwood Wo, Norwood Nth *et freq* (norð), Southwood Nf, Sx, etc. (sūð), Tanwood Wo (betwēonan), Upwood Hu (upp), Westwood Wo (west).

(vii) Descriptive adjs., as Blackwood YE (blæc), Brandwood La (brend), Evenwood Du (efen), Fulwood La (fūl), Greenwood Sx *et passim* (grēne), Horwood Bk (horu), Lightwood Wo (leoht), Manhood Sx, Manwood W, Meanwood W, YW (gemǣne), Nyewoods Sx (nīge), Roomwood Nt (rūm), Shortwood Wo (sceort), Thickwood W (þicce), Whitewood W (hwīt).

(viii) Words for buildings, topographical and other nearby features, as Bernwood Bk (byrgen), Brookwood Sx (brōc), Charnwood Lei (carn), Cheetwood La (cēto-), Hopwood La, Wo (hop), Hurstwood La (hyrst), Lockwood YW (locc), Marshwood Do (mersc), Ridgewood Sx (hrycg), Sea Wood La (sǣ), Stype Wood W (stēpe), Walkwood Wo (weorc).

(ix) Old r.ns. and p.ns., as Burtonwood, Halewood La, Kyre Wood Wo (Kyre Brook), Laxton Wood Nth, Testwood Ha (R. Test), Wistow Wood Hu, Yardley Wood Wo.

(x) Words denoting people, as Bushwood Ha (biscop), Charlwood Sr (ceorl), Earl's Wood Nth (eorl), Kingswood Wa (cyning), Ladywood Wo (hlǣfdige), Monk Wood Wo (munuc), Night Wood W (cniht), Ratchwood Nb (wrecca).

(xi) Pers.ns., as Athelstan's Wood He, Packwood Wa, Sansom Wood Nt, Simonswood La, Thurtle Wood YN.

(xii) Folk-names, as *Fildenwood* Hrt (filde), Wychwood O (Hwicce).

(*c*) As an affix *Wood* is prefixed to Ditton C, Eaton O, St, Enderby Lei, Newton Nth; and in the form *Underwood*(*s*) suffixed to Thorpe Nth, YW, Weston Bk, Db, Wotton Bk, etc. [~viðr.]

wudu-mann OE, 'a woodsman, a forester'. (*a*) Woodmancote, -cott Gl (3), Ha, Sx, Wo (cot), Woodmansey YE (sǣ), Woodminton W (tūn). [wudu, mann.]

wulf (wulfes gen.sg., wulfa gen.pl.) OE, 'a wolf', is fairly common in p.ns. denoting places haunted by, protected against or for trapping wolves. It is sometimes difficult (esp. in gen.sg.) to distinguish from the OE pers.n. *Wulf*; it interchanges with úlfr in the Danelaw. (*a*) Winfold C (hol), Wolborough D (beorg), Wolleux Co (holca). Wolfage Nth (hecg), Wolford Wa (weard), Wollage K (hæcc), Wolvey Wa (hege), Woldale YW (dæl), Woolden La (denu), Woolley Brk, Hu, YW (lēah), Woolmer Ha (mere), Wooloaks Cu (leikr).

wulf-pytt OE, 'a wolf pit or trap'. (*b*) Woolpit Sf. [wulf, pytt.]

wull OE, 'wool'. (*a*) Woolwich K (wīc).

wunden OE pa.part., 'twisted'. (*a*) Woundale Sa (wella). [~OE *windan* 'to wind'.]

wurm OE, 'a snake, a dragon', *v.* wyrm.

wylfen OE, 'a she-wolf'. (*a*) Woolman's Wood Bk 181 (hamm). [~wulf, -en.]

wylla, wyll(e) OE (WSax), 'a well, a spring', *v.* wella.

wyllere OE (WSax), 'a salt-boiler', *v.* wellere.

wylm OE (WSax), 'a spring', *v.* welm.

✱ *wynne OE, 'pasture', *v.* winn[1].

wyrhta OE, 'a wright'. (*a*) Rigbolt L (bold).

wyrm, wurm OE, 'a reptile, a snake', also 'a dragon'. In some p.ns. there may be allusion to the dragon of folk-lore (as in *Beowulf* 2287, etc.). (*a*) Wormcliff W (clif), Wormdale K (dæl), Wormhill Db, Worms Hill K (hyll), Worminghall Bk (halh), Worminster So (torr), Wormley Hrt (lēah), Wormwood Hill C (hlāw), Wormwood Scrubbs Mx (holt).

*wyrpels OE (late WSax), 'a path', *v.* werpels.

wyrt OE, 'a plant, a vegetable'. (*a*) Wortley (Barnsley) YW (lēah).

wyrt-tūn OE, 'a vegetable garden'. (*b*) Worton O, W, YN. [wyrt, tūn.]

✱ [wyrðing OE, 'cultivated land', recorded only in the gloss *occa, wealh oþþe wyrðing* (WW 495.20), where *wealh* is an error for *fealh* (falh) and *wyrðing* no doubt an alliterating error for *yrðing* 'ploughed land'; there may be a similar error in the next gloss *noualibus, wyrdelandum* (ib. 21) for *yrðelandum* 'cultivated lands'. It has, nevertheless, been suggested as an alternative for (*a*) Faldingworths La 134 (fald).]

Y

*yfer OE (Angl, WSax), *efer (Kt), 'the edge or brow of a hill', found in OE only in such names as *beneaþan yfre* BCS 756, *be yfre* ib. 802. (*b*) Iver Bk, Rivar W, River Sx (atter); Hever K (hēah). [~ofer.]

yferra OE comp.adj., 'upper, higher'. (*a*) Everthorpe YE (þorp). [~ofer.]

ylfetu OE (WSax), 'a swan', *v.* elfitu.

*ylme OE, 'an elm-tree, an elm wood'. (*a*) Ilmington Wa (tūn). [~ulm, -e.]

ynys Welsh, 'an island', *v.* inis.

yppe OE (Angl, WSax), *eppe (Kt), 'a raised place, a platform', perhaps also in p.ns. 'a look-out platform' or 'an upper place, a hill'. (*a*) Epping Ess, Uppingham R (-ingas, hām), Ipley Ha (lēah), Ipstones St (stān), Tipalt Nb (æt, wald). [~upp, -e.]

yrð OE (WSax), 'ploughed land', *v.* erð.

yrðing OE, 'ploughed land', *v.* wyrðing.

yrðling OE (WSax), 'a ploughman', *v.* erðling.

ystrad Welsh, 'a valley', *v.* strat.

ytri ON adj., 'outer'. (*a*) Itterby L (bý). [~ūt.]

INDEX

Beesthorpe L i, 30
Beeston Ch i, 72; Co, Nf, Nt, St, YW i, 33
Beetha We i, 1, 37
Beetham We i, 37
Beggary (Bedford) Bd i, 25, ii, 26
Beggearn Huish So i, 25
Beild Drove C i, 26
Bekene, The Nt i, 21
Belasis Nb i, 13, 27
Belaugh Nf i, 26, 221
Belbroughton Wo i, 28
Belchalwell Do i, 27, 78
Belchamp Ess i, 27
Beldhamland Sx i, 72
Belgar K i, 27
Belgrave Lei i, 26
Bell (Belbroughton) Wo i, 28
Bellasis Du i, 27
Bellasize YE i, 13, 27
Belleau L ii, 25
Bell Flask YW i, 175
Bell Hill Do i, 27
Bellhouse YW i, 27
Bellister Nb i, 155
Belluton So i, 27
Bellyfax YN i, 166
Belper Db ii, 82
Belsars C i, 13, 27
Belsay Du i, 257
Belsize Nf i, 13, 27
Belstead Ess, Sf i, 26, 28
Belstone D i, 27, ii, 144
Beltoft (nr Belton) L i, 26
Belton L i, 26, 27
Belton Lei, R, Sf i, 26, 27
Belvoir Nt i, 27
Belwood (nr Belton) L i, 26
Bembridge Wt i, 36
Bemerhills W i, 28
Bemersley St i, 28
Bemerton W i, 28, ii, 196
Bempton YE ii, 194; YW i, 21
Bemzells Sx ii, 118
Benacre K, Sf i, 3, 22
Benbole Co i, 32
Benchacre W i, 28
Bencroft C, Nth i, 113
Bendish Hrt i, 146
Bendysh Ess i, 146
Beneathwood Co i, 28
Beneland L i, 20, ii, 14
Benfleet Ess i, 21
Bengeworth Wo ii, 275, 276
Benhall Sf i, 22
Benham, Hoe Brk i, 257
Bennah D i, 72
Bennethead Cu i, 25
Bensham Du i, 28, 242
Bensted Ess i, 72; K i, 28, ii, 149
Benstoken Wo ii, 157
Benter So ii, 184
Bentfield Ess i, 28
Benthall Sa i, 28, 224
Bentham Gl i, 28
Bentham K i, 230; YW i, 28
Bentley St, YW ii, 21; Wo ii, 21, 94 *freq* i, 28
Bentley, Fenny Db i, 170
Bentley, Hungry Db i, 269
Benton Nb i, 28
Bents Cu i, 28
Bents, The YW i, 28
Bents, Totley Db i, 28
Bentwitchen D ii, 199
Benwell Nb i, 36
Benwick C ii, 262
Benwray Cu i, 22, ii, 233
Beoley Wo i, 28
Beorhtwaldingtune, æt i, 294
Berdestapel Hrt i, 22
Bere D i, 23, Ha i, 16
Bere Regis Do i, 124, ii, 82
Bergholt Ess i, 29
Beriow, R. Co i, 143
Berkeley Gl i, 29, 298, 300, ii, 21
Berkeley Harness Gl i, 245
Berkesdon Hrt i, 29
Berkhamstead Hrt i, 29, 232
Berkley So i, 29, ii, 21
Berkshire i, 20, ii, 111
Berne Do i, 31
Bernwood Bk i, 55, ii, 281
Berridge K i, 18
Berrier Cu i, 31, 157
Berrington Nb i, 59
Berrow Sf, So, Wo i, 29
Berse Wo i, 32
Bersted Sx i, 29
Bertie Grove Sr i, 30
Berwick Do, K, Sa i, 31
Beryl So i, 31
Bescar (Lane) La i, 36; Nt i, 25, 30
Bessacar YW i, 3, 30

Brancepeth Du ii, 58
Branchester Nb i, 87
Brand Nt, Nth i, 47
Brand Hall Wo i, 226
Brandon Du, Nf, Sf, Wa i, 52; Nb i, 49
Brandred K i, 47, ii, 90
Brandsby YN ii, 92
Brandwood La ii, 280
Brandwood Wo i, 49
Bransby L ii, 92
Bransdale YN i, 127
Bransford Wo i, 46
Bransholme YE i, 259
Bransty Cu i, 47, ii, 152
Brantbeck La i, 47
Branthill Wo i, 49, 275
Branthwaite Cu ii, 220
Brantridge Sx i, 47
Brapool Sx i, 45
Brasole K ii, 134
Brasted K ii, 149
Brathay La i, 1, 48
Bratoft L i, 48, ii, 183
Bratton W i, 48
Braughing Hrt i, 301
Braunder D i, 47
Brawne Gl i, 49
Braworth YN i, 48, ii, 230
Braxted Ess i, 45
Bray Brk i, 48; D i, 50
Braybrook Nth i, 46
Brayfield Brk i, 46
Brayford L i, 45, 148
Braygate YN i, 48, 196
Braystones Cu i, 48
Braytbuttes YE i, 65
Brayton Cu i, 48; YW i, 45, 48, ii, 193
Breach Bd, C, K, Nt, W, Wo i, 48
Breach Eau L i, 143
Breadsell Sx ii, 118
Breaks, The Nb i, 46
Bream C, Gl i, 48
Brearton YW i, 50; *freq* ii, 196
Breary YW i, 221
Breche C i, 47
Breck La, YN, YW i, 48
Breckles Nf i, 48
Bredbury Ch i, 48
Brede Sx i, 46
Brede, R. Sx i, 178
Bredenbrugge Bk, O, Wo i, 48
Bredenbury He i, 48
Bredfield Sf i, 46
Bredgar K i, 194
Bredhurst K i, 46, 48, 277
Bredon Wo i, 6, 50, 138
Bredwardine He i, 50, ii, 277
Breeches K i, 48
Breedon Lei i, 50, 139
Breightmet La i, 30, ii, 31
Breithsegges L ii, 117
Bremdean Ha i, 52
Bremeridge W i, 49
Brening Ess i, 16
Brent K i, 49
Brenthall Ess i, 49
Brenting(e) Ha i, 289
Brentwood Ess i, 49
Brenzett K i, 32, ii, 120
Brereton Ch i, 50; St i, 50, 138; *freq* ii, 196
Bretford Wa i, 48
Bretforton Wo i, 48
Bretherdale We i, 53
Bretherton La i, 53
Bretonnes Dybbyng Nth i, 131
Brettargh La i, 50
Bretton YW i, 50, ii, 197
Bretton, Monk YW ii, 45
Brewershill Bd i, 53
Brewood St i, 50
Breydon Water Nf i, 50
Brianscholes YW ii, 123
Brickhill Bd, Bk i, 50, 51, 274
Bridals Co i, 55, ii, 252
Bridborough K i, 30
Briddlesford Wt i, 51, 182
Bridekirk Cu ii, 4
Bridenbridge Wo i, 48
Bridestow D ii, 160
Bridewell W i, 55, ii, 252
Bridford D i, 55
Bridge K i, 54
Bridge End Causeway L i, 54
Bridgeford Nt, St i, 54
Bridgehampton So i, 233
Bridgemere Ch i, 50
Bridgenorth Sa i, 54
Bridgerule D i, 54
Bridge Sollers He i, 54
Bridgevear Sr i, 189
Bridge Ward Within Ln ii, 271
Bridgham Nf i, 54

Burmarsh K i, 63
Burn Co i, 49; YN i, 54; YW i, 73
Burn, Black Cu i, 37
Burnarsh K ii, 246
Burnbake W i, 21
Burnby YE i, 54
Burnecoose Co i, 53
Burnett So i, 16
Burnham Bk, Ess, Nf i, 63; L i, 54, ii, 226; So i, 230
Burnham Overy Nf ii, 54
Burnhill Bk i, 73
Burnigill Du i, 296
Burnley La i, 53
Burnside We i, 237
Burn Stocks YE ii, 156
Burnt Butts YE i, 65
Burntheath W i, 220
Burnthwaite Cu i, 49
Burntwells Nt i, 49
Burntwood Sr, St i, 49
Burpham Sx i, 228
Burracot Co i, 57, 109
Burraton D i, 57
Burrough Green C i, 59
Burrowgate Cu i, 196
Burrow on the Hill Lei i, 155
Burscough La ii, 126
Bursea YE ii, 93
Burshill YE i, 74
Burstall Sf, YE i, 62
Burstath La i, 73, ii, 147
Burstead Ess i, 62
Burston Bk ii, 205
Burstow Sr i, 60, ii, 160
Burthonspynay YE ii, 138
Burthwaite Cu i, 12, 66, ii, 220; We i, 36
Burtis Wood L ii, 183; YN i, 57
Burtoft L i, 57, ii, 183
Burton C i, 56, ii, 193; He i, 74; Sx ii, 197; YE i, 92; *passim* i, 62
Burton, Cherry YE i, 92
Burton Constable YN i, 106
Burton Extra St i, 162
Burton, Gate L i, 199
Burton in Lonsdale YW i, 281
Burton Joyce Nt i, 74
Burton on Trent St i, 62, 74, 162; ii, 55
Burton Overy Lei ii, 54
Burton upon Stather L i, 13, ii, 158
Burton, West Sx ii, 256
Burtonwood La ii, 281
Burtree YN i, 64
Burwains La i, 58
Burwardsley Ch i, 63
Burwarton Sa i, 63
Burwash Sx i, 59, 157
Burwell C i, 60, L i, 59, 60
Burwood Ess ii, 255
Bury Hu i, 59, 60; La, Sx, Wo i, 60
Bury Court Wo i, 59
Buryhill He i, 275
Bury St Edmunds Sf i, 60, ii, 159
Burythorpe YE i, 31, ii, 211
Busbridge Sr ii, 138
Busby YN i, 65
Busco YN ii, 126
Buscot Brk i, 63
Bush K i, 30, 157
Bushblades Du i, 74; Nb i, 38
Bushbury St i, 37, 61
Bushet Sr i, 74
Bushmead Bd ii, 31
Bushrubs Nth ii, 115
Bushton W i, 37
Bushwood Ha ii, 281; Wa i, 37
Busk, Stalling YW i, 65
Buskin D i, 65
Buston, High Nb i, 238
Buston, Low Nb ii, 12
Butcher Row (Beverley) YE ii, 81
Butcher Shambles ii, 100
Butcombe So i, 119
Butleigh So ii, 22
Butterby Du i, 27
Buttercrambe YN i, 65, 111
Butterhill St i, 65
Butterilket Cu i, 66
Butter Law Nb i, 250
Butterley He ii, 21; Sa i, 65
Buttermere Cu i, 65
Buttersett YN i, 64
Butterton St i, 65, ii, 194
Butterwick Do, L, La, Nb, We, YE i, 65; Do, Du, L, We, YE, YN ii, 262
Butterwork (Lincoln) L i, 65, ii, 254
Butterworth La i, 65, ii, 273; YW ii, 273
Buttery Ess i, 43
Butt Hill Wa i, 65
Buttington Tump Gl i, 65
Buttokes le W i, 65
Buttsash Ha i, 5

Cam, Cold YN i, 79
Cam, R. Gl i, 79
Cambeck Cu i, 2, 79
Cambo Nb, i, 79, 257
Cam Brook So ii, 194
Cambs YN i, 79
Camel So i, 80
Camel, R. Co i, 79
Cameley So ii, 22
Camerton So ii, 194
Cam Fell YW i, 79
Camgate Way C i, 79
Camic Pond Sx i, 79
Cammocks Wood Sr i, 79
Camp, The YE i, 79
Campden Gl i, 79, 90
Campden, Broad Gl i, 46
Campden, Chipping Gl i, 90
Camps K i, 79
Camps, Shudy C i, 80
Campsey Sf i, 79
Cams Head YN i, 79, 236
Canbury Sr i, 80
Candelshoe L i, 236
Candover (Preston) Ha i, 137, 152, ii, 73
Canford Do i, 80
Cangle Fm Ess i, 80
Cangley Mead Sr i, 80
Cank Wo i, 80
Cank Barn Wa i, 80
Cank Hill Hrt i, 80
Cann Do i, 80
Canna D i, 80
Cannamore D i, 80
Canney Ess i, 80
Cann House D i, 80
Cannings, All W i, 8
Cannington So ii, 195
Cannock Ess ii, 260, 263; St i, 120
Cannock Mill Ess i, 80
Cann Wood D i, 80
Canonbury Mx i, 80
Canonthorpe YW i, 80, ii, 209, 210, 211
Canterbury K i, 80
Canterton Ha i, 80, ii, 197
Canwell St i, 80, ii, 252
Canworthy Co ii, 276
Capel K, Sf, Sr i, 81
Capel, King's He i, 81
Capel Crag Cu ii, 2
Capel St Andrew Sf i, 81
Capenhurst Ch i, 80
Capernwray La ii, 2, 233
Capland So i, 80
Capplebeck Cu ii, 2
Capplerigg We ii, 2
Capton D i, 80
Caradoc Court He i, 76
Carcroft YW i, 113
Cardean Ch i, 81
Carden Ch ii, 277
Cardew Cu i, 76
Carfax (Oxford) O, (Horsham) Sx i, 81
Carfoix (Exeter) D i, 81
Cargo Cu i, 81
Cargo Fleet YN i, 77
Carham Nb i, 81, ii, 226
Carhampton So i, 81, ii, 195, 225, 226
Cark La i, 81
Carlbury Du ii, 2; Nb i, 61
Carlby L ii, 2
Carlecotes YW i, 90, ii, 2
Carleton Cu, La, Nf, YW i, 90, ii, 2
Carling Gill Cu ii, 3
Carlinghow YW i, 236
Carling Howe YN ii, 3
Carlisle Cu i, 76
Carlsmoor YW ii, 2
Carlton Bd, C, Du, Lei, L, Nt, Nth, Sf, YE, YN, YW i, 90, ii, 2; La, Nb, *et passim* ii, 2
Carlton, Castle L i, 87
Carlton, East Nf i, 144
Carlton, Great L i, 208
Carlton, Little L ii, 30
Carlton in Lindrick Nt i, 281
Carnaby YE i, 11
Carn Bre Co i, 51
Carnetly Cu i, 81
Carnwinnick Co i, 81
Carnyorth Co i, 81
Carp Shield Du ii, 104
Carr, Humble L i, 268
Carricawn Co i, 81
Carrick Nb i, 76
Carrington L ii, 190
Carr Lane YE i, 83
Carrock, Castle Cu i, 81
Carrock Fell Cu i, 81
Carshalton Sr i, 7, 76
Carsington Db i, 76
Carswalls Gl i, 76, ii, 252

Chelsworth Sf i, 90
Cheltenham Gl i, 88
Chelvey So i, 79, ii, 262
Chelwood So ii, 275
Chelworth W ii, 273
Chepstow Mon i, 84
Chequerbent La i, 28
Chequer Hill Coppice Nth i, 92
Chequers Bk i, 92
Chercheknabbe Nth ii, 5
Cherhill W i, 279
Cheristow D i, 95, ii, 160
Cheriton Co i, 90; K i, 95; D, Ha, So i, 95, ii, 194
Cherry Burton YE i, 92
Cherry Hinton C i, 92
Cherry Lap Nth ii, 11
Cherry Orchard Wo ii, 111
Cherry Willingham L i, 92
Chertehulle W i, 91
Cherville K i, 90
Cherwell, R. O i, 84, ii, 250
Cheselade So i, 95, 178
Cheselbourne Do i, 64, 95
Chesford Wa i, 84
Chesham Bk i, 85, 230; La i, 95, ii, 226
Cheshire ii, 109
Cheshunt Hrt i, 86, 189, 269
Cheshunt Field Ess i, 92
Chesil Bank Do i, 96
Chesland W i, 85
Chessell Down Wt i, 91
Chester Ch i, 87
Chester, Little Db i, 87
Chesterblade So i, 38, 86
Chesterfield Db i, 86; St i, 86, 168
Chesterford Ess i, 86
Chesterhope Nb i, 86
Chester le Street Du i, 87, 152, ii, 18, 162
Chesters Nb i, 87, ii, 116
Chesterton C, Gl i, 86, ii, 194; Hu, O, St, Wa i, 86
Chestham Sx i, 91
Chesthill St i, 91
Chest Wood Ess i, 85
Cheswardine Sa i, 91, ii, 277
Cheswick Nb i, 91, ii, 262; Wa ii, 262
Chettiscombe D i, 91
Chettle Do i, 91
Chetwoode Bk i, 92
Chetwynd Sa ii, 268
Cheveley C i, 84, ii, 19; Ch ii, 22
Cheverden W i, 84
Cheveridge Wo i, 84
Cheverton Wt i, 84
Chevin YW i, 87
Chew, R. So ii, 194
Chew Stoke So ii, 155
Chewton So ii, 194
Cheylesmore Wa i, 87
Chich Ess i, 93
Chichebroke Ess i, 93
Chicklade W i, 251
Chickney Ess i, 93
Chicksands Bd i, 93, ii, 97
Chickward He i, 93, ii, 277
Chidden Ha i, 130
Chiddingfold Sr i, 164, 205
Chiddingstone K ii, 145
Chidham Sx i, 89
Chieflowman D i, 94
Chieselepet Hrt i, 96
Chilbolton Ha i, 294
Chilbridge Do i, 89
Chilcombe Do, Ha i, 88
Chilcompton So i, 94
Chilcote Lei, Nth i, 94
Childerditch Ess i, 88
Childerley C i, 94, ii, 22
Childersgate L i, 94
Childer Thornton Ch i, 94
Childrebrigge Nth i, 55
Childrey Brk ii, 86
Childswickham Gl i, 94
Childwall La ii, 252
Childwick Hrt i, 93, 94
Chilford (Hundred) C i, 93, 183
Chilgrove Sx i, 89
Chillesford Sf i, 95, i, 181
Chilleyhill So i, 87
Chillmill K i, 88
Chilmark Wt i, 87, ii, 37
Chilmill K ii, 46
Chilson O i, 94, ii, 196
Chilston He, K i, 94, ii, 196
Chilsworthy Co ii, 276
Chilte, le Sx i, 88
Chilthurst Sx i, 94
Chiltington Sx i, 88
Chilton Bk, Brk, Du, Ha i, 94; Wt i, 89
Chilverton D i, 94

Crathorne YN ii, 6, 205
Crawcrook Du i, 111, ii, 7
Crawl YN ii, 252
Crawley Bd, Bk, Ess, Nb i, 111; Bd, Bk ii, 21; Nb i, 250
Cray, R. K i, 112, 183
Cray, St Mary's K i, 112
Craycombe Wo i, 111
Crayford K i, 183
Craygill YW i, 112
Crayke YN i, 112
Craythorne K i, 111, ii, 205
Creacombe D i, 111
Creake Nf i, 112
Creaton Nth i, 112
Credenhill He i, 275
Crediton D i, 10, ii, 194
Creech Do, So i, 115
Creed Sx i, 117
Creedy, R. D i, 10, ii, 194
Creegbrawse Co i, 115
Creek C ii, 6
Creeksea Ess ii, 6
Creep Wood Sx i, 118
Creighton St i, 112
Crepelstrete Ess i, 118
Creskeld YW i, 76, ii, 3
Cressage Sa i, 2, 112
Cressing Ess i, 76
Cresswell Nb, St i, 76, ii, 252
Creswell Db i, 76
Crew Cu i, 112
Crewe (Hall) Ch i, 118
Crewgarth Cu i, 112
Crewkerne So i, 4, 115
Crich Db i, 115
Crichel Do i, 115, 275
Crick Nth i, 112
Cricket So i, 161
Crickheath Sa i, 115, 220
Cricklade W ii, 9
Cridling Stubbs YW ii, 164
Cridmore Wt i, 117
Criftin Nt i, 117
Criftins YE i, 117
Crifton Nt i, 117
Crimbles La, YW i, 118
Crimple Beck YW i, 116, ii, 69
Crimsworth Dean YW i, 118
Crindledike Cu i, 132, ii, 7
Cringeldikes YE i, 132
Cringleber La ii, 7
Cringlebrook La ii, 7
Cringle Carr YN ii, 4, 7
Cringledyke Cu ii, 7
Cringleford Nf ii, 7
Cringlethwaite Cu ii, 7, 219
Cripdon D i, 118
Cripelesballe W i, 118
Cripplechurch Sr i, 146
Cripplegate, Within, Without Ln i, 118, ii, 271, 272; Wo i, 118
Cripstone Co ii, 198
Criptor D i, 118
Crisbrook K i, 52, 76
Crockenhill K i, 4
Crockerhill Ha, Sx i, 112
Crockern (Pill) D i, 112; Do i, 4, 112; So ii, 75
Crockern Tor D i, 4
Crockerton W i, 112, ii, 196
Crockford Sr i, 112
Crockhurst Sx i, 112
Crockleford Ess i, 112
Crockshard Fm K i, 113
Crockstead Sx i, 112
Croft He, L, YN i, 113; Lei i, 111
Croft, Lynn Nt i, 113
Crofton Cu, Ha, L, W, YW i, 113; K i, 114; YW ii, 194
Crofts, The YE ii, 2
Croglin Cu i, 254, ii, 7
Croichlaw La i, 115
Crollode Hu ii, 9
Cromall W i, 223
Cromer Nf ii, 39; Wo i, 111
Cromford Db i, 116
Cromhall Gl i, 116; Gl, W i, 224
Crommes, Les Sx i, 116
Crompton La i, 116
Cromwell Nt, YW i, 116, ii, 251
Cromwheel YW i, 116, 272
Crondall Ha i, 117
Cronkley Nb i, 99, 116
Cronkshaw La ii, 99
Cronuchomme Wo i, 111
Crook D, Do i, 115; La, We ii, 7
Crookake Cu i, 146
Crookbarrow Wo i, 115
Crookdale Cu i, 113
Crookham Brk i, 113, 230; Nb ii, 7, 226
Crookhurst La i, 112, ii, 7
Crooks Du, YW ii, 7
Crooksbury Sr i, 115

Dean, (The Forest of) Gl i, 130, 184
Dean, Little Gl ii, 30
Dean, Priors Ha ii, 73
Deane Bd i, 130
Deanfield Lawn Nt ii, 17
Deanham Nb i, 130, ii, 226
Deanhouse Sr i, 129
Dearham Cu i, 131
Dearnbrook YW i, 131
Dearne, R. YW i, 131
Dearsden YE ii, 228
Deaseland Wo i, 128
Debach Sf i, 24, 130
Debateable Land Cu ii, 212
Debdale Nth, Wo i, 126
Debden Sf, St i, 130
Debenham Sf i, 130
Dedmar K ii, 39
Deedle Hill YE i, 128
Deepdale Nth i, 127; YN i, 130
Deeping L i, 130, 283, 284, 289
Deerfold Wo i, 131
Deerhide Bk i, 246
Deerhurst Gl i, 131, 277
Deerplay La ii, 67
Deer Play YW ii, 67
Deerslet La ii, 129
Deeves Hall Hrt i, 140
Deeve Wood Hrt i, 140
Defford Wo i, 130, 181
Deighton YE i, 132; YN i, 132, 223, 224; *freq* ii, 194
Deighton, Kirk, North YW i, 132, ii, 4, 51
Delamere Ch ii, 17
Delapre Nth ii, 17, 73
Delf K i, 128
Delgate L i, 128
Dell Bk, Sx i, 129
Dell Bridge Ess i, 129
Delph (Bank) L, YW i, 128
Delves Ho Sx i, 128
Delvett Ess i, 141
Dembleby L i, 129
Demmyng, le YE i, 129
Denaby YW i, 71, i, 129
Denbury D i, 128
Denby Db i, 129
Denby YW i, 71, 129
Dendron La ii, 89
Denge K i, 197
Denge Marsh K i, 141, ii, 39
Denges Barn Sx i, 141
Dengie Ess i, 129
Denham Bk, St i, 130
Denhill K i, 129
Denholme YW i, 130, ii, 226
Denmead Ha i, 130
Denne Sx i, 129
Denshott Sr ii, 115
Denstroude K ii, 151
Denton Hu ii, 195; *passim* i, 130
Denver Nf i, 129, 163
Deopham Nf i, 130
Depedalemun YE ii, 45
Deptford K i, 130
Derby Db i, 71, 133, ii, 276; La i, 133
Dereham Nf i, 131
Dernestall L i, 131
Dernestall Lock L ii, 142
Dernford C i, 131
Dertren La i, 136, ii, 89
Derwent, R. Cu, Db, Nb, YE i, 131
Derwent Head YN ii, 140
Derwent Water Cu ii, 238
Derworthy D ii, 276
Desborough Bk i, 140
Detchant Nb i, 132, 152, 159
Deveral Co i, 279
Deverill, R. W i, 279
Devils Brook Do i, 203
Devil's Dyke, The C i, 132
Devizes W i, 131
Devonshire i, 128, ii, 111
Dewchurch He i, 95, ii, 40
Dewcombe Co i, 128
Dewdon D i, 128
Dewley Nb i, 128, 250
Dewsall He ii, 253
Dewsbury YW i, 70
Dexbeer D i, 131
Deyhus, le Mx i, 131
Dial, Blue Cu i, 131
Dial, Red Cu i, 131
Dial Hill Cu i, 131
Dial Post Sx i, 131
Dian House Cu i, 140
Dibb, Great YW i, 140
Dibbin's Wood Hrt i, 131
Dibble Bridge YN i, 130, 276
Dibden Ha, K i, 130
Dicker Sx i, 133
Dickering YE i, 132, 265, 283

Dove, R. Db, YN, YW i, 137
Dovehirn L i, 276
Dover K i, 137
Dover Beck Nt i, 26, 137
Dovercourt Ess i, 108, 137
Doverdale Wo i, 126, 137
Doverhay So i, 137
Doveridge Db i, 55
Dove Scar YN i, 137, ii, 124
Dow Bridge Nth, Wa, i, 137
Dowdyke L i, 137
Dowlish D i, 137
Downage Mx i, 240
Downash Sx ii, 270
Downend Co i, 152
Down Hall C i, 226
Downham La, Nb i, 138
Downhamford K i, 158
Downham Market Nf i, 185
Downhead So i, 236
Downholland La i, 139
Downholme YN i, 138, ii, 225, 226
Downton Ch, Sa i, 138; He i, 138; ii, 195
Dowreth Co i, 134
Dowthorpe YE ii, 212
Dragley La i, 249, 250
Drakedale YN i, 134
Drakehill Sr i, 134
Drakeholes Nt i, 134
Drakelow Bd, Db i, 134; Wo i, 134, 250
Drakenage Wa i, 134
Drake North W i, 134, 261
Drakepits YW i, 134, ii, 72
Drascombe D i, 136
Draughton YW i, 136
Drax YW i, 134, 135
Drax, Long YW ii, 278
Draycot(e), -cott Brk, Db, O, So, St, W, Wo i, 134; So, W, Wo i, 135; YE i, 109
Draydon So i, 135
Drayford D i, 135
Draymere Hu i, 134, 135
Drayton He, Mx, Nf, O, Sa, St, Sx, Wa i, 134; Bk, Ha, L, Nt, So, Wo i, 134, 135; C, Lei i, 134, 170; Nth i, 134, 217
Drayton, Dry/Fen(ny) C i, 170, ii, 242; Lei, i, 170
Dreibet C i, 135
Dreyefar, le C i, 136
Dreyton D i, 134
Driby L i, 68, 136
Driffield Gl, YE i, 136
Drigg Cu i, 136
Drigsell Sx i, 136, ii, 118
Dringhoe YE i, 136, 236
Dringhouses YW i, 136
Dringwell D ii, 213, 252
Drinsey L i, 136, 221; Nt i, 136
Drockbridge Ha i, 54, ii, 214
Drockmill Sx ii, 46, 214
Droitwich Wo i, 136, ii, 260, 261, 264
Dromonby YN i, 13
Dronfield Db i, 136
Drove, The L, W i, 136
Droveway W i, 136
Druckham Co ii, 214
Druridge Nb i, 136, 267
Drybeck Cu i, 136; We i, 26
Drybrook Gl i, 136
Dryburn Cu i, 64, 136; Nb i, 136
Dryland K i, 136, ii, 14
Drypool YE i, 136, ii, 69
Dry Stone Knott Cu ii, 5
Dub Beck Cu i, 137
Dubmill Cu i, 137
Dubwath Cu ii, 230
Duckaller D i, 9
Duckreed Sx i, 137
Duckworth La i, 137, ii, 275
Dudley Do i, 215
Dudswell Hrt ii, 253
Duffield Db, YE i, 137
Duffield Ings YE i, 153
Dufton We i, 137
Duggleby YE i, 71
Dukem Wt i, 128
Dukinfield Ch i, 137, 168
Dulas He i, 203
Dulford D i, 141
Duloe Bd i, 140
Dulverton So i, 133
Dulwich Sr i, 133, ii, 270
Dumble, (Crook) Nt ii, 7; Wa i, 137
Dumbleton Gl ii, 176
Dumple Street YN i, 138
Dumplington La i, 138
Dunchideock D i, 139
Dunclent Wo i, 98, 139
Duncorn Hill So i, 139
Duncotes YE i, 139

Englefield Brk i, 153
Engleton St i, 153
English St, Cu, Ha i, 153
Enham, (Knights) Ha i, 103, 143, 228
Enholmes YE i, 303
Enmore Do ii, 39; So i, 153
Ennerdale Cu i, 13, 127
Ennickford Wo ii, 224
Ennis Co i, 153
Enniscaven Co i, 153
Ennix Wood W i, 303
Ennox Wood W i, 303
Entwisle La ii, 200
Enville St i, 147, 168
Eorðbrycg Wo i, 55
Eport Wo i, 143
Epping (Forest) Ess i, 184, ii, 283
Eppleby YN i, 3
Eppleton Du i, 4
Eppleworth YE i, 156
Epscombe Hrt i, 80
Epsette Sr i, 4
Erewash, R. Db, Nt i, 304, ii, 270
Eridge Sx i, 144
Erith K i, 144, 278
Ermine Street ii, 162
Erringden YW i, 130
Eryholme YN i, 157, ii, 226
Escombe Du i, 146, ii, 226
Escowbeck La i, 160, 256
Escrick YE i, 160, ii, 83
Esh Du i, 4
Esher Sr ii, 102
Esholt Nb i, 5; YW i, 4, 259
Eshott Nb i, 5, ii, 103
Eshton YW i, 4
Esk, R. Cu i, 226, 304; YN i, 304
Eskdale Cu i, 127
Eske YE i, 5, 160
Esk Hause Cu i, 226
Eskrigg La i, 267
Espershields Nb ii, 104
Espley Nb, Sa i, 5
Esprick La i, 160
Essex ii, 109, 116
Esthallingebrouk Sx i, 302
Esthwaite Water La ii, 231
Eston (*passim*) ii, 193
Estwyke atte Flore Hrt i, 178
Etal Nb i, 161
Etchells Ch, Db i, 145
Eton Bk i, 147
Eton Wick Bk ii, 262
Ettingshall St i, 291
Euden Du i, 305; Nb i, 130
Eux(i)moor C i, 197
Evegate K ii, 202, 203
Evelith Sa i, 253, 279
Evenley Nth i, 147
Evenlode Wo ii, 9
Evenwood Du i, 147, ii, 280
Evercreech So i, 115, 154
Everdon Nth i, 154
Everingham YE i, 301
Everley W, YN i, 154
Eversden C i, 154
Evershaw Bk i, 154, ii, 99
Eversheds Sr i, 154, 237
Eversholt Bd i, 154, 259
Evershot Do i, 154, ii, 109
Eversley Ha i, 154
Everthorpe YE ii, 211, 283
Everton Bd, La, Nt i, 154; Nt ii, 196
Evesham Wo i, 231
Evesham, The Vale of Wo ii, 229
Ewanrigg Cu i, 155
Ewart Nb i, 143, ii, 274
Ewden YW i, 305
Ewehurst K i, 154, 277
Ewekene's Fm Sr ii, 234
Ewell K, Sr i, 7
Ewelme O i, 7
Ewen Gl i, 7
Ewerby Thorpe L ii, 211
Ewhurst Ha i, 277; Ha Sr, Sx i, 305
Ewood La i, 143; YW i, 305
Eworthy D ii, 276
Ewshott Ha ii, 103
Exbourne D i, 197
Exceat Sx ii, 103
Exe, R. D i, 87; D, So i, 304
Exeter D i, 87
Exfold Sx ii, 57
Exhall Wa i, 145
Exley YW i, 145
Exminster D ii, 47
Exmoor D ii, 43
Extall St i, 213
Exton Ha ii, 116, 192, 197; R ii, 57
Extons St i, 213
Extwisle La ii, 200
Exwell D i, 197
Exwick D ii, 262
Eyam Db i, 147, ii, 226

Fawcett We i, 164, ii, 122
Fawcliff Nth i, 165
Fawdington YN i, 164
Fawdon Nb i, 164
Faweather YW i, 164, 214
Fawepark Cu i, 165
Fawler Brk, O i, 164, 178
Fawley Bk, Brk i, 166; Ha i, 173; He ii, 21
Fawn Wood Hrt ii, 221
Fawside Du i, 164
Fawsley Nth i, 166
Faxfleet Ess i, 166
Faxfleet Ye i, 166, 177
Faxton Nth i, 68, 166
Faygate Sx i, 170
Fazakerley La i, 163
Fazeley St i, 166
Fearnhead La i, 237
Feasegate Yk i, 166, 196, 199
Feather Holm YE i, 174
Featherston Nb i, 171
Featherstone St, YW i, 171, ii, 144
Feathery Haugh Nb i, 172
Feetham YN i, 174
Feizor YW i, 157
Field, Home W i, 227
Felborough K i, 29
Felbrigg Nf i, 55, 174
Felderland K i, 168, ii, 246
Feldom YN i, 167
Feldon, The Wa i, 173
Felebrigge La i, 174
Felixkirk YN ii, 4
Felixstowe Sf ii, 160
Felkirk YW i, 174, ii, 4
Fellands L i, 170
Fellbeck YW i, 174
Fell Briggs YN i, 55, 174
Felley Nt i, 165, 168
Felling, (The) Du i, 168, 169
Felliscliffe YW i, 165
Fellow Sr i, 168
Fellowsfield Hrt i, 166
Felpham Sx i, 165
Felstead Ess ii, 149
Felter Lane Yk i, 169, 199
Feltham Do i, 173, Mx i, 169
Felton He, Nb, Sa, So i, 167
Felton Hill Nb i, 173
Feltwell Nf i, 169
Fen L, Wo i, 170
Fen Bank L i, 19
Fenby L i, 68, 170
Fencewood Nb i, 169
Fencote, -cott He i, 110, 170; O i, 110
Fenellane C i, 169
Fenham Nb i, 170, ii, 226
Fenhampton He i, 170, 232
Feniscowles La i, 170, ii, 123
Fenland C ii, 14
Fennedyke L i, 132
Fennel St. La i, 169
Fennelonddrove L i, 136
Fenny Wo i, 147
Fennymere Sa i, 170, ii, 39
Fenrother Nb i, 173, ii, 88
Fenstead Sf i, 173, ii, 149
Fenton Cu, Hu, L, Nb i, 170; Nt, St ii, 195
Fenton, Church YW i, 95, ii, 195
Fenwick Nb i, 170, ii, 262; YW i, 170, ii, 262
Ferdeweye, le Nth i, 171
Fernacre Co i, 3
Fern Down Do i, 171
Fernham Brk i, 166, 229
Fernilee Db i, 166
Fernworthy D ii, 276
Ferriby (North, South) L, YE i, 71, 171
Ferring Sx i, 289
Ferry Bridge YW i, 171
Ferryfield Nb i, 171
Ferryhill Du i, 171
Fersfield Nf i, 168, 190
Fethrescawe Nb i, 172
Fewcott O i, 166
Fewsome YE i, 166
Field K i, 173; St i, 167
Fielden Way C i, 173, ii, 249; O ii, 249; Wa i, 173, ii, 249
Fieldon Bridge Wa i, 173
Fieldy Wo i, 167
Fiendsfell Cu i, 171
Fifehead Do i, 172, 246
Fifhide Sr i, 172
Fifield Gl, O, W i, 172, 246
Figham YE i, 165, 193
Filands Fm W i, 168
Filborough K i, 29, 166
Fildenwood Hrt ii, 281
Filey (Brigg) YE i, 55, 172
Fillham D i, 173

Froxfield Ha, W i, 188
Froxton Co ii, 144
Froyle Ha i, 187
Frustfield Hundred W i, 190
Fryant Fm Mx i, 186
Fryerning Ess i, 186
Fryston, (Ferry, Monk, Water) YW i, 171, 187, ii, 45, 238
Fryton YN i, 188
Fryup YN i, 187
Fuge D i, 170, ii, 262
Fugglestone W i, 189
Fuidge D i, 170, ii, 262
Fulbrook Bk i, 51, 189
Fulepet Ess ii, 76
Fulfen St i, 170, 189
Fulford, (Gate/Water YE i, 196, ii, 238) D i, 181; Du i, 189; So, St, Wt, YE i, 181, 189
Fulham Palace Mx ii, 58
Fullamoor Co i, 189; D i, 179
Fulledge La ii, 10
Fullerton Ha i, 188
Fulletby L i, 189
Fullingcott D i, 188
Fulloway W ii, 249
Fulmer Bk i, 189, ii, 39
Fulnetby L i, 189
Fulney L i, 147, 189
Fulready Wa ii, 86
Fulshaw Ch i, 189, ii, 100; La ii, 100
Fulstone YW i, 189
Fulstow L i, 189, ii, 160
Fulwich K ii, 262
Fulwood La ii, 280
Furness La ii, 49
Fursdon Co i, 138, 190
Fursette, la Sr i, 190
Furtho Nth i, 185
Furze Co, D i, 190
Furzehill W i, 184
Furzenepp Co i, 101, 190
Furzen Fm Sr i, 190
Furzenhill Bk i, 190
Fusedale We i, 166
Fusehill Cu i, 166
Fyfield Brk ii, 247; Brk, Ess, Gl, Ha i, 172
Fylde, The La i, 172
Fyling Thorpe YN ii, 209
Fyning Sx i, 174
Fyvehalf W i, 222
Gable, Great Cu i, 191
Gaddesdon Hrt i, 191
Gadsey Bd i, 204
Gadshill K i, 204
Gagingwell O i, 191
Gailey St i, 148, 192
Gainford Du i, 199
Gaisgill We, YW i, 200
Gaitacre YN i, 7
Gale, The YW i, 199
Gale Bank YN i, 19, 199
Gale Hall Cu i, 199
Gale, High YN i, 199
Galemire Cu i, 192
Galford D i, 192
Galgate La i, 196
Galhampton So i, 192
Gall Drove C i, 192
Galley Lane L i, 235
Galleywood Ess, Sr i, 192
Galligill Cu i, 192
Gallow Green YN i, 192
Gallow Hill YW i, 79, 275
Galmanlythe Yk i, 253
Galmington D, So i, 192
Galphay YW i, 192, 221
Galsham D i, 192
Galton Do i, 192, ii, 194
Galtres, (The Forest of) YN i, 184, 206, 265
Gamblesby Cu i, 72
Gamelan wyrðe K i, 294
Gammersgill YN ii, 123
Gammock C i, 193
Gammon's Fm K i, 294
Gampton D i, 192
Gamston Nt ii, 197
Ganarew He ii, 82
Ganfield Hundred Brk i, 193
Gang Bridge W i, 193
Gannah He i, 193
Gannaway Wa i, 193
Gannock C, Hrt i, 193
Gannok, le YE i, 193
Gannow La, Wo i, 193
Gannoweslonde Wa i, 193
Gannowestockyng Wa i, 193
Ganstead YE i, 192, ii, 147
Ganton Peak YE ii, 60
Ganwick Mx i, 193
Garboldisham Nf i, 229
Gardenness Point Ess i, 195

Gipsey Race YE i, 202, ii, 81
Girdlergate Yk i, 202
Girnhill YW i, 209, 275
Girsby L i, 210
Girtford Bd i, 181, 209
Girton C i, 209
Girton Nt i, 209, ii, 195
Gisburn YW i, 64, 212
Gissage Lake D i, 212
Gladfen Ess i, 203
Gladley Bd i, 202
Glaisdale YN i, 203
Glamford L i, 203
Glantlees Nb i, 204
Glanton Nb i, 204
Glanty Sr i, 204
Glanville D i, 97
Glapton Nt i, 203
Glapwell Db i, 203
Glaramara Cu i, 204
Glasbury He i, 203
Glascote Wa i, 109, 203
Glasshamptom Wo i, 203
Glasson, R. La i, 203
Glassonby Cu i, 72
Glaston La i, 203
Glastonbury So i, 303
Glatton Hu i, 202
Glazebrook, R. La i, 203
Glazeley Sa i, 203
Glazenwood Ess i, 203
Gleadless YW i, 204
Gleadthorpe Nt i, 202, ii, 211
Gleden Brook Wo i, 203
Gledhill YW i, 204
Gledholt YW i, 204
Gledhow YW i, 203, 204
Glemham Sf i, 203
Glemsford Sf i, 203
Glen Lei i, 203
Glencoyne Cu i, 203
Glendford Nf i, 203
Glendon D i, 203
Glendue Nb i, 137, 203
Glenfield Lei i, 97
Glentham L i, 204
Glentworth L i, 204
Glinch Brook Wo i, 288, 289
Gloucester Gl i, 87
Glover Lane Yk i, 199, 204
Glusburn YW i, 54, 204
Glynde (Reach) Sx i, 204, ii, 83
Glyne Manor Sx i, 204
Glynleigh Sx i, 204
Glywish Sx i, 204
Gnatham Co, D i, 204
Gnipe Howe YN i, 204
Goat Cu, Sx i, 206
Goathland YN i, 205, ii, 14
Goathurst So i, 196
Godalming Sr i, 301
Godardeshant Ess i, 233
Godderthwaite Cu ii, 220
Godestoch Sa ii, 154, 156
Godley Ch i, 205
Godley YW i, 205
Godmanchester Hu i, 87
Godmanham YE i, 301
Godney So i, 205
Godshill Ha, Wt i, 204
Godstow O i, 204, ii, 160
Godswell W ii, 250, 252
Godwick Nf i, 205
Gog, The W i, 205
Gogland D i, 205
Gogmore Sr i, 205
Gogwell D i, 205
Goit Nt i, 206
Goit, East YE i, 206
Gokewell L i, 196
Golborne La i, 205
Golbourne Ch i, 205
Golcar YW i, 157
Goldbridge Sx i, 205
Gold Dyke C i, 206
Goldehord Sa i, 205
Goldencross Ess i, 205
Golden hoard Sr i, 205
Goldenlands Sr i, 205
Goldenlow Bd i, 211
Goldentoft L ii, 183
Golden Valley Gl, He i, 205
Golder O i, 205
Goldhard Sr i, 205
Gold Hill K i, 205
Goldhord Sa i, 205
Goldhordcroft Wa i, 205
Goldhorde Field Sr i, 205
Goldiford Hu i, 205
Golding Sa i, 205
Goldings Field Ess i, 205
Goldmire La ii, 47
Goldor O ii, 55
Goldpit Hu i, 205

Goldsoncott So i, 205
Goldspur Hundred Sx ii, 139
Goldsworth Sr i, 205
Goldthorn St i, 205
Gollard Ha i, 205
Golsoncott So i, 109
Gomenhulle Wo i, 193
Gomshall Sr ii, 105, 106
Gooden La i, 206, 212
Goodmanham YE i, 6
Goodmansleigh So ii, 22
Goodneston K ii, 197
Goodramgate Yk i, 196
Goole YW i, 206
Goosey Brk i, 148, 206
Goosnargh La i, 157
Gopsall Lei i, 206
Gordano So i, 130, 206
Gore W i, 194
Gore Green K i, 194
Gorepece W ii, 61
Gorfen Nb i, 206
Gormire YN i, 206, ii, 47
Gorracott Co i, 194
Gorrell D ii, 251
Gorse Hill Wo i, 206
Gorsley Gl i, 206, ii, 21; He i, 206
Gorsty Hill Wo i, 206
Gorsuch La ii, 122
Gorton La i, 206
Gosbrook St i, 51, 206
Goscote Lei i, 109, 206; St i, 110, 206
Gosford D, O, Wa i, 206; O, Sf, So, Wa i, 182
Gosforth Cu, Nb i, 182, 206
Goshenges Nth i, 153
Gosport Ha i, 206, ii, 71; YW i, 182
Gosshill K i, 206
Goswell Mx ii, 252
Goswick Nb ii, 262
Gotes Bridge L i, 206
Gotham Nt i, 196, 229
Gotherswick La ii, 263
Gotwick Sx ii, 259, 262
Goule, la So i, 206
Gowbarrow Cu i, 192, 205
Gowbusk YW i, 65
Gowdall YW i, 205
Gowerdale YN ii, 1
Gowthorpe Nf, La, YE, YW i, 196
Goxhill L, YE ii, 8
Graby L i, 209
Gracechurch Mx i, 95, 191
Gracedieu Lei i, 207
Graffham Sx i, 207
Grafham Hu i, 207, 228
Graft, Le L i, 208
Graft Drain L i, 208
Grafte, Old L i, 208
Grafton (Temple Wa) Ch, Gl, O, Sa, W, Wo, YW i, 207
Grafty K ii, 177
Grain, Isle of K i, 209
Grain Hill Cu i, 208
Grainsgill Cu i, 208
Grampound Co i, 208, ii, 70
Granary Court K i, 110
Granberry Lodge Ess i, 209
Granby Nt i, 235
Grandborough Bk, K i, 29, 209
Granehou Nt i, 235
Grange Chine, Fm C, Nt i, 208; Wt i, 94
Gransmere Ess i, 209
Granta, R. C ii, 94
Grantchester C ii, 94
Grantham L i, 208
Grappenhall Ch i, 210
Graseley St i, 191
Grasmere We i, 191, ii, 39
Grassendale La i, 191
Grassgarth Cu i, 191, 195
Grassington YW i, 191
Grass Kiln YN i, 76
Grassnop Cu i, 101
Grassoms Cu i, 191, 259
Grassthorpe Nt i, 191, ii, 211
Grateley Ha i, 208
Gratton D i, 207, 208, 210
Gravatts Sx i, 208
Graveley C i, 207
Graveney K i, 10, 143, 208
Gravenhunger He i, 233; Sa i, 208
Gravenhurst Bd i, 208
Gravesend K i, 152
Gravett(s) Sr i, 208
Graynes YN i, 208
Grayshott Ha i, 207, ii, 103
Graystone YN i, 207
Graythwaite La i, 207
Grazeley Brk i, 207, ii, 134
Greasborough YW i, 191
Greasby Ch i, 58
Greatham Du, Ha i, 209, 228; Sx i, 228

Keldholme YN ii, 3
Kelfield L, YE i, 88
Kelham Nt ii, 4, 226
Kelk YE i, 88
Kellet La ii, 3
Kelleth We i, 253, ii, 3
Kelloe Du i, 88
Kelmer YN i, 279, ii, 36
Kelsick Cu ii, 3, 122
Kelstern L ii, 205
Kelvedon Hatch Ess i, 123
Kemerton Gl i, 293, 295
Kemphill Ha i, 88
Kempland D i, 88
Kempley Gl i, 89
Kempsford Gl i, 183
Kempshot Ha i, 88
Kemsing K i, 91, 283, 286, 289
Kenchester He i, 87
Kendal We i, 127
Kenderchurch He i, 95
Kenelmstowe He ii, 161
Kennard So i, 118, 198
Kennet, R. Brk i, 120; Sf i, 183
Kennington Brk i, 297; K i, 123
Kensington Gore Mx i, 194
Kent i, 80, 120, ii, 109
Kentchurch He i, 95
Kentford Sf i, 183
Kenton Nb, i, 123, ii, 194; Sf i, 123
Kepier Du i, 124, 197
Keppel K i, 81
Kepwick YN i, 84, ii, 262
Kerlingdimple La i, 138
Kern Wt i, 122
Kerrow Co i, 76
Kersal La i, 76
Kersbrook Co i, 52, 76
Kersey Sf i, 76
Kersey Bridge Cu ii, 230
Kersham Bridge D i, 112
Kerslake Co i, 76, ii, 8
Kerswell D, Wo i, 76
Kesgrave Sf i, 76, 207
Kesteven L i, 92, ii, 150
Kestlemerris Co i, 81
Keswick Cu, Nf i, 91, ii, 262; YW ii, 262
Ketford Gl i, 124, 182
Ketmongergate Yk ii, 35
Kettlebaston Sf ii, 197
Kettleburgh Sf ii, 3
Kettleby Db, Lei i, 71; L, Lei ii, 3, 92
Kettleshulme Ch i, 268
Kettlesing YW i, 153, 283, ii, 3
Kettle Spring YW ii, 163
Kettlestang YW ii, 157
Kettlethorpe YE ii, 3; YW ii, 211
Kettlewell YW i, 91, ii, 3
Kew Sr i, 75, ii, 3
Kewstoke So ii, 155
Kex Beck (R. Wharfe) YW ii, 3, 5
Kexwith YN ii, 3, 220
Keyford So i, 75
Keyhaven Ha i, 118, 214
Keyhirst Nb i, 75, 277
Keymer Sx i, 118, ii, 39
Keynor Sx i, 118
Keynsham So i, 229, 231
Keysoe Bd i, 257
Keystone Hu ii, 145
Key Street K, Wo ii, 3
Kidbrook(e) K, Sx i, 124
Kiddal YW i, 118
Kidderminster Wo ii, 47
Kidsnape La ii, 3, 132
Kigbeare D i, 75
Kilbourne Db i, 123
Kilburn Mx i, 123
Kilby Lei i, 68, 94
Kildale YN ii, 3
Kildwick YW i, 94
Kildwick YW ii, 263
Kilham Nb, YE i, 123; YE ii, 226
Killbreece He i, 93
Killing Nab Scar YN ii, 48, 124
Kilmenorth Co ii, 3
Kilmeston Ha ii, 197
Kiln Ho C i, 123
Kilnsea YE i, 123, ii, 93
Kilpeck He i, 93
Kilpin YE i, 88, ii, 61
Kilquite Co i, 93
Kilton (Thorpe YN ii, 211) Nt, YN i, 94; So i, 123
Kilve So i, 123
Kimber D i, 88
Kimberwell Bd ii, 253
Kimble (Wick) Bk i, 27, 123, ii, 262
Kimmeridge Do i, 123
Kinder Scout Db ii, 126
Kineton Gl, Wa i, 123; Wa ii, 194
Kingcombe Do i, 119, 123
King Henry Cu i, 84

Marling Shaw Sx ii, 36
Marlow Bk ii, 12, 39
Marl Pit K ii, 36
Marlpit Shaw Sx ii, 36
Marlston Brk ii, 198
Marr, High YE i, 7
Marraton Co ii, 37
Marraway Wa ii, 43
Marrick YN i, 267, ii, 36
Marrs, The YE ii, 36
Marsden Gl, YW ii, 37; La ii, 38
Marsh Sa, Sx ii, 39
Marshal Drove C i, 224
Marshfield Gl i, 167, ii, 39
Marshwood Do ii, 39, 281
Marske YN ii, 39
Marsland Co ii, 14
Marsshedyke L i, 132
Marston, (Dry Gl i, 136) Bd, Bk, Ch, Gl, He, L, Lei, Nth, O, So, YW, *freq* ii, 195; (*passim*) ii, 39
Marston, Fleet, Long Bk i, 177; Gl, Hrt ii, 16
Marston, Potters Lei ii, 72
Marston Sicca Gl ii, 122
Marstow He ii, 159, 161
Marten W ii, 39; *freq* ii, 195
Martham Nf i, 229
Martholme La ii, 36
Martin Ha, K, L, Wo, *freq* ii, 39; Nt ii, 34
Martley Sf, Wo ii, 37
Marton Ch, La, L, Wa, Y, *freq* ii, 39; YN ii, 36; *freq* ii, 34; *freq* ii, 192, 195
Marton Doles Wa i, 126
Marvell Wt i, 168, ii, 47
Marwell D ii, 37
Marwood Du ii, 36
Marygate (Landing) Yk i, 196, ii, 23
Marystowe D ii, 161
Masborough YW i, 62
Mashamshire YN ii, 110
Matfen Nb i, 170
Mathon Wo ii, 36
Matlask Nf i, 5, 13, ii, 34
Matlock Db i, 2, ii, 34
Matterdale Cu ii, 37
Mauldon Bd i, 138, ii, 33
Maund He ii, 94
Mautby Nf i, 71
Mawbray Cu ii, 32
Mawdesley La ii, 22
Mawsley Nth ii, 35
Mawthorpe L ii, 42
Maxey Nth i, 148
Maxstoke Wa ii, 156
Maxted K ii, 41, 149
Maybridge Wo ii, 32
Mayburgh We ii, 32
Mayfield St i, 168, ii, 31; Sx ii, 32
Mayland Ess i, 14
Mayne, Fryer/Little Do i, 186, ii, 30
Maynes Cu ii, 34
Maytham K i, 230, ii, 32
Meadfield Sr ii, 37
Meadle Bk ii, 31
Meadow Place Db ii, 67
Meads Sx i, 147, ii, 31
Mealcheapen Wo i, 90
Mean, The K ii, 33
Mean, West Wt ii, 33
Meaning Way O ii, 33, 249
Meanwood W, YW ii, 280; YW ii, 33
Meare So ii, 39
Mearley La ii, 34
Measand We ii, 41
Mease, R. Lei ii, 38
Measham Co ii, 34; Lei, ii, 38
Meathop We i, 260, ii, 41
Meaux YE ii, 38, 93
Medbourne Lei, W ii, 31
Medbury Bd ii, 31, 32
Meden, R. Nt ii, 37
Medeseye Mx ii, 93
Medhone Sx i, 233
Medhurst K ii, 31
Medlar La i, 157, ii, 40
Medley O i, 148
Medlock, R. La ii, 8, 31
Medmenham (Abbey) Bk i, 225, ii, 37
Medmerry Fm Sx ii, 37
Medstead Ha ii, 149
Meece St ii, 38
Meend Gl, He, Sa ii, 41
Meering Nt i, 302, 303
Meersbrook YW ii, 34
Meesden Hrt ii, 38
Meeth(e) D ii, 34, 47
Melbourn(e) C, YE i, 64; C ii, 38; YE ii, 40
Melbury (Abbas Do i, 1) D, Do ii, 33
Melchbourne Bd ii, 37
Melcheburnfeld Mx ii, 37

Melcheheg Bd ii, 37
Melchet Ha ii, 37; W i, 92
Melcombe Do ii, 38; So ii, 46
Meldon D, Nb ii, 33; Nb i, 138
Meldreth C ii, 38, 86
Melhuish D ii, 33
Melkinthorpe We ii, 210, 212
Melkridge Nb ii, 38
Mellersh's Fm Sr ii, 33
Mellingey Co ii, 38
Mellor Db, La i, 50, ii, 37
Mell(e)s Sf ii, 46; So i, 158, ii, 46
Melmerby Cu i, 71; YN i, 12, 71, ii, 35
Melplash Do ii, 46, 66
Melton L, Lei, Nf, YE ii, 40; Nf, Sf ii, 194
Melton Ross L ii, 193
Melwood L ii, 40
Mendip Hills So ii, 41
Meneatt Wo ii, 33
Menith Wo ii, 33
Menkee Co i, 75
Menmarsh O ii, 33
Menna Co ii, 38
Menwith YW ii, 33, 232
Menwood W ii, 33
Meols, (North) Ch, La ii, 38
Meon (Hill) Gl i, 100; Ha ii, 32
Meonstoke Ha ii, 155
Meopham K i, 229
Merbach He ii, 34
Mere (Brook) Ch, L, W ii, 34, 39
Mere Brow La i, 53
Mereburn Nb ii, 34
Mereflete L i, 177
Merevale Wa ii, 47, 229
Meriden Wa i, 130, ii, 47
Merketstede YW ii, 148
Merriall Nt i, 242, ii, 47
Merridale St ii, 47
Merridge So ii, 34
Merrifield Co i, 168, ii, 47
Merrington Sa ii, 47
Merrow Sr ii, 79
Merryvale He ii, 47, 229
Mersea Ess i, 147, ii, 38
Merset Hundred Sa ii, 34, 94
Merstham Sr ii, 94
Merston K, Sx, Wt ii, 39; *freq* ii, 195
Merstow Wo ii, 33, 160
Merton D, Nf, O ii, 39
Meshaw D i, 13
Mesne Close Nt ii, 34
Messingham L i, 301
Metfeld Sf ii, 31
Metham YE ii, 34
Methwold Nf ii, 40, 241
Mettle Hill C i, 250, ii, 44
Mew Stone D ii, 34
Michaelchurch He i, 95
Michaelstow Co, Ess ii, 161
Micheldever Ha i, 137
Michel Grove Sx ii, 40
Michelmarsh Ha ii, 39, 40
Michilbreche L i, 47
Mickering La i, 153, ii, 46
Mickfield Sf ii, 40
Micklebring YW i, 51, ii, 40
Mickleby YN i, 71, ii, 41
Mickledales YN i, 128
Micklefield YW i, 40, 168, ii, 40
Micklegate *freq* i, 196
Mickleover Db ii, 54
Micklethwaite Cu, YW ii, 41, 219
Mickleton Gl i, 10; Gl, YN ii, 40; *freq* ii, 193
Mickley Nb ii, 40
Middlecote So i, 158
Middleham Du ii, 40; YN i, 228, ii, 40
Middleney So ii, 40
Middlesex ii, 40, 116
Middlethorpe Nt, YW ii, 211
Middleton Db, Du, Ess, YW ii, 40; (*passim*) ii, 193
Middlewich Ch ii, 40, 261
Middop YW i, 260, ii, 40
Middridge Du ii, 40
Midewinde, Aqua de Sx ii, 268
Midford So ii, 47
Midge Hall La ii, 46
Midgehall W i, 224
Midgeham Brk ii, 46
Midgell So ii, 46
Midgley YW ii, 46
Midhope YW ii, 40
Midhurst Sx ii, 40
Midridge So ii, 40
Midsomer Norton So ii, 168
Midsyke YN ii, 40, 122
Midwinter D ii, 269
Migley Du ii, 21, 40
Mikeldam L i, 127

Mountain Fm, Wood D, Sr ii, 42
Mount Ferrant YE ii, 42
Mount Grace YN i, 207, ii, 42
Mount, The K ii, 45
Mouseberry D ii, 45
Mousehole D ii, 45
Moustows Sx ii, 44
Mouthwaite YN ii, 220
Mow Cop Ch ii, 44
Mowshurst K ii, 45
Mowsley Lei ii, 45
Mowthorpe YE, YN ii, 45, 212
Moxhull Wa ii, 106
Moxley St i, 250
Moze Ess ii, 44
Mozergh We i, 157, ii, 44
Muchelney So ii, 40
Mucklands Nth ii, 45
Muckleford Do ii, 40
Mucklow (Hill) Wo i, 250, ii, 40
Muddipit D ii, 44
Mudford So ii, 44
Mudwall Ess ii, 44
Muggleton Wt ii, 40, 193
Muker YN i, 7, ii, 41
Mulbarton Nf i, 31, ii, 38
Mulfra Co i, 50
Mulgrave YN i, 211, ii, 45
Mulwith YW ii, 45, 230
Mumby L i, 127
Muncaster Cu i, 87
Munden Hrt ii, 45
Mundie's Fm Sr ii, 42
Mundon Ess ii, 45
Munkehaithespen YW ii, 137
Munkesdeil L i, 128
Munstead Sr ii, 45
Munster Mx ii, 44
Murcot(t) O, W ii, 43
Murk Head YN ii, 47
Murrah Cu ii, 233
Murrein Wood K ii, 43
Murston K i, 159
Murton Du, Nb, We, YN ii, 42
Murtwell D ii, 43
Musardere Gl i, 156
Musbury D i, 61, ii, 45; La i, 57, ii, 45
Muscoates, -cott Nth, YN i, 110, ii, 45
Musden La ii, 45, 46
Muston Do ii, 198; Lei, YE ii, 45, 46
Mustouwe Ess ii, 44
Muswell Bk ii, 38, 252; Mx ii, 252
Mutford Hundred Sf ii, 44
Mutley D ii, 44
Mutlow C, Ch ii, 44; Ch i, 250
Myland Ess i, 152
Mynde, The He ii, 41
Mystelfelde Sr ii, 41
Mystlehawe Sr ii, 41
Mytchett Sr ii, 103
Mytham Db, La ii, 47
Mythe, The Gl ii, 47
Mythe Hook Gl i, 255
Mytholmroyd YW ii, 47, 87
Mythop La i, 259, ii, 41
Myton (Gate) YE, YN i, 196, ii, 47; *freq* ii, 195
Mytton Sa ii, 47

Nab Cu, Nt, YE ii, 48
Nabbs Nt ii, 48
Nab Lane Nth ii, 48
Naburn YE ii, 48
Nackholt K i, 2, 259
Nackington K i, 296
Nafferton Nb, YE ii, 197
Nafford Wo i, 182, ii, 49
Nailsea So i, 148
Naithwood D i, 28
Nakedale Nb i, 149, ii, 48
Nalderswood Sr i, 9
Naldrett Sx i, 9
Nanhurst Sr i, 102
Nantwich Ch ii, 260, 262
Naplease Goyle D i, 206
Napleton Wo i, 4
Nappa YN i, 254
Nappay YW i, 254
Napsted Ess ii, 49
Napton Wa i, 254
Nareton K ii, 193
Narford Nf ii, 49
Narraway D ii, 52
Naseby Nth i, 58
Nash Bk, He i, 14; Sa i, 5, 14; So, Wo i, 5
Nashenden K i, 14, 277
Nass Gl ii, 48
Nassington Nth ii, 48
Nateley Ha ii, 48
Nathwait Cu ii, 48
Natland We ii, 28
Natsley D i, 254
Natson D i, 204

Newlod C ii, 9
Newmarket Sf ii, 36
Newnham Bd, C ii, 51; Gl i, 228, ii, 51; Ha ii, 51; Hrt, K i, 228
Newport Bk, Ess, Sa, Wt ii, 51, 71; Co, L ii, 71
Newport Pagnell Bk ii, 70, 71
Newquay Co ii, 3
Newsam, Temple YE ii, 177
Newsells Hrt ii, 117
Newsham Du, L, YN ii, 51, 226; L, YN ii, 225; La, YN i, 270, ii, 51; YN ii, 52
Newsholme Y ii, 51; YE i, 270, ii, 225, 226; YW ii, 225, 226
Newstead L, Nt ii, 51, 148, 149; Nb ii, 149; YN ii, 51, 149
Newthorpe Nt, YW ii, 211
Newtimber Sx ii, 50, 180
Newton (*passim*) ii, 194
Newton, Bank YW i, 19
Newton, Cold Lei i, 78
Newton, Kings Db i, 124
Newton, Maiden Do ii, 32
Newton, Old Sf i, 8
Newton, Out YE ii, 228
Newton, Potter YW ii, 72
Newton, Wold YE ii, 242
Newton, Wood Nth ii, 281
Newton by the Sea Nb ii, 93
Newton Garth YE i, 195
Newton le Wold L ii, 242
Newton on Ouse YN ii, 55, 169
Newton on the Moor Nb ii, 55, 169
Newton Unthank Lei ii, 227
Newton Without W ii, 272
Newtown Gl, Ha, Nb, Wt ii, 194; *freq* ii, 191, 194
Nibley, (North) Gl i, 255
Nidd, R. YN i, 13
Nidderdale YW i, 13, 127
Niddermyn YN i, 13; YW ii, 46
Nightwood W i, 103
Night Wood K ii, 281
Nikeresaker C ii, 50
Nikerpoll Sx ii, 50
Nikersmadwe Ess ii, 50
Nikirwells L ii, 50
Nill Well C i, 103
Nimmings Wo ii, 50
Nine Acre Wood Hrt ii, 50
Ninebanks Nb i, 28, ii, 50
Ninehams Sr i, 303
Ninham Wt ii, 50
Ninnings Ess, Hrt i, 304
Niton Wt ii, 50
Nizel's Heath K ii, 50, 118
Noak Wo i, 1, 2
Nobold Nth i, 45
Nobottle Nth i, 45, ii, 51
Nocton L i, 254, ii, 196
Noctorum Ch i, 103
Noddon D i, 254
Node, The Hrt i, 2
Node, atte W i, 2
Noke O i, 1, 14
Noke Bridge Ha i, 2
Nomansland Mx *et freq* ii, 14
Noman's Land Sx, Wo ii, 35
Nook, The Sx i, 103
Nookton Du i, 103
Noonstones Cu ii, 50
Norbins (Glastonbury) So i, 36
Norbiton Sr ii, 51
Norbreck La i, 48
Norbury Ch, Db, Sa i, 61, ii, 51
Norchard Wo i, 14, ii, 56
Norcross La i, 114
Nordkampe Nt i, 79
Norfolk i, 179, ii, 51, 109
Norham Nb ii, 51
Norhamshire Du ii, 110
Norke He i, 14
Norland YW ii, 51
Normanby L ii, 52; YN i, 71, ii, 52
Normancross Hu i, 114, 115, ii, 52
Normansburgh Nf ii, 52
Normanton Db, L, Lei ii, 52, 192, 197; Nt, R, YW ii, 52
Nornay Nt ii, 52
Norney Sr ii, 52
Norrington W ii, 51
Northam D, Ha i, 228
Northampton Nth i, 232, ii, 51
Northdelve Sx i, 128
Northease Sx i, 218
North End Sx i, 303
Northenden Ch ii, 277
Northgate *freq* i, 196
Northiam Sx i, 241
Northleach Gl ii, 10, 51
Northload So ii, 9
Northmostown D ii, 52
Northolt Mx i, 224, ii, 51, 224

Northorpe L ii, 211; YE ii, 208, 209, 211
Northover So ii, 54
Northowram YW ii, 54
North Pasture YW ii, 60
Northridge D i, 254
North Riding Y ii, 51, 213
North Riding of the parts of Lindsey L ii, 213
Northumberland ii, 13, 14, 52, 109
Northway D i, 33; *passim* ii, 249
North Weald Ess ii, 241
Northwich Ch ii, 260, 261, 264
Northwold Nf ii, 241
Northwood K i, 33, ii, 52; Wo ii, 280
Norðworðig Db ii, 276
Nortoft Nth ii, 183
Norton Wo i, 281, ii, 51; *passim* ii, 51, 193
Norton, Bishop L i, 37
Norton, Chipping O i, 90
Norton, Cold St i, 78
Norton in Hales Sa i, 281
Norton in le Drit YN i, 136
Norton in the Moors St ii, 43
Norton juxta Kempsey Wo ii, 1
Norton juxta Twycross Lei ii, 1
Norton le Clay YN i, 136
Norton, Midsomer So ii, 40
Norwich Nf ii, 51, 261
Norwood Nth *et freq* ii, 280
Nosterfield C i, 14; YN i, 14, 155
Notfreðing K i, 289
Notgrove Gl i, 208, ii, 48
Notley Bk i, 254, ii, 21; Hrt i, 254
Notley, Black Ess i, 37
Notter Co i, 254, ii, 184
Notter Tor Co i, 254
Nottingham Nt i, 170, 196, 285, 301, ii, 190
Notton YW i, 254
Noutdritlane YE ii, 49
Noutgate Yk ii, 49
Noutwath Cu ii, 49, ii, 230
Noven Sx ii, 53
Noverton St i, 14
Nower, The K ii, 54
Nowton Sf ii, 51
Nuffield O ii, 181
Nunburnholme YE i, 54, ii, 52
Nun Coton L ii, 226
Nuneaton Wa ii, 52
Nuneham O ii, 51
Nunley Wa ii, 52
Nunney So ii, 52
Nunriding Nb ii, 52, 91
Nunstainton Du ii, 52
Nunton Nth ii, 52
Nunwick Nb ii, 52, 263; YW i, 10, ii, 52, 263
Nursling Ha i, 254
Nurstead K i, 254, ii, 149; Sf i, 254
Nutford Do i, 254
Nuthall Nt i, 224; Wt i, 254
Nuthampstead Hrt i, 232, 254
Nuthurst La i, 254, 277; Sx i, 254; Wa i, 254, 277
Nutley Ess i, 254, ii, 211; Ha, Sx i, 254
Nutshaw La ii, 99
Nutwith YN i, 254, ii, 232
Nycharpool L ii, 50
Nyetimber Sx ii, 50, 180
Nyewoods Sx ii, 50, 280, 281
Nykerpole W ii, 50
Nyland Do i, 148
Nymandoles C i, 126
Nymet D ii, 50
Nympsfield Gl ii, 50
Nympton D ii, 50
Nynehead So i, 246, ii, 50
Nyton Sx ii, 50

Oadby Lei i, 71
Oak, Crooked Du i, 113
Oake So i, 2
Oaken Sa ii, 225; St i, 1, ii, 226
Oakenbottom La i, 43
Oakenden K i, 2, 130
Oakeneaves La i, 147
Oakengates Sa i, 2
Oakenpole K i, 2, 164
Oakenshaw YW i, 2, ii, 99
Oakerthorpe Db ii, 210, 212
Oakes, Holy Lei i, 2, 225
Oakford Do i, 2, 182
Oakhall Wo i, 259
Oakhampton Wo i, 232
Oakhanger Ha i, 233
Oakhurst Hrt i, 157
Oakleigh K ii, 21
Oakley Bd, Bk, Wo ii, 21; *freq* i, 2, ii, 21
Oakroyd YW ii, 87

Osmotherley La i, 12, 250; YN i, 12, ii, 22
Ospringe K ii, 56
Ossett YW ii, 120
Ossington Co i, 139
Ost End Ess i, 13
Osterland K ii, 56
Osterley Mx i, 155, ii, 56
Ostringe K ii, 56
Oswaldkirk YN ii, 4
Oswaldslow Hundred Wo i, 249
Oswaldtwistle La ii, 200
Oswardesbeksokene Nt ii, 134
Oswestry Sa ii, 187
Oteley Sa i, 13, ii, 21
Othecolle YE ii, 6
Otherton St, Wo ii, 56
Othery So ii, 56
Otley Sf, YW ii, 22
Otter D ii, 56
Otter, R. D i, 143; So ii, 56
Otterbourne, -burn Ha, Nb, YW i, 64, ii, 56
Ottercops Nb i, 107
Otterford So ii, 56
Otterham Co i, 230, ii, 56
Otterpley K ii, 56, 67
Otterpool K ii, 69
Ottershaw Sr ii, 56, 100
Otter's Pool La ii, 56
Otterton D ii, 56
Ottery, Venn D i, 170
Oubrough YE i, 61, ii, 224
Ouerwhart Sykes YE ii, 221
Oughterside Cu ii, 96
Oughtrington Ch i, 297
Oulton Ch, St i, 8
Ousden Sf ii, 224
Ouse, Old i, 8
Ouse, R. Sx ii, 247, 268; YE i, 177; YW i, 135
Ouse Brook Wa ii, 247
Ousefleet YW i, 177
Oustdayles YE i, 128
Ousterley Du i, 155
Outchester Nb i, 87, ii, 224
Outerness Hu ii, 48, 228
Outfield Cu ii, 228
Outgang, (The) Cu, Nt, YE ii, 228
Outgate L ii, 228
Outhwaite La ii, 220
Outwell C ii, 228
Ovangle La i, 11
Oveney K ii, 224
Over C, Ch, Db ii, 54
Overacres Nb i, 7
Overbury Wo i, 59, ii, 224
Overday D i, 131
Overdrove, le Hu i, 136
Overgrass Nb i, 194
Overpool Ch ii, 224
Overstrand Nf ii, 54, 162
Overton Ch ii, 53, 54; Db ii, 53; Ha ii, 224; La ii, 54; Lei ii, 53, 54; R, Sa ii, 53; W ii, 224; YN ii, 54
Overy O ii, 54
Ovingham Nb i, 298, 301, ii, 190
Ovington Ha i, 297; Nb i, 301, ii, 190
Ovis D ii, 54
Ower Do ii, 55
Owlacombe D ii, 224
Owlands YN ii, 28, 224
Owlerton YW i, 9
Owley K i, 224, ii, 224
Owl Head YW ii, 224
Owlpen Gl ii, 61
Owmby by Spital L i, 13
Owmers Nb ii, 40
Owsthorpe YE ii, 211
Owstmarsk YE ii, 39
Owston L, YW i, 14
Owstwick YE i, 14, ii, 261
Owthorne YE ii, 205, 228, 271
Owzlebury Ha i, 61, ii, 56
Oxborough Nf ii, 57
Oxcombe L i, 119, ii, 57
Oxcroft C i, 113
Oxenbold Sa i, 45, ii, 57
Oxendale La i, 127
Oxendon Nth i, 138, ii, 57
Oxenhall Du, Gl i, 224, ii, 57
Oxen Hoath K ii, 57
Oxenholme We i, 259
Oxenhope YW i, 260, ii, 57
Oxenton Gl i, 138, ii, 57
Oxenwood W ii, 280
Oxford O i, 182, ii, 57
Oxhall Wo ii, 252
Oxhey Hrt, Wo i, 215
Oxhill Wa ii, 105, 106
Oxley St ii, 22, 57
Oxnall Wo i, 224
Oxnead Nf i, 146
Oxnop YN i, 260, ii, 57

Quernmore La ii, 43
Quethelake Mx ii, 77
Quick La, YW i, 122
Quickbeam Hill D i, 122
Quicksbury Ess i, 118
Quickstavers YW i, 122, ii, 141
Quidhampton Ha, W i, 121
Quinton Gl, Nth, Wo i, 121
Quither D i, 121
Quob Ha i, 121
Quobbs W i, 121
Quobwell W i, 121, ii, 252
Quoditch D i, 121
Quorn(don) Lei i, 122, 138
Quy C i, 118, 148

Rableyheath Hrt i, 223
Raby Ch, Du i, 69, ii, 78; Cu ii, 78
Raceby Du i, 71
Race Dale YE ii, 124
Rackenford D i, 4, ii, 78
Rackheath Nf ii, 78
Racton Sx i, 263
Radbourn Db i, 264
Radbourne Wa i, 64, 264
Radcliffe La i, 99, ii, 81; Lei, Mx, Nt ii, 81
Radclive Bk i, 99, ii, 81
Radcot O i, 264
Raddicombe D ii, 79
Radford Nt ii, 81; O ii, 78; Wa ii, 81
Radipole Do i, 264
Radlett Hrt ii, 12
Radley Brk ii, 81
Radmanthwaite Nt i, 264
Radnage Bk i, 1, 2, ii, 81
Radstock So ii, 78
Radstone Nth ii, 87
Radway D ii, 249; Wa ii, 78, 249
Radwell Bd, Hrt ii, 251
Radwinter Ess ii, 269
Rae Burn Cu ii, 78
Ragden La ii, 78
Rag Hill Sr ii, 79
Ragill La i, 200
Ragley Wa ii, 79
Rainow Ch i, 263
Rains Brook Wa ii, 82
Rainworth Nt i, 264, ii, 82, 230
Raisdale YN i, 127
Raise Cu i, 264
Raisebeck We i, 26, 264
Raisthwaite La i, 244, ii, 220
Rake Cu, Db ii, 80
Rake D i, 263
Rake, The Sx i, 263
Rakes Fm Sr i, 263
Ramacre Ess ii, 202, 213
Rame Co i, 264
Rame Hill Co i, 264
Ramhurst K ii, 80
Rampside La i, 237, ii, 80
Rampton C, Nt ii, 80, 196
Ramsbottom La i, 43, 264, ii, 80
Ramsbury W i, 61, 263
Ramsdale Ha i, 264
Ramsden Bellhouse Ess i, 27
Ramsey Ess, Hu i, 264
Ramsgate K i, 198
Ramsgreave La i, 207
Ramshaw Du ii, 100
Ramsholt Sf i, 264
Ramshorn D i, 262; St ii, 80
Ramsnest Sr ii, 50
Rancombe Wt ii, 78
Rand L, YN ii, 80
Randall Wood K ii, 87
Randwick Gl ii, 84
Randworth Nf ii, 80
Ranell Bk ii, 80
Rangeworthy Gl i, 267, ii, 276
Ranmore Sr ii, 80
Ranskill Nt i, 263, ii, 125
Ranworth Nf ii, 274
Rasen, Market L i, 185, ii, 79
Rashwood Wo i, 5, 246
Raskelf YN ii, 78, 125
Rassler Bk ii, 129
Rastrick YW ii, 83, 88
Rat Wt ii, 91
Ratchwood Nb ii, 278, 281
Rathmell YW ii, 38, 81
Rathmoss La ii, 44
Ratley Wa ii, 88
Ratling K ii, 91
Ratsborough Ess ii, 79
Ratsbury D ii, 140
Ratsloe D ii, 129
Ratten Cu, Nb ii, 81
Rattenbury Co ii, 79
Rattery D ii, 81, 186
Ratton Row Cu, Nb ii, 81
Raughmere Sx i, 263
Raughton Cu ii, 78

Rytham YE ii, 279
Ryther YW ii, 91
Ryton Du, Sa, Wa ii, 91, 196; YN ii, 195

Sabden La, So ii, 94
Sacombe Hrt i, 80
Sacriston Heugh Du ii, 117
Sadberge Du ii, 120
Saddlesborough D ii, 92
Saddlescombe Sx ii, 92
Saddlestone D ii, 92
Saddle Tor D ii, 92
Saddleworth YW ii, 92, 274
Saffronelane C i, 169
Saham Nf i, 228, ii, 93
Saighton Ch ii, 96
St Bees Cu i, 169
Saintbridge Gl ii, 118
St Chloe Gl ii, 118
St Ellen Dub La i, 137
St Giles YE i, 196
St Helen's Well YE ii, 253
Saint Hill D, Sx ii, 118, 172
St Ives Ha i, 279; Hu ii, 127; Sx ii, 118
Saintlow Gl ii, 118
St Margaret Intra K i, 304
St Martin's Down Wt ii, 130
St Mary le Bow Ln ii, 17
St Michael's Mount Co ii, 42
St Nicholas at Wade K ii, 234
Saintoft(s) YE ii, 118, 183; YN ii, 183
St Osyth Ess i, 93, ii, 260
St Rhadegund's Path Wt i, 193, ii, 78
Salcey Forest Nth ii, 96
Salcombe Regis D ii, 96
Salcott Ess i, 109, ii, 96
Salden Bk i, 130, ii, 100, 106
Sale Ch ii, 96
Salecorner, le Nth i, 108
Salehurst Sx i, 277, ii, 96
Salem Bridge L ii, 117
Saleway Wo ii, 96
Sale Wheel La ii, 96, 249
Salford Bd, La, O, Wa i, 182, ii, 96; Wo ii, 96, 114, 252; (Hundred) La ii, 110; (Bridge) Wo ii, 113
Salisbury (Plain) W i, 100, ii, 66
Sallings Wo ii, 96
Sallow Vallets Gl i, 169
Salmonby L i, 13
Salmonsbury (Camp) Gl i, 61, 62, ii, 167
Salome (Wood) Hu ii, 96, 226
Salph End Bd ii, 96
Salt St ii, 118
Saltash Co ii, 96
Salt Ayre La i, 162
Saltburn YN ii, 97
Salt ee, le L i, 143
Salter Cu ii, 96
Salterford Nt i, 183, ii, 97
Salterforth YW i, 183, ii, 97
Saltergate L, YN, YW ii, 97
Salter Lee YW ii, 97
Salter's Bridge St ii, 97
Salterton D, W ii, 97
Saltfleet(by) L i, 69, ii, 97
Saltford So ii, 96
Salthouse Nf i, 270, ii, 96
Salthrop W i, 240, ii, 96
Saltings D ii, 97; YE i, 153, 283
Saltisford Wa ii, 97
Saltley Wa ii, 96
Saltlond L ii, 14
Saltmarsh(e) Gl, He, Sx, YE ii, 39, ii, 97
Saltney L ii, 97
Salton(stall) YN, YW ii, 96, 198
Saltram D ii, 97
Saltren's Cottages D ii, 97
Salts House YE ii, 96
Salt Way O, Wo ii, 249
Saltwell Du ii, 97
Saltwick Nb ii, 96, 262
Salwarpe, (R.) Wo ii, 19, 97, 248
Samber W i, 29
Samblesbury La ii, 100
Sambourn Wa ii, 97
Sambrook Sa ii, 97
Sampford Co, D, Ess i, 181
Sancton YE ii, 195
Sand So ii, 97
Sandal YW i, 224, ii, 97
Sandbach Ch i, 24, ii, 97
Sandbeck YW i, 26, ii, 97
Sanderstead Sr ii, 97
Sandford Brk, D, Do, We i, 181, ii, 97; O i, 181; Sa, (*passim*) ii, 97
Sandgate K i, 198, ii, 97
Sandhills Wt ii, 97
Sandhurst Brk, Gl, K i, 277, ii, 97
Sandiacre Db i, 3, ii, 97

Shipley Db, Du, Sa, Sx, YW ii, 22, 101; Nb i, 302, ii, 101
Shipmeadow Sf ii, 31
Shippen YW ii, 115
Shippon Brk ii, 115
Shipston on Stour Wo ii, 101, 195
Shipton Bk, Do, Gl, Ha, O, Sa ii, 101; Do, YE, YN, *freq* ii, 196; YE, YN i, 243
Shipton Lee Bk i, 138
Shipton under Wychwood O ii, 227
Shipway K ii, 101, 249
Shirehead La i, 237
Shiremark Sr, Sx ii, 37, 110
Shireoaks Nt i, 2, ii, 111
Shireshead La ii, 111
Shirland Db ii, 111
Shirlet Sa ii, 111
Shirlet Forest Sa i, 251
Shirley Db, Ha, He, Sr, Wa ii, 111; Wa, *freq* ii, 20
Shirrell Heath Ha i, 276
Shirwell D ii, 111
Shiter So ii, 112
Shoals, The C ii, 100
Shoart K ii, 108
Shobrooke D ii, 115
Shoby Lei i, 58
Shocklach Ch ii, 10, 115
Shode, R. K ii, 99
Shoebroad Db ii, 112
Shoebury (Shop) Ess ii, 107
Shoeland Mx ii, 107
Shofford K i, 182
Sholden K ii, 112
Shooter, The La ii, 112
Shooter's Green Hu ii, 108
Shooter's Hill K i, 242, ii, 108; Nth, Wa ii, 108
Shootersway Hrt ii, 98
Shootlands Sr ii, 109
Shopland Ess ii, 107
Shopwyke Sr ii, 101; Sx ii, 262
Shore La, YW ii, 113
Shoreditch Mx ii, 113
Shoreham K i, 228, ii, 113
Shore Moor La ii, 43
Shoresworth La, Nb ii, 113; Nb ii, 277
Shorncliffe K ii, 113
Shorncote W ii, 101
Shorne K ii, 113
Shortflatt Nb i, 175, ii, 107
Shortfurrows Sr i, 189
Shortgrove Ess ii, 107
Shorthampton O i, 232, ii, 107
Shortlands C ii, 14
Short Wait YN ii, 219
Shortwood Wo ii, 281
Shorwell Wt ii, 113
Shot Ess ii, 103
Shotley Nb, Sf ii, 107, 108
Shotover O ii, 108
Shottermill Sr ii, 46
Shottery Wa ii, 86, 108, 113
Shottesbrook Brk i, 51, ii, 108
Shottle Db ii, 108
Shotton Du ii, 108
Shotwell Mill Nth ii, 108
Shotwick Ch ii, 108
Shouldham Nf ii, 115
Shoulthwaite Cu i, 248, ii, 220
Shoulton Wo ii, 107
Showley La ii, 107
Shrawardine Sa ii, 114, 277
Shrawley Wo ii, 114
Shrawnell Wo ii, 114
Shrewley Wa ii, 114
Shrewsnest C ii, 114
Shrewton W ii, 112, 196
Shrigley Ch ii, 22, 114
Shripney Sx ii, 114
Shrivenham Brk i, 152, 231, ii, 114
Shrofield K ii, 114
Shrogg YW ii, 114
Shroner Ha ii, 114
Shroton Do ii, 112
Shrub Fm Ess, Nth, Sx ii, 115
Shrubland Sf ii, 28, 115
Shrubs Hill Sr ii, 115
Shrubs, The Sx ii, 115
Shuckborough St ii, 115
Shuckburgh Wa ii, 115
Shucknall He i, 275, ii, 115
Shudecamp Ess i, 80
Shudy Camps C i, 80, ii, 115
Shugborough St i, 61
Shulbrede Sx i, 46, ii, 112
Shunner Howe YN i, 235, ii, 123
Shurdington Gl ii, 108
Shurton So ii, 112, ii, 196
Shushions St ii, 107
Shute(lake) D, W ii, 109
Shuteley D ii, 109

Stibb (Cross) Co, D ii, 165
Stibbard Nf i, 73
Stibbington Hu i, 296, ii, 165, 194
Stickford L ii, 166
Stickleball Hill So ii, 152
Sticklepath D ii, 58, 152
Stickleton Mx ii, 152
Sticklinch So i, 252
Stickney L ii, 166
Stickwick D ii, 151
Stidd La ii, 148, 149
Stidham So ii, 157
Stiffkey Nf i, 148, ii, 166
Stifford Ess, YN i, 182, ii, 152
Stile Cu ii, 152
Stilton Hu ii, 152
Stinchcombe Gl ii, 153
Sting Head Nb ii, 150
Stiniel D i, 226, ii, 141
Stinsford Do ii, 153
Stintesford W ii, 153
Stipershill Wa ii, 153
Stippadon D ii, 165
Stirchley Sa ii, 22, 153
Stirtloe Hu ii, 151
Stisted Ess ii, 153
Stitchcombe W ii, 165
Stitches, The C ii, 166
Stittenham YN ii, 152
Stitworthy D ii, 276
Stivichall Wa ii, 166
Stixwould L ii, 241
Stobbilee Du ii, 164
Stoborough Do ii, 144; So i, 29
Stobs House Du ii, 164
Stobswood Nb ii, 164
Stock Bk, K, Wo ii, 156
Stockalls Hrt ii, 252
Stockbridge Do, Ha, YW i, 55, ii, 156; K i, 55; Sx ii, 156
Stockbury K i, 16, 302, ii, 155
Stockeld YW ii, 156
Stockenbridge D ii, 156
Stockenden Sr i, 130
Stockenham D ii, 154; Sf ii, 155
Stockerston Lei i, 163, ii, 156
Stockett Ess ii, 156
Stockett Sa i, 199, ii, 156
Stockham Ch ii, 156; Ch, St ii, 226
Stockheld YW i, 242
Stockholm YE ii, 156
Stockholt Bk i, 259, ii, 156
Stockhurst Sr ii, 156
Stocking He, St, YN, YW ii, 157
Stockingford Wa i, 296, ii, 157
Stockland D, Gl ii, 154, 155
Stockleigh, -ley D, Du, Sf ii, 156
Stocklinch So ii, 155
Stockport Ch ii, 155
Stocksfield Nb ii, 155
Stockton Ch, Du, He, Nf, Sa, W, Wo, YN ii, 155; (*passim*) ii, 156; *freq* ii, 194
Stockton on the Forest YN ii, 55
Stockwell Gl, He, Sr ii, 156, 252
Stockwith L, Nt i, 278, ii, 156
Stockwood D, Do, So ii, 155; Do ii, 154, 155
Stoddah Cu ii, 157
Stodday La i, 221, ii, 157
Stodfald Nth, YE ii, 157
Stodfold L ii, 157
Stodfold Hundred Bk ii, 157
Stodmarsh K ii, 157
Stody Nf i, 215, ii, 157
Stoford So ii, 143, 144
Stoke Bk, Ch, D, (*passim*) ii, 155; D ii, 154; K i, 302
Stoke, North/South So ii, 154
Stoke, Severn Wo ii, 155
Stoke Abbott D ii, 156
Stoke Bishop Gl ii, 156
Stoke by Nayland Sf ii, 154
Stoke Canon D ii, 155, 156
Stoke Dry R i, 136
Stoke Ferry Nf i, 171
Stokeham Nt ii, 226; Nth ii, 155
Stoke Holy Cross Nf i, 116
Stokeinteignhead D ii, 155, 178
Stokenchurch Bk i, 95, ii, 156
Stoke Newington Mx ii, 156
Stokenham D ii, 155
Stoke Prior He, Wo ii, 156
Stokes Ha ii, 155
Stoke St Gregory/Mary/Michael So ii, 156
Stoke St Milborough Sa ii, 154, 155–6
Stokesby Nf i, 69, ii, 155
Stokesley YN ii, 155
Stoketeignhead D i, 246, ii, 178
Stonal St i, 224, ii, 144
Stonar K ii, 55
Stondon Bd, Ess i, 138, ii, 144
Stone Bk, Gl, Ha, K, So, St, Wo ii, 144

Warthill YN ii, 247
Warth's Old Halves C ii, 246
Warton La, Nb ii, 247; St, Wa ii, 236
Wartop Lei ii, 183, 232
Warwick Cu ii, 246, 262; Wa ii, 255, 262
Wasdale We ii, 229
Wash, R. L–Lei ii, 238
Wash, The L–Nf ii, 237
Washall Green Hrt ii, 237
Washbourne D i, 64, ii, 237; Gl ii, 238
Washbrook Sf ii, 237
Washford D ii, 237
Washingham Sr i, 284
Washington Sx i, 303, ii, 259
Washway L ii, 237
Wass YN ii, 230
Wassand YE ii, 97, 230
Wassell Wo ii, 247
Wasthills Wo ii, 247
Watchcommon Cu ii, 229
Watendlath Cu i, 152, ii, 229
Waterbeach C ii, 13
Water Blocks Sr i, 39
Watercombe Do i, 119, ii, 238
Waterden Nf i, 130, ii, 238
Water Fm Sr, Sx ii, 238
Waterfall St, YN ii, 238
Water Flash YN i, 175
Watergall Wa i, 192
Watergalle C, Db, Nt, Nth, Wa i, 192
Waterham K i, 230, ii, 238
Waterhead La i, 237
Waterholmes YN ii, 238
Watericoddes C i, 104
Waterlode L ii, 9
Watermillock Cu ii, 37, 257
Waterperry O ii, 66
Water Sheep Ess, Hrt ii, 238
Watership Lane W ii, 238
Watership(pe) Ess, Hrt ii, 238
Water Shoot D ii, 109
Watershute D ii, 238
Waterstock O ii, 238
Waterstone Co i, 234
Waterton L ii, 238
Watervale D ii, 238
Water Yeat La i, 199
Watford Hrt, Nth ii, 247
Wath Cu, YN, YW ii, 230
Wath Cote YN ii, 229
Wathe Wt ii, 234
Watless YN ii, 17
Watling Street i, 276, ii, 162
Watton Hrt ii, 196, 234; YE i, 138, ii, 196, 234
Wauldby YE ii, 241
Waveney, R. Nf–Sf i, 143, ii, 239
Waver, R. Cu ii, 195, 235, 236
Waverley Sr ii, 235, 236; Wa ii, 238
Wavermouth Cu ii, 235
Waverton Cu ii, 195, 235
Wavertree La ii, 236
Wawne YE ii, 239
Waxham Nf i, 229
Waxholme YE i, 228, ii, 248
Waxlow Mx ii, 272
Way D ii, 249
Waye D ii, 249
Wayer, le C, Hrt ii, 257
Wayford So i, 182, ii, 249
Wayland Smith's Cave Brk ii, 131
Waystrode K i, 271, ii, 164
Waytail Gate YN ii, 239
Wayton Co ii, 249
Weaks Sx ii, 270
Weald Bk, Hu, O ii, 241
Weald (Forest), The K, Sx ii, 19, 239, 240, 241
Wealdgullet Ess i, 206
Weald Moors Sa ii, 265
Wear, R. Du i, 170
Weare D, So ii, 255
Wearmouth Du ii, 46
Weatheroak Wo ii, 257
Weaver W ii, 248
Weaver, R. Ch ii, 248
Weavercote Ch ii, 248
Weaverham Ch ii, 248
Weavern Fm W ii, 248
Weaverthorpe YE ii, 212
Webland D ii, 248
Webton He ii, 196
Wechylstone K ii, 234
Weddicar Cu i, 3, ii, 254
Wedhampton W ii, 254
Wedholme Cu ii, 230
Wedmore So ii, 43, 238
Wednesbury St ii, 272
Wednesday Market (Beverley) YE ii, 272
Wednesfield St ii, 272

Wickenlow La i, 122, 250
Wick Episcopi Wo i, 155
Wickerthwaite Cu ii, 220
Wickey Bd ii, 249, 261
Wickham Brk ii, 263; C ii, 261; Ess, Ha, Hrt, K ii, 263
Wickhampton Nf i, 233, ii, 261
Wickham Skeith Sf ii, 124
Wickhurst K i, 277
Wickmere Nf i, 161, ii, 261
Wickwar Gl ii, 261
Widcombe So i, 119, ii, 264
Widdicombe D i, 119, ii, 271
Widdington Ess ii, 196, 271; W ii, 271; YW ii, 196, 271
Widemarsh He ii, 39, 264
Widemouth Co ii, 46
Widewell D ii, 252
Widford Ess, Hrt ii, 271
Widmere Bk ii, 39, 271
Widnell Bk ii, 264
Widnes La ii, 48, 264
Widworthy D ii, 276
Wieghelmestun K i, 6, 294
Wield Ha ii, 241
Wifelinge K i, 289
Wifford D ii, 249
Wigan Hu ii, 226, 261
Wiganthorpe YN ii, 231
Wigford L ii, 261
Wiggenholt Sx i, 259
Wigginton YN ii, 231
Wighill YW i, 224, ii, 261
Wightfield Gl i, 168, ii, 265
Wighton Nf ii, 264
Wigley Db, Ha ii, 265
Wigston Lei ii, 145, 198, 231
Wigston Parva Lei ii, 265
Wigtoft L ii, 183, 231
Wigton YW ii, 261
Wigwell Db ii, 265
Wike YW ii, 261
Wilberfoss YE i, 185
Wilbraham C i, 229
Wilburton C ii, 197
Wilbury Hrt i, 61, ii, 266, 267
Wilby Nf, Nth ii, 267; Sf i, 21, ii, 267
Wilcot W i, 110, ii, 251
Wild Brk ii, 265
Wild C, K, Hrt ii, 240
Wild Fm Hrt ii, 241
Wilderehey Ess ii, 266
Wilders Moor La ii, 266
Wildhill Hrt ii, 266
Wildmore L ii, 43, 265
Wildres Mareys Wo ii, 266
Wildwood Sr ii, 266
Wilkesley Ch i, 96
Will D ii, 250
Willand D ii, 14, 266
Will Ave Cu i, 191
Willen Bk ii, 226, 267
Willenhall Wa ii, 267
Willersey Gl ii, 253
Willesden Mx ii, 251
Williamstrip Gl ii, 216
Willian Hrt ii, 267
Willingham, Cherry L i, 92
Willey Ch, He ii, 21, 267; Sa ii, 21; Sr ii, 21, 265; Wa ii, 21
Willington Bd, Db ii, 196, 267
Willitoft YE ii, 183, 267
Willock C ii, 264
Willoughby L, Lei, Nt, i, 68, ii, 267; Wa ii, 266, 267
Willoughton L ii, 196, 267
Willyards D i, 200, ii, 266
Wilmington K i, 294
Wilne Db ii, 267
Wilpshire La ii, 110
Wilsætan W ii, 94
Wilsford L, W ii, 264
Wilsill YW ii, 264
Wilsmere Down C i, 139
Wilson D ii, 254
Wilsthorpe Db, L, YE ii, 212
Wilstone Hrt ii, 205
Wilstrop YW ii, 212, 264
Wilsworthy D ii, 276
Wilton He ii, 266; So ii, 251; W ii, 94, 230, 251; YE, YN ii, 266
Wiltshire ii, 109
Wimborne Do ii, 269
Wimborne Minster Do i, 216
Wimpole Park C ii, 60
Winceby L ii, 92
Winch Nf ii, 269
Wincham K ii, 267
Winchbottom Bk ii, 267
Winchcomb(e) Gl, K i, 119, ii, 268
Winchelsea Sx ii, 268
Winchendon, Lower Bk ii, 267
Winches Hrt ii, 267, 268
Winchester Ha i, 87, 247, ii, 230

Woolmer Ha ii, 281
Wooloaks Cu ii, 23, 281
Woolpit Sf ii, 281
Wools Grove W i, 208
Woolstone Bk ii, 197
Woolwich K ii, 262, 281
Woore Sa ii, 235, 236
Wootton Bd, Brk, Do, (*passim*) ii, 280; Wt ii, 279; *freq* ii, 195
Wootton Wawen Wa ii, 280
Worcester Wo i, 87
Worden D ii, 277
Wordwell Sf ii, 279
Worf, R. Sa ii, 272
Worgret Do ii, 248
Worhope K i, 260, ii, 272
Worksop Nt i, 260
Workway W ii, 249, 254
Worlaby L i, 71
Worle So ii, 272
Worley Wo ii, 22
Worlingworth Sf i, 301, ii, 275
Wormald YW ii, 251
Wormcliff W ii, 282
Wormdale K i, 126, ii, 282
Wormhill Db ii, 282
Worminghall Bk ii, 282
Worminster So ii, 184, 282
Wormleighton Wa ii, 18
Wormley Hrt ii, 282; L ii, 22
Wormshill K ii, 118, 272, 282
Wormwood Hill C i, 250, ii, 282
Wormwood Scrubs Mx i, 259, ii, 115, 282
Worplesdon Sr ii, 256
Worrall YW i, 224, ii, 270
Worsley Wo ii, 255
Worstead Nf ii, 149, 274
Worsted's Fm Sx ii, 271
Worth Brk ii, 273; Ch, Do, K, Sx ii, 274
Wortha Co ii, 274
Wortham Sf i, 228, ii, 274
Worthen D ii, 277
Worthene, le Ess ii, 277
Worthgate K ii, 246
Worthin Sa ii, 277
Worthing Nf ii, 277
Worthy D, Gl, Ha, W ii, 276
Wortley (Barnsley) YW ii, 282
Worton O, W, YN ii, 282
Wose, atte Mx ii, 247
Wothersome YW i, 270, ii, 226, 280
Wotton Nth ii, 279; Bk, Gl, Sr ii, 280; *freq* ii, 195
Wotton under Edge Gl i, 145, ii, 227
Wotton Underwood Bk ii, 281
Wouldham K i, 229
Woundale Sa ii, 281
Wrackhill K i, 263
Wrafton D ii, 278
Wragby L i, 235
Wraggoe Wapentake L i, 235
Wragholme L ii, 229
Wragmire Cu ii, 47, 229
Wragohill L i, 235
Wrampool La ii, 278
Wrangaton D ii, 278
Wrangbrook YW i, 51, ii, 278
Wrangle L ii, 278
Wrangling C ii, 13, 14, 278
Wrangworthy D ii, 276, 278
Wrantage K ii, 277; So i, 162
Wratting C, Sf i, 289, ii, 278
Wratton Hrt ii, 278
Wratworth C ii, 275, 278
Wrautam Wa ii, 279
Wrawby L i, 71
Wrax(h)all Do, So, W i, 224, ii, 279
Wray YW ii, 232
Wraysholme La ii, 278
Wrayton La ii, 232
Wrea La ii, 232
Wreay Cu ii, 232
Wreighburn Nb ii, 247
Wreighill Nb ii, 247
Wrekendike Du i, 132, ii, 278
Wrenbury Ch i, 61, ii, 278
Wrens Nest Hill Wo ii, 278
Wrenwell D ii, 252, 278
Wressell YE ii, 277
Wrest Bd ii, 277
Wrest Wood Sx ii, 277
Wretchwick O ii, 278
Wretham Nf i, 229, ii, 278
Wretton Nf ii, 196, 278
Wring, R. So i, 289, ii, 279
Wringford Co ii, 276, 279
Wrington So ii, 279
Wringworthy D ii, 276, 279
Wrinstead K ii, 149, 277
Writtle Ess ii, 279
Wrockwardine Sa ii, 277
Wrongelond Bd ii, 14